VIEW

OF

THE STATE OF EUROPE

DURING

THE MIDDLE AGES.

By HENRY HALLAM, LL.D., F.R.A.S.,

FOREIGN ASSOCIATE OF THE INSTITUTE OF FRANCE.

IN THREE VOLUMES.

VOLUME II.

NEW YORK:

W. J. WIDDLETON, PUBLISHER.

1872.

CAMBRIDGE:
PRESSWORK BY JOHN WILSON AND SON.

CONTENTS

OF

THE SECOND VOLUME.

CHAPTER IV.

THE HISTORY OF SPAIN TO THE CONQUEST OF GRANADA.

CHAPTER V.

HISTORY OF GERMANY TO THE DIET OF WORMS IN 1495.

CHAPTER VI.

HISTORY OF THE GREEKS AND SARACENS.

CHAPTER VII.

HISTORY OF ECCLESIASTICAL POWER DURING THE MIDDLE AGES.

PART I.

PART II.

CHAPTER VIII.

THE CONSTITUTIONAL HISTORY OF ENGLAND.

PART I.

PART II.

THE ANGLO-NORMAN CONSTITUTION

VIEW

OF

THE STATE OF EUROPE

DURING THE MIDDLE AGES.

CHAPTER IV.

THE HISTORY OF SPAIN TO THE CONQUEST OF GRANADA.

Kingdom of the Visigoths — Conquest of Spain by the Moors — Gradual Revival of the Spanish Nation — Kingdoms of Leon, Aragon, Navarre, and Castile, successively formed — Chartered Towns of Castile — Military Orders — Conquest of Ferdinand III. and James of Aragon — Causes of the Delay in expelling the Moors — History of Castile continued — Character of the Government — Peter the Cruel — House of Trastamare — John II. — Henry IV. — Constitution of Castile — National Assemblies or Cortes — their constituent Parts — Right of Taxation — Legislation — Privy Council of Castile — Laws for the Protection of Liberty — Imperfections of the Constitution — Aragon — its History in the fourteenth and fifteenth Centuries — disputed Succession — Constitution of Aragon — Free Spirit of its Aristocracy — Privilege of Union — Powers of the Justiza — Legal Securities — Illustrations — other Constitutional Laws — Valencia and Catalonia — Union of two Crowns by the Marriage of Ferdinand and Isabella — Conquest of Granada.

Kingdom of Visigoths in Spain.

The history of Spain during the middle ages ought to commence with the dynasty of the Visigoths; a nation among the first that assaulted and overthrew the Roman Empire, and whose establishment preceded by nearly half a century the invasion of Clovis. Vanquished by that conqueror in the battle of Poitiers, the Gothic monarchs lost their extensive dominions in Gaul, and transferred their residence from Toulouse to Toledo. But I will not detain the reader by naming one sovereign of that obscure race. It may suffice to mention that the Visigothic monarchy differed in several respects from that of the Franks during the same period. The crown was less hereditary, or at least the regular succession was more frequently disturbed. The prelates had a still more commanding influence in temporal government. The distinction of

Romans and barbarians was less marked, the laws more uniform, and approaching nearly to the imperial code. The power of the sovereign was perhaps more limited by an aristocratical council than in France, but it never yielded to the dangerous influence of mayors of the palace. Civil wars and disputed successions were very frequent, but the integrity of the kingdom was not violated by the custom of partition.

Conquest by the Saracens.

Spain, after remaining for nearly three centuries in the possession of the Visigoths, fell under the yoke of the Saracens in 712. The fervid and irresistible enthusiasm which distinguished the youthful period of Mohammedism might sufficiently account for this conquest, even if we could not assign additional causes — the factions which divided the Goths, the resentment of disappointed pretenders to the throne, the provocations, as has been generally believed, of count Julian, and the temerity that risked the fate of an empire on the chances of a single battle.[1] It is more surprising that a remnant of this ancient monarchy should not only have preserved its national liberty and name in the northern mountains, but waged for some centuries a successful, and generally an offensive warfare against the conquerors, till the balance was completely turned in its favor, and the Moors were compelled to maintain almost as obstinate and protracted a contest for a small portion of the peninsula. But the Arabian monarchs of Cordova found in their success and imagined security a pretext for indolence; even in the cultivation of science and contemplation of the magnificent architecture of their mosques and palaces they forgot their poor but daring enemies in the Asturias; while, according to the nature of despotism, the fruits of wisdom or bravery in one generation were lost in the follies and effeminacy of the next. Their kingdom was dismembered by successful rebels, who formed the states of Toledo, Huesca, Saragosa, and others less eminent; and these, in their own mutual contests, not only relaxed their natural enmity towards the Christian princes, but sometimes sought their alliance.[2]

Kingdom of Leon

The last attack which seemed to endanger the reviving monarchy of Spain was that of Almanzor, the illustrious vizir of Haccham II., towards the end

[1] [NOTE.]
[2] Cardonne, Histoire de l'Afrique et de l'Espagne.

of the tenth century, wherein the city of Leon, and even the shrine of Compostella, were burned to the ground. For some ages before this transient reflux, gradual encroachments had been made upon the Saracens, and the kingdom originally styled of Oviedo, the seat of which was removed to Leon in 914, had extended its boundary to the Douro, and even to the mountainous chain of the Guadarrama. The province of Old Castile, thus denominated, as is generally supposed, from the castles erected while it remained a march or frontier against the Moors, was governed by hereditary counts, elected originally by the provincial aristocracy, and virtually independent, it seems probable, of the kings of Leon, though commonly serving them in war as brethren of the same faith and nation.[1]

Kingdoms of Navarre and Aragon.

While the kings of Leon were thus occupied in recovering the western provinces, another race of Christian princes grew up silently under the shadow of the Pyrenean mountains. Nothing can be more obscure than the beginnings of those little states which were formed in Navarre and the country of Soprarbe. They might perhaps be almost contemporaneous with the Moorish conquests. On both sides of the Pyrenees dwelt an aboriginal people, the last to undergo the yoke, and who had never acquired the language, of Rome. We know little of these intrepid mountaineers in the dark period which elapsed under the Gothic and Frank dynasties, till we find them cutting off the rear-guard of Charlemagne in Roncesvalles, and maintaining at least their independence, though seldom, like the kings of Asturias, waging offensive war against the Saracens. The town of Jaca, situated among long narrow valleys that intersect the southern ridges of the Pyrenees, was the capital of a little free state, which afterwards expanded into the monarchy of Aragon.[2] A territory rather more extensive be-

[1] According to Roderic of Toledo, one of the earliest Spanish historians, though not older than the beginning of the thirteenth century, the nobles of Castile, in the reign of Froila, about the year 924, sibi et posteris providerunt, et duos milites non de potentioribus, sed de prudentioribus elegerunt, quos et judices statuerunt, ut dissensiones patriæ et querelantium causæ suo judicio sopirentur. l. v. c. 1. Several other passages in the same writer prove that the counts of Castile were nearly independent of Leon, at least from the time of Ferdinand Gonsalvo about the middle of the tenth century. Ex quo iste suscepit suæ patriæ comitatum, cessaverunt reges Asturiarum insolescere in Castellam, et a flumine Pisoricâ nihil amplius vindicârunt, l. v. c. 2. Marina, in his Ensayo Historico-Critico, is disposed to controvert this fact.

[2] The Fueros, or written laws of Jaca, were perhaps more ancient than any local customary in Europe. Alfonso III. confirms them by name of the ancient usages

longed to Navarre, the kings of which fixed their seat at Pampelona. Biscay seems to have been divided between this kingdom and that of Leon. The connection of Aragon or Soprarbe and Navarre was very intimate, and they were often united under a single chief.

Kingdom of Castile.

At the beginning of the eleventh century, Sancho the Great, king of Navarre and Aragon, was enabled to render his second son Ferdinand count, or, as he assumed the title, king of Castile. This effectually dismembered that province from the kingdom of Leon; but their union soon became more complete than ever, though with a reversed supremacy. Bermudo III., king of Leon, fell in an engagement with the new king of Castile, who had married his sister; and Ferdinand, in her right, or in that of conquest, became master of the united monarchy. This cessation of hostilities between the Christian states enabled them to direct a more unremitting energy against their ancient enemies, who were now sensibly weakened by the various causes of decline to which I have already alluded. During the eleventh century the Spaniards were almost always superior in the field; the towns which they began by pillaging, they gradually possessed; their valor was heightened by the customs of chivalry and inspired by the example of the Cid; and before the end of this age Alfonso VI. recovered the ancient metropolis of the monarchy, the city of Toledo. This was the severest blow which the Moors had endured, and an unequivocal symptom of that change in their relative strength, which, from being so gradual, was the more irretrievable. Calamities scarcely inferior fell upon them in a different quarter. The kings of Aragon (a title belonging originally to a little district upon the river of that name) had been cooped up almost in the mountains by the

Capture of Toledo,

of Jaca. They prescribe the descent of lands and movables, as well as the election of municipal magistrates. The following law, which enjoins the rising in arms on a sudden emergency, illustrates, with a sort of romantic wildness, the manners of a pastoral but warlike people, and reminds us of a well-known passage in the Lady of the Lake. De appellitis ita statuimus. Cum homines de villis, vel qui stant in montanis cum suis ganatis [gregibus], audierint appellitum; omnes capiant arma, et dimissis ganatis, et omnibus aliis suis faziendis [negotiis] sequantur appellitum. Et si illi qui fuerint magis remoti, invenerint in villâ magis proximâ appellito, [deest aliquid?] omnes qui nondum fuerint egressi tunc villam illam, quæ tardius secuta est appellitum, pecent [solvant] unam baccam [vaccam]; et unusquisque homo ex illis qui tardius secutus est appellitum, et quem magis remoti præcesserint, pecet tres solidos, quomodo nobis videbitur, partiendos. Tamen in Jacâ et in aliis villis, sint aliqui nominati et certi, quos elegerint consules, qui remaneant ad villas custodiendas et defendendas. Biancæ Commentaria, in Schotti Hispania Illustrata, p. 595.

small Moorish states north of the Ebro, especially that of Huesca. About the middle of the eleventh century they began to attack their neighbors with success; the Moors lost one town after another, till, in 1118, exposed and weakened by the reduction of all these places, the city of Saragosa, in which a line of Mohammedan princes had flourished for several ages, became the prize of Alfonso I. and the capital of his kingdom. The southern parts of what is now the province of Aragon were successively reduced during the twelfth century; while all new Castile and Estremadura became annexed in the same gradual manner to the dominion of the descendants of Alfonso VI.

and Saragosa.

Mode of settling the new conquests.

Although the feudal system cannot be said to have obtained in the kingdoms of Leon and Castile, their peculiar situation gave the aristocracy a great deal of the same power and independence which resulted in France and Germany from that institution. The territory successively recovered from the Moors, like waste lands reclaimed, could have no proprietor but the conquerors, and the prospect of such acquisitions was a constant incitement to the nobility of Spain, especially to those who had settled themselves on the Castilian frontier. In their new conquests they built towns and invited Christian settlers, the Saracen inhabitants being commonly expelled or voluntarily retreating to the safer provinces of the south. Thus Burgos was settled by a count of Castile about 880; another fixed his seat at Osma; a third at Sepulveda; a fourth at Salamanca. These cities were not free from incessant peril of a sudden attack till the union of the two kingdoms under Ferdinand I., and consequently the necessity of keeping in exercise a numerous and armed population, gave a character of personal freedom and privilege to the inferior classes which they hardly possessed at so early a period in any other monarchy. Villeinage seems never to have been established in the Hispano-Gothic kingdoms, Leon and Castile; though I confess it was far from being unknown in that of Aragon, which had formed its institutions on a different pattern. Since nothing makes us forget the arbitrary distinctions of rank so much as participation in any common calamity, every man who had escaped the great shipwreck of liberty and religion in the mountains of Asturias was invested with a personal dignity, which gave him value in his own eyes and those of his country. It is probably this sentiment transmitted to posterity, and gradually fixing the national character, that has produced the elevation of manner remarked by travellers in the Castilian peasant. But while these acquisitions of the nobility promoted the grand object of winning back the peninsula from its invaders, they by no means invigorated the government or tended to domestic tranquillity.

Chartered towns or communities.

A more interesting method of securing the public defence was by the institution of chartered towns or communities. These were established at an earlier period than in France and England, and were, in some degree, of a peculiar description. Instead of purchasing their immunities, and almost their personal freedom, at the hands of a master, the burgesses of Castilian towns were invested with civil rights and extensive property on the more liberal condition of protecting their country. The earliest instance of the erection of a community is in 1020, when Alfonso V. in the cortes at Leon established the privileges of that city with a regular code of laws, by which its magistrates should be governed. The citizens of Carrion, Llanes, and other towns were incorporated by the same prince. Sancho the Great gave a similar constitution to Naxara. Sepulveda had its code of laws in 1076 from Alfonso VI.; in the same reign Logroño and Sahagun acquired their privileges, and Salamanca not long afterwards. The fuero, or original charter of a Spanish community, was properly a compact, by which the king or lord granted a town and adjacent district to the burgesses, with various privileges, and especially that of choosing magistrates and a common council, who were bound to conform themselves to the laws prescribed by the founder. These laws, civil as well as criminal, though essentially derived from the ancient code of the Visigoths, which continued to be the common law of Castile till the fourteenth or fifteenth century, varied from each other in particular usages, which had probably grown up and been established in these districts before their legal confirmation. The territory held by chartered towns was frequently very extensive, far beyond any comparison with corporations in our own country or in France; including the estates of private landholders, subject to the jurisdiction and control of the municipality as well as its inalienable demesnes, allotted to the maintenance of the magistrates and other public expenses.

In every town the king appointed a governor to receive the usual tributes and watch over the police and the fortified places within the district; but the administration of justice was exclusively reserved to the inhabitants and their elected judges. Even the executive power of the royal officer was regarded with jealousy; he was forbidden to use violence towards any one without legal process; and, by the fuero of Logroño, if he attempted to enter forcibly into a private house he might be killed with impunity. These democratical customs were altered in the fourteenth century by Alfonso XI., who vested the municipal administration in a small number of jurats, or regidors. A pretext for this was found in some disorders to which popular elections had led; but the real motive, of course, must have been to secure a greater influence for the crown, as in similar innovations of some English kings.

In recompense for such liberal concessions the incorporated towns were bound to certain money payments, and to military service. This was absolutely due from every inhabitant, without dispensation or substitution, unless in case of infirmity. The royal governor and the magistrates, as in the simple times of primitive Rome, raised and commanded the militia; who, in a service always short, and for the most part necessary, preserved that delightful consciousness of freedom, under the standard of their fellow citizens and chosen leaders, which no mere soldier can enjoy. Every man of a certain property was bound to serve on horseback, and was exempted in return from the payment of taxes. This produced a distinction between the *caballeros*, or noble class, and the *pecheros*, or payers of tribute. But the distinction appears to have been founded only upon wealth, as in the Roman equites, and not upon hereditary rank, though it most likely prepared the way for the latter. The horses of these caballeros could not be seized for debt; in some cases they were exclusively eligible to magistracy; and their honor was protected by laws which rendered it highly penal to insult or molest them. But the civil rights of rich and poor in courts of justice were as equal as in England.[1]

[1] I am indebted for this account of municipal towns in Castile to a book published at Madrid in 1808, immediately after the revolution, by the Doctor Marina, a canon of the church of St Isidor, entitled, Ensayo Historico-Critico sobre la antigua legislacion y principales cuerpos legales de los reynos de Lyon y

The progress of the Christian arms in Spain may in part be ascribed to another remarkable feature in the constitution of that country, the military orders.

Military orders.

These had already been tried with signal effect in Palestine; and the similar circumstances of Spain easily led to an adoption of the same policy. In a very few years after the first institution of the Knights Templars, they were endowed with great estates, or rather districts, won from the Moors, on condition of defending their own and the national territory. These lay chiefly in the parts of Aragon beyond the Ebro, the conquest of which was then recent and insecure.[1] So extraordinary was the respect for this order and that of St. John, and so powerful the conviction that the hope of Christendom rested upon their valor, that Alfonso the First, king of Aragon, dying childless, bequeathed to them his whole kingdom; an example of liberality, says Mariana, to surprise future times and displease his own.[2] The states of Aragon annulled, as may be supposed, this strange testament; but the successor of Alfonso was obliged to pacify the ambitious knights by immense concessions of money and territory; stipulating even not to make peace with the Moors against their will.[3] In imitation of these great military orders common to all Christendom, there arose three Spanish institutions of a similar kind, the orders of Calatrava, Santiago, and Alcantara. The first of these was established in 1158; the second and most famous had its charter from the pope in 1175, though it seems to have existed previously; the third branched off from that of Calatrava at a subsequent time.[4] These were military colleges, having their walled towns in different parts of Castile, and governed by an elective grand master, whose influence in the state was at least equal to that of any of the nobility. In the civil dissensions of the fourteenth and fifteenth centuries, the chiefs of these incorporated knights were often very prominent.

Final union of Leon and Castile.

The kingdoms of Leon and Castile were unwisely divided anew by Alfonso VII. between his sons Sancho and Ferdinand, and this produced not

Castilla, especialmente sobre el codigo de D. Alonso el Sabio, conocido con el nombre de las Siete Partidas. This work is perhaps not readily to be procured in England: but an article in the Edinburgh Review, No. XLIII., will convey a sufficient notion of its contents.

1 Mariana, Hist. Hispan. l. x. c. 10.

2 l. x. c. 15.

3 l. x. c. 18.

4 l. xi. c. 6, 13; l. xii. c. 3.

only a separation but a revival of the ancient jealousy with frequent wars for near a century. At length, in 1238, Ferdinand III., king of Castile, reunited forever the two branches of the Gothic monarchy. He employed their joint strength against the Moors, whose dominion, though it still embraced the finest provinces of the peninsula, was sinking by internal weakness, and had never recovered a tremendous defeat at Banos di Toloso, a few miles from Baylen, in 1210.[1] Ferdinand, bursting into Andalusia, took its great capital the city of Cordova, not less ennobled by the cultivation of Arabian science, and by the names of Avicenna and Averroes, than by the splendid works of a rich and munificent dynasty.[2] In a few years more Seville was added to his conquests, and the Moors lost their favorite regions on the banks of the Guadalquivir. James I. of Aragon, the victories of whose long reign gave him the surname of Conqueror, reduced the city and kingdom of Valencia, the Balearic isles, and the kingdom of Murcia; but the last was annexed, according to compact, to the crown of Castile.

Conquest of Andalusia. A.D. 1236. and Valencia.

It could hardly have been expected about the middle of the thirteenth century, when the splendid conquests of Ferdinand and James had planted the Christian banner on the three principal Moorish cities, that two hundred and fifty years were yet to elapse before the rescue of Spain from their yoke should be completed. Ambition, religious zeal, national enmity, could not be supposed to pause in a career which now seemed to be obstructed by such moderate difficulties; yet we find, on the contrary, the exertions of the Spaniards begin from this time to relax, and their acquisitions of territory to become more

Expulsion of the Moors long delayed.

1 A letter of Alfonso IX., who gained this victory, to Pope Innocent III., puts the loss of the Moors at 180,000 men. The Arabian historians, though without specifying numbers, seem to confirm this immense slaughter, which nevertheless it is difficult to conceive before the invention of gunpowder, or indeed since. Cardonne, t. ii. p. 327.

2 If we could rely on a Moorish author quoted by Cardonne (t. i. p. 337), the city of Cordova contained, I know not exactly in what century, 200,000 houses, 600 mosques, and 900 public baths. There were 12,000 towns and villages on the banks of the Guadalquivir. This, however, must be greatly exaggerated, as numerical statements generally are. The mines of gold and silver were very productive. And the revenues of the khalifs of Cordova are said to have amounted to 130,000,000 of French money; besides large contributions that, according to the practice of oriental governments, were paid in the fruits of the earth. Other proofs of the extraordinary opulence and splendor of this monarchy are dispersed in Cardonne's work, from which they have been chiefly borrowed by later writers. The splendid engravings in Murphy's Moorish Antiquities of Spain illustrate this subject.

slow. One of the causes, undoubtedly, that produced this unexpected protraction of the contest was the superior means of resistance which the Moors found in retreating. Their population, spread originally over the whole of Spain, was now condensed, and, if I may so say, become no further compressible, in a single province. It had been mingled, in the northern and central parts, with the Mozarabic Christians, their subjects and tributaries, not perhaps treated with much injustice, yet naturally and irremediably their enemies. Toledo and Saragosa, when they fell under a Christian sovereign, were full of these inferior Christians, whose long intercourse with their masters has infused the tones and dialect of Arabia into the language of Castile.[1] But in the twelfth century the Moors, exasperated by defeat and jealous of secret disaffection, began to persecute their Christian subjects, till they renounced or fled for their religion; so that in the southern provinces scarcely any professors of Christianity were left at the time of Ferdinand's invasion. An equally severe policy was adopted on the other side. The Moors had been permitted to dwell in Saragosa as the Christians had dwelt before, subjects, not slaves; but on the capture of Seville they were entirely expelled, and new settlers invited from every part of Spain. The strong fortified towns of Andalusia, such as Gibraltar, Algeciras, Tariffa, maintained also a more formidable resistance than had been experienced in Castile; they cost tedious sieges, were sometimes recovered by the enemy, and were always liable to his attacks. But the great protection of the Spanish Mohammedans was found in the alliance and ready aid of their kindred beyond the Straits. Accustomed to hear of the African Moors only as pirates, we cannot easily conceive the powerful dynasties, the warlike chiefs, the vast armies, which for seven or eight centuries illustrate the annals of that people. Their assistance was always afforded to the true believers in Spain, though their ambition was generally dreaded by those who stood in need of their valor.[2]

Probably, however, the kings of Granada were most indebted to the indolence which gradually became characteristic of their enemies. By the cession of Murcia to Castile, the kingdom of Aragon shut itself out from the possibility of

[1] Mariana, l. xi. c. 1; Gibbon, c. 51.

[2] Cardonne, t. ii. and iii. passim.

extending those conquests which had ennobled her earlier sovereigns; and their successors, not less ambitious and enterprising, diverted their attention towards objects beyond the peninsula. The Castilian, patient and undesponding in bad success, loses his energy as the pressure becomes less heavy, and puts no ordinary evil in comparison with the exertions by which it must be removed. The greater part of his country freed by his arms, he was content to leave the enemy in a single province rather than undergo the labor of making his triumph complete.

If a similar spirit of insubordination had not been found compatible in earlier ages with the aggrandizement of the Castilian monarchy, we might ascribe its want of splendid successes against the Moors to the continued rebellions which disturbed that government for more than a century after the death of Ferdinand III. His son, Alfonso X., might justly acquire the surname of Wise for his general proficiency in learning, and especially in astronomical science, if these attainments deserve praise in a king who was incapable of preserving his subjects in their duty. As a legislator, Alfonso, by his code of the Siete Partidas, sacrificed the ecclesiastical rights of his crown to the usurpation of Rome;[1] and his philosophy sunk below the level of ordinary prudence when he permitted the phantom of an imperial crown in Germany to seduce his hopes for almost twenty years. For the sake of such an illusion he would even have withdrawn himself from Castile, if the states had not remonstrated against an expedition that would probably have cost him the kingdom. In the latter years of his turbulent reign Alfonso had to contend against his son. The right of representation was hitherto unknown in Castile, which had borrowed little from the customs of feudal nations. By the received law of succession the nearer was always preferred to the more remote, the son to the grandson. Alfonso X. had established the different maxim of representation by his code of the Siete Partidas, the authority of which, however, was not universally acknowledged. The question soon came to an issue: on the death of his elder son Ferdinand, leaving two male children, Sancho their uncle asserted his claim, founded upon the ancient Castilian right of succession; and

Alfonso X. A.D. 1252.

[1] Marina, Ensayo Historico-Critico, p. 272, &c.

this, chiefly no doubt through fear of arms, though it did not want plausible arguments, was ratified by an assembly of the cortes, and secured, notwithstanding the king's reluctance, by the courage of Sancho. But the descendants of Ferdinand, generally called the infants of la Cerda, by the protection of France, to whose royal family they were closely allied, and of Aragon, always prompt to interfere in the disputes of a rival people, continued to assert their pretensions for more than half a century, and, though they were not very successful, did not fail to aggravate the troubles of their country.

Civil disturbances of Castile. Sancho IV. A.D. 1284. Ferdinand IV. A.D. 1295. Alfonso XI. A.D. 1312.

The annals of Sancho IV. and his two immediate successors, Ferdinand IV. and Alfonso XI., present a series of unhappy and dishonorable civil dissensions with too much rapidity to be remembered or even understood. Although the Castilian nobility had no pretence to the original independence of the French peers, or to the liberties of feudal tenure, they assumed the same privilege of rebelling upon any provocation from their sovereign. When such occurred, they seem to have been permitted, by legal custom, to renounce their allegiance by a solemn instrument, which exempted them from the penalties of treason.[1] A very few families composed an oligarchy, the worst and most ruinous condition of political society, alternately the favorites and ministers of the prince, or in arms against him. If unable to protect themselves in their walled towns, and by the aid of their faction, these Christian patriots retired to Aragon or Granada, and excited an hostile power against their country, and perhaps their religion. Nothing is more common in the Castilian history than instances of such defection. Mariana remarks coolly of the family of Castro, that they were much in the habit of revolting to the Moors.[2] This house and that of Lara were at one time the great rivals for power; but from the time of Alfonso X. the former seems to have declined, and the sole family that came in competition with the Laras during the tempestuous period that followed was that of Haro, which possessed the lordship of Biscay by an hereditary title. The evils of a weak gov-

[1] Mariana, l. xiii. c. 11.

[2] Alvarus Castrius patriâ aliquanto antea, uti moris erat, renunciatâ.—Castria gens per hæc tempora ad Mauros sæpe defecisse visa est. l. xii. c. 12. See also chapters 17 and 19.

ernment were aggravated by the unfortunate circumstances in which Ferdinand IV. and Alfonso XI. ascended the throne; both minors, with a disputed regency, and the interval too short to give ambitious spirits leisure to subside. There is indeed some apology for the conduct of the Laras and Haros in the character of their sovereigns, who had but one favorite method of avenging a dissembled injury, or anticipating a suspected treason. Sancho IV. assassinates Don Lope Haro in his palace at Valladolid. Alfonso XI. invites to court the infant Don Juan, his first-cousin, and commits a similar violence. Such crimes may be found in the history of other countries, but they were nowhere so usual as in Spain, which was far behind France, England, and even Germany, in civilization.

Peter the Cruel. A.D. 1350.

But whatever violence and arbitrary spirit might be imputed to Sancho and Alfonso was forgotten in the unexampled tyranny of Peter the Cruel. A suspicion is frequently intimated by Mariana, which seems, in more modern times, to have gained some credit, that party malevolence has at least grossly exaggerated the enormities of this prince.[1] It is difficult, however, to believe that a number of atrocious acts unconnected with each other, and generally notorious enough in their circumstances, have been ascribed to any innocent man. The history of his reign, chiefly derived, it is admitted, from the pen of an inveterate enemy, Lope de Ayala, charges him with the murder of his wife, Blanche of Bourbon, most of his brothers and sisters, with Eleanor Gusman, their mother, many Castilian nobles, and multitudes of the commonalty; besides continual outrages of licentiousness, and especially a pretended marriage with a noble lady of the Castrian family. At length a rebellion was headed by his illegitimate brother,

[1] There is in general room enough for scepticism as to the characters of men who are only known to us through their enemies. History is full of calumnies, and of calumnies that can never be effaced. But I really see no ground for thinking charitably of Peter the Cruel. Froissart, part i. c. 230, and Matteo Villani (in Script. Rerum Italic. t. xiv. p 53), the latter of whom died before the rebellion of Henry of Trastamare, speak of him much in the same terms as the Spanish historians. And why should Ayala be doubted, when he gives a long list of murders committed in the face of day, within the recollection of many persons living when he wrote? There may be a question whether Richard III. smothered his nephews in the Tower; but nobody can dispute that Henry VIII. cut off Anna Boleyn's head.

The passage from Matteo Villani above mentioned is as follows:—Cominciò aspramente a se far ubbidire, perchè temendo de' suoi baroni, trovò modo di far infamare l' uno l' altro, e prendendo cagione, gli cominciò ad uccidere con le sue mani. E in brieve tempo ne fece morire 25 e tre suoi fratelli fece morire, &c.

Henry count of Trastamare, with the assistance of Aragon and Portugal. This, however, would probably have failed of dethroning Peter, a resolute prince, and certainly not destitute of many faithful supporters, if Henry had not invoked the more powerful succor of Bertrand du Guesclin, and the companies of adventure, who, after the pacification between France and England, had lost the occupation of war, and retained only that of plunder. With mercenaries so disciplined it was in vain for Peter to contend; but, abandoning Spain for a moment, he had recourse to a more powerful weapon from the same armory. Edward the Black Prince, then resident at Bordeaux, was induced by the promise of Biscay to enter Spain as the ally of Castile; and at

A.D. 1367.

the great battle of Navarette he continued lord of the ascendant over those who had so often already been foiled by his prowess. Du Guesclin was made prisoner; Henry fled to Aragon, and Peter remounted the throne. But a second revolution was at hand: the Black Prince, whom he had ungratefully offended, withdrew into Guienne; and he lost his kingdom and life in a second short contest with his brother.

House of Trastamare. Henry II. A.D. 1368. John I. A.D. 1379. Henry III. A.D. 1390.

A more fortunate period began with the accession of Henry. His own reign was hardly disturbed by any rebellion; and though his successors, John I. and Henry III., were not altogether so unmolested, especially the latter, who ascended the throne in his minority, yet the troubles of their time were slight in comparison with those formerly excited by the houses of Lara and Haro, both of which were now happily extinct. Though Henry II.'s illegitimacy left him no title but popular choice, his queen was sole representative of the Cerdas, the offspring, as has been mentioned above, of Sancho IV.'s elder brother, and, by the extinction of the younger branch, unquestioned heiress of the royal line. Some years afterwards, by the marriage of Henry III. with Catherine, daughter of John of Gaunt and Constance, an illegitimate child of Peter the Cruel, her pretensions, such as they were, became merged in the crown.

John II. A.D. 1406.

No kingdom could be worse prepared to meet the disorders of a minority than Castile, and in none did the circumstances so frequently recur. John II. was but fourteen months old at his accession; and but for the disinterestedness of his uncle Ferdinand, the nobility would have been inclined to avert the danger by placing that prince upon the throne. In this instance, however, Castile suffered less from faction during the infancy of her sovereign than in his maturity. The queen dowager, at first jointly with Ferdinand, and solely after his accession to the crown of Aragon, administered the government with credit. Fifty years had elapsed at her death in 1418 since the elevation of the house of Trastamare, who had entitled themselves to public affection by conforming themselves more strictly than their predecessors to the constitutional laws of Castile, which were never so well established as during this period. In external affairs their reigns were not what is considered as glorious. They were generally at peace with Aragon and Granada; but one memorable defeat by the Portuguese at Aljubarrota disgraces the annals of John I., whose cause was as unjust as his arms were unsuccessful. This comparatively golden period ceases at the majority of John II. His reign was filled up by a series of conspiracies and civil wars, headed by his cousins John and Henry, the infants of Aragon, who enjoyed very extensive territories in Castile, by the testament of their father Ferdinand. Their brother the king of Aragon frequently lent the assistance of his arms. John himself, the elder of these two princes, by marriage with the heiress of the kingdom of Navarre, stood in a double relation to Castile, as a neighboring sovereign, and as a member of the native oligarchy. These conspiracies were all ostensibly directed against the favorite of John II., Alvaro de Luna, who retained for five-and-thirty years an absolute control over his feeble master. The adverse faction naturally ascribed to this powerful minister every criminal intention and all public mischiefs. He was certainly not more scrupulous than the generality of statesmen, and appears to have been rapacious in accumulating wealth. But there was an energy and courage about Alvaro de Luna which distinguishes him from the cowardly sycophants who usually rise by the favor of weak princes; and Castile probably would not have been happier under the administration of his enemies. His fate is among the memorable lessons of history. After a life of troubles endured for the sake of this favorite, sometimes a fugitive, sometimes a prisoner, his son heading rebellions

A.D. 1385.

Power and fall of Alvaro de Luna.

against him, John II. suddenly yielded to an intrigue of the palace, and adopted sentiments of dislike towards the man he had so long loved. No substantial charge appears to have been brought against Alvaro de Luna, except that general malversation which it was too late for the king to object to him. The real cause of John's change of affection was, most probably, the insupportable restraint which the weak are apt to find in that spell of a commanding understanding which they dare not break; the torment of living subject to the ascendant of an inferior, which has produced so many examples of fickleness in sovereigns. That of John II. is not the least conspicuous. Alvaro de Luna was brought to a summary trial and beheaded; his estates were confiscated. He met his death with the intrepidity of Strafford, to whom he seems to have borne some resemblance in character.

John II. did not long survive his minister, dying in 1454, after a reign that may be considered as inglorious, compared with any except that of his successor. If the father was not respected, the son fell completely into contempt. He had been governed by Pacheco, marquis of Villena, as implicitly as John by Alvaro de Luna. This influence lasted for some time afterwards. But the king inclining to transfer his confidence to the queen Joanna of Portugal, and to one Bertrand de Cueva, upon whom common fame had fixed as her paramour, a powerful confederacy of disaffected nobles was formed against the royal authority. In what degree Henry IV.'s government had been improvident or oppressive towards the people, it is hard to determine. The chiefs of that rebellion, Carillo archbishop of Toledo, the admiral of Castile, a veteran leader of faction, and the marquis of Villena, so lately the king's favorite, were undoubtedly actuated only by selfish ambition and revenge. They deposed Henry in an assembly of their faction at Avila with a sort of theatrical pageantry which has often been described. But modern historians, struck by the appearance of judicial solemnity in this proceeding, are sometimes apt to speak of it as a national act; while, on the contrary, it seems to have been reprobated by the majority of the Castilians as an audacious outrage upon a sovereign who, with many defects, had not been guilty of any excessive tyranny. The confederates set up Alfonso, the king's brother, and a civil war of some duration ensued,

Henry IV.

A.D. 1465.

in which they had the support of Aragon. The queen of Castile had at this time borne a daughter, whom the enemies of Henry IV., and indeed no small part of his adherents, were determined to treat as spurious. Accordingly, after the death of Alfonso, his sister Isabel was considered as heiress of the kingdom. She might have aspired, with the assistance of the confederates, to its immediate possession; but, avoiding the odium of a contest with her brother, Isabel agreed to a treaty, by which the succession was absolutely settled upon her. This arrangement was not long afterwards followed by the union of that princess with Ferdinand, son of the king of Aragon. This marriage was by no means acceptable to a part of the Castilian oligarchy, who had preferred a connection with Portugal. And as Henry had never lost sight of the interests of one whom he considered, or pretended to consider, as his daughter, he took the first opportunity of revoking his forced disposition of the crown and restoring the direct line of succession in favor of the princess Joanna. Upon his death, in 1474, the right was to be decided by arms. Joanna had on her side the common presumptions of law, the testamentary disposition of the late king, the support of Alfonso king of Portugal, to whom she was betrothed, and of several considerable leaders among the nobility, as the young marquis of Villena, the family of Mendoza, and the archbishop of Toledo, who, charging Ferdinand with ingratitude, had quitted a party which he had above all men contributed to strengthen. For Isabella were the general belief of Joanna's illegitimacy, the assistance of Aragon, the adherence of a majority both among the nobles and people, and, more than all, the reputation of ability which both she and her husband had deservedly acquired. The scale was however pretty equally balanced, till the king of Portugal having been defeated at Toro in 1476, Joanna's party discovered their inability to prosecute the war by themselves, and successively made their submission to Ferdinand and Isabella.

A.D. 1469.

Constitution of Castile. Succession of the crown.

The Castilians always considered themselves as subject to a legal and limited monarchy. For several ages the crown was elective, as in most nations of German origin, within the limits of one royal family.[1] In general, of course, the public

[1] Defuncto in pace principe, primates totius regni unà cum sacerdotibus successorum regni concilio communi constituant. Concil. Toletan. IV. c. 75.

choice fell upon the nearest heir; and it became a prevailing usage to elect a son during the lifetime of his father, till about the eleventh century a right of hereditary succession was clearly established. But the form of recognizing the heir apparent's title in an assembly of the cortes has subsisted until our own time.[1]

National councils.

In the original Gothic monarchy of Spain, civil as well as ecclesiastical affairs were decided in national councils, the acts of many of which are still extant, and have been published in ecclesiastical collections. To these assemblies the dukes and other provincial governors, and in general the principal individuals of the realm, were summoned along with spiritual persons. This double aristocracy of church and state continued to form the great council of advice and consent in the first ages of the new kingdoms of Leon and Castile. The prelates and nobility, or rather some of the more distinguished nobility, appear to have concurred in all general measures of legislation, as we infer from the preamble of their statutes. It would be against analogy, as well as without evidence, to suppose that any representation of the commons had been formed in the earlier period of the monarchy. In the preamble of laws passed in 1020, and at several subsequent times during that and the ensuing century, we find only the bishops and magnats recited as present.

Admission of deputies from towns

According to the General Chronicle of Spain, deputies from the Castilian towns formed a part of cortes in 1169, a date not to be rejected as incompatible with their absence in 1178. However, in 1188, the first year of the reign of Alfonso IX., they are expressly mentioned; and from that era were constant and necessary parts of those general assemblies.[2] It has been seen already that the corporate towns or districts of

apud Marina, Teoria de las Cortes, t. ii. p. 2. This important work, by the author of the Ensayo Historico-Critico, quoted above, contains an ample digest of the parliamentary law of Castile, drawn from original and, in a great degree, unpublished records. I have been favored with the use of a copy, from which I am the more disposed to make extracts, as the book is likely, through its liberal principles, to become almost as scarce in Spain as in England. Marina's former work (the Ensayo Hist.-Crit.) furnishes a series of testimonies (c. 66) to the elective character of the monarchy from Pelayo downwards to the twelfth century.

1 Teoria de las Cortes, t. ii. p. 7.

2 Ensayo Hist.-Crit. p. 77; Teoria de las Cortes, t. i. p. 66. Marina seems to have somewhat changed his opinion since the publication of the former work, where he inclines to assert that the commons were from the earliest times admitted into the legislature. In 1188, the first year of the reign of Alfonso IX., we find positive mention of la muchedumbre de las cibdades è embiados de cada cibdat.

Castile had early acquired considerable importance, arising less from commercial wealth, to which the towns of other kingdoms were indebted for their liberties, than from their utility in keeping up a military organization among the people. To this they probably owe their early reception into the cortes as integrant portions of the legislature, since we do not read that taxes were frequently demanded, till the extravagance of later kings, and their alienation of the domain, compelled them to have recourse to the national representatives.

Every chief town of a concejo or corporation ought perhaps, by the constitution of Castile, to have received its regular writ for the election of deputies to cortes.[1] But there does not appear to have been, in the best times, any uniform practice in this respect. At the cortes of Burgos, in 1315, we find one hundred and ninety-two representatives from more than ninety towns; at those of Madrid, in 1391, one hundred and twenty-six were sent from fifty towns; and the latter list contains names of several places which do not appear in the former.[2] No deputies were present from the kingdom of Leon in the cortes of Alcala in 1348, where, among many important enactments, the code of the Siete Partidas first obtained a legislative recognition.[3] We find, in short, a good deal more irregularity than during the same period in England, where the number of electing boroughs varied pretty considerably at every parliament. Yet the cortes of Castile did not cease to be a numerous body and a fair representation of the people till the reign of John II. The first princes of the house of Trastamare had acted in all points with the advice of their cortes. But John II., and still more his son Henry IV., being conscious of their own unpopularity, did not venture to meet a full assembly of the nation. Their writs were directed only to certain towns — an abuse for which the looseness of preceding usage had given a pretence.[4] It must be owned that the people bore it in general very patiently. Many of the corporate towns, impoverished

[1] Teoria de las Cortes, p. 139.

[2] Id. p. 148. Geddes gives a list of one hundred and twenty-seven deputies from forty-eight towns to the cortes at Madrid in 1390. — Miscellaneous Tracts, vol. iii.

[3] Id. p. 154.

[4] Sepades (says John II. in 1442) que en el ayuntamiento que yo fice en la noble villa de Valladolid . . . . los procuradores de ciertas cibdades é villas de mis reynos que por mi mandado fueron llamados. This language is repeated as to subsequent meetings. p. 156.

by civil warfare and other causes, were glad to save the cost of defraying their deputies' expenses. Thus, by the year 1480, only seventeen cities had retained privilege of representation. A vote was afterwards added for Granada, and three more in later times for Palencia, and the provinces of Estremadura and Galicia.[1] It might have been easy perhaps to redress this grievance while the exclusion was yet fresh and recent. But the privileged towns, with a mean and preposterous selfishness, although their zeal for liberty was at its height, could not endure the only means of effectually securing it, by a restoration of elective franchises to their fellow-citizens. The cortes of 1506 assert, with one of those bold falsifications upon which a popular body sometimes ventures, that "it is established by some laws, and by immemorial usage, that eighteen cities of these kingdoms have the right of sending deputies to cortes, and no more;" remonstrating against the attempts made by some other towns to obtain the same privilege, which they request may not be conceded. This remonstrance is repeated in 1512.[2]

From the reign of Alfonso XI., who restrained the government of corporations to an oligarchy of magistrates, the right of electing members of cortes was confined to the ruling body, the bailiffs or regidores, whose number seldom exceeded twenty-four, and whose succession was kept up by close election among themselves.[3] The people therefore had no direct share in the choice of representatives. Experience proved, as several instances in these pages will show, that even upon this narrow basis the deputies of Castile were not deficient in zeal for their country and its liberties. But it must be confessed that a small body of electors is always liable to corrupt influence and to intimidation. John II. and Henry IV. often invaded the freedom of election; the latter even named some of the deputies.[4] Several energetic remonstrances were made in cortes against this flagrant grievance. Laws were enacted and other precautions devised to secure the due re-

[1] The cities which retained their representation in cortes were Burgos, Toledo (there was a constant dispute for precedence between these two), Leon, Granada, Cordova, Murcia, Jaen, Zamora, Toro, Soria, Valladolid, Salamanca, Segovia, Avila, Madrid, Guadalaxara, and Cuenca. The representatives of these were supposed to vote not only for their immediate constituents, but for other adjacent towns. Thus Toro voted for Palencia and the kingdom of Galicia, before they obtained separate votes; Salamanca for most of Estremadura; Guadalaxara for Siguenza and four hundred other towns. Teoria de las Cortes, p. 160, 268

[2] Idem, p. 161.

[3] Idem, p. 86, 197.

[4] Idem, p. 199.

turn of deputies. In the sixteenth century the evil, of course, was aggravated. Charles and Philip corrupted the members by bribery.[1] Even in 1573 the cortes are bold enough to complain that creatures of government were sent thither, "who are always held for suspected by the other deputies, and cause disagreement among them."[2]

Spiritual and temporal nobility in cortes.

There seems to be a considerable obscurity about the constitution of the cortes, so far as relates to the two higher estates, the spiritual and temporal nobility. It is admitted that down to the latter part of the thirteenth century, and especially before the introduction of representatives from the commons, they were summoned in considerable numbers. But the writer to whom I must almost exclusively refer for the constitutional history of Castile contends that from the reign of Sancho IV. they took much less share and retained much less influence in the deliberation of cortes.[3] There is a remarkable protest of the archbishop of Toledo, in 1295, against the acts done in cortes, because neither he nor the other prelates had been admitted to their discussions, nor given any consent to their resolutions, although such consent was falsely recited in the laws enacted therein.[4] This protestation is at least a testimony to the constitutional rights of the prelacy, which indeed all the early history of Castile, as well as the analogy of other governments, conspires to demonstrate. In the fourteenth and fifteenth centuries, however, they were more and more excluded. None of the prelates were summoned to the cortes of 1299 and 1301; none either of the prelates or nobles to those of 1370 and 1373, of 1480 and 1505. In all the latter cases, indeed, such members of both orders as happened to be present in the court attended the cortes — a fact which seems to be established by the language of the statutes.

[1] Teoria de las Cortes, p. 218.

[2] p. 202.

[3] p. 67.

[4] Protestamos que desde aquí venimos non fuemos llamados á consejo, ni á los tratados soore los fechos del reyno, ni sobre las otras cosas que hí fueren tractadas et fechas, et sennaladamente sobre los fechos de los consejos de las hermandades et de las peticiones que fueron fechas de su parte, et sobre los otorgamentos que les ficieron, et sobre los previlegios que por esta nazon les fueron otorgados; mas ante fuemos ende apartados et estrannados et secados expresamente nos et los otros perlados et ricos homes et los fijosdalgo; et non fue hí cosa fecha con nuestro consejo. Otrosí protestamos por razon de aquello que dice en los previlegios que les otorgaron, que fueren los perlados llamados, et que eran otorgados de consentimiento et de voluntad dellos, que non fuemos hí presentes ni llamados nin fué fecho con nuestra voluntad, nin consentiemos, niu consentimos en ellos, &c. p. 72.

[5] Teoria de las Cortes, p. 74.

Other instances of a similar kind may be adduced. Nevertheless, the more usual expression in the preamble of laws reciting those summoned to and present at the cortes, though subject to considerable variation, seems to imply that all the three estates were, at least nominally and according to legitimate forms, constituent members of the national assembly. And a chronicle mentions, under the year 1406, the nobility and clergy as deliberating separately, and with some difference of judgment, from the deputies of the commons.[1] A theory, indeed, which should exclude the great territorial aristocracy from their place in cortes, would expose the dignity and legislative rights of that body to unfavorable inferences. But it is manifest that the king exercised very freely a prerogative of calling or omitting persons of both the higher orders at his discretion. The bishops were numerous, and many of their sees not rich; while the same objections of inconvenience applied perhaps to the ricoshombres, but far more forcibly to the lower nobility, the hijosdalgo or caballeros. Castile never adopted the institution of deputies from this order, as in the States General of France and some other countries, much less that liberal system of landed representation, which forms one of the most admirable peculiarities in

[1] t. ii. p. 234. Marina is influenced by a prejudice in favor of the abortive Spanish constitution of 1812, which excluded the temporal and spiritual aristocracy from a place in the legislature, to imagine a similar form of government in ancient times. But his own work furnishes abundant reasons, if I am not mistaken, to modify this opinion very essentially. A few out of many instances may be adduced from the enacting words of statutes, which we consider in England as good evidences to establish a constitutional theory. Sepades que yo hube mio acuerdo é mio consejo con mios hermanos è los arzobispos, é los obispos, é con los ricos homes de Castella, é de Leon, é con homes buenos de las villas de Castella, é de Leon, que fueron conmigo en Valladolit, sobre muchas cosas, &c. Alfonso X. in 1258.) Mandamos enviar llama por cartas del rei é nuestras á los infantes é perlados é ricos homes é infanzones é caballeros é homes buenos de las cibdades é de las villas de los reynos de Castilia et de Toledo é de Leon é de las Estramaduras, é de Gallicia é de las Asturias é del Andalusia. (Writ of summons to cortes of Burgos in 1315.) Con acuerdo de los perlados é de los ricos homes é procuradores de las cibdades é villas é logares de los nuestros reynos. (Ordinances of Toro in 1371.) Estanho hí con él el infante Don Ferrando, &c., é otros perlados é condes é ricos homes é otros caballeros é escuderos, é los procuradores de las cibdades é villas é logares de sus reynos. (Cortes of 1391.) Los tres estados que deben venir á las cortes é ayuntamientos segunt se debe facer é es de buena costumbre antigua. (Cortes of 1393.) This last passage is apparently conclusive to prove that three estates, the superior clergy, the nobility, and the commons, were essential members of the Legislature in Castile, as they were in France and England; and one is astonished to read in Marina that no faltaron á ninguna de las formalidades de derecho los monarcas que no tuvieron por oportuno llamar á cortes para semejantes actos ni al clero ni á la nobleza ni á las personas singulares de uno y otro estado. t. i. p. 69. That great citizen, Jovellanos, appears to have had much wiser notions of the ancient government of his country, as well as of the sort of reformation which she wanted: as we may infer from passages in his Memoria á sus compatriotas, Coruña, 1811, quoted by Marina for the purpose of censure.

our own constitution. It will be seen hereafter that spiritual and even temporal peers were summoned by our kings with much irregularity; and the disordered state of Castile through almost every reign was likely to prevent the establishment of any fixed usage in this and most other points.

Right of taxation.

The primary and most essential characteristic of a limited monarchy is that money can only be levied upon the people through the consent of their representatives. This principle was thoroughly established in Castile; and the statutes which enforce it, the remonstrances which protest against its violation, bear a lively analogy to corresponding circumstances in the history of our constitution. The lands of the nobility and clergy were, I believe, always exempted from direct taxation — an immunity which perhaps rendered the attendance of the members of those estates in the cortes less regular. The corporate districts or concejos, which, as I have observed already, differed from the communities of France and England by possessing a large extent of territory subordinate to the principal town, were bound by their charter to a stipulated annual payment, the price of their franchises, called moneda forera.[1] Beyond this sum nothing could be demanded without the consent of the cortes. Alfonso VIII., in 1177, applied for a subsidy towards carrying on the siege of Cuenca. Demands of money do not however seem to have been very usual before the prodigal reign of Alfonso X. That prince and his immediate successors were not much inclined to respect the rights of their subjects; but they encountered a steady and insuperable resistance. Ferdinand IV., in 1307, promises to raise no money beyond his legal and customary dues. A more explicit law was enacted by Alfonso XI. in 1328, who bound himself not to exact from his people, or cause them to pay any tax, either partial or general, not hitherto established by law, without the previous grant of all the deputies convened to the cortes.[2] This abolition of illegal impositions was several times confirmed by the same prince. The cortes, in 1393, having made a grant to

[1] Marina, Ensayo Hist.-Crit. cap. 158; Teoria de las Cortes, t. ii. p. 387. This is expressed in one of their fueros, or charters: Liberi et ingenui semper maneatis, reddendo mihi et successoribus meis in unoquoque anno in die Pentecostes de unaquaque domo 12 denarios; et, mihi cum bonâ voluntate vestrâ feceritis, nullum servitium faciatis.

[2] De los con echar nin mandar pagar pecho desaforado ninguno, especial nin general, en toda mi tierra, sin ser llamados primeramente á cortes é otorgado por todos los procuradores que hi venieren p. 388.

Henry III., annexed this condition, that "since they had granted him enough for his present necessities, and even to lay up a part for a future exigency, he should swear before one of the archbishops not to take or demand any money, service, or loan, or anything else, of the cities and towns, nor of individuals belonging to them, on any pretence of necessity, until the three estates of the kingdom should first be duly summoned and assembled in cortes according to ancient usage. And if any such letters requiring money have been written, that they shall be *obeyed and not complied with*."[1] His son, John II., having violated this constitutional privilege on the allegation of a pressing necessity, the cortes, in 1420, presented a long remonstrance, couched in very respectful but equally firm language, wherein they assert "the good custom, founded in reason and in justice, that the cities and towns of your kingdoms shall not be compelled to pay taxes or requisitions, or other new tribute, unless your highness order it by advice and with the grant of the said cities and towns, and of their deputies for them." And they express their apprehension lest this right should be infringed, because, as they say, "there remains no other privilege or liberty which can be profitable to subjects if this be shaken."[2] The king gave them as full satisfaction as they desired that his encroachment should not be drawn into precedent. Some fresh abuses during the unfortunate reign of Henry IV. produced another declaration in equally explicit language, forming part of the sentence awarded by the arbitrators to whom the differences between the king and his people had been referred at Medina del Campo in 1465.[3] The catholic kings, as they are emi nently called, Ferdinand and Isabella, never violated this

[1] Obedecidas é non cumplidas. This expression occurs frequently in provisions made against illegal acts of the crown; and is characteristic of the singular respect with which the Spaniards always thought it right to treat their sovereign, while they were resisting the abuses of his authority.

[2] La buena costumbre é possession fundada en razon é en justicia que las cibdades é villas de vuestros reinos tenian de no ser mandado coger monedas é pedidos nin otro tributo nuevo alguno en los vuestros reinos sin que la vuestra señoria lo faga é ordene de consejo é con otorgamiento de las cibdades é villas de los vuestros reinos é de sus procuradores en su nombre . . . . no queda otro previlegio ni libertad de que los subditos puedan gozar ni aprovechar quebrantado el sobre dicho. t. iii. p. 30.

[3] Declaramos é ordenamos, que el dicho señor rei nin los otros reyes que despues del fueren non echan nin repartan nin pidan pedidos nin monedas en sus reynos, salvo por gran necessidad, é seyendo primero accordado con los perlados é grandes de sus reynos, é con los otros que á la sazon residierin en su consejo, é seyendo para ello llamados los procuradores de las cibdades é villas de sus reynos, que para las tales cosas se suelen é acostumbran llamar, é seyendo per los dichos procuradores otorgado el dicho pedimento é monedas. t. ii. p. 391.

part of the constitution; nor did even Charles I., although sometimes refused money by the cortes, attempt to exact it without their consent.[1] In the Recopilacion, or code of Castilian law published by Philip II., we read a positive declaration against arbitrary imposition of taxes, which remained unaltered on the face of the statute-book till the present age.[2] The law was indeed frequently broken by Philip II.; but the cortes, who retained throughout the sixteenth century a degree of steadiness and courage truly admirable when we consider their political weakness, did not cease to remonstrate with that suspicious tyrant, and recorded their unavailing appeal to the law of Alfonso XI., "so ancient and just, and which so long time has been used and observed."[3]

Control of cortes over expenditure.

The free assent of the people by their representatives to grants of money was by no means a mere matter of form. It was connected with other essential rights indispensable to its effectual exercise; those of examining public accounts and checking the expenditure. The cortes, in the best times at least, were careful to grant no money until they were assured that what had been already levied on their constituents had been properly employed.[4] They refused a subsidy in 1390 because they had already given so much, and, "not knowing how so great a sum had been expended, it would be a great dishonor and mischief to promise any more." In 1406 they stood out a long time, and at length gave only half of what was demanded.[5] Charles I. attempted to obtain money in 1527 from the nobility as well as commons. But the former protested that "their obligation was to follow the king in war, wherefore to contribute money

[1] Marina has published two letters from Charles to the city of Toledo, in 1542 and 1548, requesting them to instruct their deputies to consent to a further grant of money, which they had refused to do without leave of their constituents. t. iii. p. 180, 187.

[2] t. ii. p. 393.

[3] En las cortes de ano de 70 y en las de 76 pedimos á v. m. fuese servide de no poner nuevos impuestos, rentas, pechos, ni derechos ni otros tributos particulares ni generales sin junta del reyno en cortes, como está dispuesto por lei del señor rei Don Alonso, y se significó á v. m. el daño grande que con las nuevas rentas habia rescibido el reino, suplicando á v. m. fuese servido de mandarle aliviar y descargar, y que en lo de adelante se les hiciesse merced de guardar las dichas leyes reales, y que ne se impusiessen nuevas rentas sin su asistencia; pues podria v. m. estar satisfecho de que el reino sirve en las cosas necessarias con toda lealtad y hasta ahora no se ha proveido lo susodicho; y el reino por la obligacion que tiene á pedir á v. m. guarde la dicha lei, y que no solamente han cessado las necessidades de los subditos y naturales de v. m. pero antes crecen de cada dia: vuelve á suplicar á v. m. sea servido concederle lo susodicho, y que las nuevas rentas pechos y derechos se quiten, y que de aquí adelante se guarde la dicha lei del señor rei Don Alonso, como tan antigua y justa y que tanto tiempo se usó y guardó. p. 395 This petition was in 1579.

[4] Marina, t. ii. p. 404, 406.

[5] p. 409.

was totally against their privilege, and for that reason they could not acquiesce in his majesty's request."[1] The commons also refused on this occasion. In 1538, on a similar proposition, the superior and lower nobility (los grandes y caballeros) "begged with all humility that they might never hear any more of that matter."[2]

The contributions granted by cortes were assessed and collected by respectable individuals (hombres buenos) of the several towns and villages.[3] This *repartition*, as the French call it, of direct taxes is a matter of the highest importance in those countries where they are imposed by means of a gross assessment on a district. The produce was paid to the royal council. It could not be applied to any other purpose than that to which the tax had been appropriated. Thus the cortes of Segovia, in 1407, granted a subsidy for the war against Granada, on condition "that it should not be laid out on any other service except this war;" which they requested the queen and Ferdinand, both regents in John II.'s minority, to confirm by oath. Part, however, of the money remaining unexpended, Ferdinand wished to apply it to his own object of procuring the crown of Aragon; but the queen first obtained not only a release from her oath by the pope, but the consent of the cortes. They continued to insist upon this appropriation, though ineffectually, under the reign of Charles I.[4]

The cortes did not consider it beyond the line of their duty, notwithstanding the respectful manner in which they always addressed the sovereign, to remonstrate against profuse expenditure even in his own household. They told Alfonso X. in 1258, in the homely style of that age, that they thought it fitting that the king and his wife should eat at the rate of a hundred and fifty maravedis a day, and no more; and that the king should order his attendants to eat more moderately than they did.[5] They remonstrated more forcibly against the prodigality of John II. Even in 1559 they spoke with an undaunted Castilian spirit to Philip II.:—"Sir, the expenses of your royal establishment and household are much increased; and we conceive it would much redound to the good of these kingdoms that your majesty should direct them to be lowered,

[1] Pero que contribuir á la guerra con ciertas sumas era totalmente opuesto á sus previlegios, é asi que no podrian acomodarse á lo que s. m. deseaba.—p. 411.

[2] Marina, t. ii. p. 411.

[3] Marina, t. ii. p. 398.

[4] p. 412.

[5] p. 417.

both as a relief to your wants, and that all the great men and other subjects of your majesty may take example therefrom to restrain the great disorder and excess they commit in that respect."[1]

Forms of the cortes.

The forms of a Castilian cortes were analogous to those of an English parliament in the fourteenth century. They were summoned by a writ almost exactly coincident in expression with that in use among us.[2] The session was opened by a speech from the chancellor or other chief officer of the court. The deputies were invited to con sider certain special business, and commonly to grant money. After the principal affairs were despatched they conferred to gether, and, having examined the instructions of their respective constituents, drew up a schedule of petitions. These were duly answered one by one; and from the petition and answer, if favorable, laws were afterwards drawn up where the matter required a new law, or promises of redress were given if the petition related to an abuse or grievance. In the struggling condition of Spanish liberty under Charles I., the crown began to neglect answering the petitions of cortes, or to use unsatisfactory generalities of expression. This gave rise to many remonstrances. The deputies insisted in 1523 on having answers before they granted money. They repeated the same contention in 1525, and obtained a general law inserted in the Recopilacion enacting that the king should answer all their petitions before he dissolved the assembly.[4] This, however, was disregarded as before; but the cortes, whose intrepid honesty under Philip II. so often attracts our admiration, continued as late as 1586 to appeal to the written statute and lament its violation.[5]

Right of cortes in legislation.

According to the ancient fundamental constitution of Castile, the king did not legislate for his subjects without their consent. The code of the Visigoths, called in Spain the Fuero Jusgo, was enacted in public councils, as were also the laws of the early kings of Leon, which appears by the reciting words of their preambles.[6] This

[1] Senhor, los gastos de vuestro real estado y mesa son muy crescidos, y entendemos que convernia mucho al bien de estos reinos que v. m. los mandasse moderar, así para algun remedio de sus necessidades, como para que de v. m. tomen egempló totos los grandes y caballeros y otros subditos de v. m. en la gran desorden y excessos que hacen en las cosas sobredichas. p. 437.

[2] Marina, t. i. p. 175; t. iii. p. 103.

[3] t. i. p. 278.

[4] p. 301.

[5] p. 288–304.

[6] t. ii. p. 202. The acts of tne cortes of Leon in 1020 run thus: Omnes pon

consent was originally given only by the higher estates, who might be considered, in a large sense, as representing the nation, though not chosen by it; but from the end of the twelfth century by the elected deputies of the commons in cortes. The laws of Alfonso X. in 1258, those of the same prince in 1274, and many others in subsequent times, are declared to be made with the consent (con acuerdo) of the several orders of the kingdom. More commonly, indeed, the preamble of Castilian statutes only recites their advice (consejo); but I do not know that any stress is to be laid on this circumstance. The laws of the Siete Partidas, compiled by Alfonso X., did not obtain any direct sanction till the famous cortes of Alcala, in 1348, when they were confirmed along with several others, forming altogether the basis of the statute-law of Spain.[1] Whether they were in fact received before that time has been a matter controverted among Spanish antiquaries, and upon the question of their legal validity at the time of their promulgation depends an important point in Castilian history, the disputed right of succession between Sancho IV. and the infants of la Cerda; the former claiming under the ancient customary law, the latter under the new dispositions of the Siete Partidas. If the king could not legally change the established laws without consent of his cortes, as seems most probable, the right of representative succession did not exist in favor of his grandchildren, and Sancho IV. cannot be considered as an usurper.

It appears, upon the whole, to have been a constitutional principle, that laws could neither be made nor annulled except in cortes. In 1506 this is claimed by the deputies as an established right.[2] John I. had long before admitted that what was done by cortes and general assemblies could not be undone by letters missive, but by such cortes and assemblies alone.[3] For the kings of Castile had adopted the English

tifices et abbates et optimates regni Hispaniæ jussu ipsius regis talia decreta decrevimus quæ firmiter teneantur futuris temporibus. So those of Salamanca, in 1178: Ego rex Fernandus inter cætera quæ cum episcopis et abbatibus regni nostri et quamplurimis aliis religiosis, cum comitibus terrarum et principibus et rectoribus provinciarum, toto posse tenenda statuimus apud Salamancam.

[1] Ensayo Hist.-Crit. p. 353; Teoria de las Cortes, t. ii. p. 77. Marina seems to have changed his opinion between the publication of these two works, in the former of which he contends for the previous authority of the Siete Partidas, and in favor of the infants of la Cerda.

[2] Los reyes establicieron que cuando hubiesen de hacer leyes, para que fuesen provechosas á sus reynos y cada provincias fuesen proveidas, se llamasen cortes y procuradores que entendiesen en ellas, y por esto se establecio lei que no se hiciesen ni renovasen leyes sino en cortes. Teoria de las Cortes, t. ii. p. 218.

[3] Lo que es fecho por cortes é por

practice of dispensing with statutes by a non obstante clause in their grants. But the cortes remonstrated more steadily against this abuse than our own parliament, who suffered it to remain in a certain degree till the Revolution. It was several times enacted upon their petition, especially by an explicit statute of Henry II., that grants and letters-patent dispensing with statutes should not be obeyed.[1] Nevertheless, John II., trusting to force or the servility of the judges, had the assurance to dispense explicitly with this very law.[2] The cortes of Valladolid, in 1442, obtained fresh promises and enactments against such an abuse. Philip I. and Charles I. began to legislate without asking the consent of cortes; this grew much worse under Philip II., and reached its height under his successors, who entirely abolished all constitutional privileges.[3] In 1555 we find a petition that laws made in cortes should be revoked nowhere else. The reply was such as became that age: "To this we answer, that we shall do what best suits our government." But even in 1619, and still afterwards, the patriot representatives of Castile continued to lift an unavailing voice against illegal ordinances, though in the form of very humble petition; perhaps the latest testimonies to the expiring liberties of their country.[4] The denial of exclusive legislative authority to the crown must, however, be understood to admit the legality of particular ordinances designed to strengthen the king's executive government.[5] These, no doubt, like the royal proclamations in England, extended sometimes very far, and subjected the people to a sort of arbitrary coercion much beyond what our enlightened notions of freedom would consider as reconcilable to it. But in the middle ages such temporary commands and prohibitions were not reckoned strictly legislative, and passed, perhaps rightly, for inevitable consequences of a scanty code and short sessions of the national council.

The kings were obliged to swear to the observance of laws enacted in cortes, besides their general coronation oath to keep the laws and preserve the liberties of their people. Of this we find several instances from the middle of the thir-

ayuntamientos que non se pueda disfacer por las tales cartas, salvo por ayuntamientos é cortes. Teoria de las Cortes, t. ii. p. 215.

[1] p. 215.

[2] p. 216; t. iii. p. 40.

[3] t. ii. p. 218.

[4] Ha suplicado el reino á v. m. no se promulguen nuevas leyes, ni en todo ni en parte las antiguas se alteren, sin que sea por cortes . . . . y por ser de tanta importancia vuelve el reino á suplicarlo humilmente á v. m. p. 220.

[5] p. 207.

teenth century, and the practice continued till the time of John II., who, in 1433, on being requested to swear to the laws then enacted, answered that he intended to maintain them, and consequently no oath was necessary; an evasion in which the cortes seem unaccountably to have acquiesced.[1] The guardians of Alfonso XI. not only swore to observe all that had been agreed on at Burgos in 1315, but consented that, if any one of them did not keep his oath, the people should no longer be obliged to regard or obey him as regent.[2]

Other rights of the cortes.

It was customary to assemble the cortes of Castile for many purposes besides those of granting money and concurring in legislation. They were summoned in every reign to acknowledge and confirm the succession of the heir apparent; and upon his accession to swear allegiance.[3] These acts were, however, little more than formal, and accordingly have been preserved for the sake of parade after all the real dignity of the cortes was annihilated. In the fourteenth and fifteenth centuries they claimed and exercised very ample powers. They assumed the right, when questions of regency occurred, to limit the prerogative, as well as to designate the persons who were to use it.[4] And the frequent minorities of Castilian kings, which were unfavorable enough to tranquillity and subordination, served to confirm these parliamentary privileges. The cortes were usually consulted upon all material business. A law of Alfonso XI. in 1328, printed in the Recopilacion or code published by Philip II., declares, "Since in the arduous affairs of our kingdom the counsel of our natural subjects is necessary, especially of the deputies from our cities and towns, therefore we ordain and command that on such great occasions the cortes shall be assembled, and counsel shall be taken of the three estates of our kingdoms, as the kings our forefathers have been used to do."[5] A cortes of John II., in 1419, claimed this right of being consulted in all matters of importance, with a warm remonstrance against the alleged violation of so wholesome a law by the reigning prince; who answered, that in weighty matters he had acted, and would continue to act, in conformity to it.[6] What should be intended by great and weighty affairs might be not at all agreed

1 Teoria de las Cortes, t. i. p. 306.
2 t. iii. p. 62.
3 t. i. p. 33; t. ii. p. 24.
4 p. 230.
5 t. i. p. 31.
6 p. 34.

upon by the two parties; to each of whose interpretations these words gave pretty full scope. However, the current usage of the monarchy certainly permitted much authority in public deliberations to the cortes. Among other instances, which indeed will continually be found in the common civil histories, the cortes of Ocana, in 1469, remonstrate with Henry IV. for allying himself with England rather than France, and give, as the first reason of complaint, that, "according to the laws of your kingdom, when the kings have anything of great importance in hand, they ought not to undertake it without advice and knowledge of the chief towns and cities of your kingdom."[1] This privilege of general interference was asserted, like other ancient rights, under Charles, whom they strongly urged, in 1548, not to permit his son Philip to depart out of the realm.[2] It is hardly necessary to observe, that, in such times, they had little chance of being regarded.

Council of Castile.

The kings of Leon and Castile acted, during the interval of the cortes, by the advice of a smaller council, answering, as it seems, almost exactly to the king's ordinary council in England. In early ages, before the introduction of the commons, it is sometimes difficult to distinguish this body from the general council of the nation; being composed, in fact, of the same class of persons, though in smaller numbers. A similar difficulty applies to the English history. The nature of their proceedings seems best to ascertain the distinction. All executive acts, including those ordinances which may appear rather of a legislative nature, all grants and charters, are declared to be with the assent of the court (curia), or of the magnats of the palace, or of the chiefs or nobles.[3] This privy council was an essential part of all European monarchies; and, though the sovereign might be considered as free to call in the advice of whomsoever he pleased, yet, in fact, the princes of the blood and most powerful nobility had anciently a constitutional right to be members of such a council, so that it formed a very material check upon his personal authority.

The council underwent several changes in progress of time, which it is not necessary to enumerate. It was justly deemed

[1] Porque, segunt leyes de nuestros reynos, cuando los reyes han de facer alguna cosa de gran importancia, non lo deben facer sin consejo é sabiduria de las cibdades e villas principales de vuestros reynos. Teoria de las Cortes, t. ii. p. 241.

[2] t. iii. p. 183.

[3] Cum assensu magnatum palatii: Cum consilio curiæ meæ: Cum consilio et beneplacito omnium principum meorum, nullo contradicente nec reclamente. Teoria de las Cortes, t. iii. p. 325.

an important member of the constitution, and the cortes showed a laudable anxiety to procure its composition in such a manner as to form a guarantee for the due execution of laws after their own dissolution. Several times, especially in minorities, they even named its members or a part of them; and in the reigns of Henry III. and John II. they obtained the privilege of adding a permanent deputation, consisting of four persons elected out of their own body, annexed as it were to the council, who were to continue at the court during the interval of cortes and watch over the due observance of the laws.[1] This deputation continued as an empty formality in the sixteenth century. In the council the king was bound to sit personally three days in the week. Their business, which included the whole executive government, was distributed with considerable accuracy into what might be despatched by the council alone, under their own seals and signatures, and what required the royal seal.[2] The consent of this body was necessary for almost every act of the crown: for pensions or grants of money, ecclesiastical and political promotions, and for charters of pardon, the easy concession of which was a great encouragement to the homicides so usual in those ages, and was restrained by some of our own laws.[3] But the council did not exercise any judicial authority, if we may believe the well-informed author from whom I have learned these particulars; unlike in this to the ordinary council of the kings of England. It was not until the days of Ferdinand and Isabella that this, among other innovations, was introduced.[4]

Administration of justice.

Civil and criminal justice was administered, in the first instance, by the alcaldes, or municipal judges of towns; elected within themselves, originally, by the community at large, but, in subsequent times, by the governing body. In other places a lord possessed the right of jurisdiction by grant from the crown, not, what we find in countries where the feudal system was more thoroughly established, as incident to his own territorial superiority The kings, however, began in the thirteenth century to appoint judges of their own, called corregidores, a name which seems to express concurrent jurisdiction with the regidores, or ordinary magistrates.[5] The cortes frequently remonstrat-

[1] Teoria de las Cortes, t. ii. p. 346.
[2] p. 354.
[3] p. 360, 362, 372.
[4] t. ii. p. 375, 379.
[5] Alfonso X. says, Ningun ome sea osado juzgar pleytos, se no fuere alcalde puesto

ed against this encroachment. Alfonso XI. consented to withdraw his judges from all corporations by which he had not been requested to appoint them.[1] Some attempts to interfere with the municipal authorities of Toledo produced serious disturbances under Henry III. and John II.[2] Even where the king appointed magistrates at a city's request, he was bound to select them from among the citizens.[3] From this immediate jurisdiction an appeal lay to the adelantado or governor of the province, and from thence to the tribunal of royal alcaldes.[4] The latter, however, could not take cognizance of any cause depending before the ordinary judges; a contrast to the practice of Aragon, where the justiciary's right of evocation (juris firma) was considered as a principal safeguard of public liberty.[5] As a court of appeal, the royal alcaldes had the supreme jurisdiction. The king could only cause their sentence to be revised, but neither alter nor revoke it.[6] They have continued to the present day as a criminal tribunal; but civil appeals were transferred by the ordinances of Toro in 1371 to a new court, styled the king's audience, which, though deprived under Ferdinand and his successors of part of its jurisdiction, still remains one of the principal judicatures in Castile.[7]

Violent actions of some kings of Castile.

No people in a half-civilized state of society have a full practical security against particular acts of arbitrary power. They were more common perhaps in Castile than in any other European monarchy which professed to be free. Laws indeed were not wanting to protect men's lives and liberties, as well as their properties. Ferdinand IV., in 1299, agreed to a petition that "justice shall be executed impartially according to law and right; and that no one shall be put to death or imprisoned, or deprived of his possessions, without trial, and that this be better observed than heretofore."[8] He renewed the same law in 1307. Nevertheless, the most remarkable circumstance of this monarch's history was a violation of so sacred

pol el rey. Id. fol. 27. This seems an encroachment on the municipal magistrates.

1 Teoria de las Cortes, t. ii. p. 251.

2 p. 255. Mariana, l. xx. c. 13.

3 p. 255.

4 p. 266.

5 p. 260.

6 p. 287, 304.

7 Teoria de las Cortes, t. ii. p. 292–302. The use of the present tense, in this and many other passages, will not confuse the attentive reader.

8 Que mandase facer la justicia en aquellos que la merecen comunalmente con fuero é con derecho é los homes que non sean muertos nin presos nin tomados lo que han sin ser oidos por derecho ó por fuero de aquel logar do acaesciere, é que sea guardado mejor que se guardó fasta aquí. Marina, Ensayo Hist.-Critico, p. 148

and apparantly so well-established a law. Two gentlemen having been accused of murder, Ferdinand, without waiting for any process, ordered them to instant execution. They summoned him with their last words to appear before the tribunal of God in thirty days; and his death within the time, which has given him the surname of the Summoned, might, we may hope, deter succeeding sovereigns from iniquity so flagrant. But from the practice of causing their enemies to be assassinated, neither law nor conscience could withhold them. Alfonso XI. was more than once guilty of this crime. Yet he too passed an ordinance in 1325 that no warrant should issue for putting any one to death, or seizing his property, till he should be duly tried by course of law. Henry II. repeats the same law in very explicit language.[1] But the civil history of Spain displays several violations of it. An extraordinary prerogative of committing murder appears to have been admitted in early times by several nations who did not acknowledge unlimited power in their sovereign.[2] Before any regular police was established, a powerful criminal might have been secure from all punishment, but for a notion, as barbarous as any which it served to counteract, that he could be lawfully killed by the personal mandate of the king. And the frequent attendance of sovereigns in their courts of judicature might lead men not accustomed to consider the indispensable necessity of legal forms to confound an act of assassination with the execution of justice.

Confederacies of the nobility.

Though it is very improbable that the nobility were not considered as essential members of the cortes, they certainly attended in smaller numbers than we should expect to find from the great legislative and deliberative authority of that assembly. This arose chiefly from the lawless spirit of that martial aristocracy which placed less confidence in the constitutional methods of resisting arbitrary encroachment than in its own armed combinations.[3] Such confederacies to obtain redress of grievances by force, of which there were five or six remarkable instances, were called Hermandad (brotherhood or union), and, though not

[1] Que non mandemos matar nin prender nin lisiar nin despechar nin tomar á alguno ninguna cosa de lo suyo, sin ser anté llamado é oido é vencido por fuero é por derecho, por querella nin por querellas que á nos fuesen dadas, segunt que esto está ordenado por el rei don Alonso nuestro padre. Teoria de las Cortes, t. ii. p. 287.

[2] Si quis hominem per jussionem regis vel ducis sui occiderit, non requiratur ei, nec sit faidosus, quia jussio domini sui fuit, et non potuit contradicere jussionem. Leges Bajuvariorum, tit. ii. in Baluz Capitularibus.

[3] Teoria de las Cortes, t. ii. p. 465.

so explicitly sanctioned as they were by the celebrated Privilege of Union in Aragon, found countenance in a law of Alfonso X., which cannot be deemed so much to have voluntarily emanated from that prince as to be a record of original rights possessed by the Castilian nobility. "The duty of subjects towards their king," he says, "enjoins them not to permit him knowingly to endanger his salvation, nor to incur dishonor and inconvenience in his person or family, nor to produce mischief to his kingdom. And this may be fulfilled in two ways: one by good advice, showing him the reason wherefore he ought not to act thus; the other by deeds, seeking means to prevent his going on to his own ruin, and putting a stop to those who give him ill counsel. forasmuch as his errors are of worse consequence than those of other men, it is the bounden duty of subjects to prevent his committing them.[1] To this law the insurgents appealed in their coalition against Alvaro de Luna; and indeed we must confess that, however just and admirable the principles which it breathes, so general a license of rebellion was not likely to preserve the tranquillity of a kingdom. The deputies of towns in a cortes of 1445 petitioned the king to declare that no construction should be put on this law inconsistent with the obedience of subjects towards their sovereign: a request to which of course he willingly acceded.

Castile, it will be apparent, bore a closer analogy to England in its form of civil polity than France or even Aragon. But the frequent disorders of its government and a barbarous state of manners rendered violations of law much more continual and flagrant than they were in England under the Plantagenet dynasty. And besides these practical mischiefs, there were two essential defects in the constitution of Castile, through which perhaps it was ultimately subverted. It wanted those two brilliants in the coronet of British liberty, the representation of freeholders among the commons, and trial by jury. The cortes of Castile became a congress of deputies from a few cities, public-spirited indeed and intrepid, as we find them in bad times, to an eminent degree, but too much limited in number, and too unconnected with the territorial aristocracy, to maintain a just balance against the crown. Yet, with every disadvantage, that country possessed a liberal form of government, and was animated with a noble spirit for its defence. Spain, in her late memorable though

1 Ensayo Hist.-Critico, p. 312

short resuscitation, might well have gone back to her ancient institutions, and perfected a scheme of policy which the great example of England would have shown to be well adapted to the security of freedom. What she did, or rather attempted, instead, I need not recall. May her next effort be more wisely planned, and more happily terminated![1]

Affairs of Aragon.

Though the kingdom of Aragon was very inferior in extent to that of Castile, yet the advantages of a better form of government and wiser sovereigns, with those of industry and commerce along a line of sea-coast, rendered it almost equal in importance. Castile rarely intermeddled in the civil dissensions of Aragon; the kings of Aragon frequently carried their arms into the heart of Castile. During the sanguinary outrages of Peter the Cruel, and the stormy revolutions which ended in establishing the house of Trastamare, Aragon was not indeed at peace, nor altogether well governed; but her political consequence rose in the eyes of Europe through the long reign of the ambitious and wily Peter IV., whose sagacity and good fortune redeemed, according to the common notions of mankind, the iniquity with which he stripped his relation the king of Majorca of the Balearic islands, and the constant perfidiousness of his character. I have mentioned in another place the Sicilian war, prosecuted with so much eagerness for many years by Peter III. and his son Alfonso III. After this object was relinquished James II. undertook an enterprise less splendid, but not much less difficult: the conquest of Sardinia. That island, long accustomed to independence, cost an incredible expense of blood and treasure to the kings of Aragon during the whole fourteenth century. It was not fully subdued till the commencement of the next, under the reign of Martin.

Disputed succession after the death of Martin.

At the death of Martin king of Aragon, in 1410, a memorable question arose as to the right of succession. Though Petronilla, daughter of Ramiro II., had reigned in her own right from 1137 to 1172, an opinion seems to have gained ground from the thirteenth century that females could not inherit the crown of Aragon. Peter IV. had excited a civil war by attempting to settle the succession upon his daughter, to the exclusion of his next brother. The birth of a son about the same time suspended the ultimate decision of this question; but it was tacitly understood that what is called the Salic law ought to

[1] The first edition of this work was published in 1818.

prevail.[1] Accordingly, on the death of John I. in 1395, his two daughters were set aside in favor of his brother Martin, though not without opposition on the part of the elder, whose husband, the count of Foix, invaded the kingdom, and desisted from his pretension only through want of force. Martin's son, the king of Sicily, dying in his father's lifetime, the nation was anxious that the king should fix upon his successor, and would probably have acquiesced in his choice. But his dissolution occurring more rapidly than was expected, the throne remained absolutely vacant. The count of Urgel had obtained a grant of the lieutenancy, which was the right of the heir apparent. This nobleman possessed an extensive territory in Catalonia, bordering on the Pyrenees. He was grandson of James, next brother to Peter IV., and, according to our rules of inheritance, certainly stood in the first place. The other claimants were the duke of Gandia, grandson of James II., who, though descended from a more distant ancestor, set up a claim founded on proximity to the royal stock, which in some countries was preferred to a representative title; the duke of Calabria, son of Violante, younger daughter of John I. (the countess of Foix being childless); Frederic count of Luna, a natural son of the younger Martin king of Sicily, legitimated by the pope, but with a reservation excluding him from royal succession; and finally, Ferdinand, infant of Castile, son of the late king's sister.[2] The count of

[1] Zurita, t. ii. f. 188. It was pretended that women were excluded from the crown in England as well as France: and this analogy seems to have had some influence in determining the Aragonese to adopt a Salic law.

[2] The subjoined pedigree will show more clearly the respective titles of the competitors :—

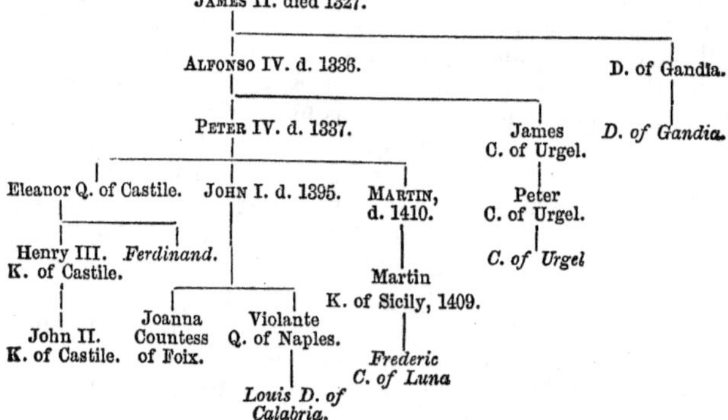

Urgel was favored in general by the Catalans, and he seemed to have a powerful support in Antonio de Luna, a baron of Aragon, so rich that he might go through his own estate from France to Castile. But this apparent superiority frustrated his hopes. The justiciary and other leading Aragonese were determined not to suffer this great constitutional question to be decided by an appeal to force, which might sweep away their liberties in the struggle. Urgel, confident of his right, and surrounded by men of ruined fortunes, was unwilling to submit his pretensions to a civil tribunal. His adherent, Antonio de Luna, committed an extraordinary outrage, the assassination of the archbishop of Saragosa, which alienated the minds of good citizens from his cause. On the other hand, neither the duke of Gandia, who was very old,[1] nor the count of Luna, seemed fit to succeed. The party of Ferdinand, therefore, gained ground by degrees. It was determined however, to render a legal sentence. The cortes of each nation agreed upon the nomination of nine persons, three Aragonese, three Catalans, and three Valencians, who were to discuss the pretensions of the several competitors, and by a plurality of six votes to adjudge the crown. Nothing could be more solemn, more peaceful, nor, in appearance, more equitable than the proceedings of this tribunal. They summoned the claimants before them, and heard them by counsel. One of these, Frederic of Luna, being ill defended, the court took charge of his interests, and named other advocates to maintain them. A month was passed in hearing arguments; a second was allotted to considering them; and at the expiration of the prescribed time it was announced to the people, by the mouth of St. Vincent Ferrier, that Ferdinand of Castile had ascended the throne.[2]

[1] This duke of Gandia died during the interregnum. His son, though not so objectionable on the score of age, seemed to have a worse claim; yet he became a competitor.

[2] Biancæ Commentaria, in Schotti Hispania Illustrata, t. ii. Zurita, t. iii. f. 1–74. Vincent Ferrier was the most distinguished churchman of his time in Spain. His influence, as one of the nine judges, is said to have been very instrumental in procuring the crown for Ferdinand. Five others voted the same way; one for the count of Urgel; one doubtfully between the count of Urgel and duke of Gandia; the ninth declined to vote. Zurita, t. iii. f. 71. It is curious enough that John king of Castile was altogether disregarded; though his claim was at least as plausible as that of his uncle Ferdinand. Indeed, upon the principles of inheritance to which we are accustomed, Louis duke of Calabria had a prior right to Ferdinand, admitting the rule which it was necessary for both of them to establish; namely, that a right of succession might be transmitted through females, which females could not personally enjoy. This, as is well known, had been advanced in the preceding age by Edward III. as the foundation of his claim to the crown of France.

In this decision it is impossible not to suspect that the judges were swayed rather by politic considerations than a strict sense of hereditary right. It was, therefore, by no means universally popular, especially in Catalonia, of which principality the count of Urgel was a native; and perhaps the great rebellion of the Catalans fifty years afterwards may be traced to the disaffection which this breach, as they thought, of the lawful succession had excited. Ferdinand however was well received in Aragon. The cortes generously recommended the count of Urgel to his favor, on account of the great expenses he had incurred in prosecuting his claim. But Urgel did not wait the effect of this recommendation. Unwisely attempting a rebellion with very inadequate means, he lost his estates, and was thrown for life into prison. Ferdinand's successor was his son, Alfonso V., more distinguished in the history of Italy than of Spain. For all the latter years of his life he never quitted the kingdom that he had acquired by his arms; and, enchanted by the delicious air of Naples, intrusted the government of his patrimonial territories to the care of a brother and an heir. John II., upon whom they devolved by the death of Alfonso without legitimate progeny, had been engaged during his youth in the turbulent revolutions of Castile, as the head of a strong party that opposed the domination of Alvaro de Luna. By marriage with the heiress of Navarre he was entitled, according to the usage of those times, to assume the title of king, and administration of government, during her life. But his ambitious retention of power still longer produced events which are the chief stain on his memory. Charles prince of Viana was, by the constitution of Navarre, entitled to succeed his mother. She had requested him in her testament not to assume the government without his father's consent. That consent was always withheld. The prince raised what we ought not to call a rebellion; but was made prisoner, and remained for some time in captivity. John's ill disposition towards his son was exasperated by a step-mother, who scarcely disguised her intention of placing her own child on the throne of Aragon at the expense of the eldest-born. After a life of perpetual oppression, chiefly passed in exile or captivity, the prince of Viana died in Catalonia, at a moment when that province

Decision in favor of Ferdinand of Castile. A.D. 1412.

Alfonso V. A.D. 1410.

John II. A.D. 1458.

A.D. 1420.

A.D. 1442.

was in open insurrection upon his account. Though it hardly seems that the Catalans had any more general provocations, they persevered for more than ten years with inveterate obstinacy in their rebellion, offering the sovereignty first to a prince of Portugal, and afterwards to Regnier duke of Anjou, who was destined to pass his life in unsuccessful competition for kingdoms. The king of Aragon behaved with great clemency towards these insurgents on their final submission.

A.D. 1461.

It is consonant to the principle of this work to pass lightly over the common details of history, in order to fix the reader's attention more fully on subjects of philosophical inquiry. Perhaps in no European monarchy except our own was the form of government more interesting than in Aragon, as a fortunate temperament of law and justice with the royal authority. So far as anything can be pronounced of its earlier period before the capture of Saragosa in 1118, it was a kind of regal aristocracy, where a small number of powerful barons elected their sovereign on every vacancy, though, as usual in other countries, out of one family; and considered him as little more than the chief of their confederacy.[1]

Constitution of Aragon.

Originally a sort of regal aristocracy.

These were the ricoshombres or barons, the first order of the state. Among these the kings of Aragon, in subsequent times, as they extended their dominions, shared the conquered territory in grants of honors on a feudal tenure.[2] For this system was fully established in the kingdom of Aragon. A ricohombre, as we read in Vitalis bishop of Huesca, about the middle of the thirteenth century,[3] must hold of the king an honor or barony capable of supporting more than three knights; and

Privileges of the ricoshombres or barons.

[1] Alfonso III. complained that his barons wanted to bring back old times, quando havia en el reyno tantos reyes como ricos hombres. Blancæ Commentaria, p. 787. The form of election supposed to have been used by these bold barons is well known. "We, who are as good as you, choose you for our king and lord, provided that you observe our laws and privileges; and if not, not." But I do not much believe the authenticity of this form of words. See Robertson's Charles V. vol. i. note 31. It is, however, sufficiently agreeable to the spirit of the old government.

[2] Los ricos hombres, por los feudos que tenian del rey, eran obligados de seguir al rey, si yva en persona á la guerra, y residir en ella tres meses en cadaun ano. Zurita, t. i. fol. 43. (Saragosa, 1610.) A fief was usually called in Aragon an honor, que en Castilla llamavan tierra, y en el principado de Cataluna feudo. fol. 46.

[3] I do not know whether this work of Vitalis has been printed; but there are large extracts from it in Blancas's history, and also in Du Cange, under the words Infancia, Mesnadarius, &c. Several illustrations of these military tenures may be found in the Fueros de Aragon, especially lib. 7.

this he was bound to distribute among his vassals in military fiefs. Once in the year he might be summoned with his feudataries to serve the sovereign for two months (Zurita says three); and he was to attend the royal court, or general assembly, as a counsellor, whenever called upon, assisting in its judicial as well as deliberative business. In the towns and villages of his barony he might appoint bailiffs to administer justice and receive penalties; but the higher criminal jurisdiction seems to have been reserved to the crown. According to Vitalis, the king could divest these ricoshombres of their honors at pleasure, after which they fell into the class of mesnadaries, or mere tenants in chief. But if this were constitutional in the reign of James I., which Blancas denies, it was not long permitted by that high-spirited aristocracy. By the General Privilege or Charter of Peter III. it is declared that no barony can be taken away without a just cause and legal sentence of the justiciary and council of barons.[1] And the same protection was extended to the vassals of the ricoshombres.

Lower nobility.

Below these superior nobles were the mesnadaries, corresponding to our mere tenants in chief, holding estates not baronial immediately from the crown; and the military vassals of the high nobility, the knights and *infanzones;* a word which may be rendered by gentlemen. These had considerable privileges in that aristocratic government; they were exempted from all taxes, they could only be tried by the royal judges for any crime; and offences committed against them were punished with additional severity.[2] The ignoble classes were, as in other countries, the burgesses of towns, and the villeins or peasantry. The peasantry seem to have been subject to territorial servitude, as in France and England. Vitalis says that some villeins were originally so unprotected that, as he expresses it, they might be divided into pieces by sword among the sons of their masters, till they were provoked to an insurrection, which ended in establishing certain stipulations, whence they obtained the denomination of villeins *ae parada*, or of convention.[3]

Burgesses and peasantry.

Liberties of the Aragonese kingdom.

Though from the twelfth century the principle of hereditary succession to the throne superseded, in Aragon as well as Castile, the original right

[1] Biancæ Comm. p. 730. [2] p. 732. [3] Biancæ Comm. p. 729

of choosing a sovereign within the royal family, it was still founded upon one more sacred and fundamental, that of compact. No king of Aragon was entitled to assume that name until he had taken a coronation oath, administered by the justiciary at Saragosa, to observe the laws and liberties of the realm.[1] Alfonso III., in 1285, being in France at the time of his father's death, named himself king in addressing the states, who immediately remonstrated on this premature assumption of his title, and obtained an apology.[2] Thus, too, Martin, having been called to the crown of Aragon by the cortes in 1395, was specially required not to exercise any authority before his coronation.[3]

Blancas quotes a noble passage from the acts of cortes in 1451. "We have always heard of old time, and it is found by experience, that, seeing the great barrenness of this land, and the poverty of the realm, if it were not for the liberties thereof, the folk would go hence to live and abide in other realms and lands more fruitful."[4] This high spirit of freedom had long animated the Aragonese. After several contests with the crown in the reign of James I., not to go back to earlier times, they compelled Peter III. in 1283 to grant a law, called the General Privilege, the Magna Charta of Aragon, and perhaps a more full and satisfactory basis of civil liberty than our own. It contains a series of provisions against arbitrary tallages, spoliations of property, secret process after the manner of the Inquisition in criminal charges, sentences of the justiciary without assent of the cortes, appointment of foreigners or Jews to judicial offices; trials of accused persons in places beyond the kingdom, the use of torture,

General Privilege of 1283.

[1] Zurita, Anales de Aragon, t. i. fol. 104, t. iii. fol. 76.

[2] Blancæ Comm. p. 661. They acknowledged, at the same time, that he was their natural lord, and entitled to reign as lawful heir to his father—so oddly were the hereditary and elective titles jumbled together. Zurita, t. i. fol. 303.

[3] Zurita, t. ii. fol. 424.

[4] Siempre havemos oydo dezir antigament, é se troba por esperiencia, que attendida la grand sterilidad de aquesta tierra, é pobreza de aqueste regno, si non fues por las libertades de aquel, se yrian á bivir, y habitar las gentes á otros regnos, é tierras mas frutieras. p. 571. Aragon was, in fact, a poor country, barren and ill-peopled. The kings were forced to go to Catalonia for money, and indeed were little able to maintain expensive contests. The wars of Peter IV. in Sardinia, and of Alfonso V. with Genoa and Naples, impoverished their people. A hearth-tax having been imposed in 1404, it was found that there were 42,683 houses in Aragon, which, according to most calculations, will give less than 300,000 inhabitants. In 1429, a similar tax being laid on, it is said that the number of houses was diminished in consequence of war. Zurita, t. iii. fol. 189. It contains at present between 600,000 and 700,000 inhabitants.

except in charges of falsifying the coin, and the bribery of judges. These are claimed as the ancient liberties of their country. "Absolute power (mero imperio è mixto), it is declared, never was the constitution of Aragon, nor of Valencia, nor yet of Ribagorça, nor shall there be in time to come any innovation made; but only the law, custom, and privilege which has been anciently used in the aforesaid kingdoms.[1]

Privilege of Union.

The concessions extorted by our ancestors from John, Henry III., and Edward I., were secured by the only guarantee those times could afford, the determination of the barons to enforce them by armed confederacies. These, however, were formed according to emergencies, and, except in the famous commission of twenty-five conservators of Magna Charta, in the last year of John, were certainly unwarranted by law. But the Aragonese established a positive right of maintaining their liberties by arms. This was contained in the Privilege of Union granted by Alfonso III. in 1287, after a violent conflict with his subjects; but which was afterwards so completely abolished, and even eradicated from the records of the kingdom, that its precise words have never been recovered.[2] According to Zurita, it consisted of two articles: first, that in the case of the king's proceeding forcibly against any member of the union without previous sentence of the justiciary, the rest should be absolved from their allegiance; secondly, that he should hold cortes every year in Saragosa.[3] During the two subsequent reigns of James II. and Alfonso IV. little pretence seems to have been given for the exercise of this right. But dissensions breaking out under Peter IV. in 1347, rather on account of his attempt to settle the crown upon his daughter than of any specific public grievances, the nobles had recours to the Union, that last voice, says Blancas, of an almost expiring state, full of weight and dignity, to chastise the presumption of kings.[4] They as-

Revolt against Peter IV.

[1] Fueros de Aragon, fol. 9; Zurita, t. i. fol. 265.

[2] Blancas says that he had discovered a copy of the Privilege of Union in the archives of the see of Tarragona, and would gladly have published it, but for his deference to the wisdom of former ages, which had studiously endeavored to destroy all recollection of that dangerous law. p. 662.

[3] Zurita, t. i. fol. 322.

[4] Priscam illam Unionis, quasi moriientis reipublicæ extremam vocem, auctoritatis et gravitatis plenam, regum insolentiæ apertum vindicem excitârunt, summâ ac singulari bonorum omnium consensione. p. 669. It is remarkable that such strong language should have been tolerated under Philip II

sembled at Saragosa, and used a remarkable seal for all their public instruments, an engraving from which may be seen in the historian I have just quoted. It represents the king sitting on his throne, with the confederates kneeling in a suppliant attitude around, to denote their loyalty and unwillingness to offend. But in the background tents and lines of spears are discovered, as a hint of their ability and resolution to defend themselves. The legend is Sigillum Unionis Aragonum. This respectful demeanor towards a sovereign against whom they were waging war reminds us of the language held out by our Long Parliament before the Presbyterian party was overthrown. And although it has been lightly censured as inconsistent and hypocritical, this tone is the safest that men can adopt, who, deeming themselves under the necessity of withstanding the reigning monarch, are anxious to avoid a change of dynasty, or subversion of their constitution. These confederates were defeated by the king at Epila in 1348.[1] But his prudence and the remaining strength of his opponents inducing him to pursue a moderate course, there ensued a more legitimate and permanent balance of the constitution from this victory of the royalists. The Privilege of Union was abrogated, Peter himself cutting to pieces with his sword the original instrument. But in return many excellent laws for the security of the subject were enacted;[2] and their preservation was intrusted to the greatest officer of the kingdom, the justiciary, whose authority and preeminence may in a great degree be dated from this period.[3] That watchfulness over public liberty, which originally belonged to the aristocracy of ricoshombres, always apt to thwart the crown or to oppress the people, and which was afterwards maintained by the dangerous Privilege of Union, became the duty of a civil magistrate, accustomed to legal rules and responsible for his actions, whose office and func-

Privilege of Union abolished. Other provisions instituted.

[1] Zurita observes that the battle of Epila was the last fought in defence of public liberty, for which it was held lawful of old to take up arms, and resist the king, by virtue of the Privileges of Union. For the authority of the justiciary being afterwards established, the former contentions and wars came to an end; means being found to put the weak on a level with the powerful, in which consists the peace and tranquillity of all states; and from thence the name of Union was, by common consent, proscribed. t. ii. fol. 226. Blancas also remarks that nothing could have turned out more advantageous to the Aragonese than their ill fortune at Epila.

[2] Fueros de Aragon. De iis, quæ Dominus rex. fol. 14, et alibi passim.

[3] Bianc. Comm. p. 671, 811; Zurita, t. ii. fol. 229.

tions are the most pleasing feature in the constitutional history of Aragon.

Office of justiciary.

The justiza or justiciary of Aragon has been treated by some writers as a sort of anomalous magistrate, created originally as an intermediate power between the king and people, to watch over the exercise of royal authority. But I do not perceive that his functions were, in any essential respect, different from those of the chief justice of England, divided, from the time of Edward I., among the judges of the King's Bench. We should undervalue our own constitution by supposing that there did not reside in that court as perfect an authority to redress the subject's injuries as was possessed by the Aragonese magistrate. In the practical exercise, indeed, of this power, there was an abundant difference. Our English judges, more timid and pliant, left to the remonstrances of parliament that redress of grievances which very frequently lay within the sphere of their jurisdiction. There is, I believe, no recorded instance of a habeas corpus granted in any case of illegal imprisonment by the crown or its officers during the continuance of the Plantagenet dynasty. We shall speedily take notice of a very different conduct in Aragon.

The office of justiciary, whatever conjectural antiquity some have assigned to it, is not to be traced beyond the capture of Saragosa in 1118, when the series of magistrates commences.[1] But for a great length of time they do not appear to have been particularly important; the judicial authority residing in the council of ricoshombres, whose suffrages the justiciary collected, in order to pronounce their sentence rather than his own. A passage in Vitalis bishop of Huesca, whom I have already mentioned, shows this to have been the practice during the reign of James I.[2] Gradually, as notions of liberty became more definite, and laws more numerous, the reverence paid to their permanent interpreter grew stronger, and there was fortunately a succession of prudent and just men in that high office, through whom it acquired dignity and stable influence. Soon after the accession of James II., on

1 Biancæ Comment. p. 638.

2 Id. p. 772. Zurita indeed refers the justiciary's preëminence to an earlier date, namely, the reign of Peter II., who took away a great part of the local jurisdictions of the ricoshombres. t. i. fol. 102. But if I do not misunderstand the meaning of Vitalis, his testimony seems to be beyond dispute. By the General Privilege of 1283, the justiciary was to advise with the ricoshombres, in all cases where the king was a party against any of his subjects. Zurita, f. 281. See also f. 180.

some dissensions arising between the king and his barons, he called in the justiciary as a mediator whose sentence, says Blancas, all obeyed.[1] At a subsequent time in the same reign the military orders, pretending that some of their privileges were violated, raised a confederacy or union against the king. James offered to refer the dispute to the justiciary, Ximenes Salanova, a man of eminent legal knowledge. The knights resisted his jurisdiction, alleging the question to be of spiritual cognizance. He decided it, however, against them in full cortes at Saragosa, annulled their league, and sentenced the leaders to punishment.[2] It was adjudged also that no appeal could lie to the spiritual court from a sentence of the justiciary passed with assent of the cortes. James II. is said to have frequently sued his subjects in the justiciary's court, to show his regard for legal measures; and during the reign of this good prince its authority became more established.[3] Yet it was not perhaps looked upon as fully equal to maintain public liberty against the crown, till in the cortes of 1348, after the Privilege of Union was forever abolished, such laws were enacted, and such authority given to the justiciary, as proved eventually a more adequate barrier against oppression than any other country could boast. All the royal as well as territorial judges were bound to apply for his opinion in case of legal difficulties arising in their courts, which he was to certify within eight days. By subsequent statutes of the same reign it was made penal for any one to obtain letters from the king, impeding the execution of the justiza's process, and they were declared null. Inferior courts were forbidden to proceed in any business after his prohibition.[4] Many other laws might be cited, corroborating the authority of this great magistrate; but there are two parts of his remedial jurisdiction which deserve special notice.

Processes of a jurisfirma and manifestation. These are the processes of jurisfirma, or firma del derecho, and of manifestation. The former bears some analogy to the writs of *pone* and *certiorari*

[1] Zurita, p. 663.

[2] Zurita, t. i. f. 403; t. ii. f. 34; Bian. p. 666. The assent of the cortes seems to render this in the nature of a legislative, rather than a judicial proceeding; but it is difficult to pronounce anything about a transaction so remote in time, and in a foreign country, the native historians writing rather concisely.

[3] Bianc. p. 663. James acquired the surname of Just, el Justiciero, by his fair dealings towards his subjects. Zurita, t. ii. fol. 82. El Justiciero properly denotes his exercise of civil and criminal justice.

[4] Fueros de Aragon: Quod in dubiis non crassis. (A.D. 1348.) Quod impetrans (1372), &c. Zurita, t. ii. fol. 229. Bianc p. 671 and 811.

in England, through which the Court of King's Bench exer cises its right of withdrawing a suit from the jurisdiction of inferior tribunals. But the Aragonese jurisfirma was of more extensive operation. Its object was not only to bring a cause commenced in an inferior court before the justiciary, but to prevent or inhibit any process from issuing against the person who applied for its benefit, or any molestation from being offered to him; so that, as Blancas expresses it, when we have entered into a recognizance (firmè et graviter asseveremus) before the justiciary of Aragon to abide the decision of law, our fortunes shall be protected, by the interposition of his prohibition, from the intolerable iniquity of the royal judges.[1] The process termed manifestation afforded as ample security for personal liberty as that of jurisfirma did for property. "To *manifest* any one," says the writer so often quoted, "is to wrest him from the hands of the royal officers, that he may not suffer any illegal violence; not that he is at liberty by this process, because the merits of his case are still to be inquired into; but because he is now detained publicly, instead of being as it were concealed, and the charge against him is investigated, not suddenly or with passion, but in calmness and according to law, therefore this is called manifestation."[2] The power of this

[1] p. 751. Fueros de Aragon, f. 137.

[2] Est apud nos manifestare, reum subito sumere, atque è regiis manibus extorquere, ne qua ipsi contra jus vis inferatur. Non quod tunc reus judicio liberetur; nihilominus tamen, ut loquimur, de meritis causæ ad plenum cognoscitur. Sed quod deinceps manifesto teneatur, quasi antea celatus extitisset; necesseque deinde sit de ipsius culpâ, non impetu et cum furore, sed sedatis prorsus animis, et juxta constitutas leges judicari. Ex eo autem, quod hujusmodi judicium manifesto deprehensum, omnibus jam patere debeat, Manifestationis sibi nomen arripuit. p. 675.

Ipsius Manifestationis potestas tam solida est et repentina, ut homini jam collum in laqueum inserenti subveniat. Illius enim præsidio, damnatus, dum per leges licet, quasi experiendi juris gratiâ, de manibus judicum confestim extorquetur, et in carcerem ducitur ad id ædificatum, ibidemque asservatur tamdiu, quamdiu jurene, an injuriâ, quid in eâ causâ factum fuerit, judicatur. Propterea carcer hic vulgari linguâ, la carcel de los manifestados nuncupatur. p. 751.

Fueros de Aragon, fol 60 De Manifestationibus personarum. Independently of this right of manifestation by writ of the justiciary, there are several statutes in the Fueros against illegal detention, or unnecessary severity towards prisoners. (De Custodiâ reorum, f. 163.) No judge could proceed secretly in a criminal process; an indispensable safeguard to public liberty, and one of the most salutary, as well as most ancient, provisions in our own constitution. (De judiciis.) Torture was abolished, except in cases of coining false money, and then only in respect of vagabonds. (General Privilege of 1283.)

Zurita has explained the two processes of jurisfirma and manifestation so perspicuously, that, as the subject is very interesting, and rather out of the common way, I shall both quote and translate the passage. Con firmar de derecho, que es dar caution á estar á justicia, se conseden literas inhibitorias por el justicia de Aragon, para que no puedan sur presos, ni privados, ni despojados de su possession, hasta que judicialmente se conozca, y declare sobre la pretension, y justicia de las partes, y parezca por processo legitimo, que se deve revocar la tal inhibition.

writ (if I may apply our term) was such, as he elsewhere asserts, that it would rescue a man whose neck was in the halter. A particular prison was allotted to those detained for trial under this process.

Instances of their application.

Several proofs that such admirable provisions did not remain a dead letter in the law of Aragon appear in the two historians, Blancas and Zurita, whose noble attachment to liberties, of which they had either witnessed or might foretell the extinction, continually displays itself. I cannot help illustrating this subject by two remarkable instances. The heir apparent of the kingdom of Aragon had a constitutional right to the lieutenancy or regency during the sovereign's absence from the realm. The title and office indeed were permanent, though the functions must of course have been superseded during the personal exercise of royal authority. But as neither Catalonia nor Valencia, which often demanded the king's presence, were considered as parts of the kingdom, there were pretty frequent occasions for this anticipated reign of the eldest prince. Such a regulation was not likely to diminish the mutual and almost inevitable jealousies between kings and their heirs apparent, which have so often disturbed the tranquillity of a court and a nation. Peter IV. removed his eldest son, afterwards John I., from the lieutenancy of the kingdom. The

Esta fué la suprema y principal autoridad del Justicia de Aragond esde que este magistrado tuvo origen, y lo que llama manifestation; porque assí como la firma de derecho por privilegio general del reyno impide, que no puede ninguno ser preso, ó agraviado contra razon y justicia, de la misma manera la manifestacion, que es otro privilegio, y remedia muy principal, tiene fuerca, quando alguno es preso sin preceder processo legitimo, ó quando lo prenden de hecho sin orden de justiciâ; y en estos casos solo el Justicia de Aragon, quando se tiene recurso al el, se interpone, manifestando il preso, que es tomarlo á su mano, de poder de qualquiera juez, aunque sea el mas supremo; y es obligado el Justicia de Aragon, y sus lugartenientes de proveer la manifestacion en el mismo instante, que les es pedida sin preceder informacion; y basta que se pida por qualquiere persona que se diga procurador del que quiere que lo tengan por manifesto. t. ii. fol. 386. "Upon a firma de derecho, which is to give security for abiding the decision of the law, the Justiciary of Aragon issues letters inhibiting all persons to arrest the party, or deprive him of his possession, until the matter shall be judicially inquired into, and it shall appear that such inhibition ought to be revoked. This process and that which is called manifestation have been the chief powers of the justiciary, ever since the commencement of that magistracy. And as the firma de derecho by the general privilege of the realm secures every man from being arrested or molested against reason and justice, so the manifestation, which is another principal and remedial right takes place when any one is actually arrested without lawful process; and in such cases only the Justiciary of Aragon, when recourse is had to him, interposes by *manifesting* the person arrested, that is, by taking him into his own hands, out of the power of any judge, however high in authority; and this manifestation the justiciary, or his deputies in his absence, are bound to issue at the same instant it is demanded, without further inquiry; and it may be demanded by any one as attorney of the party requiring to be manifested."

prince entered into a firma del derecho before the justiciary, Dominic de Cerda, who, pronouncing in his favor, enjoined the king to replace his son in the lieutenancy as the undoubted right of the eldest born. Peter obeyed, not only in fact, to which, as Blancas observes, the law compelled him, but with apparent cheerfulness.[1] There are indeed no private persons who have so strong an interest in maintaining a free constitution and the civil liberties of their countrymen as the members of royal families, since none are so much exposed, in absolute governments, to the resentment and suspicion of a reigning monarch.

John I., who had experienced the protection of law in his weakness, had afterwards occasion to find it interposed against his power. This king had sent some citizens of Saragosa to prison without form of law. They applied to Juan de Cerda, the justiciary, for a manifestation. He issued his writ accordingly; nor, says Blancas, could he do otherwise without being subject to a heavy fine. The king, pretending that the justiciary was partial, named one of his own judges, the vice-chancellor, as coadjutor. This raised a constitutional question, whether, on suspicion of partiality, a coadjutor to the justiciary could be appointed. The king sent a private order to the justiciary not to proceed to sentence upon this interlocutory point until he should receive instructions in the council, to which he was directed to repair. But he instantly pronounced sentence in favor of his exclusive jurisdiction without a coadjutor. He then repaired to the palace. Here the vice-chancellor, in a long harangue, enjoined him to suspend sentence till he had heard the decision of the council. Juan de Cerda answered that, the case being clear, he had already pronounced upon it. This produced some expressions of anger from the king, who began to enter into an argument on the merits of the question. But the justiciary answered that, with all deference to his majesty, he was bound to defend his conduct before the cortes, and not elsewhere. On a subsequent day the king, having drawn the justiciary to his country palace on pretence of hunting, renewed the conversation with the assistance of his ally the vice-chancellor; but no impression was made on the venerable magistrate, whom John at length, though much pressed by his advisers to violent courses, dismissed with civility. The king was

[1] Zurita, ubi supra. Blancas, p. 678.

probably misled throughout this transaction, which I have thought fit to draw from obscurity, not only in order to illustrate the privilege of manifestation, but as exhibiting an instance of judicial firmness and integrity, to which, in the fourteenth century, no country perhaps in Europe could offer a parallel.[1]

Office of justiciary held for life.

Before the cortes of 1348 it seems as if the justiciary might have been displaced at the king's pleasure. From that time he held his station for life. But in order to evade this law, the king sometimes exacted a promise to resign upon request. Ximenes Cerdan, the justiciary in 1420, having refused to fulfil this engagement, Alfonso V. gave notice to all his subjects not to obey him, and, notwithstanding the alarm which this encroachment created, eventually succeeded in compelling him to quit his office. In 1439 Alfonso insisted with still greater severity upon the execution of a promise to resign made by another justiciary, detaining him in prison until his death. But the cortes of 1442 proposed a law, to which the king reluctantly acceded, that the justiciary should not be compellable to resign his office on account of any previous engagement he might have made.[2]

Responsibility of this magistrate.

But lest these high powers, imparted for the prevention of abuses, should themselves be abused, the justiciary was responsible, in case of an unjust sentence, to the extent of the injury inflicted;[3] and was also subjected, by a statute of 1390, to a court of inquiry, composed of four persons chosen by the king out of eight named by the cortes; whose office appears to have been that of examining and reporting to the four estates in cortes, by whom he was ultimately to be acquitted or condemned. This superintendence of the cortes, however, being thought dilatory and inconvenient, a court of seventeen persons was appointed in 1461 to hear complaints against the justiciary. Some alterations were afterwards made in this tribunal.[4] The justiciary was always a knight, chosen from the second

[1] Blancæ Commentar. ubi supra. Zurita relates the story, but not so fully.

[2] Fueros de Aragon, fol. 22; Zurita, t. iii. fol. 140, 255, 272; Blanc. Comment. p. 701.

[3] Fueros de Aragon, fol. 25.

[4] Blancas; Zurita, t. iii. fol. 321; t. iv. f. 108. These regulations were very acceptable to the nation. In fact, the justiza of Aragon had possessed much more unlimited powers than ought to be intrusted to any single magistrate. The Court of King's Bench in England, besides its consisting of four coördinate judges, is checked by the appellant jurisdictions of the Exchequer Chamber and House of Lords, and still more importantly by the rights of juries.

order of nobility, the barons not being liable to personal punishment. He administered the coronation oath to the king and in the cortes of Aragon the justiciary acted as a sort of royal commissioner, opening or proroguing the assembly by the king's direction.

Rights of legislation and taxation.

No laws could be enacted or repealed, nor any tax imposed, without the consent of the estates duly assembled.[1] Even as early as the reign of Peter II., in 1205, that prince having attempted to impose a general tallage, the nobility and commons united for the preservation of their franchises; and the tax was afterwards granted in part by the cortes.[2] It may easily be supposed that the Aragonese were not behind other nations in statutes to secure these privileges, which upon the whole appear to have been more respected than in any other monarchy.[3] The general privilege of 1283 formed a sort of groundwork for this legislation, like the Great Charter in England. By a clause in this law, cortes were to be held every year at Saragosa. But under James II. their time of meeting was reduced to once in two years, and the place was left to the king's discretion.[4] Nor were the cortes of Aragon less vigilant than those of Castile in claiming a right to be consulted in all important deliberations of the executive power, or in remonstrating against abuses of government, or in superintending the proper expenditure of public money.[5] A vari-

[1] Majores nostri, quæ de omnibus statuenda essent, noluerunt juberi, vetarive posse, nisi vocatis, descriptisque ordinibus, ac cunctis eorum adhibitis suffragiis, re ipsâ cognitâ et promulgatâ. Unde perpetuum illud nobis comparatum est jus, ut communes et publicæ leges neque tolli, neque rogari possint, nisi prius universus populus una voce comitiis institutis suum eâ de re liberum suffragium ferat; idque postea ipsius regis assensu comprobetur. Biancæ, p. 761.

[2] Zurita, t. i. fol. 92.

[3] Fueros de Aragon: Quod sissæ in Aragoniâ removeantur. (A.D. 1372.) De prohibitione sissarum. (1398.) De conservatione patrimonii. (1461.) I have only remarked two instances of arbitrary taxation in Zurita's history, which is singularly full of information; one, in 1343, when Peter IV. collected money from various cities, though not without opposition; and the other a remonstrance of the cortes in 1383 against heavy taxes; and it is not clear that this refers to general unauthorized taxation Zurita, t. ii. f. 168 and 382. Blancas mentions that Alfonso V. set a tallage upon his towns for the marriage of his natural daughters, which he might have done had they been legitimate; but they appealed to the justiciary's tribunal, and the king receded from his demand. p. 701.

Some instances of tyrannical conduct in violation of the constitutional laws occur, as will naturally be supposed, in the annals of Zurita. The execution of Bernard Cabrera under Peter IV., t. ii. f. 336, and the severities inflicted on queen Forcia by her son-in-law John I., f. 391, are perhaps as remarkable as any.

[4] Zurita, t. i. f. 426. In general the session lasted from four to six months. One assembly was prorogued from time to time, and continued six years, from 1446 to 1452, which was complained of as a violation of the law for their biennial renewal. t. iv. f. 6.

[5] The Sicilian war of Peter III. was very unpopular, because it had been undertaken without consent of the barons, contrary to the practice of the kingdom ·

ety of provisions, intended to secure these parliamentary privileges and the civil liberties of the subject, will be found dispersed in the collection of Aragonese laws,[1] which may be favorably compared with those of our own statute-book.

Cortes of Aragon.

Four estates, or, as they were called, arms (brazos), formed the cortes of Aragon — the prelates and commanders of military orders, who passed for ecclesiastics;[2] the barons or ricoshombres; the equestrian order or infanzones, and the deputies of royal towns.[3] The two former had a right of appearing by proxy. There was no representation of the infanzones, or lower nobility. But it must be remembered that they were not numerous, nor was the kingdom large. Thirty-five are reckoned by Zurita as present in the cortes of 1395, and thirty-three in those of 1412; and as upon both occasions an oath of fealty to a new monarch was to be taken, I presume that nearly all the nobility of the kingdom were present.[4] The ricoshombres do not seem to have exceeded twelve or fourteen in number. The ecclesiastical estate was not much, if at all, more numerous. A few principal towns alone sent deputies to the cortes; but their representation was very full; eight or ten, and sometimes more, sat for Saragosa, and no town appears to have had less than four representatives. During the interval of the cortes a permanent commission, varying a good deal as to numbers, but chosen out of the four estates, was empowered to sit with very considerable authority, receiving

porque ningun negocio arduo emprendian, sin acuerdo y consejo de sus ricoshombres. Zurita, t. i. fol. 264. The cortes, he tells us, were usually divided into two parties, whigs and tories; estava ordinariamente dividida en dos partas, la una que pensava procurar el beneficio del reyno, y la otra que el servicio del rey. t. iii. fol. 321.

[1] Fueros y observancias del reyno de Aragon. 2 vols. in fol. Saragosa, 1667. The most important of these are collected by Blancas, p. 750.

[2] It is said by some writers that the ecclesiastical arm was not added to the cortes of Aragon till about the year 1300. But I do not find mention in Zurita of any such constitutional change at that time; and the prelates, as we might expect from the analogy of other countries, appear as members of the national council long before. Queen Petronilla, in 1142, summoned á los perlados, ricoshombres, y cavalleros, y procuradores de las ciudades y villas, que le juntassen á cortes generales en la ciudad de Huesca. Zurita, t. i. fol. 71. So in the cortes of 1275, and on other occasions.

[3] Popular representation was more ancient in Aragon than in any other monarchy. The deputies of towns appear in the cortes of 1133, as Robertson has remarked from Zurita. Hist. of Charles V. note 32. And this cannot well be called in question, or treated as an anomaly; for we find them mentioned in 1142 (the passage cited in the last note), and again in 1164, when Zurita enumerates many of their names, fol. 74. The institution of consejos, or corporate districts under a presiding town, prevailed in Aragon as it did in Castile.

[4] Zurita, t. ii. f. 490; t. iii. f. 76.

and managing the public revenue, and protecting the justiciary in his functions.[1]

The kingdom of Valencia, and principality of Catalonia, having been annexed to Aragon, the one by conquest, the other by marriage, were always kept distinct from it in their laws and government. Each had its cortes, composed of three estates, for the division of the nobility into two orders did not exist in either country. The Catalans were tenacious of their ancient usages, and averse to incorporation with any other people of Spain. Their national character was high-spirited and independent; in no part of the peninsula did the territorial aristocracy retain, or at least pretend to, such extensive privileges,[2] and the citizens were justly proud of wealth acquired by industry, and of renown achieved by valor. At the accession of Ferdinand I., which they had not much desired, the Catalans obliged him to swear three times successively to maintain their liberties, before they would take the reciprocal oath of allegiance.[3] For Valencia it seems to have been a politic design of James the Conqueror to establish a constitution nearly analogous to that of Aragon, but with such limitations as he should impose, taking care that the nobles of the two kingdoms should not acquire strength by union. In the reigns of Peter III. and Alfonso III., one of the principal objects contended for by the barons of Aragon was the establishment of their own laws in Valencia; to which the kings never acceded.[4] They permitted, however, the possessions of the natives of Aragon in the latter kingdom to be governed by the law of Aragon.[5] These three states, Aragon, Valencia, and Catalonia, were perpetually united by a law of Alfonso III.; and every king on his accession was bound to swear that he would never separate them.[6] Sometimes general cortes of the kingdoms and principality were convened; but the members did not, even in this case, sit together, and were no otherwise united than as they met in the same city.[7]

Government of Valencia and Catalonia.

[1] Biancæ, p. 762; Zurita, t. iii. f. 76, f. 182 et alibi.

[2] Zurita, t. ii. f. 360. The villenage of the peasantry in some parts of Catalonia was very severe, even near the end of the fifteenth century. t. iv. f. 327.

[3] Zurita, t. iii. f. 81.

[4] Id. t. i. f. 281, 310, 333. There was originally a justiciary in the kingdom of Valencia, f. 281; but this, I believe, did not long continue.

[5] Zurita, t. ii. f. 433.

[6] t. ii. f. 91.

[7] Biancæ, Comment. p. 760; Zurita, t. iii. fol. 289.

I do not mean to represent the actual condition of society in Aragon as equally excellent with the constitutional laws. Relatively to other monarchies, as I have already observed, there seem to have been fewer excesses of the royal prerogative in that kingdom. But the licentious habits of a feudal aristocracy prevailed very long. We find in history instances of private war between the great families, so as to disturb the peace of the whole nation, even near the close of the fifteenth century.[1] The right of avenging injuries by arms, and the ceremony of diffidation, or solemn defiance of an enemy, are preserved by the laws. We even meet with the ancient barbarous usage of paying a composition to the kindred of a murdered man.[2] The citizens of Saragosa were sometimes turbulent, and a refractory nobleman sometimes defied the ministers of justice. But owing to the remarkable copiousness of the principal Aragonese historian, we find more frequent details of this nature than in the scantier annals of some countries. The internal condition of society was certainly far from peaceable in other parts of Europe.

State of police.

By the marriage of Ferdinand with Isabella, and by the death of John II., in 1479, the two ancient and rival kingdoms of Castile and Aragon were forever consolidated in the monarchy of Spain. There had been some difficulty in adjusting the respective rights of the husband and wife over Castile. In the middle ages it was customary for the more powerful sex to exercise all the rights which it derived from the weaker, as much in sovereignties as in private possessions. But the Castilians were determined to maintain the positive and distinct prerogatives of their queen, to which they attached the independence of their nation. A compromise therefore was concluded, by which, though, according to our notions, Ferdinand obtained more than a due share, he might consider himself as more strictly limited than his father had been in Navarre. The names of both were to appear jointly in their style and upon the coin, the king's taking the precedence in respect of his sex. But in the royal scutcheon the arms of Castile were preferred on account of the kingdom's dignity. Isabella had the appointment to all civil offices in Castile; the nom-

Union of Castile and Aragon.

1 Zurita, t. iv. fol. 189.

2 Fueros de Aragon, f. 1660, &c.

ination to spiritual benefices ran in the name of both. The government was to be conducted by the two conjointly when they were together, or by either singly in the province where one or other might happen to reside.[1] This partition was well preserved throughout the life of Isabel without mutual encroachments or jealousies. So rare an unanimity between persons thus circumstanced must be attributed to the superior qualities of that princess, who, while she maintained a constant good understanding with a very ambitious husband, never relaxed in the exercise of her paternal authority over the kingdoms of her ancestors.

Conquest of Granada.

Ferdinand and Isabella had no sooner quenched the flames of civil discord in Castile than they determined to give an unequivocal proof to Europe of the vigor which the Spanish monarchy was to display under their government. For many years an armistice with the Moors of Granada had been uninterrupted. Neither John II. nor Henry IV. had been at leisure to think of aggressive hostilities; and the Moors themselves, a prey, like their Christian enemies, to civil war and the feuds of their royal family, were content with the unmolested enjoyment of the finest province in the peninsula. If we may trust historians, the sovereigns of Granada were generally usurpers and tyrants. But I know not how to account for that vast populousness, that grandeur and magnificence, which distinguished the Mohammedan kingdom of Spain, without ascribing some measure of wisdom and beneficence to their governments. These southern provinces have dwindled in later times; and in fact Spain itself is chiefly interesting to many travellers for the monuments which a foreign and odious race of conquerors have left behind them. Granada was, however, disturbed by a series of revolutions about the time of Ferdinand's accession, which naturally encouraged his designs. The Moors, contrary to what might have been expected from their relative strength, were the aggressors by attacking a town in Andalusia.[2] Predatory inroads of this nature had hitherto been only retaliated by the Christians. But Ferdinand was conscious that his resources extended to the conquest of Granada, the consummation of a struggle protracted through nearly eight centuries. Even in the last stage of the Moorish dominion, exposed on

[1] Zurita, t. iv. fol. 224; Mariana, l. xxiv. c. 5.

[2] Zurita, t. iv. fol. 314.

every side to invasion, enfeebled by civil dissension that led one party to abet the common enemy, Granada was not subdued without ten years of sanguinary and unremitting contest. Fertile beyond all the rest of Spain, that kingdom contained seventy walled towns; and the capital is said, almost two centuries before, to have been peopled by 200,000 inhabitants.[1] Its resistance to such a force as that of Ferdinand is perhaps the best justification of the apparent negligence of earlier monarchs. But Granada was ultimately to undergo the yoke. The city surrendered on the 2nd of January 1492—an event glorious not only to Spain but to Christendom—and which, in the political combat of the two religions, seemed almost to counterbalance the loss of Constantinople. It raised the name of Ferdinand and of the new monarchy which he governed to high estimation throughout Europe. Spain appeared an equal competitor with France in the lists of ambition. These great kingdoms had for some time felt the jealousy natural to emulous neighbors. The house of Aragon loudly complained of the treacherous policy of Louis XI. He had fomented the troubles of Castile, and given, not indeed an effectual aid, but all promises of support, to the princess Joanna, the competitor of Isabel. Rousillon, a province belonging to Aragon, had been pledged to France by John II. for a sum of money. It would be tedious to relate the subsequent events, or to discuss their respective claims to its possession.[2] At the accession of Ferdinand, Louis XI. still held Rousillon, and showed little intention to resign it. But Charles VIII., eager to smooth every impediment to his Italian expedition, restored the province to Ferdinand in 1493. Whether by such a sacrifice he was able to lull the king of Aragon into acquiescence, while he dethroned his relation at Naples, and alarmed for a moment all Italy with the apprehension of French dominion, it is not within the limits of the present work to inquire.

1 Zurita, t. iv. fol. 314.

2 For these transactions see Garnier, Hist. de France, or Gaillard, Rivalité de France et d'Espagne, t. iii. The latter is the most impartial French writer I have ever read, in matters where his own country is concerned.

NOTE TO CHAPTER IV.

NOTE. Page 2.

THE story of Cava, daughter of count Julian, whose seduction by Roderic, the last Gothic king, impelled her father to invite the Moors into Spain, enters largely into the cycle of Castilian romance and into the grave narratives of every historian. It cannot, however, be traced in extant writings higher than the eleventh century, when it appears in the Chronicle of the Monk of Silos. There are Spanish historians of the eighth and ninth centuries; in the former, Isidore bishop of Beja (Pacensis), who wrote a chronicle of Spain; in the latter, Paulus Diaconus of Merida, Sebastian of Salamanca, and an anonymous chronicler. It does not appear, however, that these dwell much on Roderic's reign. (See Masdeu, Historia Critica de España, vol. xiii. p. 882.) The most critical investigators of history, therefore, have treated the story as too apocryphal to be stated as a fact. A sensible writer in the History of Spain and Portugal, published by the Society for the Diffusion of Useful Knowledge, has defended its probability, quoting a passage from Ferreras, a Spanish writer of the eighteenth century, whose authority stands high, and who argues in favor of the tradition from the brevity of the old chroniclers who relate the fall of Spain, and from the want of likelihood that Julian, who had hitherto defended his country with great valor, would have invited the Saracens, except through some strong motives. This, if we are satisfied as to the last fact, appears plausible; but another hypothesis has been suggested, and is even mentioned by one of the early writers, that Julian, being of Roman descent, was ill-affected to the Gothic dynasty, who had never attached to themselves the native inhabitants. This I cannot but reckon the less likely explanation of the two. Roderic, who became archbishop of Toledo in 1208, and our earliest authority after the monk of Silos, calls Julian "vir nobilis de nobili Gothorum prosapia ortus, illustris in officio Palatino, in armis exercitatus," &c. (See Schottus, Hispania Illustrata, ii. 63.) Few, however, of those who deny the truth of the story as it relates to Cava admit the defection of count Julian to the Moors, and his existence has been doubted. The two parts of the story cohere together, and we have no better evidence for one than for the other.

Southey, in his notes to the poem of Roderic, says, "The best Spanish historians and antiquaries are persuaded that there is no cause for disbelieving the uniform and concurrent tradition of both Moors and Christians." But this is on the usual assumption, that those are the best who agree best with ourselves. Southey took generally the credulous side, and his critical judgment is of no superlative value. Masdeu, in learning and laboriousness the first Spanish antiquary, calls the story of Julian's daughter "a ridiculous tale, framed in the age of romance, when histories were thrust aside (arrinconadas) and any love-tale was preferred to the most serious truth." (Hist. Crit. de España, vol. x. p. 223.) And when, in another passage (vol. xii. p. 6), he recounts the story at large, he says that the silence of all writers before the monk of Silos "should be sufficient in my opinion to expel from our history a romance so destitute of foundation, which the Arabian romancers doubtless invented for their ballads."

A modern writer of extensive learning says, "This fable, which has found its way into most of the sober histories of Spain, was first introduced by the monk of Silos, a chronicler of the eleventh century. There can be no doubt that he borrowed it from the Arabs, but it seems hard to believe that it was altogether a tale of their invention. There are facts in it which an Arab could not have invented, unless he drew them from Christian sources; and, as I shall show hereafter, the Arabs knew and consulted the writings of the Christians." (Gayangos, History of the Mohammedan Dynasties of Spain, vol. i. p. 513.) It does not appear to be a conclusion from this passage that the story is a fable. For if a chronicler of the eleventh century borrowed it from the Arabs, and they again from Christian sources, we get over a good deal of the chasm of time. But if writers antecedent to the monk of Silos have related the Arabian invasion and the fall of Roderic without alluding to so important a point as the treachery of a great Gothic noble, it seems difficult to resist the inference from their silence.

Gayangos investigates in a learned note (vol. i. p. 537) the following points: — By whom and when was the name of Ilyan, the Arabic form of Julian, first introduced into Spanish history? Did such a man ever exist? What were his country and religion? Was he an independent prince, or a tributary to the Gothic monarchs? What part did he take in the conquest of Spain by the Arabs?

The account of Julian in the Chronicon Silense appears to Gayangos indisputably borrowed from some Arabian authority; and this he proves by several writers from the ninth century downwards, "all of whom mention, more or less explicitly, the existence of a man living in Africa, and named Ilyan, who helped the Arabs to make a conquest of Spain; to which I ought to add that the rape of Ilyan's daughter, and the circumstances attending it, may also be read in detail in the Mohammedan authors who preceded the monk of Silos." The result of this learned writer's investigation is, that Ilyan really existed, that he was a Christian chief, settled, not in Spain, but on the African coast, and that he betrayed, not his country (except indeed as he was probably of Spanish descent), but the interests of his religion, by assisting the Saracens to subjugate the Gothic kingdom.[1]

The story of Cava is not absolutely overthrown by this hypothesis, though it certainly may be the invention of some Christian or Arabian romancer. It is perfectly true that of itself it contains no apparent improbability. Injuries have been thus inflicted by kings, and thus resented by subjects. But for this very reason it was likely to be invented; and the unwillingness with which many seem to surrender so romantic a tale attests the probability of its obtaining currency in an uncritical period. We must reject it as false or not, according as we lay stress on the negative argument from the silence of very early writers (an argument, strong even as it is, and which would be insuperable if they were less brief and im-

[1] The Arabian writer whom Gayangos translates, one of late date, speaks of Ilyan as governor of Ceuta, but tells the story of Cava in the usual manner. The Goths may very probably have possessed some of the African coast; so that the residence of Julian on that side of the straits would not be incompatible with his being truly a Spaniard. Ilyan is evidently not an European form of the name.

perfect) and on the presumptions adduced by Gayangos that Julian was not a noble Spaniard; but we cannot receive this celebrated legend at any rate with more than a very sceptical assent, not sufficient to warrant us in placing it among the authentic facts of history.

CHAPTER V.

HISTORY OF GERMANY TO THE DIET OF WORMS IN 1495.

Sketch of German History under the Emperors of the House of Saxony — House of Franconia — Henry IV. — House of Suabia — Frederic Barbarossa — Fall of Henry the Lion — Frederic II. — Extinction of House of Suabia — Changes in the Germanic Constitution — Electors — Territorial Sovereignty of the Princes — Rodolph of Hapsburg — State of the Empire after his Time — Causes of Decline of Imperial Power — House of Luxemburg — Charles IV. — Golden Bull — House of Austria — Frederic III. — Imperial Cities — Provincial States — Maximilian — Diet of Worms — Abolition of Private Wars — Imperial Chamber — Aulic Council — Bohemia — Hungary — Switzerland.

AFTER the deposition of Charles the Fat in 888, which finally severed the connection between France and Germany,[1] Arnulf, an illegitimate descendant of Charlemagne, obtained the throne of the latter country, in which he was succeeded by his son Louis.[2] But upon the death of this prince in 911, the German branch of that dynasty became extinct. There remained indeed Charles the Simple, acknowledged as king in some parts of France, but rejected in others, and possessing no personal claims to respect. The Germans therefore wisely determined to choose a sovereign from among themselves. They were at this time divided into five nations, each under its own duke, and distinguished by difference of laws, as well as of origin; the Franks, whose territory, comprising Franconia and the modern Palatinate, was considered as the cradle of the empire, and who seem to have arrogated some superiority over the rest, the Suabians, the Bavarians, the Saxons, under which name the

Separation of Germany from France.

1 There can be no question about this in a general sense. But several German writers of the time assert that both Eudes and Charles the Simple, rival kings of France, acknowledged the feudal superiority of Arnulf. Charles, says Regino, regnum quod usurpaverit ex manu ejus percepit. Struvius, Corpus Hist. German. p. 202, 203. This acknowledgment of sovereignty in Arnulf king of Germany, who did not even pretend to be emperor, by both the claimants of the throne of France, for such it virtually was, though they do not appear to have rendered homage, cannot affect the independence of the crown in that age, which had been established by the treaty of Verdun in 843, but proves the weakness of the competitors, and their want of patriotism. In Eudes it is more remarkable than in Charles the Simple, a man of feeble character, and a Carlovingian by birth.

2 The German princes had some hesitation about the choice of Louis, but their partiality to the Carlovingian line prevailed. Struvius, p. 208: quia reges Francorum semper ex uno genere procedebant, says an archbishop Hatto, in writing to the pope.

inhabitants of Lower Saxony alone and Westphalia were included, and the Lorrainers, who occupied the left bank of the Rhine as far as its termination. The choice of these nations in their general assembly fell upon Conrad, duke of Franconia, according to some writers, or at least a man of high rank, and descended through females from Charlemagne.[1]

Election of Conrad. A.D. 911.

Conrad dying without male issue, the crown of Germany was bestowed upon Henry the Fowler, duke of Saxony, ancestor of the three Othos, who followed him in direct succession. To Henry, and to the first Otho, Germany was more indebted than to any sovereign since Charlemagne. The conquest of Italy, and recovery of the imperial title, are indeed the most brilliant trophies of Otho the Great; but he conferred far more unequivocal benefits upon his own country by completing what his father had begun, her liberation from the inroads of the Hungarians. Two marches, that of Misnia, erected by Henry the Fowler, and that of Austria, by Otho, were added to the Germanic territories by their victories.[2]

House of Saxony. Henry the Fowler. A.D. 919. Otho I. A.D. 936. Otho II. A.D. 973. Otho III. A.D. 983.

A lineal succession of four descents without the least opposition seems to show that the Germans were disposed to consider their monarchy as fixed in the Saxon family. Otho II. and III. had been chosen each in his father's lifetime, and during legal infancy. The formality of election subsisted at that time in every European kingdom; and the imperfect rights of birth required a ratification by public assent. If at least France and England were hereditary monarchies in the tenth century, the same may surely be said of Germany; since we find the lineal succession fully as well observed in the last as in the former. But upon the early and unexpected decease of Otho III., a momentary opposition was offered to Henry duke of Bavaria, a collateral branch of the reigning family. He ob-

Henry II. A.D. 1002.

[1] Schmidt, Hist. des Allemands, t. ii. p. 288. Struvius, Corpus Historiæ Germanicæ, p. 210. The former of these writers does not consider Conrad as duke of Franconia.

[2] Many towns in Germany, especially on the Saxon frontier, were built by Henry I., who is said to have compelled every ninth man to take up his residence in them. This had a remarkable tendency to promote the improvement of that territory, and, combined with the discovery of the gold and silver mines of Goslar under Otho I., rendered it the richest and most important part of the empire. Struvius, p. 225 and 251. Schmidt, t. ii. p. 322. Putter, Historical Development of the German Constitution, vol. i. p. 115.

tained the crown, however, by what contemporary historians call an hereditary title,[1] and it was not until his death in 1024 that the house of Saxony was deemed to be extinguished.

House of Franconia. Conrad II. A.D. 1024. Henry III. A.D. 1039. Henry IV A.D. 1056. Henry V. A.D. 1106.

No person had now any pretensions that could interfere with the unbiassed suffrages of the nation; and accordingly a general assembly was determined by merit to elect Conrad, surnamed the Salic, a nobleman of Franconia.[2] From this prince sprang three successive emperors, Henry III., IV., and V. Perhaps the imperial prerogatives over that insubordinate confederacy never reached so high a point as in the reign of Henry III., the second emperor of the house of Franconia. It had been, as was natural, the object of all his predecessors, not only to render their throne hereditary, which, in effect, the nation was willing to concede, but to surround it with authority sufficient to control the leading vassals. These were the dukes of the four nations of Germany, Saxony, Bavaria, Suabia, and Franconia, and the three archbishops of the Rhenish cities, Mentz, Treves, and Cologne. Originally, as has been more fully shown in another place, duchies, like counties, were temporary governments, bestowed at the pleasure of the crown. From this first stage they advanced to hereditary offices, and finally to patrimonial fiefs. But their progress was much slower in Germany than in France. Under the Saxon line of emperors, it appears probable that, although it was usual, and consonant to the prevailing notions of equity, to confer a duchy upon the nearest heir, yet no positive rule enforced this upon the emperor, and some instances of a contrary proceeding occurred.[3] But, if the royal prerogative in this respect stood higher than in France, there was a countervailing principle that prohibited the emperor from uniting a fief to his domain, or even retaining one which he had possessed before his accession. Thus Otho the Great granted

[1] A maximâ multitudine vox una respondit; Henricum, Christi adjutorio, et jure hæreditario, regnaturum. Ditmar apud Struvium, p. 273. See other passages quoted in the same place. Schmidt, t. ii. p. 410.

[2] Conrad was descended from a daughter of Otho the Great, and also from Conrad I. His first-cousin was duke of Franconia. Struvius; Schmidt; Pfeffel.

[3] Schmidt, t. ii. p. 393, 403. Struvius, p. 214, supposes the hereditary rights of dukes to have commenced under Conrad I.; but Schmidt is perhaps a better authority; and Struvius afterwards mentions the refusal of Otho I. to grant the duchy of Bavaria to the sons of the last duke, which, however, excited a rebellion. p. 235.

away his duchy of Saxony, and Henry II. that of Bavaria. Otho the Great endeavored to counteract the effects of this custom by conferring the duchies that fell into his hands upon members of his own family. This policy, though apparently well conceived, proved of no advantage to Otho, his son and brother having mixed in several rebellions against him. It was revived, however, by Conrad II. and Henry III. The latter was invested by his father with the two duchies of Suabia and Bavaria. Upon his own accession he retained the former for six years, and even the latter for a short time. The duchy of Franconia, which became vacant, he did not regrant, but endeavored to set a precedent of uniting fiefs to the domain. At another time, after sentence of forfeiture against the duke of Bavaria, he bestowed that great province on his wife, the empress Agnes.[1] He put an end altogether to the form of popular concurrence, which had been usual when the investiture of a duchy was conferred; and even deposed dukes by the sentence of a few princes, without the consent of the diet.[2] If we combine with these proofs of authority in the domestic administration of Henry III. his almost unlimited control over papal elections, or rather the right of nomination that he acquired, we must consider him as the most absolute monarch in the annals of Germany.

Unfortunate reign of Henry IV.

These ambitious measures of Henry III. prepared fifty years of calamity for his son. It is easy to perceive that the misfortunes of Henry IV. were primarily occasioned by the jealousy with which repeated violations of their constitutional usages had inspired the nobility.[3] The mere circumstance of Henry IV.'s minority, under the guardianship of a woman, was enough to dissipate whatever power his father had acquired. Hanno, archbishop of Mentz, carried the young king away by force from his mother, and governed Germany in his name; till another archbishop, Adalbert of Bremen, obtained greater influence over him. Through the neglect of his education, Henry grew up with a character not well fitted to retrieve the mischief of so unprotected a minority; brave indeed,

1 Schmidt, t. iii. p. 25, 37.

2 Id. p. 207.

3 In the very first year of Henry's reign, while he was but six years old, the princes of Saxony are said by Lambert of Aschaffenburg to have formed a conspiracy to depose him, out of resentment for the injuries they had sustained from his father. Struvius, p. 306. St. Marc, t. iii. p. 248.

well-natured, and affable, but dissolute beyond measure, and addicted to low and debauched company. He was soon involved in a desperate war with the Saxons, a nation valuing itself on its populousness and riches, jealous of the house of Franconia, who wore a crown that had belonged to their own dukes, and indignant at Henry's conduct in erecting fortresses throughout their country.

A.D. 1073.

In the progress of this war many of the chief princes evinced an unwillingness to support the emperor.[1] Notwithstanding this, it would probably have terminated, as other rebellions had done, with no permanent loss to either party. But in the middle of this contest another far more memorable broke out with the Roman see, concerning ecclesiastical investitures. The motives of this famous quarrel will be explained in a different chapter of the present work. Its effect in Germany was ruinous to Henry. A sentence, not only of excommunication, but of deposition, which Gregory VII. pronounced against him, gave a pretence to all his enemies, secret as well as avowed, to withdraw their allegiance.[2] At the head of these was Rodolph duke of Suabia, whom an assembly of revolted princes raised to the throne. We may perceive, in the conditions of Rodolph's election, a symptom of the real principle that animated the German aristocracy against Henry IV. It was agreed that the kingdom should no longer be hereditary, not conferred on the son of a reigning monarch, unless his merit should challenge the popular approbation.[3] The pope strongly encouraged this plan of rendering the empire elective, by which he hoped either eventually to secure the nomination of its chief for the Holy See, or at least, by sowing the seed of civil dissensions in Germany, to render

A.D. 1077.

[1] Struvius. Schmidt.

[2] A party had been already formed, who were meditating to depose Henry. His excommunication came just in time to confirm their resolutions. It appears clearly, upon a little consideration of Henry IV.'s reign, that the ecclesiastical quarrel was only secondary in the eyes of Germany. The contest against him was a struggle of the aristocracy, jealous of the imperial prerogatives which Conrad II. and Henry III. had strained to the utmost. Those who were in rebellion against Henry were not pleased with Gregory VII. Bruno, author of a history of the Saxon war, a furious invective, manifests great dissatisfaction with the court of Rome, which he reproaches with dissimulation and venality.

[3] Hoc etiam ibi consensu communi comprobatum, Romani pontificis auctoritate est corroboratum, ut regia potestas nulli per hæreditatem, sicut antea fuit consuetudo, cederet, sed filius regis, etiamsi valde dignus esset, per electionem spontaneam, non per successionis lineam, rex proveniret: si vero non esset dignus regis filius, vel si nollet eum populus, quem regem facere vellet, haberet in potestate populus. Bruno de Bello Saxonico, apud Struvium, p. 327.

Italy more independent. Henry IV., however, displayed greater abilities in his adversity than his early conduct had promised. In the last of several decisive battles, Rodolph, though victorious, was mortally wounded; and no one cared to take up a gauntlet which was to be won with so much trouble and uncertainty. The Germans were sufficiently disposed to submit; but Rome persevered in her unrelenting hatred. At the close of Henry's long reign she excited against him his eldest son, and, after more than thirty years of hostility, had the satisfaction of wearing him down with misfortune, and casting out his body, as excommunicated, from its sepulchre.

A.D. 1080.

In the reign of his son Henry V. there is no event worthy of much attention, except the termination of the great contest about investitures. At his death in 1125 the male line of the Franconian emperors was at an end. Frederic duke of Suabia, grandson by his mother of Henry IV., had inherited their patrimonial estates, and seemed to represent their dynasty. But both the last emperors had so many enemies, and a disposition to render the crown elective prevailed so strongly among the leading princes, that Lothaire duke of Saxony was elevated to the throne, though rather in a tumultuous and irregular manner.[1] Lothaire, who had been engaged in a revolt against Henry V., and the chief of a nation that bore an inveterate hatred to the house of Franconia, was the natural enemy of the new family that derived its importance and pretensions from that stock. It was the object of his reign, accordingly, to oppress the two brothers, Frederic and Conrad, of the Hohenstauffen or Suabian family. By this means he expected to secure the succession of the empire for his son-in-law. Henry, surnamed the Proud, who married Lothaire's only child, was fourth in descent from Welf, son of Azon marquis of Este, by Cunegonda, heiress of a distinguished family, the Welfs of Altorf in Suabia. Her son was invested with the duchy

Extinction of the house of Franconia.

A.D. 1125.

Election of Lothaire.

1 See an account of Lothaire's election by a contemporary writer in Struvius, p. 357. See also proofs of the dissatisfaction of the aristocracy at the Franconian government. Schmidt, t. iii. p. 328. It was evidently their determination to render the empire truly elective (Id. p. 335): and perhaps we may date that fundamental principle of the Germanic constitution from the accession of Lothaire. Previously to that era, birth seems to have given not only a fair title to preference, but a sort of inchoate right, as in France, Spain, and England. Lothaire signed a capitulation at his accession.

of Bavaria in 1071. His descendant, Henry the Proud, represented also, through his mother, the ancient dukes of Saxony, surnamed Billung, from whom he derived the duchy of Luneburg. The wife of Lothaire transmitted to her daughter the patrimony of Henry the Fowler, consisting of Hanover and Brunswic. Besides this great dowry, Lothaire bestowed upon his son-in-law the duchy of Saxony in addition to that of Bavaria.[1]

This amazing preponderance, however, tended to alienate the princes of Germany from Lothaire's views in favor of Henry; and the latter does not seem to have possessed abilities adequate to his eminent station. On the death of Lothaire in 1138 the partisans of the house of Suabia made a hasty and irregular election of Conrad, in which the Saxon faction found itself obliged to acquiesce.[2] The new emperor availed himself of the jealousy which Henry the Proud's aggrandizement had excited. Under pretence that two duchies could not legally be held by the same person, Henry was summoned to resign one of them; and on his refusal, the diet pronounced that he had incurred a forfeiture of both. Henry made but little resistance, and before his death, which happened soon afterwards, saw himself stripped of all his hereditary as well as acquired possessions. Upon this occasion the famous names of Guelf and Ghibelin were first heard, which were destined to keep alive the flame of civil dissension in far distant countries, and after their meaning had been forgotten. The Guelfs, or Welfs, were, as I have said, the ancestors of Henry, and the name has become a sort of patronymic in his family. The word Ghibelin is derived from Wibelung, a town in Franconia, whence the emperors of that line are said to have sprung. The house of Suabia were considered in Germany as representing that of Franconia; as the Guelfs may, without much impropriety, be deemed to represent the Saxon line.[3]

House of Suabia. Conrad III. A.D 1138.

Origin of Guelfs and Ghibelins.

Though Conrad III. left a son, the choice of the electors fell, at his own request, upon his nephew Frederic Barbarossa.[4] The most conspicuous events of this great emperor's life belong to the history of Italy. At home

Frederic Barbarossa.

1 Pfeffel, Abrégé Chronologique de l'Histoire d'Allemagne, t. i. p. 269. (Paris, 1777.) Gibbon's Antiquities of the House of Brunswic

2 Schmidt.

3 Struvius, p 370 and 378.

4 Struvius.

he was feared and respected; the imperial prerogatives stood as high during his reign as, after their previous decline, it was possible for a single man to carry them.[1] But the only circumstance which appears memorable enough for the present sketch is the second fall of the Guelfs. Henry the Lion, son of Henry the Proud, had been restored by Conrad III. to his father's duchy of Saxony, resigning his claim to that of Bavaria which had been conferred on the margrave of Austria. This renunciation, which indeed was only made in his name during childhood, did not prevent him from urging the emperor Frederic to restore the whole of his birthright; and Frederic, his first-cousin, whose life he had saved in a sedition at Rome, was induced to comply with this request in 1156. Far from evincing that political jealousy which some writers impute to him, the emperor seems to have carried his generosity beyond the limits of prudence. For many years their union was apparently cordial. But, whether it was that Henry took umbrage at part of Frederic's conduct,[2] or that mere ambition rendered him ungrateful, he certainly abandoned his sovereign in a moment of distress, refusing to give any assistance in that expedition into Lombardy which ended in the unsuccessful battle of Legnano. Frederic could not forgive this injury, and, taking advantage of complaints, which Henry's power and haughtiness had produced, summoned him to answer charges in a general diet. The duke refused to appear, and, being adjudged contumacious, a sentence of confiscation, similar to that which ruined his father, fell upon his head; and the vast imperial fiefs that he possessed were shared among some potent enemies.[3] He made an ineffectual resistance; like his father, he appears to have owed more to fortune than to nature; and after three years' exile, was obliged to remain content with the restoration of his alodial estates in Saxony. These, fifty years afterwards, were converted into imperial fiefs, and became the two duchies of the house

Fall of Henry the Lion.

A.D. 1178.

1 Pfeffel, p. 341.

2 Frederic had obtained the succession of Wolf marquis of Tuscany, uncle of Henry the Lion, who probably considered himself as entitled to expect it. Schmidt, p. 427.

3 Putter, in his Historical Development of the Constitution of the German Empire, is inclined to consider Henry the Lion as sacrificed to the emperor's jealousy of the Guelfs, and as illegally proscribed by the diet. But the provocations he had given Frederic are undeniable; and, without pretending to decide on a question of German history, I do not see that there was any precipitancy or manifest breach of justice in the course of proceedings against him. Schmidt, Pfeffel, and Struvius do not represent the condemnation of Henry as unjust.

of Brunswic, the lineal representatives of Henry the Lion, and inheritors of the name of Guelf.[1]

Notwithstanding the prevailing spirit of the German oligarchy, Frederic Barbarossa had found no difficulty in procuring the election of his son Henry, even during infancy, as his successor.[2] The fall of Henry the Lion had greatly weakened the ducal authority in Saxony and Bavaria; the princes who acquired that title, especially in the former country, finding that the secular and spiritual nobility of the first class had taken the opportunity to raise themselves into an immediate dependence upon the empire. Henry VI. came, therefore, to the crown with considerable advantages in respect of prerogative; and these inspired him with the bold scheme of declaring the empire hereditary. One is more surprised to find that he had no contemptible prospect of success in this attempt: fifty-two princes, and even what appears hardly credible, the See of Rome, under Clement III., having been induced to concur in it. But the Saxons made so vigorous an opposition, that Henry did not think it advisable to persevere.[3] He procured, however, the election of his son Frederic, an infant only two years old. But, the emperor dying almost immediately, a powerful body of princes, supported by Pope Innocent III., were desirous to withdraw their consent. Philip duke of Suabia, the late king's brother, unable to secure his nephew's succession, brought about his own election by one party, while another chose Otho of Brunswic, younger son of Henry the Lion. This double election renewed the rivalry between the Guelfs and Ghibelins, and threw Germany into confusion for several years. Philip, whose pretensions appear to be the more legitimate of the two, gained ground upon his adversary, notwithstanding the opposition of the pope, till he was assassinated in consequence of a private resentment. Otho IV. reaped the benefit of a crime in which he did not participate, and became for some years undisputed sovereign. But, having offended the pope by not entirely abandoning his imperial rights over Italy, he had, in the latter part of his reign, to contend against Frederic, son of Henry VI., who,

Henry VI. A.D. 1190.

Philip and Otho IV. A.D. 1197.

A.D. 1208.

[1] Putter, p. 220.

[2] Struvius, p. 418.

[3] Struvius, p. 424. Impetravit a subditis, ut cessante pristinâ Palatinorum electione, imperium in ipsius posteritatem, distinctâ proximorum successione, transiret, et sic in ipso terminus esset electionis, principiumque successivæ dignitatis. Gervas. Tilburiens. ibidem.

having grown up to manhood, came into Germany as heir of the house of Suabia, and, what was not very usual in his own history, or that of his family, the favored candidate of the Holy See. Otho IV. had been almost entirely deserted except by his natural subjects, when his death, in 1218, removed every difficulty, and left Frederic II. in the peaceable possession of Germany.

Frederic II.

The eventful life of Frederic II. was chiefly passed in Italy. To preserve his hereditary dominions, and chastise the Lombard cities, were the leading objects of his political and military career. He paid therefore but little attention to Germany, from which it was in vain for any emperor to expect effectual assistance towards objects of his own. Careless of prerogatives which it seemed hardly worth an effort to preserve, he sanctioned the independence of the princes, which may be properly dated from his reign. In return, they readily elected his son Henry king of the Romans; and on his being implicated in a rebellion, deposed him with equal readiness, and substituted his brother Conrad at the emperor's request.[1] But in the latter part of Frederic's reign the deadly hatred of Rome penetrated beyond the Alps. After his solemn deposition in the council of Lyons, he was incapable, in ecclesiastical eyes, of holding the imperial sceptre. Innocent IV. found, however, some difficulty in setting up a rival emperor. Henry landgrave of Thuringia made an indifferent figure in this character. Upon his death, William count of Holland was chosen by the party adverse to Frederic and his son Conrad; and after the emperor's death he had some success against the latter. It is hard indeed to say that any one was actually sovereign for twenty-two years that followed the death of Frederic II.: a period of contested title and universal anarchy, which is usually denominated the grand interregnum. On the decease of William of Holland, in 1256, a schism among the electors produced the double choice of Richard earl of Cornwall, and Alfonso X. king of Castile. It seems not easy to determine which of these candidates had a legal majority of votes;[2] but the subsequent recognition of almost all Germany,

Consequences of the council of Lyons.

A.D. 1245.

A.D. 1248.

Grand interregnum. A.D. 1250.

A.D. 1272.

Richard of Cornwall.

[1] Struvius, p. 457.

[2] The election ought legally to have been made at Frankfort. But the elector of Treves, having got possession of the town, shut out the archbishops of Mentz and Cologne and the count palatine, on

and a sort of possession evidenced by public acts, which have been held valid, as well as the general consent of contemporaries, may justify us in adding Richard to the imperial list. The choice indeed was ridiculous, as he possessed no talents which could compensate for his want of power; but the electors attained their objects; to perpetuate a state of confusion by which their own independence was consolidated, and to plunder without scruple a man, like Didius at Rome, rich and foolish enough to purchase the first place upon earth.

State of the Germanic constitution.

That place indeed was now become a mockery of greatness. For more than two centuries, notwithstanding the temporary influence of Frederic Barbarossa and his son, the imperial authority had been in a state of gradual decay. From the time of Frederic II. it had bordered upon absolute insignificance; and the more prudent German princes were slow to canvass for a dignity so little accompanied by respect. The changes wrought in the Germanic constitution during the period of the Suabian emperors chiefly consist in the establishment of an oligarchy of electors, and of the territorial sovereignty of the princes.

Electors.

1. At the extinction of the Franconian line by the death of Henry V. it was determined by the German nobility to make their empire practically elective, admitting no right, or even natural pretension, in the eldest son of a reigning sovereign. Their choice upon former occasions had been made by free and general suffrage. But it may be presumed that each nation voted unanimously, and according to the disposition of its duke. It is probable, too, that the leaders, after discussing in previous deliberations the merits of the several candidates, submitted their own resolutions to the assembly, which would generally concur in them without hesitation. At the election of Lothaire, in 1124, we

pretence of apprehending violence. They met under the walls, and there elected Richard. Afterwards Alfonso was chosen by the votes of Treves, Saxony, and Brandenburg. Historians differ about the vote of Ottocar king of Bohemia, which would turn the scale. Some time after the election it is certain that he was on the side of Richard. Perhaps we may collect from the opposite statements in Struvius, p. 504, that the proxies of Ottocar had voted for Alfonso, and that he did not think fit to recognize their act.

There can be no doubt that Richard was *de facto* sovereign of Germany; and it is singular that Struvius should assert the contrary, on the authority of an instrument of Rodolph, which expressly designates him king, per quondam Richardum regem illustrem. Struv. p. 502.

find an evident instance of this previous choice, or, as it was called, *prætaxation*, from which the electoral college of Germany has been derived. The princes, it is said, trusted the choice of an emperor to ten persons, in whose judgment they promised to acquiesce.[1] This precedent was, in all likelihood, followed at all subsequent elections. The proofs indeed are not perfectly clear. But in the famous privilege of Austria, granted by Frederic I. in 1156, he bestows a rank upon the newly-created duke of that country, immediately after the electing princes (post principes electores);[2] a strong presumption that the right of pretaxation was not only established, but limited to a few definite persons. In a letter of Innocent III., concerning the double election of Philip and Otho in 1198, he asserts the latter to have had a majority in his favor of those to whom the right of election chiefly belongs (ad quos principaliter spectat electio).[3] And a law of Otho in 1208, if it be genuine, appears to fix the exclusive privilege of the seven electors.[4] Nevertheless, so obscure is this important part of the Germanic system, that we find four ecclesiastical and two secular princes concurring with the regular electors in the act, as reported by a contemporary writer, that creates Conrad, son of Frederic II., king of the Romans.[5] This, however, may have been an irregular deviation from the principle already established. But it is admitted that all the princes retained, at least during the twelfth century, their consenting suffrage; like the laity in an episcopal election, whose approbation continued to be necessary long after the real power of choice had been withdrawn from them.[6]

It is not easy to account for all the circumstances that gave to seven spiritual and temporal princes this distinguished preëminence. The three archbishops, Mentz, Treves, and Cologne, were always indeed at the head of the German church. But the secular electors should naturally have been the dukes of four nations: Saxony, Franconia, Suabia, and Bavaria. We find, however, only the first of these in the

1 Struvius, p. 357. Schmidt, t. iii. p. 331.

2 Schmidt, t. iii. p. 390.

3 Pfeffel, p. 360.

4 Schmidt, t. iv. p. 80.

5 This is not mentioned in Struvius, or the other German writers. But Denina (Rivoluzioni d'Italia, l. ix. c. 9) quotes the style of the act of election from the Chronicle of Francis Pippin.

6 This is manifest by the various passages relating to the elections of Philip and Otho, quoted by Struvius, p. 428, 430. See, too, Pfeffel, ubi supra. Schmidt, t. iv. p. 79.

undisputed exercise of a vote. It seems probable that, when the electoral princes came to be distinguished from the rest, their privilege was considered as peculiarly connected with the discharge of one of the great offices in the imperial court. These were attached, as early as the diet of Mentz in 1184, to the four electors, who ever afterwards possessed them: the duke of Saxony having then officiated as arch-marshal, the count palatine of the Rhine as arch-steward, the king of Bohemia as arch-cupbearer, and the margrave of Brandenburg as arch-chamberlain of the empire.[1] But it still continues a problem why the three latter offices, with the electoral capacity as their incident, should not rather have been granted to the dukes of Franconia, Suabia, and Bavaria. I have seen no adequate explanation of this circumstance; which may perhaps lead us to presume that the right of pre-election was not quite so soon confined to the precise number of seven princes. The final extinction of two great original duchies, Franconia and Suabia, in the thirteenth century, left the electoral rights of the count palatine and the margrave of Brandenburg beyond dispute. But the dukes of Bavaria continued to claim a vote in opposition to the kings of Bohemia. At the election of Rodolph in 1272 the two brothers of the house of Wittelsbach voted separately, as count palatine and duke of Lower Bavaria. Ottocar was excluded upon this occasion; and it was not till 1290 that the suffrage of Bohemia was fully recognized. The Palatine and Bavarian branches, however, continued to enjoy their family vote conjointly, by a determination of Rodolph; upon which Louis of Bavaria slightly innovated, by rendering the suffrage alternate. But the Golden Bull of Charles IV. put an end to all doubts on the rights of electoral houses, and absolutely excluded Bavaria from voting. The limitation to seven electors, first perhaps fixed by accident, came to be invested with a sort of mysterious importance, and certainly was considered, until times comparatively recent, as a fundamental law of the empire.[2]

Princes and untitled inferior nobility.

2. It might appear natural to expect that an oligarchy of seven persons, who had thus excluded their equals from all share in the election of a sovereign, would assume still greater authority, and trespass fur-

[1] Schmidt, t. iv. p. 78.
[2] Ibid. p. 78, 568; Putter, p. 274; Pfeffel, p. 435, 565; Struvius, p. 511.

ther upon the less powerful vassals of the empire. But while the electors were establishing their peculiar privilege, the class immediately inferior raised itself by important acquisitions of power. The German dukes, even after they became hereditary, did not succeed in compelling the chief nobility within their limits to hold their lands in fief so completely as the peers of France had done. The nobles of Suabia refused to follow their duke into the field against the emperor Conrad II.[1] Of this aristocracy the superior class were denominated princes; an appellation which, after the eleventh century, distinguished them from the untitled nobility, most of whom were their vassals. They were constituent parts of all diets; and though gradually deprived of their original participation in electing an emperor, possessed, in all other respects, the same rights as the dukes or electors. Some of them were fully equal to the electors in birth as well as extent of dominions; such as the princely houses of Austria, Hesse, Brunswic, and Misnia. By the division of Henry the Lion's vast territories,[2] and by the absolute extinction of the Suabian family in the following century, a great many princes acquired additional weight. Of the ancient duchies, only Saxony and Bavaria remained; the former of which especially was so dismembered, that it was vain to attempt any renewal of the ducal jurisdiction. That of the emperor, formerly exercised by the counts palatine, went almost equally into disuse during the contest between Philip and Otho IV. The princes accordingly had acted with sovereign independence within their own fiefs before the reign of Frederic II.; but the legal recognition of their immunities was reserved for two edicts of that emperor; one, in 1220, relating to ecclesiastical, and the other, in 1232, to secular princes. By these he engaged neither to levy the customary imperial dues, nor to permit the jurisdiction of the palatine judges, within the limits of a state of the empire;[3] concessions that amounted to little less than an abdication of his own sovereignty. From this epoch the territorial independence of the states may be dated.

A class of titled nobility, inferior to the princes, were the counts of the empire, who seem to have been separated from the former in the twelfth century, and to have lost at the same

1 Pfeffel, p. 209.

2 See the arrangements made in consequence of Henry's forfeiture, which gave quite a new face to Germany, in Pfeffel, p. 234; also p. 437.

3 Pfeffel, p. 384; Putter, p. 233.

time their right of voting in the diets.[1] In some parts of Germany, chiefly in Franconia and upon the Rhine, there always existed a very numerous body of lower nobility; untitled at least till modern times, but subject to no superior except the emperor. These are supposod to have become *immediate*, after the destruction of the house of Suabia, within whose duchies they had been comprehended.[2]

Election of Rodolph of Hapsburg. A.D. 1272.

A short interval elapsed after the death of Richard of Cornwall before the electors could be induced, by the deplorable state of confusion into which Germany had fallen, to fill the imperial throne. Their choice was however the best that could have been made. It fell upon Rodolph count of Hapsburg, a prince of very ancient family, and of considerable possessions as well in Switzerland as upon each bank of the Upper Rhine, but not sufficiently powerful to alarm the electoral oligarchy. Rodolph was brave, active, and just; but his characteristic quality appears to have been good sense, and judgment of the circumstances in which he was placed. Of this he gave a signal proof in relinquishing the favorite project of so many preceding emperors, and leaving Italy altogether to itself. At home he manifested a vigilant spirit in administering justice, and is said to have destroyed seventy strongholds of noble robbers in Thuringia and other parts, bringing many of the criminals to capital punishment.[3] But he wisely avoided giving offence to the more powerful princes; and during his reign there were hardly any rebellions in Germany.

Investment of his son Albert with duchy of Austria.

It was a very reasonable object of every emperor to aggrandize his family by investing his near kindred with vacant fiefs; but no one was so fortunate in his opportunities as Rodolph. At his accession, duchy of Austria, Styria, and Carniola were in the hands of Ottocar king of Bohemia. These extensive and fertile countries had been formed into a march or margraviate, after the victories of Otho the Great over the Hungarians. Frederic Barbarossa erected them into a duchy, with many distinguish ed privileges, especially that of female succession, hithert

[1] In the instruments relating to the election of Otho IV. the princes sign their names, Ego N. elegi et subscripsi. But the counts only as follows: Ego N. consensi et subscripsi. Pfeffel, p. 360.

[2] Pfeffel, p. 455; Putter, p. 254; Struvius, p. 511.

[3] Struvius, p. 530. Coxe's Hist. of House of Austria, p. 57. This valuable work contains a full and interesting account of Rodolph's reign.

unknown in the feudal principalities of Germany.[1] Upon the extinction of the house of Bamberg, which had enjoyed this duchy, it was granted by Frederic II. to a cousin of his own name; after whose death a disputed succession gave rise to several changes, and ultimately enabled Ottocar to gain possession of the country. Against this king of Bohemia Rodolph waged two successful wars, and recovered the Austrian provinces, which, as vacant fiefs, he conferred, with the consent of the diet, upon his son Albert.[2]

A.D. 1283.

State of the empire after Rodolph.

Notwithstanding the merit and popularity of Rodolph, the electors refused to choose his son king of the Romans in his lifetime; and, after his death, determined to avoid the appearance of hereditary succession, put Adolphus of Nassau upon the throne. There is very little to attract notice in the domestic history of the empire during the next two centuries. From Adolphus to Sigismund every emperor had either to struggle against a competitor claiming the majority of votes at his election, or against a combination of the electors to dethrone him. The imperial authority became more and more ineffective; yet it was frequently made a subject of reproach against the emperors that they did not maintain a sovereignty to which no one was disposed to submit.

Adolphus. A.D. 1292. Albert I. A.D. 1298. Henry VII. A.D. 1308. Louis IV. A.D. 1314. Charles IV. A.D. 1347. Wenceslaus. A.D. 1378. Robert. A.D. 1400. Sigismund. A.D. 1414.

It may appear surprising that the Germanic confederacy under the nominal supremacy of an emperor should have been preserved in circumstances apparently so calculated to dissolve it. But, besides the natural effect of prejudice and a famous name, there were sufficient reasons to induce the electors to preserve a form of government in which they bore so

1 The privileges of Austria were granted to the margrave Henry in 1156, by way of indemnity for his restitution of Bavaria to Henry the Lion. The territory between the Inn and the Ems was separated from the latter province, and annexed to Austria at this time. The dukes of Austria are declared equal in rank to the palatine archdukes (archiducibus palatinis). This expression gave a hint to the duke Rodolph IV. to assume the title of archduke of Austria. Schmidt, t. iii. p. 390. Frederic II. even created the duke of Austria king: a very curious fact, though neither he nor his successors ever assumed the title. Struvius, p. 463. The instrument runs as follows: Ducatus Austriæ et Styriæ, cum pertinentiis et terminis suis quot hactenus habuit, ad nomen et honorem regium transferentes, te hactenus ducatuum prædictorum ducem, de potestatis nostræ plenitudine et magnificentiâ speciali promovemus in regem, per libertates et jura prædictum regnum tuum præsentis epigrammatis auctoritate donantes, quæ regiam deceant dignitatem; ut tamen ex honore quem tibi libenter addimus, nihil honoris et juris nostri diadematis aut imperii subtrahatur.

2 Struvius, p. 525; Schmidt; Coxe.

decided a sway. Accident had in a considerable degree restricted the electoral suffrages to seven princes. Without the college there were houses more substantially powerful than any within it. The duchy of Saxony had been subdivided by repeated partitions among children, till the electoral right was vested in a prince who possessed only the small territory of Wittenberg. The great families of Austria, Bavaria, and Luxemburg, though not electoral, were the real heads of the German body; and though the two former lost much of their influence for a time through the pernicious custom of partition, the empire seldom looked for its head to any other house than one of these three.

Custom of partition.

While the duchies and counties of Germany retained their original character of offices or governments, they were of course, even though considered as hereditary, not subject to partition among children. When they acquired the nature of fiefs, it was still consonant to the principles of a feudal tenure that the eldest son should inherit according to the law of primogeniture; an inferior provision or appanage, at most, being reserved for the younger children. The law of England favored the eldest exclusively; that of France gave him great advantages. But in Germany a different rule began to prevail about the thirteenth century.[1] An equal partition of the inheritance, without the least regard to priority of birth, was the general law of its principalities. Sometimes this was effected by undivided possession, or tenancy in common, the brothers residing together, and reigning jointly. This tended to preserve the integrity of dominion; but as it was frequently incommodious, a more usual practice was to divide the territory. From such partitions are derived those numerous independent principalities of the same house, many of which still subsist in Germany. In 1589 there were eight reigning princes of the Palatine family; and fourteen, in 1675, of that of Saxony.[2] Originally these partitions were in general absolute and without reversion; but, as their effect in weakening families became evident, a practice was introduced of making compacts of reciprocal succession, by which a fief was prevented from escheating to the empire, until all

[1] Schmidt, t. iv. p. 66. Pfeffel, p. 289, maintains that partitions were not introduced till the latter end of the thirteenth century. This may be true as a general rule; but I find the house of Baden divided into two branches, Baden and Hochberg, in 1190, with rights of mutual reversion.

[2] Pfeffel, p. 289; Putter, p. 189

the male posterity of the first feudatory should be extinct. Thus, while the German empire survived, all the princes of Hesse or of Saxony had reciprocal contingencies of succession, or what our lawyers call cross-remainders, to each other's dominions. A different system was gradually adopted. By the Golden Bull of Charles IV. the electoral territory, that is, the particular district to which the electoral suffrage was inseparably attached, became incapable of partition, and was to descend to the eldest son. In the fifteenth century the present house of Brandenburg set the first example of establishing primogeniture by law; the principalities of Anspach and Bayreuth were dismembered from it for the benefit of younger branches; but it was declared that all the other dominions of the family should for the future belong exclusively to the reigning elector. This politic measure was adopted in several other families; but, even in the sixteenth century, the prejudice was not removed, and some German princes denounced curses on their posterity, if they should introduce the impious custom of primogeniture.[1] Notwithstanding these subdivisions, and the most remarkable of those which I have mentioned are of a date rather subsequent to the middle ages, the antagonist principle of consolidation by various means of acquisition was so actively at work that several princely houses, especially those of Hohenzollern or Brandenburg, of Hesse, Wirtemburg, and the Palatinate, derive their importance from the same era, the fourteenth and fifteenth centuries, in which the prejudice against primogeniture was the strongest. And thus it will often be found in private patrimonies; the tendency to consolidation of property works more rapidly than that to its disintegration by a law of gavelkind.

Weakened by these subdivisions, the principalities of Germany in the fourteenth and fifteenth centuries shrink to a more and more diminutive size in the scale of nations. But one family, the most illustrious of the former age, was less exposed to this enfeebling system. Henry VII. count of Luxemburg, a man of much more personal merit than hereditary importance, was elevated to the empire in 1308. Most part of his short reign he passed in Italy; but he had a fortunate opportunity of obtaining the crown of Bohemia for his son. John king of Bohemia did not himself

House of Luxemburg.

1 Pfeffel, p. 280.

wear the imperial crown; but three of his descendants possessed it, with less interruption than could have been expected. His son Charles IV. succeeded Louis of Bavaria in 1347; not indeed without opposition, for a double election and a civil war were matters of course in Germany. Charles IV. has been treated with more derision by his contemporaries, and consequently by later writers, than almost any prince in history; yet he was remarkably successful in the only objects that he seriously pursued. Deficient in personal courage, insensible of humiliation, bending without shame to the pope, to the Italians, to the electors, so poor and so little reverenced as to be arrested by a butcher at Worms for want of paying his demand, Charles IV. affords a proof that a certain dexterity and cold-blooded perseverance may occasionally supply, in a sovereign, the want of more respectable qualities. He has been reproached with neglecting the empire. But he never designed to trouble himself about the empire, except for his private ends. He did not neglect the kingdom of Bohemia, to which he almost seemed to render Germany a province. Bohemia had been long considered as a fief of the empire, and indeed could pretend to an electoral vote by no other title. Charles, however, gave the states by law the right of choosing a king, on the extinction of the royal family, which seems derogatory to the imperial prerogative.[1] It was much more material that, upon acquiring Brandenburg, partly by conquest, and partly by a compact of succession in 1373, he not only invested his sons with it, which was conformable to usage, but tried to annex that electorate forever to the kingdom of Bohemia.[2] He constantly resided at Prague, where he founded a celebrated university, and embellished the city with buildings. This kingdom, augmented also during his reign by the acquisition of Silesia, he bequeathed to his son Wenceslaus, for whom, by pliancy towards the electors and the court of Rome, he had procured, against all recent example, the imperial succession.[3]

The reign of Charles IV. is distinguished in the constitutional history of the empire by his Golden Bull; an instrument which finally ascertained the prerogatives of the electoral college. The Golden Bull terminated the disputes which had arisen between different

Golden Bull. A.D. 1355.

1 Struvius, p. 641.
2 Pfeffel, p. 575; Schmidt, t. iv. p. 595
3 Struvius, p. 637.

members of the same house as to their right of suffrage, which was declared inherent in certain definite territories. The number was absolutely restrained to seven. The place of legal imperial elections was fixed at Frankfort; of coronations, at Aix-la-Chapelle; and the latter ceremony was to be performed by the archbishop of Cologne. These regulations, though consonant to ancient usage, had not always been observed, and their neglect had sometimes excited questions as to the validity of elections. The dignity of elector was enhanced by the Golden Bull as highly as an imperial edict could carry it; they were declared equal to kings, and conspiracy against their persons incurred the penalty of high treason.[1] Many other privileges are granted to render them more completely sovereign within their dominions. It seems extraordinary that Charles should have voluntarily elevated an oligarchy, from whose pretensions his predecessors had frequently suffered injury. But he had more to apprehend from the two great families of Bavaria and Austria, whom he relatively depressed by giving such a preponderance to the seven electors, than from any members of the college. By his compact with Brandenburg he had a fair prospect of adding a second vote to his own; and there was more room for intrigue and management, which Charles always preferred to arms, with a small number, than with the whole body of princes.

Deposition of Wenceslaus.

The next reign, nevertheless, evinced the danger of investing the electors with such preponderating authority. Wenceslaus, a supine and voluptuous man, less respected, and more negligent of Germany, if possible, than his father, was regularly deposed by a majority of the electoral college in 1400. This right, if it is to be considered as a right, they had already used against Adolphus of Nassau in 1298, and against Louis of Bavaria in 1346. They chose Robert count palatine instead of Wenceslaus; and though the latter did not cease to have some adherents, Robert has generally been counted among the lawful emperors.[2] Upon his death the empire returned

[1] Pfeffel, p. 565; Putter, p. 271; Schmidt, t. iv. p. 566. The Golden Bull not only fixed the Palatine vote, in absolute exclusion of Bavaria, but settled a controversy of long standing between the two branches of the house of Saxony, Wittenberg and Lauenburg, in favor of the former.

[2] Many of the cities besides some princes, continued to recognize Wenceslaus throughout the life of Robert; and the latter was so much considered as an usurper by foreign states, that his ambassadors were refused admittance at the council of Pisa. Struvius, p. 658.

to the house of Luxemburg; Wenceslaus himself waiving his rights in favor of his brother Sigismund of Hungary.[1]

House of Austria.

The house of Austria had hitherto given but two emperors to Germany, Rodolph its founder, and his son Albert, whom a successful rebellion elevated in the place of Adolphus. Upon the death of Henry of Luxemburg, in 1313, Frederic, son of Albert, disputed the election of Louis duke of Bavaria, alleging a majority of genuine votes. This produced a civil war, in which the Austrian party were entirely worsted. Though they advanced no pretensions to the imperial dignity during the rest of the fourteenth century, the princes of that line added to their possessions Carinthia, Istria, and the Tyrol. As a counterbalance to these acquisitions, they lost a great part of their ancient inheritance by unsuccessful wars with the Swiss. According to the custom of partition, so injurious to princely houses, their dominions were divided among three branches: one reigning in Austria, a second in Styria and the adjacent provinces, a third in the Tyrol and Alsace. This had in a considerable degree eclipsed the glory of the house of Hapsburg. But it was now its destiny to revive, and to enter upon a career of prosperity which has never since been permanently interrupted. Albert duke of Austria, who had married Sigismund's only daughter, the queen of Hungary and Bohemia, was raised to the imperial throne upon the death of his father-in-law in 1437. He died in two years, leaving his wife pregnant with a son, Ladislaus Posthumus, who afterwards reigned in the two kingdoms just mentioned; and the choice of the electors fell upon Frederic duke of Styria, second-cousin of the last emperor, from whose posterity it never departed, except in a single instance, upon the extinction of his male line in 1740.

Albert II. A.D. 1438.

Reign of Frederic III. A.D. 1440—1493.

Frederic III. reigned fifty-three years, a longer period than any of his predecessors; and his personal character was more insignificant. With better fortune than could be expected, considering both these circumstances, he escaped any overt attempt

[1] This election of Sigismund was not uncontested: Josse, or Jodocus, margrave of Moravia, having been chosen, as far as appears, by a legal majority. However, his death within three months removed the difficulty; and Josse, who was not crowned at Frankfort, has never been reckoned among the emperors, though modern critics agree that his title was legitimate. Struvius, p. 684; Pfeffel, p. 612.

to depose him, though such a project was sometimes in agitation. He reigned during an interesting age, full of remarkable events, and big with others of more leading importance. The destruction of the Greek empire, and appearance of the victorious crescent upon the Danube, gave an unhappy distinction to the earlier years of his reign, and displayed his mean and pusillanimous character in circumstances which demanded a hero. At a later season he was drawn into contentions with France and Burgundy, which ultimately produced a new and more general combination of European politics. Frederic, always poor, and scarcely able to protect himself in Austria from the seditions of his subjects, or the inroads of the king of Hungary, was yet another founder of his family, and left their fortunes incomparably more prosperous than at his accession.[1] The marriage of his son Maximilian with the heiress of Burgundy began that aggrandizement of the house of Austria which Frederic seems to have anticipated.[2] The electors, who had

[1] Ranke has drawn the character of Frederic III. more favorably, on the whole, than preceding historians, and with a discrimination which enables us to account better for his success in the objects which he had at heart. "From his youth he had been inured to trouble and adversity. When compelled to yield, he never gave up a point, and always gained the mastery in the end. The maintenance of his prerogatives was the governing principle of all his actions, the more because they acquired an ideal value from their connection with the imperial dignity. It cost him a long and severe struggle to allow his son to be crowned king of the Romans; he wished to take the supreme authority undivided with him to the grave: in no case would he grant Maximilian any independent share in the administration of government; but kept him, even after he was king, still as 'son of the house'; nor would he ever give him anything but the countship of Cilli; 'for the rest he would have time enough.' His frugality bordered on avarice, his slowness on inertness, his stubbornness on the most determined selfishness; yet all these faults are removed from vulgarity by high qualities. He had at bottom a sober depth of judgment, a sedate and inflexible honor; the aged prince, even when a fugitive imploring succor, had a personal bearing which never allowed the majesty of the empire to sink." Hist. Reformation (Translation), vol. ii. p. 103. A character of such obstinate passive resistance was well fitted for his station in that age; spite of his poverty and weakness, he was hereditary sovereign of extensive and fertile territories; he was not loved, feared, or respected, but he was necessary; he was a German, and therefore not to be exchanged for a king of Hungary or Bohemia; he was, not as Frederic of Austria, but as elected emperor, the sole hope for a more settled rule, for public peace, for the maintenance of a confederacy so ill held together by any other tie. Hence he succeeded in what seemed so difficult — in procuring the election of Maximilian as king of the Romans; and interested the German diet in maintaining the Burgundian inheritance, the western provinces of the Netherlands, which the latter's marriage brought into the house of Austria.

[2] The famous device of Austria, A. E. I. O. U., was first used by Frederic III., who adopted it on his plate, books, and buildings. These initials stand for, Austriæ Est Imperare Orbi Universo; or, in German, Alles Erdreich Ist Osterreich Unterthan: a bold assumption for a man who was not safe in an inch of his dominions. Struvius, p. 722. He confirmed the archiducal title of his family, which might seem implied in the original grant of Frederic I.; and bestowed other high privileges above all princes of the empire. These are enumerated in Coxe's House of Austria, vol. i. p. 263.

lost a good deal of their former spirit, and were grown sensible of the necessity of choosing a powerful sovereign, made no opposition to Maximilian's becoming king of the Romans in his father's lifetime. The Austrian provinces were reunited either under Frederic, or in the first years of Maximilian; so that, at the close of that period which we denominate the Middle Ages, the German empire, sustained by the patrimonial dominions of its chief, became again considerable in the scale of nations, and capable of preserving a balance between the ambitious monarchies of France and Spain.

Progress of free imperial cities.

The period between Rodolph and Frederic III. is distinguished by no circumstance so interesting as the prosperous state of the free imperial cities, which had attained their maturity about the commencement of that interval. We find the cities of Germany, in the tenth century, divided into such as depended immediately upon the empire, which were usually governed by their bishop as imperial vicar, and such as were included in the territories of the dukes and counts.[1] Some of the former, lying principally upon the Rhine and in Franconia, acquired a certain degree of importance before the expiration of the eleventh century. Worms and Cologne manifested a zealous attachment to Henry IV., whom they supported in despite of their bishops.[2] His son Henry V. granted privileges of enfranchisement to the inferior townsmen or artisans, who had hitherto been distinguished from the upper class of freemen, and particularly relieved them from oppressive usages, which either gave the whole of their movable goods to the lord upon their decease, or at least enabled him to seize the best chattel as his heriot.[3] He took away the temporal authority of the bishop, at least in several instances, and restored the cities to a more immediate dependence upon the empire. The citizens were classed in companies, according to their several occupations; an institution which was speedily adopted in other commercial countries. It does not appear that any German city had obtained, under this emperor, those privileges of choosing its own magistrates, which were conceded

[1] Pfeffel, p. 187. The Othos adopted the same policy in Germany which they had introduced in Italy, conferring the temporal government of cities upon the bishops; probably as a counterbalance to the lay aristocracy. Putter, p. 136; Struvius, p. 252.

[2] Schmidt, t. iii. p. 239.

[3] Schmidt, p. 242; Pfeffel, p. 293; Dumont, Corps Diplomatique, t. i. p. 64.

about the same time, in a few instances, to those of France.[1] Gradually, however, they began to elect councils of citizens, as a sort of senate and magistracy. This innovation might perhaps take place as early as the reign of Frederic I.;[2] at least it was fully established in that of his grandson. They were at first only assistants to the imperial or episcopal bailiff, who probably continued to administer criminal justice. But in the thirteenth century the citizens, grown richer and stronger, either purchased the jurisdiction, or usurped it through the lord's neglect, or drove out the bailiff by force.[3] The great revolution in Franconia and Suabia occasioned by the fall of the Hohenstauffen family completed the victory of the cities. Those which had depended upon mediate lords became immediately connected with the empire; and with the empire in its state of feebleness, when an occasional present of money would easily induce its chief to acquiesce in any claims of immunity which the citizens might prefer.

It was a natural consequence of the importance which the free citizens had reached, and of their immediacy, that they were admitted to a place in the diets, or general meetings of the confederacy. They were tacitly acknowledged to be equally sovereign with the electors and princes. No proof exists of any law by which they were adopted into the diet. We find it said that Rodolph of Hapsburg, in 1291, renewed his oath with the princes, lords, and cities. Under the emperor Henry VII. there is unequivocal mention of the three orders composing the diet; electors, princes, and deputies from cities.[4] And in 1344 they appear as a third distinct college in the diet of Frankfort.[5]

The inhabitants of these free cities always preserved their respect for the emperor, and gave him much less vexation than his other subjects. He was indeed their natural friend. But the nobility and prelates were their natural enemies; and the western parts of Germany were the scenes of irreconcilable warfare between the possessors of fortified castles

[1] Schmidt, p. 245.

[2] In the charter granted by Frederic I. to Spire in 1182, confirming and enlarging that of Henry V., though no express mention is made of any municipal jurisdiction, yet it seems implied in the following words: Causam in civitate jam lite contestatam non episcopus aut alia potestas extra civitatem determinari compellet. Dumont, p. 108.

[3] Schmidt, t. iv. p. 96; Pfeffel, p. 441.

[4] Mansit ibi rex sex hebdomadibus cum principibus electoribus et aliis principibus *et civitatum nuntiis*, de suo transitu et de præstandis servitiis in Italiam disponendo. Auctor apud Schmidt, t. vi p. 31.

[5] Pfeffel, p. 552.

and the inhabitants of fortified cities. Each party was frequently the aggressor. The nobles were too often mere robbers, who lived upon the plunder of travellers. But the citizens were almost equally inattentive to the rights of others. It was their policy to offer the privileges of burghership to all strangers. The peasantry of feudal lords, flying to a neighboring town, found an asylum constantly open. A multitude of aliens, thus seeking as it were sanctuary, dwelt in the suburbs or liberties, between the city walls and the palisades which bounded the territory. Hence they were called Pfahlbürger, or burgesses of the palisades; and this encroachment on the rights of the nobility was positively, but vainly, prohibited by several imperial edicts, especially the Golden Bull. Another class were the Ausbürger, or outburghers, who had been admitted to privileges of citizenship, though resident at a distance, and pretended in consequence to be exempted from all dues to their original feudal superiors. If a lord resisted so unreasonable a claim, he incurred the danger of bringing down upon himself the vengeance of the citizens. These outburghers are in general classed under the general name of Pfahlbürger by contemporary writers.[1]

Leagues of the cities.

As the towns were conscious of the hatred which the nobility bore towards them, it was their interest to make a common cause, and render mutual assistance. From this necessity of maintaining, by united exertions, their general liberty, the German cities never suffered the petty jealousies, which might no doubt exist among them, to ripen into such deadly feuds as sullied the glory, and ultimately destroyed the freedom, of Lombardy. They withstood the bishops and barons by confederacies of their own, framed expressly to secure their commerce against rapine, or unjust exactions of toll. More than sixty cities, with three ecclesiastical electors at their head, formed the league of the Rhine, in 1255, to repel the inferior nobility, who, having now become immediate, abused that independence by perpetual robberies.[2] The Hanseatic Union owes its origin to no other cause, and may be traced perhaps to rather a higher date. About the year 1370 a league was formed,

[1] Schmidt, t. iv. p. 98; t. vi. p. 76; Pfeffel, p. 402; Du Cange, Gloss. v. Pfahlbürger. Faubourg is derived from this word.

[2] Struvius, p. 498; Schmidt, t. iv. p. 101; Pfeffel, p. 416.

which, though it did not continue so long, seems to have produced more striking effects in Germany. The cities of Suabia and the Rhine united themselves in a strict confederacy against the princes, and especially the families of Wirtemburg and Bavaria. It is said that the emperor Wenceslaus secretly abetted their projects. The recent successes of the Swiss, who had now almost established their republic, inspired their neighbors in the empire with expectations which the event did not realize; for they were defeated in this war, and ultimately compelled to relinquish their league. Counter-associations were formed by the nobles, styled Society of St. George, St. William, the Lion, or the Panther.[1]

Provincial states of the empire.

The spirit of political liberty was not confined to the free immediate cities. In all the German principalities a form of limited monarchy prevailed, reflecting, on a reduced scale, the general constitution of the empire. As the emperors shared their legislative sovereignty with the diet, so all the princes who belonged to that assembly had their own provincial states, composed of their feudal vassals and of their mediate towns within their territory. No tax could be imposed without consent of the states; and, in some countries, the prince was obliged to account for the proper disposition of the money granted. In all matters of importance affecting the principality, and especially in cases of partition, it was necessary to consult them; and they sometimes decided between competitors in a disputed succession, though this indeed more strictly belonged to the emperor. The provincial states concurred with the prince in making laws, except such as were enacted by the general diet. The city of Wurtzburg, in the fourteenth century, tells its bishop that, if a lord would make any new ordinance, the custom is that he must consult the citizens, who have always opposed his innovating upon the ancient laws without their consent.[2]

Alienation of the imperial domain.

The ancient imperial domain, or possessions which belonged to the chief of the empire as such, had originally been very extensive. Besides large estates in every province, the territory upon each bank of the Rhine, afterwards occupied by the counts palatine and ecclesiastical electors, was, until the

[1] Struvius, p. 649; Pfeffel, p. 586; Schmidt, t. v. p. 10; t. vi. p. 78. Putter, p. 298.
[2] Schmidt, t. vi. p. 8. Putter, p. 286.

thirteenth century, an exclusive property of the emperor. This imperial domain was deemed so adequate to the support of his dignity that it was usual, if not obligatory, for him to grant away his patrimonial domains upon his election. But the necessities of Frederic II., and the long confusion that ensued upon his death, caused the domain to be almost entirely dissipated. Rodolph made some efforts to retrieve it, but too late; and the poor remains of what had belonged to Charlemagne and Otho were alienated by Charles IV.[1] This produced a necessary change in that part of the constitution which deprived an emperor of hereditary possessions, It was, however, some time before it took place. Even Albert I. conferred the duchy of Austria upon his son, when he was chosen emperor.[2] Louis of Bavaria was the first who retained his hereditary dominions, and made them his residence.[3] Charles IV. and Wenceslaus lived almost wholly in Bohemia, Sigismund chiefly in Hungary, Frederic III. in Austria. This residence in their hereditary countries, while it seemed rather to lower the imperial dignity, and to lessen their connection with the general confederacy, gave them intrinsic power and influence. If the emperors of the houses of Luxemburg and Austria were not like the Conrads and Frederics, they were at least very superior in importance to the Williams and Adolphuses of the thirteenth century.

Accession of Maximilian. Diet of Worms. A.D. 1495.

The accession of Maximilian nearly coincides with the expedition of Charles VIII. against Naples; and I should here close the German history of the middle age, were it not for the great epoch which is made by the diet of Worms in 1495. This assembly is celebrated for the establishment of a perpetual public peace, and of a paramount court of justice, the Imperial Chamber.

Establishment of public peace.

The same causes which produced continual hostilities among the French nobility were not likely to operate less powerfully on the Germans, equally warlike with their neighbors, and rather less civilized. But while the imperial government was still vigorous, they were kept under some restraint. We find Henry III., the most powerful of the Franconian emperors,

1 Pfeffel, p. 580.

2 Id. p. 494. Struvius, p. 546.

3 Struvius, p. 611. In the capitulation of Robert it was expressly provided that he should retain any escheated fief for the domain, instead of granting it away; so completely was the public policy of the empire reversed. Schmidt, t. v. p. 44.

forbidding all private defiances, and establishing solemnly a general peace.[1] After his time the natural tendency of manners overpowered all attempts to coerce it, and private war raged without limits in the empire. Frederic I. endeavored to repress it by a regulation which admitted its legality. This was the law of defiance (jus diffidationis), which required a solemn declaration of war, and three days' notice, before the commencement of hostile measures. All persons contravening this provision were deemed robbers and not legitimate enemies.[2] Frederic II. carried the restraint further, and limited the right of self-redress to cases where justice could not be obtained. Unfortunately there was, in later times, no sufficient provision for rendering justice. The German empire indeed had now assumed so peculiar a character, and the mass of states which composed it were in so many respects sovereign within their own territories, that wars, unless in themselves unjust, could not be made a subject of reproach against them, nor considered, strictly speaking, as private. It was certainly most desirable to put it an end to them by common agreement, and by the only means that could render war unnecessary, the establishment of a supreme jurisdiction. War indeed, legally undertaken, was not the only nor the severest grievance. A very large proportion of the rural nobility lived by robbery.[3] Their castles, as the ruins still bear witness, were erected upon inaccessible hills, and in defiles that command the public road. An archbishop of Cologne having built a fortress of this kind, the governor inquired how he was to maintain himself, no revenue having been assigned for that purpose: the prelate only desired him to remark that the castle was situated near the junction of four roads.[4] As commerce increased, and the example of French and Italian civilization rendered the Germans more sensible to their own rudeness, the preservation of public peace was loudly demanded. Every diet under Frederic III. professed to occupy itself with the two great objects of domestic reformation, peace

1 Pfeffel, p. 212.

2 Schmidt, t. iv. p. 108, et infra; Pfeffel, p. 340; Putter, p. 205.

3 Germani atque Alemanni, quibus census patrimonii ad victum suppetit, et hos qui procul urbibus, aut qui castellis et oppidulis dominantur, *quorum magna pars latrocinio deditur*, nobiles censent. Pet. de Andlo. apud Schmidt, t. v p. 490.

4 Quem cum officiatus suus interrogans, de quo castrum deberet retinere, cum annuis careret reditibus, dicitur respondisse; Quatuor viæ sunt trans castrum situatæ. Auctor apud Schmidt, p. 492.

and law. Temporary cessations, during which all private hostility was illegal, were sometimes enacted; and, if observed, which may well be doubted, might contribute to accustom men to habits of greater tranquillity. The leagues of the cities were probably more efficacious checks upon the disturbers of order. In 1486 a ten years' peace was proclaimed, and before the expiration of this period the perpetual abolition of the right of defiance was happily accomplished in the diet of Worms.[1]

These wars, incessantly waged by the states of Germany, seldom ended in conquest. Very few princely houses of the middle ages were aggrandized by such means. That small and independent nobility, the counts and knights of the empire whom the revolutions of our own age have annihilated, stood through the storms of centuries with little diminution of their numbers. An incursion into the enemy's territory, a pitched battle, a siege, a treaty, are the general circumstances of the minor wars of the middle ages, as far as they appear in history. Before the invention of artillery, a strongly fortified castle or walled city, was hardly reduced except by famine, which a besieging army, wasting improvidently its means of subsistence, was full as likely to feel. That invention altered the condition of society, and introduced an inequality of forces, that rendered war more inevitably ruinous to the inferior party. Its first and most beneficial effect was to bring the plundering class of the nobility into control; their castles were more easily taken, and it became their interest to deserve the protection of law. A few of these continued to follow their old profession after the diet of Worms; but they were soon overpowered by the more efficient police established under Maximilian.

Imperial Chamber.

The next object of the diet was to provide an effectual remedy for private wrongs which might supersede all pretence for taking up arms. The administration of justice had always been a high prerogative as well as bounden duty of the emperors. It was exercised originally by themselves in person, or by the count palatine, the judge who always attended their court. In the provinces of Germany the dukes were intrusted with this duty; but, in order to control their influence, Otho the Great appointed provincial counts palatine, whose jurisdiction was in some respects

[1] Schmidt, t. iv. p. 116; t. v. p. 338, 371; t. vi. p. 34; Putter, p. 292, 348.

exclusive of that still possessed by the dukes. As the latter became more independent of the empire, the provincial counts palatine lost the importance of their office, though their name may be traced to the twelfth and thirteenth centuries.[1] The ordinary administration of justice by the emperors went into disuse; in cases where states of the empire were concerned, it appertained to the diet, or to a special court of princes. The first attempt to reëstablish an imperial tribunal was made by Frederic II. in a diet held at Mentz in 1235. A judge of the court was appointed to sit daily, with certain assessors, half nobles, half lawyers, and with jurisdiction over all causes where princes of the empire were not concerned.[2] Rodolph of Hapsburg endeavored to give efficacy to this judicature; but after his reign it underwent the fate of all those parts of the Germanic constitution which maintained the prerogatives of the emperors. Sigismund endeavored to revive this tribunal; but as he did not render it permanent, nor fix the place of its sittings, it produced little other good than as it excited an earnest anxiety for a regular system. This system, delayed throughout the reign of Frederic III., was reserved for the first diet of his son.[3]

The Imperial Chamber, such was the name of the new tribunal, consisted, at its original institution, of a chief judge, who was to be chosen among the princes or counts, and of sixteen assessors, partly of noble or equestrian rank, partly professors of law. They were named by the emperor with the approbation of the diet. The functions of the Imperial Chamber were chiefly the two following. They exercised an appellant jurisdiction over causes that had been decided by the tribunals established in states of the empire. But their jurisdiction in private causes was merely appellant According to the original law of Germany, no man could be sued except in the nation or province to which he belonged. The early emperors travelled from one part of their dominions to another, in order to render justice consistently with this fundamental privilege. When the Luxemburg emperors fixed their residence in Bohemia, the jurisdiction of the im perial court in the first instance would have ceased of itself

1 Pfeffel, p. 180.
2 Idem, p. 386; Schmidt, t. iv. p. 56.
3 Pfeffel, t. ii. p. 66.

by the operation of this ancient rule. It was not, however, strictly complied with; and it is said that the emperors had a concurrent jurisdiction with the provincial tribunals even in private causes. They divested themselves, nevertheless, of this right by granting privileges *de non evocando;* so that no subject of a state which enjoyed such a privilege could be summoned into the imperial court. All the electors possessed this exemption by the terms of the Golden Bull; and it was specially granted to the burgraves of Nuremberg, and some other princes. This matter was finally settled at the diet of Worms; and the Imperial Chamber was positively restricted from taking cognizance of any causes in the first instance, even where a state of the empire was one of the parties. It was enacted, to obviate the denial of justice that appeared likely to result from the regulation in the latter case, that every elector and prince should establish a tribunal in his own dominions, where suits against himself might be entertained.[1]

The second part of the chamber's jurisdiction related to disputes between two states of the empire. But these two could only come before it by way of appeal. During the period of anarchy which preceded the establishment of its jurisdiction, a custom was introduced, in order to prevent the constant recurrence of hostilities, of referring the quarrels of states to certain arbitrators, called Austregues, chosen among states of the same rank. This conventional reference became so popular that the princes would not consent to abandon it on the institution of the Imperial Chamber; but, on the contrary, it was changed into an invariable and universal law, that all disputes between different states must, in the first instance, be submitted to the arbitration of Austregues.[2]

Establishment of circles.

The sentences of the chamber would have been very idly pronounced, if means had not been devised to carry them into execution. In earlier times the want of coercive process had been more felt than that of actual jurisdiction. For a few years after the establishment of the chamber this deficiency was not supplied. But in 1501 an institution, originally planned under Wenceslaus, and attempted by Albert II., was carried into effect. The

[1] Schmidt, t. v. p. 373; Putter, p. 372.

[2] Putter, p. 361; Pfeffel, p. 452.

empire, with the exception of the electorates and the Austrian dominions, was divided into six circles; each of which had its council of states, its director whose province it was to convoke them, and its military force to compel obedience. In 1512 four more circles were added, comprehending those states which had been excluded in the first division. It was the business of the police of the circles to enforce the execution of sentences pronounced by the Imperial Chamber against refractory states of the empire.[1]

Aulic Council.

As the judges of the Imperial Chamber were appointed with the consent of the diet, and held their sittings in a free imperial city, its establishment seemed rather to encroach on the ancient prerogatives of the emperors. Maximilian expressly reserved these in consenting to the new tribunal. And, in order to revive them, he soon afterwards instituted an Aulic Council at Vienna, composed of judges appointed by himself, and under the political control of the Austrian government. Though some German patriots regarded this tribunal with jealousy, it continued until the dissolution of the empire. The Aulic Council had, in all cases, a concurrent jurisdiction with the Imperial Chamber; an exclusive one in feudal and some other causes. But it was equally confined to cases of appeal; and these, by multiplied privileges *de non appellando*, granted to the electoral and superior princely houses, were gradually reduced into moderate compass.[2]

The Germanic constitution may be reckoned complete, as to all its essential characteristics, in the reign of Maximilian. In later times, and especially by the treaty of Westphalia, it underwent several modifications. Whatever might be its defects, and many of them seem to have been susceptible of reformation without destroying the system of government, it had one invaluable excellence: it protected the rights of the weaker against the stronger powers. The law of nations was first taught in Germany, and grew out of the public law of the empire. To narrow, as far as possible, the rights of war and of conquest, was a natural principle of those who belonged to petty states, and had nothing to tempt them in ambition. No revolution of our own eventful age, except the fall of the ancient French system of government, has been so

1 Putter, p. 355, t. ii. p. 100.

2 Putter, p. 357; Pfeffel, p. 102.

extensive, or so likely to produce important consequences, as the spontaneous dissolution of the German empire. Whether the new confederacy that has been substituted for that venerable constitution will be equally favorable to peace, justice, and liberty, is among the most interesting and difficult problems that can occupy a philosophical observer.[1]

At the accession of Conrad I. Germany had by no means reached its present extent on the eastern frontier. Henry the Fowler and the Othos made great acquisitions upon that side. But tribes of Sclavonian origin, generally called Venedic, or less properly, Vandal, occupied the northern coast from the Elbe to the Vistula. These were independent, and formidable both to the kings of Denmark and princes of Germany, till, in the reign of Frederic Barbarossa, two of the latter, Henry the Lion, duke of Saxony, and Albert the Bear, margrave of Brandenburg, subdued Mecklenburg and Pomerania, which afterwards became duchies of the empire. Bohemia was undoubtedly subject, in a feudal sense, to Frederic I. and his successors; though its connection with Germany was always slight. The emperors sometimes assumed a sovereignty over Denmark, Hungary, and Poland. But what they gained upon this quarter was compensated by the gradual separation of the Netherlands from their dominion, and by the still more complete loss of the kingdom of Arles. The house of Burgundy possessed most part of the former, and paid as little regard as possible to the imperial supremacy; though the German diets in the reign of Maximilian still continued to treat the Netherlands as equally subject to their lawful control with the states on the right bank of the Rhine. But the provinces between the Rhone and the Alps were absolutely separated; Switzerland had completely succeeded in establishing her own independence; and the kings of France no longer sought even the ceremony of an imperial investiture for Dauphiné and Provence.

Limits of the empire.

Bohemia, which received the Christian faith in the tenth century, was elevated to the rank of a kingdom near the end of the twelfth. The dukes and kings of Bohemia were feudally dependent upon the emperors, from whom they received investiture. They possessed, in return, a suffrage among the seven electors, and held one

Bohemia — its constitution.

[1] The first edition of this work was published early in 1818

of the great offices in the imperial court. But separated by a rampart of mountains, by a difference of origin and language, and perhaps by national prejudices from Germany, the Bohemians withdrew as far as possible from the general politics of the confederacy. The kings obtained dispensations from attending the diets of the empire, nor were they able to reinstate themselves in the privilege thus abandoned till the beginning of the last century.[1] The government of this kingdom, in a very slight degree partaking of the feudal character,[2] bore rather a resemblance to that of Poland; but the nobility were divided into two classes, the baronial and the equestrian, and the burghers formed a third state in the national diet. For the peasantry, they were in a condition of servitude, or predial villeinage. The royal authority was restrained by a coronation oath, by a permanent senate, and by frequent assemblies of the diet, where a numerous and armed nobility appeared to secure their liberties by law or force.[3] The sceptre passed, in ordinary times, to the nearest heir of the royal blood; but the right of election was only suspended, and no king of Bohemia ventured to boast of it as his inheritance.[4] This mixture of elective and hereditary monarchy was common, as we have seen, to most European kingdoms in their original constitution, though few continued so long to admit the participation of popular suffrages.

House of Luxemburg.

The reigning dynasty having become extinct in 1306, by the death of Wenceslaus, son of that Ottocar who, after extending his conquests to the Baltic Sea, and almost to the Adriatic, had lost his life in an unsuccessful contention with the emperor Rodolph, the Bohemians chose John of Luxemburg, son of Henry VII. Under the kings of this family in the fourteenth century, and especially Charles IV., whose character appeared in a far more advantageous light in his native domains than in the empire, Bohemia imbibed some portion of refinement and science.[5] An university

1 Pfeffel, t. ii. p. 497.

2 Bona ipsorum totâ Bohemiâ pleraque omnia hæreditaria sunt seu alodialia, perpauca feudalia. Stransky, Resp. Bohemica, p. 392. Stransky was a Bohemian protestant, who fled to Holland after the subversion of the civil and religious liberties of his country by the fatal battle of Prague in 1621.

3 Dubravius, the Bohemian historian relates (lib. xviii.) that, the kingdom having no written laws, Wenceslaus, one of the kings, about the year 1300, sent for an Italian lawyer to compile a code. But the nobility refused to consent to this: aware, probably, of the consequences of letting in the prerogative doctrines of the civilians. They opposed, at the same time, the institution of an university at Prague; which, however took place afterwards under Charles IV.

4 Stransky, Resp. Bohem. Coxe's House of Austria, p. 487.

5 Schmidt; Coxe

erected by Charles at Prague, became one of the most celebrated in Europe. John Huss, rector of the university, who had distinguished himself by opposition to many abuses then prevailing in the church, repaired to the council of Constance, under a safe-conduct from the emperor Sigismund. In violation of this pledge, to the indelible infamy of that prince and of the council, he was condemned to be burned; and his disciple, Jerome of Prague, underwent afterwards the same fate. His countrymen, aroused by this atrocity, flew to arms. They found at their head one of those extraordinary men whose genius, created by nature and called into action by fortuitous events, appears to borrow no reflected light from that of others. John Zisca had not been trained in any school which could have initiated him in the science of war; that indeed, except in Italy, was still rude, and nowhere more so than in Bohemia. But, self-taught, he became one of the greatest captains who had appeared hitherto in Europe. It renders his exploits more marvellous that he was totally deprived of sight. Zisca has been called the inventor of the modern art of fortification; the famous mountain near Prague, fanatically called Tabor, became, by his skill, an impregnable entrenchment. For his stratagems he has been compared to Hannibal. In battle, being destitute of cavalry, he disposed at intervals ramparts of carriages filled with soldiers, to defend his troops from the enemy's horse. His own station was by the chief standard; where, after hearing the circumstances of the situation explained, he gave his orders for the disposition of the army. Zisca was never defeated; and his genius inspired the Hussites with such enthusiastic affection, that some of those who had served under him refused to obey any other general, and denominated themselves Orphans in commemoration of his loss. He was indeed a ferocious enemy, though some of his cruelties might, perhaps, be extenuated by the law of retaliation; but to his soldiers affable and generous, dividing among them all the spoil.[1]

John Huss. A.D. 1416.

Hussite war.

John Zisca.

Even during the lifetime of Zisca the Hussite sect was disunited; the citizens of Prague and many of the nobility contenting themselves with moderate demands, while the Taborites, his peculiar followers, were actu-

Calixtins. A.D. 1424.

[1] Lenfant, Hist. de la Guerre des Hussites; Schmidt; Coxe

ated by a most fanatical frenzy. The former took the name of Calixtins, from their retention of the sacramental cup, of which the priests had latterly thought fit to debar laymen an abuse so totally without pretence or apology, that nothing less than the determined obstinacy of the Romish church could have maintained it to this time. The Taborites, though no longer led by Zisca, gained some remarkable victories, but were at last wholly defeated; while the Catholic and Calixtin parties came to an accommodation, by which Sigismund was acknowledged as king of Bohemia, which he had claimed by the title of heir to his brother Wenceslaus, and a few indul-
A.D. 1433. gences, especially the use of the sacramental cup, conceded to the moderate Hussites. But this compact, though concluded by the council of Basle, being ill observed, through the perfidious bigotry of the see of Rome, the reformers armed again to defend their religious liberties, and ultimately elected a nobleman of their own party, by
A.D. 1458. name George Podiebrad, to the throne of Bohemia, which he maintained during his life with great vigor and prudence.[1] Upon his death they chose Uladislaus,
A.D. 1471. son of Casimir king of Poland, who afterwards
A.D. 1527. obtained also the kingdom of Hungary. Both these crowns were conferred on his son Louis, after whose death, in the unfortunate battle of Mohacz, Ferdinand of Austria became sovereign of the two kingdoms.

The Hungarians, that terrible people who laid waste the
Hungary. Italian and German provinces of the empire in the tenth century, became proselytes soon afterwards to the religion of Europe, and their sovereign, St. Stephen, was admitted by the pope into the list of Christian kings. Though the Hungarians were of a race perfectly distinct from either the Gothic or the Sclavonian tribes, their system of government was in a great measure analogous. None indeed could be more natural to rude nations who had but recently accustomed themselves to settled possessions, than a territorial aristocracy, jealous of unlimited or even hereditary power in their chieftain, and subjugating the inferior people to that servitude which, in such a state of society, is the unavoidable consequence of poverty.

The marriage of an Hungarian princess with Charles II

[1] Lenfant; Schmidt; Coxe.

king of Naples, eventually connected her country far more than it had been with the affairs of Italy. I have mentioned in a different place the circumstances which led to the invasion of Naples by Louis king of Hungary, and the wars of that powerful monarch with Venice. By marrying the eldest daughter of Louis, Sigismund, afterwards emperor, acquired the crown of Hungary, which upon her death without issue he retained in his own right, and was even able to transmit to the child of a second marriage, and to her husband Albert duke of Austria. From this commencement is deduced the connection between Hungary and Austria. In two years, however, Albert dying left his widow pregnant; but the states of Hungary, jealous of Austrian influence, and of the intrigues of a minority, without waiting for her delivery, bestowed the crown upon Uladislaus king of Poland. The birth of Albert's posthumous son, Ladislaus, produced an opposition in behalf of the infant's right; but the Austrian party turned out the weaker, and Uladislaus, after a civil war of some duration, became undisputed king. Meanwhile a more formidable enemy drew near. The Turkish arms had subdued all Servia, and excited a just alarm throughout Christendom. Uladislaus led a considerable force, to which the presence of the cardinal Julian gave the appearance of a crusade, into Bulgaria, and, after several successes, concluded an honorable treaty with Amurath II. But this he was unhappily persuaded to violate, at the instigation of the cardinal, who abhorred the impiety of keeping faith with infidels.[1] Heaven judged of this otherwise, if the judgment of Heaven was pronounced upon the field of Warna. In that fatal battle Uladislaus was killed, and the Hungarians utterly routed. The crown was now permitted to rest on the head of young Ladislaus; but the regency was allotted by the states of Hungary to a native warrior, John Hunniades.[2] This hero stood in the breach for

Sigismund. A.D. 1392.

A.D. 1437.

Uladislaus. A.D. 1440.

Battle of Warna. A.D. 1444.

Hunniades.

[1] Æneas Sylvius lays this perfidy on Pope Eugenius IV. Scripsit cardinali, nullum valere fœdus, quod *se inconsulto* cum hostibus religionis percussum esset, p. 397. The words in italics are slipped in, to give a slight pretext for breaking the treaty.

[2] Hunniades was a Wallachian, of a small family. The poles charged him with cowardice at Warna. (Æneas Sylvius, p. 398.) And the Greeks impute the same to him, or at least desertion of his troops, at Cossova, where he was defeated in 1448. (Spondanus, ad ann. 1448.) Probably he was one of those prudently brave men who, when victory is out of their power, reserve themselves to fight another day; which is the character of all partisans accustomed to desultory warfare. This is the apology

twelve years against the Turkish power, frequently defeated but unconquered in defeat. If the renown of Hunniades may seem exaggerated by the partiality of writers who lived under the reign of his son, it is confirmed by more unequivocal evidence, by the dread and hatred of the Turks, whose children were taught obedience by threatening them with his name, and by the deference of a jealous aristocracy to a man of no distinguished birth. He surrendered to young Ladislaus a trust that he had exercised with perfect fidelity; but his merit was too great to be forgiven, and the court never treated him with cordiality. The last and the most splendid service of Hunniades was the relief of Belgrade. That strong city was besieged by Mahomet II. three years after the fall of Constantinople; its capture would have laid open all Hungary. A tumultuary army, chiefly collected by the preaching of a friar, was intrusted to Hunniades: he penetrated into the city, and, having repulsed the Turks in a fortunate sally wherein Mahomet was wounded, had the honor of compelling him to raise the siege in confusion. The relief of Belgrade was more important in its effect than in its immediate circumstances. It revived the spirits of Europe, which had been appalled by the unceasing victories of the infidels. Mahomet himself seemed to acknowledge the importance of the blow, and seldom afterwards attacked the Hungarians. Hunniades died soon after this achievement, and was followed by the king Ladislaus.[1] The states of Hungary, although the emperor Frederic III. had secured to himself, as he thought, the reversion, were justly averse to his character, and to Austrian connections. They conferred their crown on Matthias Corvinus, son of their great Hunniades. This prince reigned above thirty years with considerable reputation, to which his patronage

Relief of Belgrade. A.D. 1456.

Matthias Corvinus. A.D. 1458.

made for him by Æneas Sylvius: fortasse rei militaris perito nulla in pugnâ salus visa, et salvare aliquos quàm omnes perire maluit. Poloni acceptam eo prælio cladem Hunniadis vecordiæ atque ignaviæ tradiderunt; ipse sua concilia spreta conquestus est. I observe that all the writers upon Hungarian affairs have a party bias one way or other. The best and most authentic account of Hunniades seems to be, still allowing for this partiality, in the chronicle of John Thwrocz, who lived under Matthias. Bonfinius, an Italian compiler of the same age, has amplified this original authority in his three decads of Hungarian history.

1 Ladislaus died at Prague, at the age of twenty-two, with great suspicion of poison, which fell chiefly on George Podiebrad and the Bohemians. Æneas Sylvius was with him at the time, and in a letter written immediately after plainly hints this; and his manner carries with it more persuasion than if he had spoken out. Epist. 324. Mr. Coxe, however, informs us that the Bohemian historians have fully disproved the charge.

of learned men, who repaid his munificence with very profuse eulogies, did not a little contribute.[1] Hungary, at least in his time, was undoubtedly formidable to her neighbors, and held a respectable rank as an independent power in the republic of Europe.

The kingdom of Burgundy or Arles comprehended the whole mountainous region which we now call Switzerland. It was accordingly reunited to the Germanic empire by the bequest of Rodolph along with the rest of his dominions. A numerous and ancient nobility, vassals one to another, or to the empire, divided the possession with ecclesiastical lords hardly less powerful than themselves. Of the former we find the counts of Zahringen, Kyburg, Hapsburg, and Tokenburg, most conspicuous; of the latter, the bishop of Coire, the abbot of St. Gall, and abbess of Seckingen. Every variety of feudal rights was early found and long preserved in Helvetia; nor is there any country whose history better illustrates that ambiguous relation, half property and half dominion, in which the territorial aristocracy, under the feudal system, stood with respect to their dependents. In the twelfth century the Swiss towns rise into some degree of importance. Zurich was eminent for commercial activity, and seems to have had no lord but the emperor. Basle, though subject to its bishop, possessed the usual privileges of municipal government. Berne and Friburg, founded only in that century, made a rapid progress; and the latter was raised, along with Zurich, by Frederic II. in 1218, to the rank of a free imperial city. Several changes in the principal Helvetian families took place in the thirteenth century, before the end of which the house of Hapsburg, under the politic and enterprising Rodolph and his son Albert, became possessed, through various titles, of a great ascendency in Switzerland.[2]

Switzerland — its early history. A.D. 1032.

Of these titles none was more tempting to an ambitious

[1] Spondanus frequently blames the Italians, who received pensions from Matthias, or wrote at his court, for exaggerating his virtues, or dissembling his misfortunes. And this was probably the case. However, Spondanus has rather contracted a prejudice against the Corvini. A treatise of Galeotus Martius, an Italian *littérateur*, De dictis et factis Mathiæ, though it often notices an ordinary saying as jocosè or facetè dictum, gives a favorable impression of Matthias's ability, and also of his integrity.

[2] Planta's History of the Helvetic Confederacy, vol. i. chaps. 2-5.

Albert of Austria.

chief than that of advocate to a convent. That specious name conveyed with it a kind of indefinite guardianship, and right of interference, which frequently ended in reversing the conditions of the ecclesiastical sovereign and its vassal. But during times of feudal anarchy there was perhaps no other means to secure the rich abbeys from absolute spoliation; and the free cities in their early stage sometimes adopted the same policy. Among other advocacies, Albert obtained that of some convents which had estates in the valleys of Schweitz and Underwald. These sequestered regions in the heart of the Alps had been for ages the habitation of a pastoral race, so happily forgotten, or so inaccessible in their fastnesses, as to have acquired a virtual independence, regulating their own affairs in their general assembly with a perfect equality, though they acknowledged the sovereignty of the empire.[1] The people of Schweitz had made Rodolph their advocate. They distrusted Albert, whose succession to his father's inheritance spread alarm through Helvetia. It soon appeared that their suspicions were well founded. Besides the local rights which his ecclesiastical advocacies gave him over part of the forest cantons, he pretended, after his election to the empire, to send imperial bailiffs into their valleys, as administrators of criminal justice. Their oppression of a people unused to control, whom it was plainly the design of Albert to reduce into servitude, excited those generous emotions of resentment which a brave and simple race have seldom the discretion to repress. Three men, Stauffacher of Schweitz, Furst of Uri, Melchthal of Underwald, each with ten chosen associates, met by night in a sequestered field, and swore to assert the common cause of their liberties, without bloodshed or injury to the rights of others. Their success was answerable to the justice of their undertaking; the three cantons unanimously took up arms, and expelled their oppressors without a contest. Albert's assassination by his nephew, which followed soon afterwards, fortunately gave them leisure to consolidate their union.[2] He was succeeded in the empire by Henry VII., jealous of the Austrian family, and not at all

The Swiss.

Their insurrection.

A.D. 1308.

1 Planta's History of the Helvetic Confederacy, vol. i. c. 4.
2 Planta, c. 6.

displeased at proceedings which had been accompanied with so little violence or disrespect for the empire. But Leopold duke of Austria, resolved to humble the peasants who had rebelled against his father, led a considerable force into their country. The Swiss, commending themselves to Heaven, and determined rather to perish than undergo that yoke a second time, though ignorant of regular discipline, and unprovided with defensive armor, utterly discomfitted the assailants at Morgarten.[1]

Battle of Morgarten. A.D. 1315.

This great victory, the Marathon of Switzerland, confirmed the independence of the three original cantons. After some years, Lucerne, contiguous in situation and alike in interests, was incorporated into their confederacy. It was far more materially enlarged about the middle of the fourteenth century, by the accession of Zurich, Glaris, Zug, and Berne, all which took place within two years. The first and last of these cities had already been engaged in frequent wars with the Helvetian nobility, and their internal polity was altogether republican.[2] They acquired, not independence, which they already enjoyed, but additional security, by this union with the Swiss, properly so called, who in deference to their power and reputation ceded to them the first rank in the league. The eight already enumerated are called the ancient cantons, and continued, till the late reformation of the Helvetic system, to possess several distinctive privileges and even rights of sovereignty over subject territories, in which the five cantons of Friburg, Soleure, Basle, Schaffhausen, and Appenzell did not participate. From this time the united cantons, but especially those of Berne and Zurich, began to extend their territories at the expense of the rural nobility. The same contest between these parties, with the same termination, which we know generally to have taken place in Lombardy during the eleventh and twelfth centuries, may be traced with more minuteness in the annals of Switzerland.[3] Like the Lombards, too, the Helvetic cities acted with policy and moderation towards the nobles whom they overcame, admitting them to the franchises of their community as co-burghers (a privilege which virtually implied a defensive alliance against any assailant), and uniformly respecting the legal rights of property. Many

Formation of Swiss Confederacy.

[1] Planta, c. 7. [2] Id. cc. 8, 9. [3] Id. c. 10.

feudal superiorities they obtained from the owners in a more peaceable manner, through purchase or mortgage. Thus the house of Austria, to which the extensive domains of the counts of Kyburg had devolved, abandoning, after repeated defeats, its hopes of subduing the forest cantons, alienated a great part of its possessions to Zurich and Berne.[1] And the last remnant of their ancient Helvetic territories in Argovia was wrested in 1417 from Frederic count of Tyrol, who, imprudently supporting pope John XXIII. against the council of Constance, had been put to the ban of the empire. These conquests Berne could not be induced to restore, and thus completed the independence of the confederate republics.[2] The other free cities, though not yet incorporated, and the few remaining nobles, whether lay or spiritual, of whom the abbot of St. Gall was the principal, entered into separate leagues with different cantons. Switzerland became, therefore, in the first part of the fifteenth century, a free country, acknowledged as such by neighboring states, and subject to no external control, though still comprehended within the nominal sovereignty of the empire.

The affairs of Switzerland occupy a very small space in the great chart of European history. But in some respects they are more interesting than the revolutions of mighty kingdoms. Nowhere besides do we find so many titles to our sympathy, or the union of so much virtue with so complete success. In the Italian republics a more splendid temple may seem to have been erected to liberty; but, as we approach, the serpents of faction hiss around her altar, and the form of tyranny flits among the distant shadows behind the shrine. Switzerland, not absolutely blameless, (for what republic has been so?) but comparatively exempt from turbulence, usurpation, and injustice, has well deserved to employ the native pen of an historian accounted the most eloquent of the last age.[3] Other nations displayed an insuperable resolu-

1 Planta, c. 11.

2 Id. vol. ii. c. 1.

3 I am unacquainted with Muller's history in the original language; but, presuming the first volume of Mr. Planta's History of the Helvetic Confederacy to be a free translation or abridgment of it, I can well conceive that it deserves the encomiums of Madame de Staël and other foreign critics. It is very rare to meet with such picturesque and lively delineation in a modern historian of distant times. But I must observe that, if the authentic chronicles of Switzerland have enabled Muller to embellish his narration with so much circumstantial detail, he has been remarkably fortunate in his authorities. No man could write the annals of England or France in the fourteenth century with such particularity, if he was scrupulous not to fill up the meagre sketch of chroniclers from

tion in the defence of walled towns; but the steadiness of the Swiss in the field of battle was without a parallel, unless we recall the memory of Lacedæmon. It was even established as a law, that whoever returned from battle after a defeat should forfeit his life by the hands of the executioner. Sixteen hundred men, who had been sent to oppose a predatory invasion of the French in 1444, though they might have retreated without loss, determined rather to perish on the spot, and fell amidst a far greater heap of the hostile slain.[1] At the famous battle of Sempach in 1385, the last which Austria presumed to try against the forest cantons, the enemy's knights, dismounted from their horses, presented an impregnable barrier of lances, which disconcerted the Swiss; till Winkelried, a gentleman of Underwald, commending his wife and children to his countrymen, threw himself upon the opposite ranks, and collecting as many lances as he could grasp, forced a passage for his followers by burying them in his bosom.[2]

Excellence of the Swiss troops.

The burghers and peasants of Switzerland, ill provided with cavalry, and better able to dispense with it than the natives of champaign countries, may be deemed the principal restorers of the Greek and Roman tactics, which place the strength of armies in a steady mass of infantry. Besides their splendid victories over the dukes of Austria and their own neighboring nobility, they had repulsed, in the year 1375, one of those predatory bodies of troops, the scourge of Europe in that age, and to whose licentiousness kingdoms and free states yielded alike a passive submission. They gave the dauphin, afterwards Louis XI., who entered their country in 1444 with a similar body of ruffians, called Armagnacs, the disbanded mercenaries of the English war, sufficient reason to desist from his invasion and to respect their valor. That able prince formed indeed so high a notion of the Swiss, that he sedulously cultivated their alliance during the rest of his life. He was made abundantly sensible of the wisdom of this policy when he saw his greatest enemy, the duke of Burgundy, routed at Granson and Morat, and his affairs irrecoverably ruined, by these hardy repub-

the stores of his invention. The striking scenery of Switzerland, and Muller's exact acquaintance with it, have given him another advantage as a *painter* of history.

1 Planta, vol. ii. c. 2.

2 Id. vol. i. c. 10.

licans. The ensuing age is the most conspicuous, though not the most essentially glorious, in the history of Switzerland. Courted for the excellence of their troops by the rival sovereigns of Europe, and themselves too sensible both to ambitious schemes of dominion and to the thirst of money, the united cantons came to play a very prominent part in the wars of Lombardy, with great military renown, but not without some impeachment of that sterling probity which had distinguished their earlier efforts for independence. These events, however, do not fall within my limits; but the last year of the fifteenth century is a leading epoch, with which I shall close this sketch. Though the house of Austria had ceased to menace the liberties of Helvetia, and had even been for many years its ally, the emperor Maximilian, aware of the important service he might derive from the cantons in his projects upon Italy, as well as of the disadvantage he sustained by their partiality to French interest, endeavored to revive the unextinguished supremacy of the empire. That supremacy had just been restored in Germany by the establishment of the Imperial Chamber, and of a regular pecuniary contribution for its support, as well as for other purposes, in the diet of Worms. The Helvetic cantons were summoned to yield obedience to these imperial laws; an innovation, for such the revival of obsolete prerogatives must be considered, exceedingly hostile to their republican independence, and involving consequences not less material in their eyes, the abandonment of a line of policy, which tended to enrich, if not to aggrandize them. Their refusal to comply brought on a war, wherein the Tyrolese subjects of Maximilian, and the Suabian league, a confederacy of cities in that province lately formed under the emperor's auspices, were principally engaged against the Swiss. But the success of the latter was decisive; and after a terrible devastation of the frontiers of Germany, peace was concluded upon terms very honorable for Switzerland. The cantons were declared free from the jurisdiction of the Imperial Chamber, and from all contributions imposed by the diet. Their right to enter into foreign alliance, even hostile to the empire, if it was not expressly recognized, continued unimpaired in practice; nor am I aware that they were at any time afterwards supposed to incur the crime of rebellion by such proceedings. Though, perhaps, in the strictest letter

Ratification of their independence in 1500.

of public law, the Swiss cantons were not absolutely released from their subjection to the empire until the treaty of Westphalia, their real sovereignty must be dated by an historian from the year when every prerogative which a government can exercise was finally abandoned.[1]

1 Planta, vol. ii. c. 4.

CHAPTER VI.

HISTORY OF THE GREEKS AND SARACENS.

Rise of Mohammedism — Causes of its Success — Progress of Saracen Arms — Greek Empire — Decline of the Khalifs — The Greeks recover Part of their Losses — The Turks — The Crusades — Capture of Constantinople by the Latins — Its Recovery by the Greeks — The Moguls — The Ottomans — Danger at Constantinople — Timur — Capture of Constantinople by Mahomet II. — Alarm of Europe.

THE difficulty which occurs to us in endeavoring to fix a natural commencement of modern history even in the Western countries of Europe is much enhanced when we direct our attention to the Eastern empire. In tracing the long series of the Byzantine annals we never lose sight of antiquity; the Greek language, the Roman name, the titles, the laws, all the shadowy circumstance of ancient greatness, attend us throughout the progress from the first to the last of the Constantines; and it is only when we observe the external condition and relations of their empire, that we perceive ourselves to be embarked in a new sea, and are compelled to deduce, from points of bearing to the history of other nations, a line of separation which the domestic revolutions of Constantinople would not satisfactorily afford. The appearance of Mohammed, and the conquests of his disciples, present an epoch in the history of Asia still more important and more definite than the subversion of the Roman empire in Europe; and hence the boundary-line between the ancient and modern divisions of Byzantine history will intersect the reign of Heraclius. That prince may be said to have stood on the verge of both hemispheres of time, whose youth was crowned with the last victories over the successors of Artaxerxes, and whose age was clouded by the first calamities of Mohammedan invasion.

Appearance of Mohammed.

Of all the revolutions which have had a permanent influence upon the civil history of mankind, none could so little be anticipated by human prudence as that effected by the religion of Arabia. As the seeds of invisible disease grow up sometimes in silence to maturity, till they manifest themselves hopeless and irresistible, the gradual propagation of a new faith in a barbarous country beyond the limits of the empire was hardly known perhaps, and certainly disregarded, in the court of Constantinople. Arabia, in the age of Mohammed, was divided into many small states, most of which, however, seem to have looked up to Mecca as the capital of their nation and the chief seat of their religious worship. The capture of that city accordingly, and subjugation of its powerful and numerous aristocracy, readily drew after it the submission of the minor tribes, who transferred to the conqueror the reverence they were used to show to those he had subdued. If we consider Mohammed only as a military usurper, there is nothing more explicable or more analogous, especially to the course of oriental history, than his success. But as the author of a religious imposture, upon which, though avowedly unattested by miraculous powers, and though originally discountenanced by the civil magistrate, he had the boldness to found a scheme of universal dominion, which his followers were half enabled to realize, it is a curious speculation by what means he could inspire so sincere, so ardent, so energetic, and so permanent a belief.

Causes of his success.

A full explanation of the causes which contributed to the progress of Mohammedism is not perhaps, at present, attainable by those most conversant with this department of literature.[1] But we may point out several of leading importance: in the first place, those just and elevated notions of the divine nature and of moral duties, the gold-ore that pervades the dross of the Koran, which were calculated to strike a serious and reflecting people, already perhaps disinclined, by intermixture with their Jewish and Christian fellow-citizens, to the superstitions of their ancient idolatry;[2] next, the artful incorporation of tenets, usages, and traditions

[1] We are very destitute of satisfactory materials for the history of Mohammed himself. Abulfeda, the most judicious of his biographers, lived in the fourteenth century, when it must have been morally impossible to discriminate the truth amidst the torrent of fabulous tradition. Al Jannabi, whom Gagnier translated, is a mere legend writer; it would be as rational to rely on the Acta Sanctorum as his romance. It is therefore difficult to ascertain the real character of the prophet, except as it is deducible from the Koran.

[2] The very curious romance of Antar written, perhaps, before the appearanc of Mohammed, seems to render it proba ble that, however idolatry, as we are told by Sale, might prevail in some parts of Arabia, yet the genuine religion of the descendants of Ishmael was a belief in the unity of God as strict as is laid down in the Koran itself, and accompanied by the same antipathy, partly re-

from the various religions that existed in Arabia;[1] and thirdly, the extensive application of the precepts in the Koran, a book confessedly written with much elegance and purity, to all legal transactions and all the business of life. It may be expected that I should add to these what is commonly considered as a distinguishing mark of Mohammedism, its indulgence to voluptuousness. But this appears to be greatly exaggerated. Although the character of its founder may have been tainted by sensuality as well as ferociousness, I do not think that he relied upon inducements of the former kind for the diffusion of his system. We are not to judge of this by rules of Christian purity, or of European practice. If polygamy was a prevailing usage in Arabia, as is not questioned, its permission gave no additional license to the proselytes of Mohammed, who will be found rather to have narrowed the unbounded liberty of oriental manners in this respect; while his decided condemnation of adultery, and of incestuous connections, so frequent among barbarous nations, does not argue a very lax and accommodating morality. A devout Mussulman exhibits much more of the Stoical than the Epicurean character. Nor can any one read the Koran without being sensible that it breathes an austere and scrupulous spirit. And, in fact, the founder of a new religion or sect is little likely to obtain permanent success by indulging the vices and luxuries of mankind. I should rather be disposed to reckon the severity of Mohammed's discipline among the causes of its influence. Precepts of ritual observance, being always definite and unequivocal, are less likely to be neglected, after their obligation has been acknowledged, than those of

ligious, partly national, towards the Fire-worshippers which Mohammed inculcated. This corroborates what I had said in the text before the publication of that work.

[1] I am very much disposed to believe, notwithstanding what seems to be the general opinion, that Mohammed had never read any part of the New Testament. His knowledge of Christianity appears to be wholly derived from the apocryphal gospels and similar works. He admitted the miraculous conception and prophetic character of Jesus, but not his divinity or preëxistence. Hence it is rather surprising to read, in a popular book of sermons by a living prelate, that all the heresies of the Christian church (I quote the substance from memory) are to be found in the Koran, but especially that of Arianism. No one who knows what Arianism is, and what Mohammedism is, could possibly fall into so strange an error. The misfortune has been, that the learned writer, while accumulating a mass of reading upon this part of his subject, neglected what should have been the *nucleus* of the whole, a perusal of the single book which contains the doctrine of the Arabian impostor. In this strange chimera about the Arianism of Mohammed, he has been led away by a misplaced trust in Whitaker; a writer almost invariably in the wrong, and whose bad reasoning upon all the points of historical criticism which he attempted to discuss is quite notorious.

moral virtue. Thus the long fasting, the pilgrimages, the regular prayers and ablutions, the constant alms-giving, the abstinence from stimulating liquors, enjoined by the Koran, created a visible standard of practice among its followers, and preserved a continual recollection of their law.

But the prevalence of Islâm in the lifetime of its prophet, and during the first ages of its existence, was chiefly owing to the spirit of martial energy that he infused into it. The religion of Mohammed is as essentially a military system as the institution of chivalry in the west of Europe. The people of Arabia, a race of strong passions and sanguinary temper, inured to habits of pillage and murder, found in the law of their native prophet, not a license, but a command, to desolate the world, and the promise of all that their glowing imaginations could anticipate of Paradise annexed to all in which they most delighted upon earth. It is difficult for us in the calmness of our closets to conceive that feverish intensity of excitement to which man may be wrought, when the animal and intellectual energies of his nature converge to a point, and the buoyancy of strength and courage reciprocates the influence of moral sentiment or religious hope. The effect of this union I have formerly remarked in the Crusades; a phenomenon perfectly analogous to the early history of the Saracens. In each, one hardly knows whether most to admire the prodigious exertions of heroism, or to revolt from the ferocious bigotry that attended them. But the Crusades were a temporary effort, not thoroughly congenial to the spirit of Christendom, which, even in the darkest and most superstitious ages, was not susceptible of the solitary and overruling fanaticism of the Moslem. They needed no excitement from pontiffs and preachers to achieve the work to which they were called; the precept was in their law, the principle was in their hearts, the assurance of success was in their swords. "O prophet," exclaimed Ali, when Mohammed, in the first years of his mission, sought among the scanty and hesitating assembly of his friends a vizir and lieutenant in command, "I am the man; whoever rises against thee, I will dash out his teeth, tear out his eyes, break his legs, rip up his belly. O prophet, I will be thy vizir over them."[1] These words of Mohammed's early and

[1] Gibbon, vol. ix. p. 284.

illustrious disciple are, as it were, a text, upon which the commentary expands into the whole Saracenic history. They contain the vital essence of his religion, implicit faith and ferocious energy. Death, slavery, tribute to unbelievers, were the glad tidings of the Arabian prophet. To the idolaters, indeed, or those who acknowledged no special revelation, one alternative only was proposed, conversion or the sword. The people of the Book, as they are termed in the Koran, or four sects of Christians, Jews, Magians, and Sabians, were permitted to redeem their adherence to their ancient law by the payment of tribute, and other marks of humiliation and servitude. But the limits which Mohammedan intolerance had prescribed to itself were seldom transgressed; the word pledged to unbelievers was seldom forfeited; and with all their insolence and oppression, the Moslem conquerors were mild and liberal in comparison with those who obeyed the pontiffs of Rome or Constantinople.

First conquests of the Saracens.

At the death of Mohammed in 632 his temporal and religious sovereignty embraced, and was limited by, the Arabian peninsula. The Roman and Persian empires, engaged in tedious and indecisive hostility upon the rivers of Mesopotamia and the Armenian mountains, were viewed by the ambitious fanatics of his creed as their quarry. In the very first year of Mohammed's immediate successor, Abubeker, each of these mighty empires was invaded. The latter opposed but a short resistance. The crumbling fabric of eastern despotism is never secure against rapid and total subversion; a few victories, a few sieges, carried the Arabian arms from the Tigris to the Oxus, and overthrew, with the Sassanian dynasty, the ancient and famous religion they had professed. Seven years of active and unceasing warfare sufficed to subjugate the rich province of Syria, though defended by numerous armies and fortified cities; and the khalif Omar had scarcely returned thanks for the accomplishment of this conquest, when Amrou, his lieutenant, announced to him the entire reduction of Egypt. After some interval the Saracens won their way along the coast of Africa as far as the Pillars of Hercules, and a third province was irretrievably torn from the Greek empire. These western conquests introduced them

A.D. 632-639.

A.D. 647-698.

to fresh enemies, and ushered in more splendid successes; encouraged by the disunion of the Visigoths, and perhaps invited by treachery, Musa, the general of a master who sat beyond the opposite extremity of the Mediterranean Sea, passed over into Spain, and within about two years the name of Mohammed was invoked under the Pyrenees.[1]

A.D. 710.

These conquests, which astonish the careless and superficial, are less perplexing to a calm inquirer than their cessation, the loss of half the Roman empire, than the preservation of the rest. A glance from Medina to Constantinople in the middle of the seventh century would probably have induced an indifferent spectator, if such a being may be imagined, to anticipate by eight hundred years the establishment of a Mohammedan dominion upon the shores of the Hellespont. The fame of Heraclius had withered in the Syrian war; and his successors appeared as incapable to resist, as they were unworthy to govern. Their despotism, unchecked by law, was often punished by successful rebellion; but not a whisper of civil liberty was ever heard, and the vicissitudes of servitude and anarchy consummated the moral degeneracy of the nation. Less ignorant than the western barbarians, the Greeks abused their ingenuity in theological controversies, those especially which related to the nature and incarnation of our Saviour; wherein the disputants, as is usual, became more positive and rancorous as their creed receded from the possibility of human apprehension. Nor were these confined to the clergy, who had not, in the East, obtained the prerogative of guiding the national faith; the sovereigns sided alternately with opposing factions; Heraclius was not too brave, nor Theodora too infamous, for discussions of theology; and the dissenters from an imperial decision were involved in the double proscription of treason and heresy. But the persecutors of their opponents at home pretended to cowardly scrupulousness in the field; nor was

State of the Greek empire.

[1] Ockley's History of the Saracens; Cardonne, Révolutions de l'Afrique et de l'Espagne. The former of these works is well known and justly admired for its simplicity and picturesque details. Scarcely any narrative has ever excelled in beauty that of the death of Hossein. But these do not tend to render it more deserving of confidence. On the contrary, it may be laid down as a pretty general rule, that *circumstantiality*, which enhances the credibility of a witness, diminishes that of an historian remote in time or situation. And I observe that Reiske, in his preface to Abulfeda, speaks of Wakidi, from whom Ockley's book is but a translation, as a mere fabulist.

the Greek church ashamed to require the lustration of a canonical penance from the soldier who shed the blood of his enemies in a national war.

Decline of the Saracens.

But this depraved people were preserved from destruction by the vices of their enemies, still more than by some intrinsic resources which they yet possessed. A rapid degeneracy enfeebled the victorious Moslem in their career. That irresistible enthusiasm, that earnest and disinterested zeal of the companions of Mohammed, was in a great measure lost, even before the first generation had passed away. In the fruitful valleys of Damascus and Bassora the Arabs of the desert forgot their abstemious habits. Rich from the tributes of an enslaved people, the Mohammedan sovereigns knew no employment of riches but in sensual luxury, and paid the price of voluptuous indulgence in the relaxation of their strength and energy. Under the reign of Moawiah, the fifth khalif, an hereditary succession was substituted for the free choice of the faithful, by which the first representatives of the prophet had been elevated to power; and this regulation, necessary as it plainly was to avert in some degree the dangers of schism and civil war, exposed the kingdom to the certainty of being often governed by feeble tyrants. But no regulation could be more than a temporary preservative against civil war. The dissensions which still separate and render hostile the followers of Mohammed may be traced to the first events that ensued upon his death, to the rejection of his son-in-law Ali by the electors of Medina. Two reigns, those of Abubeker and Omar, passed in external glory and domestic reverence; but the old age of Othman was weak and imprudent, and the conspirators against him established the first among a hundred precedents of rebellion and regicide. Ali was now chosen; but a strong faction disputed his right; and the Saracen empire was, for many years, distracted with civil war, among competitors who appealed, in reality, to no other decision than that of the sword. The family of Ommiyah succeeded at last in establishing an unresisted, if not an undoubted title. But rebellions were perpetually afterwards breaking out in that vast extent of dominion, till one of these revolters acquired by success a better name than rebel, and founded the dynasty of the Abbassides.

A.D. 750.

Damascus had been the seat of empire under the Ommiades; it was removed by the succeeding family to their new city of Bagdad. There are not any names in the long line of khalifs, after the companions of Mohammed, more renowned in history than some of the earlier sovereigns who reigned in this capital — Almansor, Haroun Alraschid, and Almamùn. Their splendid palaces, their numerous guards, their treasures of gold and silver, the populousness and wealth of their cities, formed a striking contrast to the rudeness and poverty of the western nations in the same age. In their court learning, which the first Moslem had despised as unwarlike or rejected as profane, was held in honor.[1] The khalif Almamùn especially was distinguished for his patronage of letters; the philosophical writings of Greece were eagerly sought and translated; the stars were numbered, the course of the planets was measured. The Arabians improved upon the science they borrowed, and returned it with abundant interest to Europe in the communication of numeral figures and the intellectual language of algebra.[2] Yet the merit of the Abbassides has been exaggerated by adulation or gratitude. After all the vague praises of hireling poets, which have sometimes been repeated in Europe, it is very rare to read the history of an eastern sovereign unstained by atrocious crimes. No Christian government, except perhaps that of Constantinople, exhibits such a series of tyrants as the khalifs of Bagdad; if deeds of blood, wrought through unbridled passion or jealous policy, may challenge the name of tyranny. These are ill redeemed by ceremonious devotion and acts of trifling, perhaps ostentatious, humility, or even by the best attribute of Mohammedan princes — a rigorous justice in chastising the offences of others. Anecdotes of this description give as imperfect a sketch of an oriental sovereign as monkish chroniclers sometimes draw of one in Europe who founded monasteries and

Khalifs of Bagdad.

[1] The Arabian writers date the origin of their literature (except those works of fiction which had always been popular) from the reign of Almansor, A.D. 758. Abulpharagius, p. 160; Gibbon, c. 52.

[2] Several very recent publications contain interesting details on Saracen literature; Berington's Literary History of the Middle Ages, Mill's History of Mohammedanism, chap. vi., Turner's History of England, vol. i. Harris's Philological Arrangement is perhaps a book better known; and though it has since been much excelled, was one of the first contributions in our own language to this department, in which a great deal yet remains for the oriental scholars of Europe. Casiri's admirable catalogue of Arabic MSS. in the Escurial ought before this to have been followed up by a more accurate examination of their contents than it was possible for him to give.

obeyed the clergy; though it must be owned that the former are in much better taste.

Though the Abbassides have acquired more celebrity, they never attained the real strength of their predecessors. Under the last of the house of Ommiyah, one command was obeyed almost along the whole diameter of the known world, from the banks of the Sihon to the utmost promontory of Portugal. But the revolution which changed the succession of khalifs produced another not less important. A fugitive of the vanquished family, by name Abdalrahman, arrived in Spain and the Moslem of that country, not sharing in the prejudices which had stirred up the Persians in favor of the line of Abbas, and conscious that their remote situation entitled them to independence, proclaimed him khalif of Cordova. There could be little hope of reducing so distant a dependency; and the example was not unlikely to be imitated. In the reign of Haroun Alraschid two principalities were formed in Africa — of the Aglabites, who reigned over Tunis and Tripoli; and of the Edrisites in the western parts of Barbary. These yielded in about a century to the Fatimites, a more powerful dynasty, who afterwards established an empire in Egypt.[1]

Separation of Spain and Africa.

The loss, however, of Spain and Africa was the inevitable effect of that immensely extended dominion, which their separation alone would not have enfeebled. But other revolutions awaited it at home. In the history of the Abbassides of Bagdad we read over again the decline of European monarchies, through their various symptoms of ruin; and find successive analogies to the insults of the barbarians towards imperial Rome in the fifth century, to the personal insignificance of the Merovingian kings, and to the feudal usurpations that dismembered the inheritance of Charlemagne. 1. Beyond the northeastern frontier of the Saracen empire dwelt a warlike and powerful nation of the Tartar family, who defended the independence of Turkestan from the sea of Aral to the great central chain of mountains. In the wars which the khalifs or their lieutenants waged against them many of these Turks were led into captivity, and dispersed over the empire. Their strength and courage dis-

Decline of the khalifs.

[1] For these revolutions, which it is not very easy to fix in the memory, consult Cardonne, who has made as much of them as the subject would bear.

tinguished them among a people grown effeminate by luxury; and that jealousy of disaffection among his subjects so natural to an eastern monarch might be an additional motive with the khalif Motassem to form bodies of guards out of these prisoners. But his policy was fatally erroneous. More rude and even more ferocious than the Arabs, they contemned the feebleness of the khalifate, while they grasped at its riches. The son of Motassem, Motawakkel, was murdered in his palace by the barbarians of the north; and his fate revealed the secret of the empire, that the choice of its sovereign had passed to their slaves. Degradation and death were frequently the lot of succeeding khalifs; but in the East the son leaps boldly on the throne which the blood of his father has stained, and the prætorian guards of Bagdad rarely failed to render a fallacious obedience to the nearest heir of the house of Abbas. 2. In about one hundred years after the introduction of the Turkish soldiers the sovereigns of Bagdad sunk almost into oblivion. Al Radi, who died in 940, was the last of these that officiated in the mosque, that commanded the forces in person, that addressed the people from the pulpit, that enjoyed the pomp and splendor of royalty.[1] But he was the first who appointed, instead of a vizir, a new officer — a mayor, as it were, of the palace — with the title of Emir al Omra, commander of commanders, to whom he delegated by compulsion the functions of his office. This title was usually seized by active and martial spirits; it was sometimes hereditary, and in effect irrevocable by the khalifs, whose names hardly appear after this time in Oriental annals. 3. During these revolutions of the palace every province successively shook off its allegiance; new principalities were formed in Syria and Mesopotamia, as well as in Khorasan and Persia, till the dominion of the Commander of the Faithful was literally confined to the city of Bagdad and its adjacent territory. For a time some of these princes, who had been appointed as governors by the khalifs, professed to respect his supremacy by naming him in the public prayers and upon the coin; but these tokens of dependence were gradually obliterated.[2]

[1] Abulfeda, p. 261; Gibbon, c. 52; Modern Univ. Hist. vol. ii. Al Radi's command of the army is only mentioned by the last.

[2] The decline of the Saracens is fully discussed in the 52nd chapter of Gibbon, which is, in itself, a complete philosophical dissertation upon this part of history

Revival of the Greek empire.

Such is the outline of Saracenic history for three centuries after Mohammed; one age of glorious conquest; a second of stationary but rather precarious greatness; a third of rapid decline. The Greek empire meanwhile survived, and almost recovered from the shock it had sustained. Besides the decline of its enemies, several circumstances may be enumerated tending to its preservation. The maritime province of Cilicia had been overrun by the Mohammedans; but between this and the Lesser Asia Mount Taurus raises its massy buckler, spreading as a natural bulwark from the sea-coast of the ancient Pamphylia to the hilly district of Isauria, whence it extends in an easterly direction, separating the Cappadocian and Cilician plains, and, after throwing off considerable ridges to the north and south, connects itself with other chains of mountains that penetrate far into the Asiatic continent. Beyond this barrier the Saracens formed no durable settlement, though the armies of Alraschid wasted the country as far as the Hellespont, and the city of Amorium, in Phrygia, was razed to the ground by Al Motassem. The position of Constantinople, chosen with a sagacity to which the course of events almost gave the appearance of prescience, secured her from any immediate danger on the side of Asia, and rendered her as little accessible to an enemy as any city which valor and patriotism did not protect. Yet
A.D. 668. in the days of Arabian energy she was twice attacked by great naval armaments. The first siege,
A.D. 716. or rather blockade, continued for seven years; the second, though shorter, was more terrible, and her walls, as well as her port, were actually invested by the combined forces of the khalif Waled, under his brother Moslema.[1] The final discomfiture of these assailants showed the resisting force of the empire, or rather of its capital; but perhaps the abandonment of such maritime enterprises by the Saracens may be in some measure ascribed to the removal of their metropolis from Damascus to Bagdad. But the Greeks in their turn determined to dispute the command of the sea. By possessing the secret of an inextinguishable fire, they fought on superior terms; their wealth, perhaps their skill, enabled them to employ larger and better appointed vessels; and they ultimately expelled their enemies from the islands of Crete and

[1] Gibbon, c. 52

Cyprus. By land they were less desirous of encountering the Moslem. The science of tactics is studied by the pusillanimous, like that of medicine by the sick; and the Byzantine emperors, Leo and Constantine, have left written treatises on the art of avoiding defeat, of protracting contest, of resisting attack.[1] But this timid policy, and even the purchase of armistices from the Saracens, were not ill calculated for the state of both nations. While Constantinople temporized, Bagdad shook to her foundations; and the heirs of the Roman name might boast the immortality of their own empire when they contemplated the dissolution of that which had so rapidly sprung up and perished. Amidst all the crimes and revolutions of the Byzantine government — and its history is but a series of crimes and revolutions — it was never dismembered by intestine war. A sedition in the army, a tumult in the theatre, a conspiracy in the palace, precipitated a monarch from the throne; but the allegiance of Constantinople was instantly transferred to his successor, and the provinces implicitly obeyed the voice of the capital. The custom too of partition, so baneful to the Latin kingdoms, and which was not altogethor unknown to the Saracens, never prevailed in the Greek empire. It stood in the middle of the tenth century, as vicious indeed and cowardly, but more wealthy, more enlightened, and far more secure from its enemies than under the first successors of Heraclius. For about one hundred years preceding there had been only partial wars with the Mohammedan potentates; and in these the emperors seem gradually to have gained the advantage, and to have become more frequently the aggressors. But the increasing distractions of the East encouraged two brave usurpers, Nicephorus Phocas and John Zimisces, to attempt the actual recovery of the lost provinces. They carried the Roman arms (one may use the term with less reluctance than usual) over Syria; Antioch and Aleppo were taken by storm; Damascus submitted; even the cities of Mesopotamia, beyond the ancient boundary of the Euphrates, were added to the trophies of Zimisces, who unwillingly spared the capital of the khalifate. From such distant conquests it was expedient, and indeed necessary, to withdraw; but Cilicia

A.D. 963-975.

[1] Gibbon, c. 53. Constantine Porphyrogenitus, in his advice to his son as to the administration of the empire, betrays a mind not ashamed to confess weakness and cowardice, and pleasing itself in petty arts to elude the rapacity or divide the power of its enemies

and Antioch were permanently restored to the empire. At the close of the tenth century the emperors of Constantinople possessed the best and greatest portion of the modern kingdom of Naples, a part of Sicily, the whole European dominions of the Ottomans, the province of Anatolia or Asia Minor, with some part of Syria and Armenia.[1]

These successes of the Greek empire were certainly much rather due to the weakness of its enemies than to any revival of national courage and vigor; yet they would probably have been more durable if the contest had been only with the khalifate, or the kingdoms derived from it. But a new actor was to appear on the stage of Asiatic tragedy. The same Turkish nation, the slaves and captives from which had become arbiters of the sceptre of Bagdad, passed their original limits of the Iaxartes or Sihon. The sultans of Ghazna, a dynasty whose splendid conquests were of very short duration, had deemed it politic to divide the strength of these formidable allies by inviting a part of them into Khorasan. They covered that fertile province with their pastoral tents, and beckoned their compatriots to share the riches of the south. The Ghaznevides fell the earliest victims; but Persia, violated in turn by every conqueror, was a tempting and unresisting prey. Togrol Bek, the founder of the Seljukian dynasty of Turks, overthrew the family of Bowides, who had long reigned at Ispahan, respected the pageant of Mohammedan sovereignty in the khalif of Bagdad, embraced with all his tribes the religion of the vanquished, and commenced the attack upon Christendom by an irruption into Armenia. His nephew and successor Alp Arslan defeated and took prisoner the emperor Romanus Diogenes; and the conquest of Asia Minor was almost completed by princes of the same family, the Seljukians of Rûm,[2] who were permitted by Malek Shah, the third sultan of the Turks, to form an independent kingdom. Through their own exertions, and the selfish impolicy of rival competitors for the throne of Constantinople, who bartered the strength of the empire for assistance, the Turks became masters of the Asiatic cities and

The Turks.

Their conquests. A.D. 1038.

A.D. 1071.

[1] Gibbon, c. 52 and 53. The latter of these chapters contains as luminous a sketch of the condition of Greece as the former does of Saracenic history. In each, the facts are not grouped historically, according to the order of time but philosophically, according to their relations.

[2] Rûm, i. e. country of the Romans.

fortified passes; nor did there seem any obstacle to the invasion of Europe.[1]

In this state of jeopardy the Greek empire looked for aid to the nations of the West, and received it in fuller measure than was expected, or perhaps desired. The deliverance of Constantinople was indeed a very secondary object with the crusaders. But it was necessarily included in their scheme of operations, which, though they all tended to the recovery of Jerusalem, must commence with the first enemies that lay on their line of march. The Turks were entirely defeated, their capital of Nice restored to the empire. As the Franks passed onwards, the emperor Alexius Comnenus trod on their footsteps, and secured to himself the fruits for which their enthusiasm disdained to wait. He regained possession of the strong places on the Ægean shores, of the defiles of Bithynia, and of the entire coast of Asia Minor, both on the Euxine and Mediterranean seas, which the Turkish armies, composed of cavalry and unused to regular warfare, could not recover.[2] So much must undoubtedly be ascribed to the first crusade. But I think that the general effect of these expeditions has been overrated by those who consider them as having permanently retarded the progress of the Turkish power. The Christians in Palestine and Syria were hardly in contact with the Seljukian kingdom of Rûm, the only enemies of the empire; and it is not easy to perceive that their small and feeble principalities, engaged commonly in defending themselves against the Mohammedan princes of Mesopotamia, or the Fatimite khalifs of Egypt, could obstruct the arms of a sovereign of Iconium upon the Mæander or the Halys. Other causes are adequate to explain the equipoise in which the balance of dominion in Anatolia was kept during the twelfth century: the valor and activity of the two Comneni, John and Manuel, especially the former; and the frequent partitions and internal feuds, through which the Seljukians of Iconium, like all other Oriental governments, became incapable of foreign aggression.

The first Crusade.

Progress of the Greeks.

But whatever obligation might be due to the first crusaders from the Eastern empire was cancelled by their descend-

1 Gibbon, c. 57; De Guignes, Hist. des Huns, t. ii. l. 2.

2 It does not seem perfectly clear whether the sea-coast, north and south, was reannexed to the empire during the reign of Alexius, or of his gallant son John Comnenus. But the doubt is hardly worth noticing.

ants one hundred years afterwards, when the fourth in number of those expeditions was turned to the subjugation of Constantinople itself. One of those domestic revolutions which occur perpetually in Byzantine history had placed an usurper on the imperial throne. The lawful monarch was condemned to blindness and a prison; but the heir escaped to recount his misfortunes to the fleet and army of crusaders assembled in the Dalmatian port of Zara. This armament had been collected for the usual purposes, and through the usual motives, temporal and spiritual, of a crusade; the military force chiefly consisted of French nobles; the naval was supplied by the republic of Venice, whose doge commanded personally in the expedition. It was not apparently consistent with the primary object of retrieving the Christian affairs in Palestine to interfere in the government of a Christian empire; but the temptation of punishing a faithless people, and the hope of assistance in their subsequent operations, prevailed. They turned their prows up the Archipelago; and, notwithstanding the vast population and defensible strength of Constantinople, compelled the usurper to fly, and the citizens to surrender. But animosities springing from religious schism and national jealousy were not likely to be allayed by such remedies; the Greeks, wounded in their pride and bigotry, regarded the legitimate emperor as a creature of their enemies, ready to sacrifice their church, a stipulated condition of his restoration, to that of Rome. In a few months a new sedition and conspiracy raised another usurper in defiance of the crusaders' army encamped without the walls. The siege instantly recommenced; and after three months the city of Constantinople was taken by storm. The tale of pillage and murder is always uniform; but the calamities of ancient capitals, like those of the great, impress us more forcibly. Even now we sympathize with the virgin majesty of Constantinople, decked with the accumulated wealth of ages, and resplendent with the monuments of Roman empire and of Grecian art. Her populousness is estimated beyond credibility: ten, twenty, thirty-fold that of London or Paris; certainly far beyond the united capitals of all European kingdoms in that age.[1] In

Capture of Constantinople by the Latins.

A.D. 1202.

A.D. 1204.

[1] Ville Hardouin reckons the inhabitants of Constantinople at quatre cens mil nommes ou plus, by which Gibbon understands him to mean men of a mili-

magnificence she excelled them more than in numbers; instead of the thatched roofs, the mud walls, the narrow streets, the pitiful buildings of those cities, she had marble and gilded palaces, churches and monasteries, the works of skilful architects, through nine centuries, gradually sliding from the severity of ancient taste into the more various and brilliant combinations of eastern fancy.[1] In the libraries of Constantinople were collected the remains of Grecian learning; her forum and hippodrome were decorated with those of Grecian sculpture; but neither would be spared by undistinguishing rapine; nor were the chiefs of the crusaders more able to appreciate the loss than their soldiery. Four horses, that breathe in the brass of Lysippus, were removed from Constantinople to the square of St. Mark at Venice; destined again to become the trophies of war, and to follow the alternate revolutions of conquest. But we learn from a contemporary Greek to deplore the fate of many other pieces of sculpture, which were destroyed in wantonness, or even coined into brass money.[2]

Partition of the empire.

The lawful emperor and his son had perished in the rebellion that gave occasion to this catastrophe; and there remained no right to interfere with that of conquest. But the Latins were a promiscuous multitude, and what their independent valor had earned was not to be transferred to a single master. Though the name of emperor seemed necessary for the government of Constantinople, the unity of despotic power was very foreign to the principles and the interests of the crusaders. In their selfish schemes of aggrandizement they tore in pieces the Greek empire. One fourth only was allotted to the emperor, three eighths were the share of the republic of Venice, and the remainder was divided among the chiefs. Baldwin count of Flanders obtained the imperial title, with the feudal sovereignty over the minor principalities. A monarchy thus dismembered had

tary age. Le Beau allows a million for the whole population. Gibbon, vol. xi. p. 213. We should probably rate London, in 1204, too high at 60,000 souls. Paris had been enlarged by Philip Augustus, and stood on more ground than London. Delamare sur la Police, t. i. p. 76.

[1] O quanta civitas, exclaims Fulk of Chartres a hundred years before, nobilis et decora! quot monasteria quotque palatia sunt in eâ, opere mero fabrefacta! quo etiam in plateis vel in vicis opera ad spectandum mirabilia! Tædium est quidem magnum recitare, quanta sit ibi opulentia bonorum omnium, auri et argenti palliorum multiformium, sacrarumque reliquiarum. Omni etiam tempore, navigio frequenti cuncta hominum necessaria illuc afferuntur. Du Chesne, Scrip. Rerum Gallicarum, t. iv. p. 822

[2] Gibbon, c. 60.

little prospect of honor or durability. The Latin emperors of Constantinople were more contemptible and unfortunate, not so much from personal character as political weakness, than their predecessors; their vassals rebelled against sovereigns not more powerful than themselves; the Bulgarians, a nation who, after being long formidable, had been subdued by the imperial arms, and only recovered independence on the eve of the Latin conquest, insulted their capital; the Greeks viewed them with silent hatred, and hailed the dawning deliverance from the Asiatic coast. On that side of the Bosphorus the Latin usurpation was scarcely for a moment acknowledged; Nice became the seat of a Greek dynasty, who reigned with honor as far as the Mæander; and crossing into Europe, after having established their dominion throughout Romania and other provinces, expelled the last Latin emperors from Constantinople in less than sixty years from its capture.

The Greeks recover Constantinople.

A.D. 1261.

During the reign of these Greeks at Nice they had fortunately little to dread on the side of their former enemies, and were generally on terms of friendship with the Seljukians of Iconium. That monarchy indeed had sufficient objects of apprehension for itself. Their own example in changing the upland plains of Tartary for the cultivated valleys of the south was imitated in the thirteenth century by two successive hordes of northern barbarians. The Karismians, whose tents had been pitched on the lower Oxus and Caspian Sea, availed themselves of the decline of the Turkish power to establish their dominion in Persia, and menaced, though they did not overthrow, the kingdom of Iconium. A more tremendous storm ensued in the eruption of Moguls under the sons of Zingis Khan. From the farthest regions of Chinese Tartary issued a race more fierce and destitute of civilization than those who had preceded, whose numbers were told by hundreds of thousands, and whose only test of victory was devastation. All Asia, from the sea of China to the Euxine, wasted beneath the locusts of the north. They annihilated the phantom of authority which still lingered with the name of khalif at Bagdad. They reduced into dependence and finally subverted the Seljukian dynasties of Persia, Syria, and Iconium. The Turks of the latter kingdom betook themselves to the mountainous country,

Invasions of Asia by the Karismians,

and Moguls.

A.D. 1218.

A.D. 1272.

where they formed several petty principalities, which subsisted by incursions into the territory of the Moguls or the Greeks. The chief of one of these, named Othman, at the end of the thirteenth century, penetrated into the province of Bithynia, from which his posterity were never withdrawn.[1]

A.D. 1299

The empire of Constantinople had never recovered the blow it received at the hands of the Latins. Most of the islands in the Archipelago, and the provinces of proper Greece from Thessaly southward, were still possessed by those invaders. The wealth and naval power of the empire had passed into the hands of the maritime republics; Venice, Genoa, Pisa, and Barcelona were enriched by a commerce which they carried on as independent states within the precincts of Constantinople, scarcely deigning to solicit the permission or recognize the supremacy of its master. In a great battle fought under the walls of the city between the Venetian and Genoese fleets, the weight of the Roman empire, in Gibbon's expression, was scarcely felt in the balance of these opulent and powerful republics. Eight galleys were the contribution of the emperor Cantacuzene to his Venetian allies; and upon their defeat he submitted to the ignominy of excluding them forever from trading in his dominions. Meantime the remains of the empire in Asia were seized by the independent Turkish dynasties, of which the most illustrious, that of the Ottomans, occupied the province of Bithynia. Invited by a Byzantine faction into Europe, about the middle of the fourteenth century, they fixed themselves in the neighborhood of the capital, and in the thirty years' reign of Amurath I. subdued, with little resistance, the province of Romania and the small Christian kingdoms that had been formed on the lower Danube. Bajazet, the successor of Amurath, reduced the independent emirs of Anatolia to subjection, and, after long threatening Constantinople, invested it by sea and land. The Greeks called loudly upon their brethren of the West for aid against the common enemy of Christendom; but the flower of French chivalry had been slain or taken in the battle of Nicopolis in Bulgaria,[2] where the king of Hun-

Declining state of the Greek empire.

A.D. 1352.

The Ottomans.

A.D. 1431.

A.D. 1396.

[1] De Guignes, Hist. des Huns, t. iii. l. 15; Gibbon, c. 64.

[2] The Hungarians fled in this battle and deserted their allies, according to

gary, notwithstanding the heroism of these volunteers, was entirely defeated by Bajazet. The emperor Manuel left his capital with a faint hope of exciting the courts of Europe to some decided efforts by personal representations of the danger; and, during his absence, Constantinople was saved, not by a friend, indeed, but by a power more formidable to her enemies than to herself.

The Tartars or Moguls of Timur.

The loose masses of mankind, that, without laws, agricul ture, or fixed dwellings, overspread the vast centra regions of Asia, have, at various times, been impelled by necessity of subsistence, or through the casual appearance of a commanding genius, upon the domain of culture and civilization. Two principal roads connect the nations of Tartary with those of the west and south; the one into Europe along the sea of Azoph and northern coast of the Euxine; the other across the interval between the Bukharian mountains and the Caspian into Persia. Four times at least within the period of authentic history the Scythian tribes have taken the former course and poured themselves into Europe, but each wave was less effectual than the preceding. The first of these was in the fourth and fifth centuries, for we may range those rapidly successive migrations of the Goths and Huns together, when the Roman empire fell to the ground, and the only boundary of barbarian conquest was the Atlantic ocean upon the shores of Portugal. The second wave came on with the Hungarians in the tenth century, whose ravages extended as far as the southern provinces of France. A third attack was sustained from the Moguls under the children of Zingis at the same period as that which overwhelmed Persia. The Russian monarchy was destroyed in this invasion, and for two hundred years that great country lay prostrate under the yoke of the Tartars. As they advanced, Poland and Hungary gave little opposi tion; and the farthest nations of Europe were appalled by the tempest. But Germany was no longer as she had been in the anarchy of the tenth century; the Moguls were un-

the Mémoires de Boucicaut, c. 25. But Froissart, who seems a fairer authority, imputes the defeat to the rashness of the French. Part iv. ch. 79. The count de Nevers (Jean Sans Peur, afterwards duke of Burgundy), who commanded the French, was made prisoner with others of the royal blood, and ransomed at a very high price. Many of eminent birth and merit were put to death; a fate from which Boucicaut was saved by the interference of the count de Nevers, who might better himself have perished with honor on that occasion than survived to plunge his country into civil war and his name into infamy

used to resistance, and still less inclined to regular warfare; they retired before the emperor Frederic II., and the utmost points of their western invasion were the cities of Lignitz in Silesia and Neustadt in Austria. In the fourth and last aggression of the Tartars their progress in Europe is hardly perceptible; the Moguls of Timur's army could only boast the destruction of Azoph and the pillage of some Russian provinces. Timur, the sovereign of these Moguls and founder of their second dynasty, which has been more permanent and celebrated than that of Zingis, had been the prince of a small tribe in Transoxiana, between the Gihon and Sirr, the doubtful frontier of settled and pastoral nations. His own energy and the weakness of his neighbors are sufficient to explain the revolution he effected. Like former conquerors, Togrol Bek and Zingis, he chose the road through Persia; and, meeting little resistance from the disordered governments of Asia, extended his empire on one side to the Syrian coast, while by successes still more renowned, though not belonging to this place, it reached on the other to the heart of Hindostan. In his old age the restlessness of ambition impelled him against the Turks of Anatolia. Bajazet hastened from the siege of Constantinople to a more perilous contest: his defeat and captivity in the plains of Angora clouded for a time the Ottoman crescent, and preserved the wreck of the Greek empire for fifty years longer.

A.D. 1245.

Defeat of Bajazet. A.D. 1402.

The Moguls did not improve their victory; in the western parts of Asia, as in Hindostan, Timur was but a barbarian destroyer, though at Samarcand a sovereign and a legislator. He gave up Anatolia to the sons of Bajazet; but the unity of their power was broken; and the Ottoman kingdom, like those which had preceded, experienced the evils of partition and mutual animosity. For about twenty years an opportunity was given to the Greeks of recovering part of their losses; but they were incapable of making the best use of this advantage, and, though they regained possession of part of Romania, did not extirpate a strong Turkish colony that held the city of Gallipoli in the Chersonesus. When Amurath II., therefore, reunited under his vigorous sceptre the Ottoman monarchy, Constantinople was exposed to another siege and to fresh losses. Her walls, however, repelled the enemy;

Danger of Constantinople.

A.D. 1421.

and during the reign of Amurath she had leisure to repeat those signals of distress which the princes of Christendom refused to observe. The situation of Europe was, indeed, sufficiently inauspicious; France, the original country of the crusades and of chivalry, was involved in foreign and domestic war; while a schism, apparently interminable, rent the bosom of the Latin church and impaired the efficiency of the only power that could unite and animate its disciples in a religious war. Even when the Roman pontiffs were best disposed to rescue Constantinople from destruction, it was rather as masters than as allies that they would interfere; their ungenerous bigotry, or rather pride, dictated the submission of her church and the renunciation of her favorite article of distinctive faith. The Greeks yielded with reluctance and insincerity in the council of Florence; but soon rescinded their treaty of union. Ugenius IV. procured a short diversion on the side of Hungary; but after the unfortunate battle of Warna the Hungarians were abundantly employed in self-defence.

A.D. 1444.

The two monarchies which have successively held their seat in the city of Constantine may be contrasted in the circumstances of their decline. In the present day we anticipate, with an assurance that none can deem extravagant, the approaching subversion of the Ottoman power; but the signs of internal weakness have not yet been confirmed by the dismemberment of provinces; and the arch of dominion, that long since has seemed nodding to its fall and totters at every blast of the north, still rests upon the landmarks of ancient conquest, and spans the ample regions from Bagdad to Belgrade. Far different were the events that preceded the dissolution of the Greek empire. Every province was in turn subdued — every city opened her gates to the conqueror: the limbs were lopped off one by one; but the pulse still beat at the heart, and the majesty of the Roman name was ultimately confined to the walls of Constantinople. Before Mahomet II. planted his cannon against them, he had completed every smaller conquest and deprived the expiring empire of every hope of succor or delay. It was necessary that Constantinople should fall; but the magnanimous resignation of her emperor bestows an honor upon her fall which her prosperity seldom earned. The long deferred but inevitable moment arrived; and

Its fall.

A.D. 1453.

the last of the Cæsars (I will not say of the Palæologi) folded round him the imperial mantle, and remembered the name which he represented in the dignity of heroic death. It is thus that the intellectual principle, when enfeebled by disease or age, is found to rally its energies in the presence of death, and pour the radiance of unclouded reason around the last struggles of dissolution.

Alarm excited by it in Europe.

Though the fate of Constantinople had been protracted beyond all reasonable expectation, the actual intelligence operated like that of sudden calamity. A sentiment of consternation, perhaps of self-reproach, thrilled to the heart of Christendom. There seemed no longer anything to divert the Ottoman armies from Hungary; and if Hungary should be subdued, it was evident that both Italy and the German empire were exposed to invasion.[1] A general union of Christian powers was required to withstand this common enemy. But the popes, who had so often armed them against each other, wasted their spiritual and political counsels in attempting to restore unanimity. War was proclaimed against the Turks at the diet of Frankfort, in 1454; but no efforts were made to carry the menace into execution. No prince could have sat on the imperial throne more unfitted for the emergency than Frederic III.; his mean spirit and narrow capacity exposed him to the contempt of mankind — his avarice and duplicity ensured the hatred of Austria and Hungary. During the papacy of Pius II., whose heart was thoroughly engaged in this legitimate crusade, a more specious attempt was made by convening an European congress at Mantua. Almost all the sovereigns attended by their envoys; it was concluded that 50,000 men-at-arms should be raised, and a tax levied for three years of one tenth from the revenues of the clergy, one thirtieth from those of the laity, and one twentieth from the capital of the Jews.[2] Pius engaged to head this arma-

A.D. 1459.

[1] Sive vincitur Hungaria, sive coacta jungitur Turcis, neque Italia neque Germania tuta erit, neque satis Rhenus Gallos securos reddet. Æn. Sylv. p. 678. This is part of a discourse pronounced by Æneas Sylvius before the diet of Frankfort; which, though too declamatory, like most of his writings, is an interesting illustration of the state of Europe and of the impression produced by that calamity. Spondanus, ad ann. 1454, has given large extracts from this oration

[2] Spondanus. Neither Charles VII. nor even Philip of Burgundy, who had made the loudest professions, and pledged himself in a fantastic pageant at his court, soon after the capture of Constantinople, to undertake this crusade, were sincere in their promises. The former pretended apprehensions of invasion from England, as an excuse for sending no troops; which, considering the situation of England in 1459, was a bold attempt upon the credulity of mankind.

ment in person; but when he appeared next year at Ancona, the appointed place of embarkation, the princes had failed in all their promises of men and money, and he found only a headlong crowd of adventurers, destitute of every necessary, and expecting to be fed and paid at the pope's expense. It was not by such a body that Mahomet could be expelled from Constantinople. If the Christian sovereigns had given a steady and sincere coöperation, the contest would still have been arduous and uncertain. In the early crusades the superiority of arms, of skill, and even of discipline, had been uniformly on the side of Europe. But the present circumstances were far from similar. An institution, begun by the first and perfected by the second Amurath, had given to the Turkish armies what their enemies still wanted, military subordination and veteran experience. Aware, as it seems, of the real superiority of Europeans in war, these sultans selected the stoutest youths from their Bulgarian, Servian, or Albanian captives, who were educated in habits of martial discipline, and formed into a regular force with the name of Janizaries. After conquest had put an end to personal captivity, a tax of every fifth male child was raised upon the Christian population for the same purpose. The arm of Europe was thus turned upon herself; and the western nations must have contended with troops of hereditary robustness and intrepidity, whose emulous enthusiasm for the country that had adopted them was controlled by habitual obedience to their commanders.[1]

Institution of Janizaries.

[1] In the long declamation of Æneas Sylvius before the diet of Frankfort in 1454, he has the following contrast between the European and Turkish militia; a good specimen of the artifice with which an ingenious orator can disguise the truth, while he seems to be stating it most precisely. Conferamus nunc Turcos et vos invicem; et quid sperandum sit si cum illis pugnetis, examinemus. Vos nati ad arma, illi tracti. Vos armati. illi inermes; vos gladios versatis, illi cultris utuntur; vos balistas tenditis, illi arcus trahunt; vos loricæ thoracesque protegunt, illos culcitra tegit; vos equos regitis, illi ab equis reguntur; vos nobiles in bellum ducitis, illi servos aut artifices cogunt, &c. &c. p. 685. This, however, had little effect upon the hearers, who were better judges of military affairs than the secretary of Frederic III. Pius II., or Æneas Sylvius, was a lively writer and a skilful intriguer. Long experience had given him a considerable insight into European politics; and his views are usually clear and sensible Though not so learned as some popes, he knew much better what was going forward in his own time. But the vanity of displaying his eloquence betrayed him into a strange folly, when he addressed a very long letter to Mahomet II., explaining the Catholic faith, and urging him to be baptized; in which case, so far from preaching a crusade against the Turks, he would gladly make use of their power to recover the rights of the church. Some of his inducements are curious, and must, if made public, have been highly gratifying to his friend Frederic III. Quippe ut arbitramur, si Christianus fuisses, mortuo Ladislao Ungariæ et Bohemiæ rege, nemo præter te sua regna fuisset adeptus. Sperassent Ungari post diuturna bellorum mala sub tuo regimine pacem, et illos Bohemi secuti fuissent; sed cum esses nostræ religionis hostis, elegerunt Ungari, &c. Epist. 396.

Yet forty years after the fall of Constantinople, at the epoch of Charles VIII.'s expedition into Italy, the just apprehensions of European statesmen might have gradually subsided. Except the Morea, Negropont, and a few other unimportant conquests, no real progress had been made by the Ottomans. Mahomet II. had been kept at bay by the Hungarians; he had been repulsed with some ignominy by the knights of St. John from the island of Rhodes. A petty chieftain defied this mighty conqueror for twenty years in the mountains of Epirus; and the persevering courage of his desultory warfare with such trifling resources, and so little prospect of ultimate success, may justify the exaggerated admiration with which his contemporaries honored the name of Scanderbeg. Once only the crescent was displayed on the Calabrian coast; but the city of Otranto remained but a year in the possession of Mahomet. On his death a disputed succession involved his children in civil war. Bajazet, the eldest, obtained the victory; but his rival brother Zizim fled to Rhodes, from whence he was removed to France, and afterwards to Rome. Apprehensions of this exiled prince seem to have dictated a pacific policy to the reigning sultan, whose character did not possess the usual energy of Ottoman sovereigns.

Suspension of the Ottoman conquests.

A.D. 1480.

CHAPTER VII.

HISTORY OF ECCLESIASTICAL POWER DURING THE MIDDLE AGES.

PART I.

Wealth of the Clergy — its Sources — Encroachments on Ecclesiastical Property — their Jurisdiction — arbitrative — coercive — their political Power — Supremacy of the Crown — Charlemagne — Change after his Death, and Encroachments of the Church in the ninth Century — Primacy of the See of Rome — its early Stage — Gregory I. — Council of Frankfort — false Decretals — Progress of Papal Authority — Effects of Excommunication — Lothaire — State of the Church in the tenth Century — Marriage of Priests — Simony — Episcopal Elections — Imperial Authority over the Popes — Disputes concerning Investitures — Gregory VII. and Henry IV. — Concordat of Calixtus — Election by Chapters — general System of Gregory VII. — Progress of Papal Usurpations in the twelfth Century — Innocent III. — his Character and Schemes.

Wealth of the church under the empire.

AT the irruption of the northern invaders into the Roman empire they found the clergy already endowed with extensive possessions. Besides the spontaneous oblations upon which the ministers of the Christian church had originally subsisted, they had obtained, even under the pagan emperors, by concealment or connivance — for the Roman law did not permit a tenure of lands in mortmain — certain immovable estates, the revenues of which were applicable to their own maintenance and that of the poor.[1] These indeed were precarious and liable to confiscation in times of persecution. But it was among the first effects of the conversion of Constantine to give not only a security, but a legal sanction, to the territorial acquisitions of the church. The edict of Milan, in 313, recognizes the actual estates of ecclesiastical corporations.[2] Another, published in 321, grants to all the subjects of the empire the power of bequeathing their property to the church.[3] His

[1] Giannone, Istoria di Napoli, l. ii. c. 8; Gibbon, c. 15 and c. 20; F. Paul's Treatise on Benefices, c. 4. The last writer does not wholly confirm this position; but a comparison of the three seems to justify my text.

[2] Giannone; Gibbon, ubi supra; F Paul, c. 5.

[3] Idem.

own liberality and that of his successors set an example which did not want imitators. Passing rapidly from a condition of distress and persecution to the summit of prosperity, the church degenerated as rapidly from her ancient purity, and forfeited the respect of future ages in the same proportion as she acquired the blind veneration of her own. Covetousness, especially, became almost a characteristic vice. Valentinian I., in 370, prohibited the clergy from receiving the bequests of women — a modification more discreditable than any general law could have been. And several of the fathers severely reprobate the prevailing avidity of their contemporaries.[1]

Increased after its subversion.

The devotion of the conquering nations, as it was still less enlightened than that of the subjects of the empire, so was it still more munificent. They left indeed the worship of Hesus and Taranis in their forests; but they retained the elementary principles of that and of all barbarous idolatry, a superstitious reverence for the priesthood, a credulity that seemed to invite imposture, and a confidence in the efficacy of gifts to expiate offences. Of this temper it is undeniable that the ministers of religion, influenced probably not so much by personal covetousness as by zeal for the interests of their order, took advantage. Many of the peculiar and prominent characteristics in the faith and discipline of those ages appear to have been either introduced or sedulously promoted for the purposes of sordid fraud. To those purposes conspired the veneration for relics, the worship of images, the idolatry of saints and martyrs, the religious inviolability of sanctuaries, the consecration of cemeteries, but, above all, the doctrine of purgatory and masses for the relief of the dead. A creed thus contrived, operating upon the minds of barbarians, lavish though rapacious, and devout though dissolute, naturally caused a torrent of opulence to pour in upon the church. Donations of land were continually made to the bishops, and, in still more ample proportion, to the monastic foundations. These had not been very numerous in the West till the beginning of the sixth century, when Benedict established his celebrated rule.[2] A more remarkable show of piety, a more absolute seclusion from

[1] Giannnone, ubi supra; F. Paul, c. 6.

[2] Giannone, l. iii. c. 6; l. iv. c. 12; Treatise on Benefices, c. 8; Fleury, Huitième Discours sur l'Hist. Ecclésiastique; Muratori, Dissert. 65.

the world, forms more impressive and edifying prayers and masses more constantly repeated, gave to the professed in these institutions an advantage, in public esteem, over the secular clergy.

The ecclesiastical hierarchy never received any territorial endowment by law, either under the Roman empire or the kingdoms erected upon its ruins. But the voluntary munificence of princes, as well as their subjects, amply supplied the place of a more universal provision. Large private estates, or, as they were termed, patrimonies, not only within their own dioceses, but sometimes in distant countries, sustained the dignity of the principal sees, and especially that of Rome.[1] The French monarchs of the first dynasty, the Carlovingian family and their great chief, the Saxon line of emperors, the kings of England and Leon, set hardly any bounds to their liberality, as numerous charters still extant in diplomatic collections attest. Many churches possessed seven or eight thousand mansi; one with but two thousand passed for only indifferently rich.[2] But it must be remarked that many of these donations are of lands uncultivated and unappropriated. The monasteries acquired legitimate riches by the culture of these deserted tracts and by the prudent management of their revenues, which were less exposed to the ordinary means of dissipation than those of the laity. Their wealth, continually accumulated, enabled them to become the regular purchasers of landed estates, especially in the time of the crusades, when the fiefs of the nobility were constantly in the market for sale or mortgage.[4]

Sometimes improperly acquired.

If the possessions of ecclesiastical communities had all been as fairly earned, we could find nothing in them to reprehend. But other sources of wealth were less pure, and they derived their wealth from many sources. Those who entered into a monastery threw frequently their whole estates into the common stock; and even the children of rich parents were expected to make a donation of land on assuming the cowl. Some gave their property to the church before entering on military expeditions; gifts were made by some to take effect after their lives, and bequests by many in the terrors of dissolution.

[1] St. Marc, t. i. p. 281; Giannone, l. v. c. 12.

[2] Schmidt, t. ii. p. 205.

[3] Muratori, Dissert. 65; Du Cange. v Eremus.

[4] Heeren, Essai sur les Croisades, p 166; Schmidt, t. iii. p. 293.

Even those legacies to charitable purposes, which the clergy could with more decency and speciousness recommend, and of which the administration was generally confined to them, were frequently applied to their own benefit.[1] They failed not, above all, to inculcate upon the wealthy sinner that no atonement could be so acceptable to Heaven as liberal presents to its earthly delegates.[2] To die without allotting a portion of worldly wealth to pious uses was accounted almost like suicide, or a refusal of the last sacraments; and hence intestacy passed for a sort of fraud upon the church, which she punished by taking the administration of the deceased's effects into her own hands. This, however, was peculiar to England, and seems to have been the case there only from the reign of Henry III. to that of Edward III., when the bishop took a portion of the intestate's personal estate for the advantage of the church and poor, instead of distributing it among his next of kin.[3] The canonical penances imposed upon repentant offenders, extravagantly severe in themselves, were commuted for money or for immovable possessions — a fertile though scandalous source of monastic wealth, which the popes afterwards diverted into their own coffers by the usage of dispensations and indulgences.[4] The church lands enjoyed an immunity from taxes, though not in general from military service, when of a feudal tenure.[5] But their tenure was frequently in what was called frankalmoign, without any obligation of service. Hence it became a customary fraud

1 Primò sacris pastoribus data est facultas, ut hæreditatis portio in pauperes et egenos dispergeretur; sed sensim ecclesiæ quoque in pauperum censum venerunt, atque intestatæ gentis mens credita est proclivior in eas futura fuisse: quâ ex re pinguius illarum patrimonium evasit. Immò episcopi ipsi in rem suam ejusmodi consuetudinem interdum convertebant: ac tributum evasit, quod antea pii moris fuit. Muratori, Antiquitates Italiæ, t. v. Dissert. 67.

2 Muratori, Dissert. 67 (Antiquit. Italiæ, t. v. p. 1055), has preserved a curious charter of an Italian count, who declares that, struck with reflections upon his sinful state, he had taken counsel with certain religious how he should atone for his offences. Accepto consilio ab iis, excepto si renunciare sæculo possem, nullum esse melius inter eleemosinarum virtutes, quàm si de propriis meis substantiis in monasterium concederem. Hoc consilium ab iis libenter, et ardentissimo animo ego accepi.

3 Selden, vol. iii. p. 1676; Prynne's Constitutions, vol. iii. p. 18; Blackstone, vol. ii. chap. 32. In France the lord of the fief seems to have taken the whole spoil. Du Cange, v. Intestatus.

4 Muratori, Dissert. 68.

5 Palgrave has shown that the Anglo-Saxon clergy were not exempt, originally at least, from the *trinoda necessitas* imposed on all alodial proprietors. They were better treated on the Continent; and Boniface exclaims that in no part of the world was such servitude imposed on the church as among the English. English Commonwealth, i. 158. But when we look at the charters collected in Kemble's Codex Diplomaticus (most or nearly all of them in favor of the church), we shall hardly think they were ill off, though they might be forced sometimes to repair a bridge, or send their tenants against the Danes.

of lay proprietors to grant estates to the church, which they received again by way of fief or lease, exempted from public burdens. And, as if all these means of accumulating what they could not legitimately enjoy were insufficient, the monks prostituted their knowledge of writing to the purpose of forging charters in their own favor, which might easily impose upon an ignorant age, since it has required a peculiar science to detect them in modern times. Such rapacity might seem incredible in men cut off from the pursuits of life and the hope of posterity, if we did not behold every day the unreasonableness of avarice and the fervor of professional attachments.[1]

Tithes.

As an additional source of revenue, and in imitation of the Jewish law, the payment of tithes was recommended or enjoined. These, however, were not applicable at first to the maintenance of a resident clergy. Parochial divisions, as they now exist, did not take place, at least in some countries, till several centuries after the establishment of Christianity.[2] The rural churches, erected successively as the necessities of a congregation required, or the piety of a landlord suggested, were in fact a sort of chapels dependent on the cathedral, and served by itinerant ministers at the bishop's discretion.[3] The bishop himself

1 Muratori's 65th, 67th, and 68th Dissertations on the Antiquities of Italy have furnished the principal materials of my text, with Father Paul's Treatise on Benefices, especially chaps. 19 and 29. Giannone, loc. cit. and l. iv. c. 12; l. v. c. 6; l. x. c. 12. Schmidt, Hist. des. Allemands, t. i. p. 370; t. ii. p. 203, 462; t. iv. p. 202. Fleury, III. Discours sur l'Hist. Ecclés. Du Cange, voc. Precaria.

2 Muratori, Dissert. 74, and Fleury, Institutions au Droit ecclésiastique, t. i. p. 162, refer the origin of parishes to the fourth century; but this must be limited to the most populous part of the empire.

3 These were not always itinerant; commonly, perhaps, they were dependants of the lord, appointed by the bishop on his nomination. — Lehuerou, Institut. Carolingiennes, p. 526, who quotes a capitulary of the emperor Lothaire in 825. "De clericis vero laicorum, unde nonnulli eorum conqueri videantur, eo quod quidam episcopi ad eorum preces nolint in ecclesiis suis eos, cum utiles sint, ordinare, visum nobis fuit, ut . . . . et cum caritate et ratione utiles et idonei eligantur; et si laicus idoneum utilemque clericum obtulerit nulla qualibet occasione ab episcopo sine ratione certa repellatur; et si rejiciendus est, propter scandalum vitandum evidenti ratione manifestetur." Another capitulary of Charles the Bald, in 864, forbids the establishment of priests in the churches of patrons, or their ejection without the bishop's consent: — "De his qui sine consensu episcopi presbyteros in ecclesiis *suis* constituunt, vel de ecclesiis dejiciunt." Thus the churches are recognized as the property of the lord; and the parish may be considered as an established division, at least very commonly. so early as the Carlovingian empire. I do not by any means deny that it was partially known in France before that time.

Guizot reckons the patronage of churches by the laity among the circumstances which diminished or retarded ecclesiastical power. (Leçon 13.) It may have been so; but without this patronage there would have been very few parish churches. It separated, in some degree, the interests of the secular clergy from those of the bishops and the regulars.

received the tithes, and apportioned them as he thought fit. A capitulary of Charlemagne, however, regulates their division into three parts; one for the bishop and his clergy, a second for the poor, and a third for the support of the fabric of the church.[1] Some of the rural churches obtained by episcopal concessions the privileges of baptism and burial, which were accompanied with a fixed share of tithes, and seem to imply the residence of a minister. The same privileges were gradually extended to the rest; and thus a complete parochial division was finally established. But this was hardly th case in England till near the time of the conquest.[2]

The slow and gradual manner in which parochial churches became independent appears to be of itself a sufficient answer to those who ascribe a great antiquity to the universal payment of tithes. There are, however, more direct proofs that this species of ecclesiastical property was acquired not only by degrees but with considerable opposition. We find the payment of tithes first enjoined by the canons of a provincial council in France near the end of the sixth century. From the ninth to the end of the twelfth, or even later, it is continually enforced by similar authority.[3] Father Paul remarks that most of the sermons preached about the eighth century inculcate this as a duty, and even seem to place the summit of Christian perfection in its performance.[4] This reluctant submission of the people to a general and permanent tribute is perfectly consistent with the eagerness displayed by them in accumulating voluntary donations upon the church. Charlemagne was the first who gave the confirmation of a civil statute to these ecclesiastical injunctions; no one at least has, so far as I know, adduced any earlier law for the payment of tithes than one of his capitularies.[5] But it would be precipitate to infer either that the practice had not already gained ground to a considerable extent, through the influence of ecclesiastical authority, or, on the other hand, that it became

1 Schmidt, t. ii. p 206. This seems to have been founded on an ancient canon, F. Paul, c. 7.

2 Collier's Ecclesiastical History, p. 229.

3 Selden's History of Tithes, vol. iii. p. 1108, edit. Wilkins. Tithes are said by Giannone to have been enforced by some papal decrees in the sixth century. l. iii c. 6.

4 Treatise on Benefices, c. 11.

5 Mably, (Observations sur l'Hist. de France, t. i. p. 238 et 438) has, with remarkable rashness, attacked the current opinion that Charlemagne established the legal obligation of tithes, and denied that any of his capitularies bear such an interpretation. Those which he quotes have indeed a different meaning; but he has overlooked an express enactment in 789 (Baluzii Capitularia, t. i. p. 253), which admits of no question; and I believe that there are others in confirmation.

universal in consequence of the commands of Charlemagne.[1] In the subsequent ages it was very common to appropriate tithes, which had originally been payable to the bishop, either towards the support of particular churches, or, according to the prevalent superstition, to monastic foundations.[2] These arbitrary consecrations, though the subject of complaint, lasted, by a sort of prescriptive right of the landholder, till about the year 1200. It was nearly at the same time that the obligation of paying tithes, which had been originally confined to those called predial, or the fruits of the earth, was extended, at least in theory, to every species of profit, and to the wages of every kind of labor.[3]

Spoliation of church property.

Yet there were many hindrances that thwarted the clergy in their acquisition of opulence, and a sort of reflux that set sometimes very strongly against them. In times of barbarous violence nothing can thoroughly compensate for the inferiority of physical strength and prowess. The ecclesiastical history of the middle ages presents one long contention of fraud against robbery; of acquisitions made by the church through such means as I have described, and torn from her by lawless power. Those very men who in the hour of sickness and impending death showered the gifts of expiatory devotion upon her altars, had passed the sunshine of their lives in sacrilegious plunder. Notwithstanding the frequent instances of extreme reverence for religious institutions among the nobility, we should be deceived in supposing this to be their general character. Rapacity, not less insatiable than that of the abbots, was commonly united with a daring fierceness that the abbots could not resist.[4] In every country we find continual lamen-

[1] The grant of Ethelwolf in 855 has appeared to some antiquaries the most probable origin of the general right to tithes in England [NOTE I.] It is said by Marina that tithes were not legally established in Castile till the reign of Alfonso X. Ensayo sobre les Siete Partidas, c. 359.

[2] Selden, p. 1114 et seq.; Coke, 2 Inst. p. 641.

[3] Selden's History of Tithes; Treatise on Benefices, c. 28; Giannone, l. x. c. 12.

[4] The church was often compelled to grant leases of her lands, under the name of *precariæ*, to laymen, who probably rendered little or no service in return, though a rent or *census* was expressed in he instrument. These *precariæ* seem to have been for life, but were frequently renewed. They are not to be confounded with *terræ censuales*, or lands let to a tenant at rack-rent, which of course formed a considerable branch of revenue. The grant was called *precaria* from being obtained at the prayer of a grantee; and the uncertainty of its renewal seems to have given rise to the adjective *precarious*.

In the ninth century, though the pretensions of the bishops were never higher, the church itself was more pillaged under pretext of these *precariæ*, and in other ways, than at any former time. — See Du Cange for a long article on Precariæ.

tation over the plunder of ecclesiastical possessions. Charles Martel is reproached with having given the first notorious example of such spoliation. It was not, however, commonly practised by sovereigns. But the evil was not the less universally felt. The parochial tithes especially, as the hand of robbery falls heaviest upon the weak, were exposed to unlawful seizure. In the tenth and eleventh centuries nothing was more common than to see the revenues of benefices in the hands of lay impropriators, who employed curates at the cheapest rate; an abuse that has never ceased in the church.[1] Several attempts were made to restore these tithes; but even Gregory VII. did not venture to proceed in it;[2] and indeed it is highly probable that they might be held in some instances by a lawful title.[3] Sometimes the property of monasteries was dilapidated by corrupt abbots, whose acts, however clandestine and unlawful, it was not easy to revoke. And both the bishops and convents were obliged to invest powerful lay protectors, under the name of advocates, with considerable fiefs, as the price of their assistance against depredators. But these advocates became too often themselves the spoilers, and oppressed the helpless ecclesiastics for whose defence they had been engaged.[4]

If it had not been for these drawbacks, the clergy must, one would imagine, have almost acquired the exclusive property of the soil. They did enjoy, according to some authorities, nearly one half of England, and, I believe, a greater proportion in some countries of Europe.[5] They had reached, perhaps, their zenith in respect of territorial prop-

[1] Du Cange, voc. Abbas.

[2] Schmidt, t iv. p. 204. At an assembly held at St. Denis in 997 the bishops proposed to restore the tithes to the secular clergy; but such a tumult was excited by this attempt, that the meeting was broken up. Recueil des Historiens, t. xi. præfat. p. 212.

[3] Selden's Hist. of Tithes, p. 1136. The third council of Lateran restrains laymen from transferring their impropriated tithes to other laymen. Velly, Hist. de France, t. iii. p. 235. This seems tacitly to admit that their possession was lawful, at least by prescription.

[4] For the injuries sustained by ecclesiastical proprietors, see Muratori, Dissert. 72. Du Cange, v. Advocatus. Schmidt, t. ii. p. 220, 470; t. iii. p. 290; t. iv. p. 188, 202. Recueil des Historiens, t. xi. præfat. p. 184. Martenne, Thesaurus Anecdotorum, t. i. p. 595. Vaissette, Hist. de Languedoc, t. ii. p. 109, and Appendix, passim.

[5] Turner's Hist. of England, vol. ii. p. 413, from Avesbury. According to a calculation founded on a passage in Knyghton, the revenue of the English church in 1337 amounted to 730,000 marks per annum. Macpherson's Annals of Commerce, vol. i. p. 519; Histoire du Droit public Ecclés. François, t. i. p. 214. Anthony Harmer (Henry Wharton) says that the monasteries did not possess one fifth of the land; and I incline to think that he is nearer the truth than Mr. Turner, who puts the wealth of the church at above 28,000 knights' fees out of 53,215. The bishops' lands could not by any means account for the difference; so that Mr. Turner was probably deceived by his authority.

erty about the conclusion of the twelfth century.[1] After that time the disposition to enrich the clergy by pious donations grew more languid, and was put under certain legal restraints, to which I shall hereafter advert; but they became rather more secure from forcible usurpations.

Ecclesiastical jurisdiction.

The acquisitions of wealth by the church were hardly so remarkable, and scarcely contributed so much to her greatness, as those innovations upon the ordinary course of justice which fall under the head of ecclesiastical jurisdiction and immunity. It is hardly, perhaps, necessary to caution the reader that rights of territorial justice, possessed by ecclesiastics in virtue of their fiefs, are by no means included in this description. Episcopal jurisdiction, properly so called, may be considered as depending upon the choice of litigant parties, upon their condition, and upon the subject-matter of their differences.

Arbitrative.

1. The arbitrative authority of ecclesiastical pastors, if not coeval with Christianity, grew up very early in the church, and was natural, or even necessary, to an insulated and persecuted society.[2] Accustomed to feel a strong aversion to the imperial tribunals, and even to consider a recurrence to them as hardly consistent with their profession, the early Christians retained somewhat of a similar prejudice even after the establishment of their religion. The arbitration of their bishops still seemed a less objectionable mode of settling differences. And this arbitrative jurisdiction was powerfully supported by a law of Constantine, which directed the civil magistrate to enforce the execution of episcopal awards. Another edict, ascribed to the same emperor, and annexed to the Theodosian code, extended the jurisdiction of the bishops to all causes which either party chose to refer to it, even where they had already commenced in a secular court, and declared the bishop's sentence not subject to appeal. This edict has clearly been proved to be a forgery. It is evident, by a novel of Valentinian III., about 450, that the church had still no jurisdiction in questions of a temporal

[1] The great age of monasteries in England was the reigns of Henry I., Stephen, and Henry II. Lyttelton's Henry II. vol. ii. p. 329. David I. of Scotland, contemporary with Henry II., was also a noted founder of monasteries. Dalrymple's Annals.

[2] 1 Corinth. v. 4. The word *ἐξουθενημένους*, rendered in our version "of no reputation," has been interpreted by some to mean persons destitute of coercive authority, referees. The passage at least tends to discourage suits before a secular judge.

nature, except by means of the joint reference of contending parties. Some expressions, indeed, used by the emperor, seem intended to repress the spirit of encroachment upon the civil magistrates, which had probably begun to manifest itself. Charlemagne, indeed, in one of his capitularies, is said by some modern writers to have repeated all the absurd and enormous provisions of the spurious constitution in the Theodosian code.[1] But this capitulary is erroneously ascribed to Charlemagne. It is only found in one of the three books subjoined by Benedict Levita to the four books of capitularies collected by Ansegisus; these latter relating only to Charlemagne and Louis, but the others comprehending many of later emperors and kings. And, what is of more importance, it seems exceedingly doubtful whether this is any genuine capitulary at all. It is not referred to any prince by name, nor is it found in any other collection. Certain it is that we do not find the church, in her most arrogant temper, asserting the full privileges contained in this capitulary.[2]

Coercive over the clergy in civil

2. If it was considered almost as a general obligation upon the primitive Christians to decide their civil disputes by internal arbitration, much more would this be incumbent upon the clergy. The canons of several councils, in the fourth and fifth centuries, sentence a bishop or priest to deposition, who should bring any suit, civil or even criminal, before a secular magistrate. This must, it should appear, be confined to causes where the defendant was a clerk; since the ecclesiastical court had hitherto no coercive jurisdiction over the laity. It was not so easy to induce laymen, in their suits against clerks, to prefer the episcopal tribunal. The emperors were not at all disposed to favor this species of encroachment till the reign of Justinian, who ordered civil suits against ecclesiastics to be carried only before the bishops. Yet this was accompanied by a provision that a party dissatisfied with the sentence might apply to the secular magistrate, not as an appellant, but a coördinate jurisdiction; for if different judgments were given in the two courts, the process was ultimately referred to the emperor.[3] But the early Merovingian kings adopted

[1] Baluzii Capitularia, t. i. p. 9018.

[2] Gibbon, c. xx. Giannone, l. ii. c. 8; l. iii. c. 6; l. vi. c. 7. Schmidt, t. ii. p. 208. Fleury, 7me Discours, and Institutions au Droit Ecclésiastique, t. ii. p. 1. Mémoires de l'Académie des Inscriptions, t. xxxix. p. 566.

[3] This was also established about the same time by Athalaric king of the Ostrogoths, and of course affected the

the exclusive jurisdiction of the bishop over causes wherein clerks were interested, without any of the checks which Justinian had provided. Many laws enacted during their reigns, and under Charlemagne, strictly prohibit the temporal magistrates from entertaining complaints against the children of the church.

and criminal suits.

This jurisdiction over the civil causes of clerks was not immediately attended with an equally exclusive cognizance of criminal offences imputed to them, wherein the state is so deeply interested, and the church could inflict so inadequate a punishment. Justinian appears to have reserved such offences for trial before the imperial magistrate, though with a material provision that the sentence against a clerk should not be executed without the consent of the bishop or the final decision of the emperor. The bishop is not expressly invested with this controlling power by the laws of the Merovingians; but they enact that he must be present at the trial of one of his clerks; which probably was intended to declare the necessity of his concurrence in the judgment. The episcopal order was indeed absolutely exempted from secular jurisdiction by Justinian; a privilege which it had vainly endeavored to establish under the earlier emperors. France permitted the same immunity; Chilperic, one of the most arbitrary of her kings, did not venture to charge some of his bishops with treason, except before a council of their brethren. Finally, Charlemagne seems to have extended to the whole body of the clergy an absolute exemption from the judicial authority of the magistrate.[1]

Over particular causes.

3. The character of a cause, as well as of the parties engaged, might bring it within the limits of ecclesiastical jurisdiction. In all questions simply religious the church had an original right of decision; in those of a temporal nature the civil magistrate had, by the imperial constitution, as exclusive an authority.[2]

popes who were his subjects. St. Marc, t. i. p. 60; Fleury, Hist. Ecclés. t. vii. p. 292.

1 Mémoires de l'Académie, ubi supra; Giannone, l. iii. c. 6; Schmidt, t. ii. p. 236; Fleury, ubi supra.

Some of these writers do not state the law of Charlemagne so strongly. Nevertheless the words of a capitulary in 789, Ut clerici ecclesiastici ordinis si culpam incurrerint apud ecclesiasticos judicentur, non apud sæculares, are sufficiently general (Baluz. Capitul. t. i. p. 227); and the same is expressed still more forcibly in the collection published by Ansegisus under Louis the Debonair. (Id. p. 904 and 1115.) See other proofs in Fleury, Hist. Ecclés. t. ix. p. 607.

2 Quoties de religione agitur, episcopos oportet judicare; alteras vero causas quæ ad ordinarios cognitores vel ad usum publici juris pertinent, legibus oportet audiri. Lex Arcadii et Honorii apud Mém. de l'Académie, t. xxxix. p. 571.

Later ages witnessed strange innovations in this respect, when the spiritual courts usurped, under sophistical pretences, almost the whole administration of justice. But these encroachments were not, I apprehend, very striking till the twelfth century; and as about the same time measures, more or less vigorous and successful, began to be adopted in order to restrain them, I shall defer this part of the subject for the present.

Political power of clergy.

In this sketch of the riches and jurisdiction of the hierarchy I may seem to have implied their political influence, which is naturally connected with the two former. They possessed, however, more direct means of acquiring temporal power. Even under the Roman emperors they had found their road into palaces; they were sometimes ministers, more often secret counsellors, always necessary but formidable allies, whose support was to be conciliated, and interference to be respected. But they assumed a far more decided influence over the new kingdoms of the West. They were entitled, in the first place, by the nature of those free governments, to a privilege unknown under the imperial despotism, that of assisting in the deliberative assemblies of the nation. Councils of bishops, such as had been convoked by Constantine and his successors, were limited in their functions to decisions of faith or canons of ecclesiastical discipline. But the northern nations did not so well preserve the distinction between secular and spiritual legislation. The laity seldom, perhaps, gave their suffrage to the canons of the church; but the church was not so scrupulous as to trespassing upon the province of the laity. Many provisions are found in the canons of national and even provincial councils which relate to the temporal constitution of the state. Thus one held at Calcluith (an unknown place in England), in 787, enacted that none but legitimate princes should be raised to the throne, and not such as were engendered in adultery or incest. But it is to be observed that, although this synod was strictly ecclesiastical, being summoned by the pope's legate, yet the kings of Mercia and Northumberland, with many of their nobles, confirmed the canons by their signature. As for the councils held under the Visigoth kings of Spain during the seventh century, it is not easy to determine whether they are to be considered as ecclesiastical or temporal assemblies.[1] No kingdom was so

[1] Marina, Teoria de las Cortes, t. i. p. 9

thoroughly under the bondage of the hierarchy as Spain.[1] The first dynasty of France seem to have kept their national convention, called the Field of March, more distinct from merely ecclesiastical councils.

The bishops acquired and retained a great part of their ascendency by a very respectable instrument of power, intellectual superiority. As they alone were acquainted with the art of writing, they were naturally entrusted with political correspondence, and with the framing of the laws. As they alone knew the elements of a few sciences, the education of royal families devolved upon them as a necessary duty. In the fall of Rome their influence upon the barbarians wore down the asperities of conquest, and saved the provincials half the shock of that tremendous revolution. As captive Greece is said to have subdued her Roman conqueror, so Rome, in her own turn of servitude, cast the fetters of a moral captivity upon the fierce invaders of the north. Chiefly through the exertions of the bishops, whose ambition may be forgiven for its effects, her religion, her language, in part even her laws, were transplanted into the courts of Paris and Toledo, which became a degree less barbarous by imitation.[2]

Supremacy of the state;

Notwithstanding, however, the great authority and privileges of the church, it was decidedly subject to the supremacy of the crown, both during the continuance of the Western empire and after its subversion. The emperors convoked, regulated, and dissolved universal councils; the kings of France and Spain exercised the same right over the synods of their national churches.[3] The Ostrogoth kings of Italy fixed by their edicts the limits within which matrimony was prohibited on account of consanguinity, and granted dispensations from them.[4] Though the Roman emperors left episcopal elections to the clergy and people of the diocese, in which they were followed by the Ostrogoths and Lombards, yet they often interfered so far as to confirm a

[1] See instances of the temporal power of the Spanish bishops in Fleury, Hist. Ecclés. t. viii. p. 368, 397; t. ix. p. 68, &c.

[2] Schmidt, t. i. p. 365.

[3] Encyclopédie, art. Concile. Schmidt, t. i. p. 384. De Marca, De Concordantiâ Sacerdotii et Imperii, l. ii. c. 9, 11; et l. iv. passim.

The last of these sometimes endeavors to extenuate the royal supremacy, but his own work furnishes abundant evidence of it; especially l. vi. c. 19, &c. For the ecclesiastical independence of Spain, down to the eleventh century, see Marina, Ensayo sobre las Siete Partidas, c. 322, &c.; and De Marca, l. vi. c 23.

[4] Giannone, l. iii. c. 6.

decision or to determine a contest. The kings of France went further, and seem to have invariably either nominated the bishops, or, what was nearly tantamount, recommended their own candidate to the electors.

especially of Charlemagne.

But the sovereign who maintained with the greatest vigor his ecclesiastical supremacy was Charlemagne. Most of the capitularies of his reign relate to the discipline of the church; principally indeed taken from the ancient canons, but not the less receiving an additional sanction from his authority.[1] Some of his regulations, which appear to have been original, are such as men of high church principles would, even in modern times, deem infringments of spiritual independence; that no legend of doubtful authority should be read in the churches, but only the canonical books, and that no saint should be honored whom the whole church did not acknowledge. These were not passed in a synod of bishops, but enjoined by the sole authority of the emperor, who seems to have arrogated a legislative power over the church which he did not possess in temporal affairs. Many of his other laws relating to the ecclesiastical constitution are enacted in a general council of the lay nobility as well as of prelates, and are so blended with those of a secular nature, that the two orders may appear to have equally consented to the whole. His father Pepin, indeed, left a remarkable precedent in a council held in 744, where the Nicene faith is declared to be established, and even a particular heresy condemned, with the consent of the bishops and nobles. But whatever share we may imagine the laity in general to have had in such matters, Charlemagne himself did not consider even theological decisions as beyond his province; and, in more than one instance, manifested a determination not to surrender his own judgment, even in questions of that nature, to any ecclesiastical authority.[2]

1 Baluzii Capitularia, passim; Schmidt, t. ii. p. 239; Gaillard, Vie de Charlemagne, t. iii.

2 Charlemagne had apparently devised an ecclesiastical theory, which would now be called Erastian, and perhaps not very short of that of Henry VIII. He directs the clergy what to preach in his own name, and uses the first person in ecclesiastical canons. Yet, if we may judge by the events, the bishops lost no part of their permanent ascendency in the state through this interference, though compelled to acknowledge the supremacy of a great mind. By a vigorous repression of those secular propensities which were displaying themselves among the superior clergy, he endeavored to render their moral influence more effective. This, however, could not be achieved in the ninth century; nor could it have been brought about by any external power. Nor was it easily consistent with the continual presence of the bishops in national assemblies, which had become essential to the polity of his age, and

This part of Charlemagne's conduct is duly to be taken into the account before we censure his vast extension of ecclesiastical privileges. Nothing was more remote from his character than the bigotry of those weak princes who have suffered the clergy to reign under their names. He acted upon a systematic plan of government, conceived by his own comprehensive genius, but requiring too continual an application of similar talents for durable execution. It was the error of a superior mind, zealous for religion and learning to believe that men dedicated to the functions of the one, and possessing what remained of the other, might, through strict rules of discipline, enforced by the constant vigilance of the sovereign, become fit instruments to reform and civilize a barbarous empire. It was the error of a magnanimous spirit to judge too favorably of human nature, and to presume that great trusts would be fulfilled, and great benefits remembered.

Pretensions of the hierarchy in the ninth century.

It is highly probable, indeed, that an ambitious hierarchy did not endure without reluctance this imperial supremacy of Charlemagne, though it was not expedient for them to resist a prince so formidable, and from whom they had so much to expect. But their dissatisfaction at a scheme of government incompatible with their own objects of perfect independence produced a violent recoil under Louis the Debonair, who attempted to act the censor of ecclesiastical abuses with as much earnestness as his father, though with very inferior qualifications for so delicate an undertaking. The bishops accordingly were among the chief instigators of those numerous revolts of his children which harrassed this emperor. They set, upon one occasion, the first example of an usurpation which was to become very dangerous to society — the deposition of sovereigns by ecclesiastical authority. Louis, a prisoner in the hands of his enemies, had been intimidated enough to undergo a public penance; and the bishops pretended that, according to a canon of the church, he was incapable of returning

with which he would not, for several reasons, have wholly dispensed. Yet it appears, by a remarkable capitulary of 811, that he had perceived the inconvenience of allowing the secular and spiritual powers to clash with each other: — Discutiendum est atque interveniendum in quantum se episcopus aut abbas rebus secularibus debeat inserere, vel in quantum comes, vel alter laicus, in ecclesiastica negotia. But as the laity, himself excepted, had probably interfered very little in church affairs, this capitulary seems to be restrictive of the prelates.

afterwards to a secular life or preserving the character of sovereignty.[1] Circumstances enabled him to retain the empire in defiance of this sentence; but the church had tasted the pleasure of trampling upon crowned heads, and was eager to repeat the experiment. Under the disjointed and feeble administration of his posterity in their several kingdoms, the bishops availed themselves of more than one opportunity to exalt their temporal power. Those weak Carlovingian princes, in their mutual animosities, encouraged the pretensions of a common enemy. Thus Charles the Bald and Louis of Bavaria, having driven their brother Lothaire from his dominions, held an assembly of some bishops, who adjudged him unworthy to reign, and, after exacting a promise from the two allied brothers to govern better than he had done, permitted and commanded them to divide his territories.[2] After concurring in this unprecedented encroachment, Charles the Bald had little right to complain when, some years afterwards, an assembly of bishops declared himself to have forfeited his crown, released his subjects from their allegiance, and transferred his kingdom to Louis of Bavaria. But, in truth, he did not pretend to deny the principle which he had contributed to maintain. Even in his own behalf he did not appeal to the rights of sove-

[1] Habitu sæculi se exuens habitum pœnitentis per impositionem manuum episcoporum suscepit; ut post tantam talemque pœnitentiam nemo ultra ad militiam sæcularem redeat. Acta exauctorationis Ludovici, apud Schmidt, t. ii. p. 68. There was a sort of precedent, though not, I think, very apposite, for this doctrine of implied abdication, in the case of Wamba king of the Visigoths in Spain, who, having been clothed with a monastic dress, according to a common superstition, during a dangerous illness, was afterwards adjudged by a council incapable of resuming his crown; to which he voluntarily submitted. The story, as told by an original writer, quoted in Baronius ad A.D. 681, is too obscure to warrant any positive inference; though I think we may justly suspect a fraudulent contrivance between the bishops and Ervigius, the successor of Wamba. The latter, besides his monastic attire, had received the last sacraments; after which he might be deemed civilly dead. Fleury, 3me Discours sur l'Hist. Ecclésiast., puts this case too strongly when he tells us that the bishops *deposed* Wamba; it may have been a voluntary abdication, influenced by superstition, or, perhaps, by disease. A late writer has taken a different view of this event, the deposition of Louis at Compiègne. It was not, he thinks, une hardiesse sacerdotale, une témérité ecclésiastique, mais bien une lâcheté politique. Ce n'était point une tentative pour élever l'autorité religieuse au-dessus de l'autorité royale dans les affaires temporelles; c'était, au contraire, un abaissement servile de la première devant le monde. Fauriel, Hist. de la Gaule Méridionale, iv. 150. In other words, the bishops lent themselves to the aristocratic faction which was in rebellion against Louis. Ranke, as has been seen in an early note, thinks that they acted out of revenge for his deviation from the law of 817, which established the unity of the empire. The bishops, in fact, had so many secular and personal interests and sympathies, that we cannot always judge of their behavior upon general principles.

[2] Schmidt, t. ii. p. 77. Velly t. ii p. 61; see, too, p. 74.

reigns, and of the nation whom they represent. "No one," says this degenerate grandson of Charlemagne, "ought to have degraded me from the throne to which I was consecrated, until at least I had been heard and judged by the bishops, through whose ministry I was consecrated, who are called the thrones of God, in which God sitteth, and by whom he dispenses his judgments; to whose paternal chastisement I was willing to submit, and do still submit myself."[1]

These passages are very remarkable, and afford a decisive proof that the power obtained by national churches, through the superstitious prejudices then received, and a train of favorable circumstances, was as dangerous to civil government as the subsequent usurpations of the Roman pontiff, against which Protestant writers are apt too exclusively to direct their animadversions. Voltaire, I think, has remarked that the ninth century was the age of the bishops, as the eleventh and twelfth were of the popes. It seemed as if Europe was about to pass under as absolute a domination of the hierarchy as had been exercised by the priesthood of ancient Egypt or the Druids of Gaul. There is extant a remarkable instrument recording the election of Boson king of Arles, by which the bishops alone appear to have elevated him to the throne, without any concurrence of the nobility.[2] But it is inconceivable that such could have really been the case; and if the instrument is genuine, we must suppose it to have been framed in order to countenance future pretensions. For the clergy, by their exclusive knowledge of Latin, had it in their power to mould the language of public documents for their own purposes; a circumstance which should be cautiously kept in mind when we peruse instruments drawn up during the dark ages.

It was with an equal defiance of notorious truth that the bishop of Winchester, presiding as papal legate at an assemby of the clergy in 1141, during the civil war of Stephen and Matilda, asserted the right of electing a king of England to appertain principally to that order; and, by virtue of this unprecedented claim, raised Matilda to the throne.[3] England,

1 Schmidt, t. ii. p. 217.

2 Recueil des Historiens, t. ix. p. 304.

3 Ventilata est causa, says the Legate, coram majori parte cleri Angliæ, ad cujus jus potissimùm spectat principem eligere, simulque ordinare. Invocatâ itaque primò in auxlium Divinitate, filiam pacifici regis, &c., in Anglia Normanniæque dominam eligimus, et ei fidem et manutenementum promittimus. Gul Malmsb. p. 188.

indeed, has been obsequious, beyond most other countries, to the arrogance of her hierarchy; especially during the Anglo-Saxon period, when the nation was sunk in ignorance and effeminate superstition. Every one knows the story of king Edwy in some form or other, though I believe it impossible to ascertain the real circumstances of that controverted anecdote.[1] But, upon the supposition least favorable to the king, the behavior of Archbishop Odo and Dunstan was an intolerable outrage of spiritual tyranny.

Rise of the papal power. Its commencement.

But while the prelates of these nations, each within his respective sphere, were prosecuting their system of encroachment upon the laity, a new scheme was secretly forming within the bosom of the church, to enthral both that and the temporal governments of the world under an ecclesiastical monarch. Long before the earliest epoch that can be fixed for *modern* history, and, indeed, to speak fairly, almost as far back as ecclesiastical testimonies can carry us, the bishops of Rome had been venerated as first in rank among the rulers of the church. The nature of this primacy is doubtless a very controverted subject. It is, however, reduced by some moderate catholics to little more than a precedency attached to the see of Rome in consequence of its foundation by the chief of the apostles, as well as the dignity of the imperial city.[2] A sort of general superintendence was admitted as an attribute of this primacy, so that the bishops of Rome were entitled, and indeed bound, to remonstrate, when any error or irregularity came to their knowledge, especially in the western churches, a greater part of which had been planted by them, and were connected, as it were by filiation, with the common capital of the Roman empire and of Christendom.[4] Various causes

[1] [NOTE II.]

[2] These foundations of the Roman primacy are indicated by Valentinian III., a great favorer of that see, in a novel of the year 455: Cum igitur sedis apostolicæ primatum B. Petri meritum, qui est princeps sacerdotalis coronæ et Romanæ dignitas civitatis, sacræ etiam synodi firmavit auctoritas. The last words allude to the sixth canon of the Nicene council, which establishes or recognizes the patriarchal supremacy, in their respective districts, of the churches of Rome, Antioch, and Alexandria. De Marca, de Concordantiâ Sacerdotii et Imperii, l. i. c. 8. At a much earlier period, Irenæus rather vaguely, and Cyprian more positively, admit, or rather assert, the primacy of the church of Rome, which the latter seems even to have considered as a kind of centre of Catholic unity, though he resisted every attempt of that church to arrogate a controlling power.— See his treatise De Unitate Ecclesiæ. [1818.] [NOTE III.]

[3] Dupin, De antiquâ Ecclesiæ Disciplinâ, p. 306 et seqq.; Histoire du Droit public ecclésiastique Francois, p. 149. The opinion of the Roman see's supremacy, though apparently rather a vague and general notion, as it still continues in those Catholics who deny its infalli-

had a tendency to prevent the bishops of Rome from augmenting their authority in the East, and even to diminish that which they had occasionally exercised; the institution of patriarchs at Antioch, Alexandria, and afterwards at Constantinople, with extensive rights of jurisdiction; the difference of rituals and discipline; but, above all, the many disgusts taken by the Greeks, which ultimately produced an irreparable schism between the two churches in the ninth century. But within the pale of the Latin church every succeeding age enhanced the power and dignity of the Roman see. By the constitution of the church, such at least as it became in the fourth century, its divisions being arranged in conformity to those of the empire, every province ought to have its metropolitan, and every vicariate its ecclesiastical exarch or primate. The bishop of Rome presided, in the latter capacity, over the Roman vicariate, comprehending southern Italy, and the three chief Mediterranean islands. But as it happened, none of the ten provinces forming this division had any metropolitan; so that the popes exercised all metropolitical functions within them, such as the consecration of bishops, the convocation of synods, the ultimate decision of appeals, and many other sorts of authority. These provinces are sometimes called the Roman patriarchate; the bishops of Rome having always been reckoned one, generally indeed the first, of the patriarchs; each of whom was at the head of all the metropolitans within his limits, but without exercising those privileges which by the ecclesiastical constitution appertained to the latter. Though the Roman patriarchate, properly so called, was comparatively very small in extent, it gave its chief, for the reason mentioned, advantages in point of authority which the others did not possess.[1]

Patriarchate of Rome.

I may perhaps appear to have noticed circumstances interesting only to ecclesiastical scholars. But it is important to apprehend this distinction of the patriarchate from the primacy of Rome, because it was by extending the bounda-

bility, seems to have prevailed very much in the fourth century. Fleury brings remarkable proofs of this from the writings of Socrates, Sozomen, Ammianus Marcellinus, and Optatus. Hist. Ecclés. t. iii. p. 282, 320, 449; t. iv. p. 227.

[1] Dupin, De Antiquâ Eccles. Disciplinâ, p. 39, &c.; Giannone, Ist. di Napoli, l. ii. c. 8; l. iii c. 6.; De Marca, l. i. c. 7 et alibi. There is some disagreement among these writers as to the extent of the Roman patriarchate, which some suppose to have even at first comprehended all the western churches, though they admit that, in a more particular sense, it was confined to the vicariate of Rome

ries of the former, and by applying the maxims of her administration in the south of Italy to all the western churches, that she accomplished the first object of her scheme of usurpation, in subverting the provincial system of government under the metropolitans. Their first encroachment of this kind was in the province of Illyricum, which they annexed in a manner to their own patriarchate, by not permitting any bishops to be consecrated without their consent.[1] This was before the end of the fourth century. Their subsequent advances were, however, very gradual. About the middle of the sixth century we find them confirming the elections of archbishops of Milan.[2] They came by degrees to exercise, though not always successfully, and seldom without opposition, an appellant jurisdiction over the causes of bishops deposed or censured in provincial synods. This, indeed, had been granted, if we believe the fact, by the canons of a very early council, that of Sardica, in 347, so far as to permit the pope to order a revision of the process, but not to annul the sentence.[3] Valentinian III., influenced by Leo the Great, one of the most ambitious of pontiffs, had gone a great deal further, and established almost an absolute judicial supremacy in the Holy See.[4] But the metropolitans

[1] Dupin, p. 66; Fleury, Hist. Ecclés. t. v. p. 373. The ecclesiastical province of Illyricum included Macedonia. Siricius, the author of this encroachment, seems to have been one of the first usurpers. In a letter to the Spanish bishops (A.D. 375) he exalts his own authority very high. De Marca, l. i. c. 8.

[2] St. Marc, t. i. p. 139, 153.

[3] Dupin, p. 109; De Marca, l. vi. c. 14. These canons have been questioned, and Dupin does not seem to lay much stress on their authority, though I do not perceive that either he, or Fleury (Hist. Ecclés. t. iii. p. 372), doubts their genuineness. Sardica was a city of Illyricum, which the translator of Mosheim has confounded with Sardes.

Consultations or references to the bishop of Rome, in difficult cases of faith or discipline, had been common in early ages, and were even made by provincial and national councils. But these were also made to other bishops emiment for personal merit, or the dignity of their sees. The popes endeavored to claim this as a matter of right. Innocent I. asserts (A.D. 402) that he was to be consulted, quoties fidei ratio ventilatur; and Gelasius (A.D. 492), quantum ad religionem pertinet, non nisi apostolicæ sedi, juxtà canones, debetur summa judicii totius. As the oak is in the acorn, so did these maxims contain the system of Bellarmin. De Marca, l. i. c. 10; and l. vii. c. 12. Dupin.

[4] Some bishops belonging to the province of Hilary, metropolitan of Arles, appealed from his sentence to Leo, who not only entertained their appeal, but presumed to depose Hilary. This assumption of power would have had little effect, if it had not been seconded by the emperor in very unguarded language; hoc perenni sanctione decernimus, ne quid tam episcopis Gallicanis, quam aliarum provinciarum, contra consuetudinem veterem liceat sine auctoritate viri venerabilis papæ urbis æternæ tentare; sed illis omnibusque pro lege sit, quidquid sanxit vel sanxerit apostolicæ sedis auctoritas. De Marca, De Concordantiâ Sacerdotii et Imperii, l. i. c. 8. The same emperor enacted that any bishop who refused to attend the tribunal of the pope when summoned should be compelled by the governor of his province; ut quisquis episcoporum ad judicium Romani episcopi evocatus venire neglexerit, per moderatorem ejusdem provinciæ adesse cogatur. Id. l. vii. c. 13; Dupin, De Ant. Discipl. p. 29 et 171.

were not inclined to surrender their prerogatives; and, upon the whole, the papal authority had made no decisive progress in France, or perhaps anywhere beyond Italy, till the pontificate of Gregory I.

Gregory I. A.D. 590–604.

This celebrated person was not distinguished by learning, which he affected to depreciate, nor by his literary performances, which the best critics consider as below mediocrity, but by qualities more necessary for his purpose, intrepid ambition and unceasing activity. He maintained a perpetual correspondence with the emperors and their ministers, with the sovereigns of the western kingdoms, with all the hierarchy of the Catholic church; employing, as occasion dictated, the language of devotion, arrogance, or adulation.[1] Claims hitherto disputed, or half preferred, assumed under his hands a more definite form; and nations too ignorant to compare precedents or discriminate principles yielded to assertions confidently made by the authority which they most respected. Gregory dwelt more than his predecessors upon the power of the keys, exclusively, or at least principally, committed to St. Peter, which had been supposed in earlier times, as it is now by the Gallican Catholics, to be inherent in the general body of bishops, joint sharers of one indivisible episcopacy. And thus the patriarchal rights, being manifestly of mere ecclesiastical institution, were artfully confounded, or as it were merged, in the more paramount supremacy of the papal chair. From the time of Gregory the popes appear in a great measure to have thrown away that scaffolding, and relied in preference on the pious veneration of the people, and on the opportunities which might occur for enforcing their dominion with the pretence of divine authority.[2]

1 The flattering style in which this pontiff addressed Brunehaut and Phocas, the most flagitious monsters of his time, is mentioned in all civil and ecclesiastical histories. Fleury quotes a remarkable letter to the patriarchs of Antioch and Alexandria wherein he says that St. Peter has one see, divided into three, Rome, Antioch, and Alexandria; stooping to this absurdity, and inconsistence with his real system, in order to conciliate their alliance against his more immediate rival, the patriarch of Constantinople. Hist. Ecclés. t. viii. p. 124.

2 Gregory seems to have established the appellant jurisdiction of the see of Rome, which had been long in suspense. Stephen, a Spanish bishop, having been deposed, appealed to Rome. Gregory sent a legate to Spain, with full powers to confirm or rescind the sentence. He says in his letter on this occasion, à sede apostolicâ, quæ omnium ecclesiarum caput est, causa hæc audienda ac dirimenda fuerat. De Marca, l. vii. c. 18. In writing to the bishops of France he enjoins them to obey Virgilius bishop of Arles, whom he has appointed his legate in France, secundùm antiquam consuetudinem; so that, if any contention should arise in the church, he may appease it by his authority, as vicegerent

It cannot, I think, be said that any material acquisitions of ecclesiastical power were obtained by the successors of Gregory for nearly one hundred and fifty years.[1] As none of them possessed vigor and reputation equal to his own, it might even appear that the papal influence was retrograde.

of the apostolic see; auctoritatis suæ vigore, vicibus nempe apostolicæ sedis functus, discretâ moderatione compescat. Gregorii Opera, t. ii. p. 783 (edit. Benedict.); Dupin, p. 34; Pasquier, Recherches de la France, l. iii. c. 9.

[1] I observe that some modern publications annex considerable importance to a supposed concession of the title of Universal Bishop, made by the emperor Phocas in 606 to Boniface III., and even appear to date the papal supremacy from this epoch. Those who have imbibed this notion may probably have been misled by a loose expression in Mosheim's Ecclesiastical History, vol. ii. p. 169; though the general tenor of that passage by no means gives countenance to their opinion. But there are several strong objections to our considering this as a leading fact, much less as marking an era in the history of the papacy. 1. Its truth, as commonly stated, appears more than questionable. The Roman pontiffs, Gregory I. and Boniface III., had been vehemently opposing the assumption of this title by the patriarch of Constantinople, not as due to themselves, but as one to which no bishop could legitimately pretend. There would be something almost ridiculous in the emperor's immediately conferring an appellation on themselves which they had just disclaimed; and though this objection would not stand against evidence, yet when we find no better authority quoted for the fact than Baronius, who is no authority at all, it retains considerable weight. And indeed the want of early testimony is so decisive an objection to any alleged historical fact, that, but for the strange prepossessions of some men, one might rest the case here. Fleury takes no notice of this part of the story, though he tells us that Phocas compelled the patriarch of Constantinople to resign his title. 2. But if the strongest proof could be advanced for the authenticity of this circumstance, we might well deny its importance. The concession of Phocas could have been of no validity in Lombardy, France, and other western countries, where nevertheless the papal supremacy was incomparably more established than in the East. 3. Even within the empire it could have had no efficacy after the violent death of that usurper, which followed soon afterwards. 4. The title of Universal Bishop is not very intelligible; but, whatever it meant, the patriarchs of Constantinople had borne it before, and continued to bear it ever afterwards. (Dupin, De Antiquâ Disciplinâ, p. 329.) 5. The preceding popes, Pelagius II. and Gregory I. had constantly disclaimed the appellation, though it had been adopted by some towards Leo the Great in the council of Chalcedon (Fleury, t. viii. p. 95); nor does it appear to have been retained by the successors of Boniface. It is even laid down in the decretum of Gratian that the pope is not styled universal: nec etiam Romanus pontifex universalis appellatur (p. 303, edit. 1591), though some refer its assumption to the ninth century. Nouveau Traité de Diplomatique, t. v. p. 93. In fact it has never been an usual title. 6. The popes had unquestionably exercised a species of supremacy for more than two centuries before this time, which had lately reached a high point of authority under Gregory I. The rescript of Valentinian III. in 455, quoted in a former note, would certainly be more to the purpose than the letter of Phocas. 7. Lastly, there are no sensible marks of this supremacy making a more rapid progress for a century and a half after the pretended grant of that emperor. [1818.] The earliest mention of this transaction that I have found, and one which puts an end to the pretended concession of such a title as Universal Bishop, is in a brief general chronology, by Bede, entitled 'De Temporum Ratione.' He only says of Phocas, — Hic, rogante papa Bonifacio, statuit sedem Romanæ et apostolicæ ecclesiæ caput esse omnium ecclesiarum, quia ecclesia Constantinopolitana primam se omnium ecclesiarum scribebat. Bedæ Opera, curâ Giles, vol. vi. p. 323. This was probably the exact truth; and the subsequent additions were made by some zealous partisans of Rome, to be seized hold of in a later age, and turned against her by some of her equally zealous enemies. The distinction generally made is, that the pope is "universalis ecclesiæ episcopus," but not "episcopus universalis;" that is, he has no immediate jurisdiction in the dioceses of other bishops, though he can correct them for the undue exercise of their own. The Ultramontanes of course go further.

But in effect the principles which supported it were taking deeper root, and acquiring strength by occasional though not very frequent exercise. Appeals to the pope were sometimes made by prelates dissatisfied with a local sentence; but his judgment of reversal was not always executed, as we perceive by the instance of bishop Wilfrid.[1] National councils were still convoked by princes, and canons enacted under their authority by the bishops who attended. Though the church of Lombardy was under great subjection during this period, yet those of France, and even of England, planted as the latter had been by Gregory, continued to preserve a tolerable measure of independence.[2] The first striking infringement of this was made through the influence of an Englishman, Winfrid, better known as St. Boniface, the apostle of Germany. Having undertaken the conversion of Thuringia, and other still heathen countries, he applied to the pope for a commission, and was consecrated bishop without any determinate see. Upon this occasion he took an oath of obedience, and became ever afterwards a zealous upholder of the apostolical chair. His success in the conversion of Germany was great, his reputation eminent, which enabled him to effect a material revolution in ecclesiastical government. Pelagius II. had, about 580, sent a pallium, or vest peculiar to metropolitans, to the bishop of Arles, perpetual vicar of the Roman see in Gaul.[3]

St. Boniface.

[1] I refer to the English historians for the history of Wilfrid, which neither altogether supports, nor much impeaches, the independency of our Anglo-Saxon church in 700; a matter hardly worth so much contention as Usher and Stillingfleet seem to have thought. The consecration of Theodore by pope Vitalian in 668 is a stronger fact, and cannot be got over by those injudicious protestants who take the bull by the horns. The history of Wilfrid has been lately put in a light as favorable as possible to himself and to the authority of Rome by Dr. Lingard. We have for this to rely on Eddius (published in Gale's Scriptores), a panegyrist in the usual style of legendary biography, — a style which has, on me at least, the effect of producing utter distrust. Mendacity is the badge of all the tribe. Bede is more respectable; but in this case we do not learn much from him. It seems impossible to deny that, if Eddius is a trustworthy historian, Dr. Lingard has made out his case; and that we must own appeals to Rome to have been recognized in the Anglo-Saxon church. Nor do I perceive any improbability in this, considering that the church had been founded by Augustin, and restored by Theodore, both under the authority of the Roman see. This intrinsic presumption is worth more than the testimony of Eddius. But we see by the rest of Wilfrid's history that it was not easy to put the sentence of Rome in execution. The plain facts are, that, having gone to Rome claiming the see of York, and having had his claim recognized by the pope, he ended his days as bishop of Hexham.

[2] Schmidt, t. i. p. 386, 394.

[3] Ut ad instar suum, in Galliarum partibus primi sacerdotis locum obtineat, et quidquid ad gubernationem vel dispensationem ecclesiastici status gerendum est, servatis patrum regulis, et sedis apostolicæ constitutis, faciat. Præterea, pallium illi concedit, &c. Dupin, p. 84. Gregory I. confirmed this vicariate to Virgilius bishop of Arles, and gave him the power of convoking synods. De Marca, l. vi. c. 7.

Gregory I. had made a similar present to other metropolitans. But it was never supposed that they were obliged to wait for this favor before they received consecration, until a synod of the French and German bishops, held at Frankfort in 742, by Boniface, as legate of pope Zachary. It was here enacted that, as a token of their willing subjection to the see of Rome, all metropolitans should request the pallium at the hands of the pope, and obey his lawful commands.[1] This was construed by the popes to mean a promise of obedience before receiving the pall, which was changed in after times by Gregory VII. into an oath of fealty.[2]

Synod of Frankfort.

This council of Frankfort claims a leading place as an epoch in the history of the papacy. Several events ensued, chiefly of a political nature, which rapidly elevated that usurpation almost to its greatest height. Subjects of the throne of Constantinople, the popes had not as yet interfered, unless by mere admonition, with the temporal magistrate. The first instance wherein the civil duties of a nation and the rights of a crown appear to have been submitted to his decision was in that famous reference as to the deposition of Childeric. It is impossible to consider this in any other light than as a point of casuistry laid before the first religious judge in the church. Certainly, the Franks who raised the king of their choice upon their shields never dreamed that a foreign priest had conferred upon him the right of governing. Yet it was easy for succeeding advocates of Rome to construe this transaction very favorably for its usurpation over the thrones of the earth.[3]

1 Decrevimus, says Boniface, in nostro synodali conventu, et confessi sumus fidem catholicam, et unitatem et subjectionem Romanæ ecclesiæ fine tenus servare, S. Petro et vicario ejus velle subjici, metropolitanos pallia ab illâ sede quærere, et, per omnia, præcepta S. Petri canonicè sequi. De Marca, l. vi. c. 7; Schmidt, t. i. p. 424, 438, 446. This writer justly remarks the obligation which Rome had to St. Boniface, who anticipated the system of Isidore. We have a letter from him to the English clergy, with a copy of canons passed in one of his synods, for the exaltation of the apostolic see, but the church of England was not then inclined to acknowledge so great a supremacy in Rome. Collier's Eccles. History, p. 128.

In the eighth general council, that of Constantinople in 872, this prerogative of sending the pallium to metropolitans was not only confirmed to the pope, but extended to the other patriarchs, who had every disposition to become as great usurpers as their more fortunate elder brother.

2 De Marca, ubi supra. Schmidt, t. ii. p. 262. According to the latter, this oath of fidelity was exacted in the ninth century; which is very probable, since Gregory VII. himself did but fill up the sketch which Nicholas I. and John VIII. had delineated. I have since found this confirmed by Gratian, p. 305.

3 Eginhard says that Pepin was made king per *auctoritatem* Romani pontificis; an ambiguous word, which may rise to *command*, or sink to *advice*, according to the disposition of the interpreter.

I shall but just glance at the subsequent political revolutions of that period; the invasion of Italy by Pepin, his donation of the exarchate to the Holy See, the conquest of Lombardy by Charlemagne, the patriarchate of Rome conferred upon both these princes, and the revival of the Western empire in the person of the latter. These events had a natural tendency to exalt the papal supremacy, which it is needless to indicate. But a circumstance of a very different nature contributed to this in a still greater degree. About the conclusion of the eighth century there appeared, under the name of one Isidore, an unknown person, a collection of ecclesiastical canons, now commonly denominated the False Decretals.[1] These purported to be rescripts or decrees of the early bishops of Rome; and their effect was to diminish the authority of metropolitans over their suffragans, by establishing an appellant jurisdiction of the Roman See in all causes, and by forbidding national councils to be holden without its consent. Every bishop, according to the decretals of Isidore, was amenable only to the immediate tribunal of the pope; by which one of the most ancient rights of the provincial synod was abrogated. Every accused person might not only appeal from an inferior sentence, but remove an unfinished process before the supreme pontiff. And the latter, instead of directing a revision of the proceedings by the original judges, might annul them by his own authority; a strain of jurisdiction beyond the canons of Sardica, but certainly warranted by the more recent practice of Rome. New sees were not to be erected, nor bishops translated from one see to another, nor their resignations accepted, without the sanction of the pope. They were still indeed to be consecrated by the metropolitan, but in the pope's name. It has been plausibly suspected that these decretals were forged by some bishop, in jealousy or resentment; and

False Decretals.

[1] The era of the False Decretals has not been precisely fixed; they have seldom been supposed, however, to have appeared much before 800. But there is a genuine collection of canons published by Adrian I. in 785, which contain nearly the same principles, and many of which are copied by Isidore, as well as Charlemagne in his Capitularies. De Marca, l. vii. c. 20; Giannone, l. v. c. 6; Dupin, De Antiquâ Disciplinâ, p. 133. Fleury, Hist. Ecclés. t. ix. p. 500, seems to consider the decretals as older than this collection of Adrian; but I have not observed the same opinion in any other writer. The right of appeal from a sentence of the metropolitan deposing a bishop to the Holy See is positively recognized in the Capitularies of Louis the Debonair (Baluze, p. 1000); the three last books of which, according to the collection of Ansegisus, are said to be apostolicâ auctoritate roborata, quia his cudendis maximè apostolica interfuit legatio. p. 1132.

their general reception may at least be partly ascribed to such sentiments. The archbishops were exceedingly powerful, and might often abuse their superiority over inferior prelates; but the whole episcopal aristocracy had abundant reason to lament their acquiescence in a system of which the metropolitans were but the earliest victims. Upon these spurious decretals was built the great fabric of papal supremacy over the different national churches; a fabric which has stood after its foundation crumbled beneath it; for no one has pretended to deny, for the last two centuries, that the imposture is too palpable for any but the most ignorant ages to credit.[1]

Papal encroachments on the hierarchy,

The Gallican church made for some time a spirited though unavailing struggle against this rising despotism. Gregory IV., having come into France to abet the children of Louis the Debonair in their rebellion, and threatened to excommunicate the bishops who adhered to the emperor, was repelled with indignation by those prelates. "If he comes here to excommunicate," said they, "he shall depart hence excommunicated."[2] In the subsequent reign of Charles the Bald a bold defender of ecclesiastical independence was found in Hincmar archbishop of Rheims, the most distinguished statesman of his age. Appeals to the pope even by ordinary clerks had become common, and the provincial councils, hitherto the supreme spiritual tribunal, as well as legislature, were falling rapidly into decay. The frame of church government, which had lasted from the third or fourth century, was nearly dissolved; a refractory bishop was sure to invoke the supreme court of appeal, and generally met there with a more favorable judicature. Hincmar, a man equal in ambition, and almost in public estimation, to any pontiff, sometimes came off successfully in his contentions with Rome.[3] But time is fatal to the

[1] I have not seen any account of the decretals so clear and judicious as in Schmidt's History of Germany, t. ii. p. 249. Indeed all the ecclesiastical part of that work is executed in a very superior manner. See also De Marca, l. iii. c. 5; l. vii. c. 20. The latter writer, from whom I have derived much information, is by no means a strenuous adversary of ultramontane pretensions. In fact, it was his object to please both in France and at Rome, to become both an archbishop and a cardinal. He failed nevertheless of the latter hope; it being impossible at that time (1650) to satisfy the papal court, without sacrificing al together the Gallican church and the crown.

[2] De Marca, l. iv. c. 11; Velly, &c.

[3] De Marca l. iv. c. 68, &c.; l. vi. c. 14, 28; l. vii. c. 21. Dupin, p. 133, &c. Hist. du Droit Ecclés. François, p. 188, 224. Velly, &c. Hincmar however was not consistent; for, having obtained the see of Rheims in an equivocal manner, he had applied for confirmation at Rome, and in other respects impaired the Gallican rights. Pasquier, Recherches de la France, l. iii. c. 12.

unanimity of coalitions; the French bishops were accessible to superstitious prejudice, to corrupt influence, to mutual jealousy. Above all, they were conscious that a persuasion of the pope's omnipotence had taken hold of the laity. Though they complained loudly, and invoked, like patriots of a dying state, names and principles of a freedom that was no more, they submitted almost in every instance to the continual usurpations of the Holy See. One of those which most annoyed their aristocracy was the concession to monasteries of exemption from episcopal authority. These had been very uncommon till about the eighth century, after which they were studiously multiplied.[1] It was naturally a favorite object with the abbots; and sovereigns, in those ages of blind veneration for monastic establishments, were pleased to see their own foundations rendered, as it would seem, more respectable by privileges of independence. The popes had a closer interest in granting exemptions, which attached to them the regular clergy, and lowered the dignity of the bishops. In the eleventh and twelfth centuries whole orders

[1] The earliest instance of a papal exemption is in 455, which indeed is a respectable antiquity. Others scarcely occur till the pontificate of Zachary in the middle of the eighth century, who granted an exemption to Monte Casino, ita ut nullius juri subjaceat, nisi solius Romani pontificis. See this discussed in Giannone, l. v. c. 6. Precedents for the exemption of monasteries from episcopal jurisdiction occur in Marculfus's forms compiled towards the end of the seventh century, but these were by royal authority. The kings of France were supreme heads of their national church. Schmidt, t. i. p. 382; De Marca, l. iii. c. 16; Fleury, Institutions au Droit, t. i. p. 228. Muratori, Dissert. 70 (t. iii. p. 104, Italian), is of opinion that exemptions of monasteries from episcopal visitation did not become frequent in Italy till the eleventh century; and that many charters of this kind are forgeries. It is held also by some English antiquaries that no Anglo-Saxon monastery was exempt, and that the first instance is that of Battle Abbey under the Conqueror; the charters of an earlier date having been forged. Hody on Convocations, p. 20 and 170. It is remarkable that this grant is made by William, and confirmed by Lanfranc. Collier, p. 256. Exemptions became very usual in England afterwards. Henry, vol. v. p. 337. It is nevertheless to be admitted that the bishops had exercised an arbitrary, and sometimes a tyrannical power over the secular clergy; and after the monks became part of the church, which was before the close of the sixth century, they also fell under a control not always fairly exerted. Both complained greatly, as the acts of councils bear witness: — Un fait important et trop peu remarque se révèle çà et là dans le cours de cette époque; c'est la lutte des prêtres de paroisse contre les évêques. Guizot, Hist. de la Civilis. en France, Leçon 13. In this contention the weaker must have given way: but the regulars, sustained by public respect, and having the countenance of the see of Rome, which began to encroach upon episcopal authority, came out successful in securing themselves by exemptions from the jurisdiction of the bishops. The latter furnished a good pretext by their own relaxation of manners. The monasteries in the eighth and ninth centuries seem not to have given occasion to much reproach, at least in comparison with the prelacy. Au commencement du huitième siècle, l'église était elle tombée dans un désordre presque égal à celui de la société civile. Sans supérieurs et sans inférieurs à redouter, dégagés de la surveillance des métropolitains comme des conciles et de l'influence des prêtres, une foule d'évê ques se livraient aux plus scandaleux excès.

of monks were declared exempt at a single stroke; and the abuse began to awaken loud complaints, though it did not fail to be aggravated afterwards.

The principles of ecclesiastical supremacy were readily applied by the popes to support still more insolent usurpations. Chiefs by divine commission of the whole church, every earthly sovereign must be subject to their interference. The bishops indeed had, with the common weapons of their order, kept their own sovereigns in check; and it could not seem any extraordinary stretch in their supreme head to assert an equal prerogative. Gregory IV., as I have mentioned, became a party in the revolt against Louis I., but he never carried his threats of excommunication into effect. The first instance where the Roman pontiffs actually tried the force of their arms against a sovereign was the excommunication of Lothaire king of Lorraine, and grandson of Louis the Debonair. This prince had repudiated his wife, upon unjust pretexts, but with the approbation of a national council, and had subsequently married his concubine. Nicolas I., the actual pope, despatched two legates to investigate this business, and decide according to the canons. They hold a council at Metz, and confirm the divorce and marriage. Enraged at this conduct of his ambassadors, the pope summons a council at Rome, annuls the sentence, deposes the archbishops of Treves and Cologne, and directs the king to discard his mistress. After some shuffling on the part of Lothaire he is excommunicated; and, in a short time, we find both the king and his prelates, who had begun with expressions of passionate contempt towards the pope, suing humbly for absolution at the feet of Adrian II., successor of Nicolas, which was not granted without difficulty. In all its most impudent pretensions the Holy See has attended to the circumstances of the time. Lothaire had powerful neighbors, the kings of France and Germany, eager to invade his dominions on the first intimation from Rome; while the real scandalousness of his behavior must have intimidated his conscience, and disgusted his subjects.

and upon civil governments.

Lothaire.

Excommunication, whatever opinions may be entertained as to its religious efficacy, was originally nothing more in appearance than the exercise of a right which every society claims, the expulsion of refractory members from its body. No direct temporal disadvantages attended

Excommunications.

this penalty for several ages; but as it was the most severe of spiritual censures, and tended to exclude the object of it not only from a participation in religious rites, but in a considerable degree from the intercourse of Christian society, it was used sparingly and upon the gravest occasions. Gradually, as the church became more powerful and more imperious, excommunications were issued upon every provocation, rather as a weapon of ecclesiastical warfare than with any regard to its original intention. There was certainly some pretext for many of these censures, as the only means of defence within the reach of the clergy when their possessions were lawlessly violated.[1] Others were founded upon the necessity of enforcing their contentious jurisdiction, which, while it was rapidly extending itself over almost all persons and causes, had not acquired any proper coercive process. The spiritual courts in England, whose jurisdiction is so multifarious, and, in general, so little of a religious nature, had till lately no means even of compelling an appearance, much less of enforcing a sentence, but by excommunication.[2] Princes who felt the inadequacy of their own laws to secure obedience called in the assistance of more formidable sanctions. Several capitularies of Charlemagne denounce the penalty of excommunication against incendiaries or deserters from the army. Charles the Bald procured similar censures against his revolted vassals. Thus the boundary between temporal and spiritual offences grew every day less distinct; and the clergy were encouraged to fresh encroachments, as they discovered the secret of rendering them successful.[3]

The civil magistrate ought undoubtedly to protect the just rights and lawful jurisdiction of the church. It is not so evident that he should attach temporal penalties to her censures. Excommunication has never carried such a presumption of moral turpitude as to disable a man, upon any solid principles, from the usual privileges of society. Superstition and tyranny, however, decided otherwise. The support due to church censures by temporal judges is vaguely declared in the capitularies of Pepin and Charlemagne. It became in later ages a more established principle in France and Eng-

[1] Schmidt, t. iv. p. 217; Fleury, Institutions au Droit, t. ii. p. 192.

[2] By a recent statute, 53 G. III. c. 127, the writ De excommunicato capiendo, as a process in contempt, was abolished in England, but retained in Ireland.

[3] Mém. de l'Acad. des Inscript. t. xxxix. p. 596, &c.

land, and, I presume, in other countries. By our common law an excommunicated person is incapable of being a witness or of bringing an action; and he may be detained in prison until he obtains absolution. By the Establishments of St. Louis, his estate or person might be attached by the magistrate.[1] These actual penalties were attended by marks of abhorrence and ignominy still more calculated to make an impression on ordinary minds. They were to be shunned, like men infected with leprosy, by their servants, their friends, and their families. Two attendants only, if we may trust a current history, remained with Robert king of France, who, on account of an irregular marriage, was put to this ban by Gregory V., and these threw all the meats which had passed his table into the fire.[2] Indeed the mere intercourse with a proscribed person incurred what was called the lesser excommunication, or privation of the sacraments, and required penitence and absolution. In some places a bier was set before the door of an excommunicated individual, and stones thrown at his windows: a singular method of compelling his submission.[3] Everywhere the excommunicated were debarred of a regular sepulture, which, though obviously a matter of police, has, through the superstition of consecrating burial-grounds, been treated as belonging to ecclesiastical control. Their carcasses were supposed to be incapable of corruption, which seems to have been thought a privilege unfit for those who had died in so irregular a manner.[4]

Interdicts.

But as excommunication, which attacked only one and perhaps a hardened sinner, was not always efficacious, the church had recourse to a more comprehensive punishment. For the offence of a nobleman she put a county, for that of a prince his entire kingdom, under an interdict or suspension of religious offices. No stretch of her tyranny was perhaps so outrageous as this. During an interdict the churches were closed, the bells silent, the dead

[1] Ordonnances des Rois, t. i. p. 121. But an excommunicated person might sue in the lay, though not in the spiritual court. No law seems to have been so severe in this respect as that of England; though it is not strictly accurate to say with Dr. Cosens (Gibson's Codex, p. 1102), that the writ De excommun. capiendo is a privilege peculiar to the English church.

[2] Velly, t. ii.

[3] Vaissette, Hist. de Languedoc, t. iii. Appendix, p 350; Du Cange, v. Excommunicatio.

[4] Du Cange, v. Imblocatus: where several authors are referred to, for the constant opinion among the members of the Greek church, that the bodies of excommunicated persons remain in statu quo.

unburied, no rite but those of baptism and extreme unction performed. The penalty fell upon those who had neither partaken nor could have prevented the offence; and the offence was often but a private dispute, in which the pride of a pope or bishop had been wounded. Interdicts were so rare before the time of Gregory VII., that some have referred them to him as their author; instances may however be found of an earlier date, and especially that which accompanied the above-mentioned excommunication of Robert king of France. They were afterwards issued not unfrequently against king doms; but in particular districts they continually occurred.[1]

This was the mainspring of the machinery that the clergy set in motion, the lever by which they moved the world. From the moment that these interdicts and excommunications had been tried the powers of the earth might be said to have existed only by sufferance. Nor was the validity of such denunciations supposed to depend upon their justice. The imposer indeed of an unjust excommunication was guilty of a sin; but the party subjected to it had no remedy but submission. He who disregards such a sentence, says Beaumanoir, renders his good cause bad.[2] And indeed, without annexing so much importance to the direct consequences of an ungrounded censure, it is evident that the received theory of religion concerning the indispensable obligation and mysterious efficacy of the rights of communion and confession must have induced scrupulous minds to make any temporal sacrifice rather than incur their privation. One is rather surprised at the instances of failure than of success in the employment of these spiritual weapons against sovereigns or the laity in general. It was perhaps a fortunate circumstance for Europe that they were not introduced, upon a large scale, during the darkest ages of superstition. In the eighth or ninth centuries they would probably have met with a more implicit obedience. But after Gregory VII., as the spirit of ecclesiastical usurpation became more violent, there grew up by slow degrees an opposite feeling in the laity, which ripened into an alienation of sentiment from the church, and a conviction of that sacred truth which superstition and sophistry have endeavored to eradicate from the heart of man,

[1] Giannone, l. vii. c. 1; Schmidt, t. iv. p. 220; Dupin, De antiquâ Eccl. Disciplinâ, p. 288; St. Marc, t. ii. p. 585; Fleury, Institutions, t. ii. p. 200.

[2] p. 261.

that no tyrannical government can be founded on a divine commission.

Further usurpation of the popes.

Excommunications had very seldom, if ever, been levelled at the head of a sovereign before the instance of Lothaire. His ignominious submission and the general feebleness of the Carlovingian line produced a repetition of the menace at least, and in cases more evidently beyond the cognizance of a spiritual authority. Upon the death of this Lothaire, his uncle Charles the Bald having possessed himself of Lorraine, to which the emperor Louis II. had juster pretensions, the pope Adrian II. warned him to desist, declaring that any attempt upon that country would bring down the penalty of excommunication. Sustained by the intrepidity of Hincmar, the king did not exhibit his usual pusillanimity, and the pope in this instance failed of success.[1] But John VIII., the next occupier of the chair of St. Peter, carried his pretensions to a height which none of his predecessors had reached. The Carlovingian princes had formed an alliance against Boson, the usurper of the kingdom of Arles. The pope writes to Charles the Fat, "I have adopted the illustrious prince Boson as my son; be content therefore with your own kingdom, for I shall instantly excommunicate all who attempt to injure my son."[2] In another letter to the same king, who had taken some property from a convent, he enjoins him to restore it within sixty days, and to certify by an envoy that he had obeyed the command, else an excommunication would immediately ensue, to be followed by still severer castigation, if the king should not repent upon the first punishment.[3] These expressions seem to intimate a sentence of deposition from his throne, and thus anticipate by two hundred years the famous era of Gregory VII., at which we shall soon arrive. In some respects John VIII. even advanced pretensions beyond those of Gregory. He asserts very plainly a right of choosing the emperor, and may seem indirectly to have exercised it in the election of Charles the Bald, who had not primogeniture in his favor.[4] This prince, whose restless ambition was united with meanness as well as insincerity, consented to sign a capitulation,

1 De Marca, l. iv. c. 11.

2 Schmidt, t. ii. p. 260.

3 Durioribus deinceps sciens te verberibus erudiendum. Schmidt, p. 261.

4 Baluz. Capitularia, t. ii. p. 251; Schmidt, t. ii. p. 197.

on his coronation at Rome, in favor of the pope and church, a precedent which was improved upon in subsequent ages.[1] Rome was now prepared to rivet her fetters upon sovereigns, and at no period have the condition of society and the circumstances of civil government been so favorable for her ambition. But the consummation was still suspended, and even her progress arrested, for more than a hundred and fifty years. This dreary interval is filled up, in the annals of the papacy, by a series of revolutions and crimes. Six popes were deposed, two murdered, one mutilated. Frequently two or even three competitors, among whom it is not always possible by any genuine criticism to distinguish the true shepherd, drove each other alternately from the city. A few respectable names appear thinly scattered through this darkness; and sometimes, perhaps, a pope who had acquired estimation by his private virtues may be distinguished by some encroachment on the rights of princes or the privileges of national churches. But in general the pontiffs of that age had neither leisure nor capacity to perfect the great system of temporal supremacy, and looked rather to a vile profit from the sale of episcopal confirmations, or of exemptions to monasteries.[2]

Their degeneracy in the tenth century.

The corruption of the head extended naturally to all other members of the church. All writers concur in stigmatizing the dissoluteness and neglect of decency that prevailed among the clergy. Though several codes of ecclesiastical discipline had been compiled by particular prelates, yet neither these nor the ancient canons were much regarded. The bishops, indeed, who were to enforce them had most occasion to dread their severity. They were obtruded upon their sees, as the supreme pontiffs were upon that of Rome, by force or corruption. A child of five years old was made archbishop of Rheims. The see of Narbonne was purchased for another at the age of ten.[3] By this relaxation of morals the priesthood began to lose its hold upon the prejudices of mankind. These are nourished chiefly indeed by shining examples of piety and virtue, but also, in a superstitious age, by ascetic observances, by the fast-

Corruption of morals.

1 Schmidt, t. ii. p. 199.

2 Schmidt, t. ii. p. 414; Mosheim; St. Marc; Muratori, Ann. d'Italia, passim.

3 Vaissette, Hist. de Languedoc, t. ii. p. 252. It was almost general in the church to have bishops under twenty years old. Id. p. 149. Even the pope Benedict IX. is said to have been only twelve, but this has been doubted.

ing and watching of monks and hermits, who have obviously so bad a lot in this life, that men are induced to conclude that they must have secured a better reversion in futurity. The regular clergy accordingly, or monastic orders, who practised, at least apparently, the specious impostures of self-mortification, retained at all times a far greater portion of respect than ordinary priests, though degenerated themselves, as was admitted, from their primitive strictness.

Two crimes, of at least violations of ecclesiastical law, had become almost universal in the eleventh century, and excited general indignation — the marriage or concubinage of priests, and the sale of benefices. By an effect of those prejudices in favor of austerity to which I have just alluded, celibacy had been, from very early times, enjoined as an obligation upon the clergy. It was perhaps permitted that those already married for the first time, and to a virgin, might receive ordination; and this, after prevailing for a length of time in the Greek church, was sanctioned by the council of Trullo in 691,[1] and has ever since continued

Neglect of the rules of celibacy.

[1] This council was held at Constantinople in the dome of the palace, called Trullus, by the Latins. The nominative Trullo, though solœcistical, is used, I believe, by ecclesiastical writers in English. St. Marc, t. i. p. 294; Art de vérifier les Dates, t. i. p. 157; Fleury, Hist. Ecclés. t. x. p. 110. Bishops are not within this permission, and cannot retain their wives by the discipline of the Greek church. Lingard says of the Anglo-Saxon church, — "During more than 200 years from the death of Augustin the laws respecting clerical celibacy, so galling to the natural propensities of man, but so calculated to enforce an elevated idea of the sanctity which becomes the priesthood, were enforced with the utmost rigor: but during part of the ninth century and most of the tenth, when the repeated and sanguinary devastations of the Danes threatened the destruction of the hierarchy no less than of the government, the ancient canons opposed but a feeble barrier to the impulse of the passions." Ang.-Sax. Church, p. 176. Whatever may have been the case in England, those who look at the abstract of the canons of French and Spanish councils, in Dupin's Ecclesiastical History, from the sixth to the eleventh century, will find hardly one wherein there is not some enactment against bishops or priests retaining wives in their houses. Such provisions were not repeated certainly without reason; so that the remark of Fleury, t. xi. p. 594, that he has found no instance of clerical marriage before 893, cannot weigh for a great deal. It is probable that bishops did not often marry after their consecration; but this cannot be presumed of priests. Southey, in his Vindiciæ Ecclesiæ Anglicanæ, p. 290, while he produces some instances of clerical matrimony, endeavors to mislead the reader into the supposition that it was even conformable to ecclesiastical canons.*

* A late writer, who has glosed over every fact in ecclesiastical history which could make against his own particular tenets, asserts, — "In the earliest ages of the church no restriction whatever had been placed on the clergy in this respect." Palmer's Compendious Ecclesiastical History, p. 115. This may be, and I believe it is, very true of the Apostolical period; but the "earliest *ages*" are generally understood to go further: and certainly the prohibition of marriage to priests was an established custom of some antiquity at the time of the Nicene council. The question agitated there was, not whether priests should marry, contrary as it was admitted by their advocate to ἀρχαία ἐκκλησίας παράδοσις, but whether married men should be ordained. I do not see any difference in principle; but the church had made one.

one of the distinguishing features of its discipline. The Latin church, however, did not receive these canons, and has uniformly persevered in excluding the three orders of priests, deacons, and subdeacons, not only from contracting matrimony, but from cohabiting with wives espoused before their ordination. The prohibition, however, during some ages existed only in the letter of her canons. In every country the secular or parochial clergy kept women in their houses, upon more or less acknowledged terms of intercourse, by a connivance of their ecclesiastical superiors, which almost amounted to a positive toleration. The sons of priests were capable of inheriting by the law of France and also of Castile.[1] Some vigorous efforts had been made in England by Dunstan, with the assistance of King Edgar, to dispossess the married canons, if not the parochial clergy, of their benefices; but the abuse, if such it is to be considered, made incessant progress, till the middle of the eleventh century. There was certainly much reason for the rulers of the church to restore this part of their discipline, since it is by cutting off her members from the charities of domestic life that she secures their entire affection to her cause, and renders them, like veteran soldiers, independent of every feeling but that of fidelity to their commander and regard to the interests of their body. Leo IX. accordingly, one of the first pontiffs who retrieved the honor of the apostolic chair, after its long period of ignominy, began in good earnest the difficult work of enforcing celibacy among the clergy.[2] His successors never lost sight of this essential point of discipline. It was a struggle against the natural rights and strongest affections of mankind, which lasted for several ages, and succeeded only by the toleration of greater evils than those it was intended to remove. The laity, in general, took part against the married priests, who were reduced to infamy and want, or obliged to renounce their dearest connections. In many parts of Germany no ministers were left to perform divine services.[3] But perhaps there was no country where the

[1] Recueil des Historiens, t. xi. preface. Marina, Ensayo sobre las Siete Partidas, c. 221, 223. This was by virtue of the general indulgence shown by the customs of that country to concubinage, or *baragania*; the children of such an union always inheriting in default of those born in solemn wedlock. Ibid.

[2] St. Marc, t. iii. p. 152, 164, 219, 602, &c.

[3] Schmidt, t. iii. p. 279; Martenne, Thesaurus Anecdotorum, t. i. p. 230. A Danish writer draws a still darker picture of the tyranny exercised towards the married clergy, which, if he does not exaggerate, was severe indeed: alii mem-

rules of celibacy met with so little attention as in England. It was acknowledged in the reign of Henry I. that the greater and better part of the clergy were married, and that prince is said to have permitted them to retain their wives.[1]

bris truncabantur, alii occidebantur, alii de patriâ expellebantur, pauci sua retinuere. Langebek, Script. Rerum Danicarum, t. i. p. 380. The prohibition was repeated by Waldemar II. in 1222, so that there seems to have been much difficulty found. Id. p. 287 and p. 272.

1 Wilkins, Concilia, p. 387; Chronicon Saxon; Collier, p. 248, 286, 294; Lyttelton, vol. iii. p. 328. The third Lateran council fifty years afterwards speaks of the detestable custom of keeping concubines long used by the English clergy. Cum in Angliâ pravâ et detestabili consuetudine et longo tempore fuerit obtentum, ut clerici in domibus suis fornicarias habeant. Labbé, Concilia, t. x. p. 1633. Eugenius IV. sent a legate to impose celibacy on the Irish clergy. Lyttelton's Henry II. vol. ii. p. 42.

The English clergy long set at nought the fulminations of the pope against their domestic happiness; and the common law, or at least irresistible custom, seems to have been their shield. There is some reason to believe that their children were legitimate for the purposes of inheritance, which, however, I do not assert. The sons of priests are mentioned in several instruments of the twelfth and thirteenth centuries; but we cannot be sure that they were not born before their fathers' ordination, or that they were reckoned legitimate.*

An instance however occurs in the Rot. Cur. Regis, A.D. 1194, where the assize find that there has been no presentation to the church of Dunstan, but the parsons have held it from father to son. Sir Francis Palgrave, in his Introduction to these records (p. 29), gives other proofs of this hereditary succession in benefices. Giraldus Cambrensis, about the end of Henry II.'s reign (*apud* Wright's Political Songs of England, p. 353), mentions the marriage of the parochial clergy as almost universal. More sacerdotum parochialium Angliæ fere cunctorum damnabili quidem et detestabili, publicam secum habebat comitem individuam, et in foco focariam, et in cubiculo concubinam. They were called *focariæ*, as living at the same hearth; and this might be tolerated, perhaps, on pretence of service; but the fellowship, we perceive, was not confined to the fireside. It was about this time that a poem, De Concubinis Sacerdotum, commonly attributed to Walter Mapes, but alluding by name to Pope Innocent III., humorously defends the uncanonical usage. It begins thus: —

"Prisciani regula penitus cassatur,
Sacerdos per *hic* et *hæc* olim declinabatur,
Sed per *hic* solummodo nunc articulatur,
Cum per nostrum præsulem *hæc* amoveatur."

The last lines are better known, having been often quoted: —

"Ecce jam pro clericis multum allegavi,
Necnon pro presbyteris multa comprobavi;
Pater-noster nunc pro me, quoniam peccavi,
Dicat quisque presbyter cum suâ suavi."

Poems ascribed to Mapes, p. 171. (Camden Society, 1841.)

Several other poems in this very curious volume allude to the same subject. In a dialogue between a priest and a scholar, the latter having taxed him with keeping a *presbytera* in his house, the parson defends himself by recrimination: —

"Malo cum presbytera pulcra fornicari,
Servituros domino filios lucrari,
Quam vagas satellites per antra sectari;
Est inhonestissimum sic dehonestari."
(p. 256.)

John, on occasion of the interdict pronounced against him in 1208, seized the concubines of the priests and compelled them to redeem themselves by a fine. Presbyterorum et clericorum focariæ per totam Angliam a ministris regis captæ sunt, et ad se redimendum graviter compulsæ. Matt. Paris, p. 190. This is omitted by Lingard.

It is said by Raumer (Gesch. der Hohenstauffen, vi. 235) that there was a

* Among the witnesses to some instruments in the reign of Edward I., printed by Mr. Hudson Gurney from the court-rolls of the manor of Keswick in Norfolk, we have more than once Walter filius presbyteri. But the rest are described by the father's surname, except one, who is called filius Beatricis; and as he may be suspected of being illegitimate, we cannot infer the contrary as to the priest's son.

But the hierarchy never relaxed in their efforts; and all the councils, general or provincial, of the twelfth century, utter denunciations against *concubinary* priests.[1] After that age we do not find them so frequently mentioned; and the abuse by degrees, though not suppressed, was reduced within limits at which the church might connive.

Simony.

Simony, or the corrupt purchase of spiritual benefices, was the second characteristic reproach of the clergy in the eleventh century. The measures taken to repress it deserve particular consideration, as they produced effects of the highest importance in the history of the middle ages.

Episcopal elections.

According to the primitive custom of the church, an episcopal vacancy was filled up by election of the clergy and people belonging to the city or diocese. The subject of their choice was, after the establishment of the federate or provincial system, to be approved or rejected by the metropolitan and his suffragans; and, if approved, he was consecrated by them.[2] It is probable that, in almost every case, the clergy took a leading part in the selection of their bishops; but the consent of the laity was absolutely necessary to render it valid.[3] They were, however, by degrees, excluded from any real participation, first in the Greek, and finally in the western church. But this was not effected till pretty late times; the people fully preserved their elective rights at Milan in the eleventh century, and traces of their concurrence may be found both in France and Germany in the next age.[4]

married bishop of Prague during the pontificate of Innocent III., and that the custom of clerical marriages lasted in Hungary and Sweden to the end of the thirteenth century.

The marriages of English clergy are noticed and condemned in some provincial constitutions of 1237. Matt. Paris, p. 381. And there is, even so late as 1404, a mandate by the bishop of Exeter against married priests. Wilkins, Concilia, t. iii. p. 277.

[1] Quidam sacerdotes Latini, says Innocent III., in domibus suis habent concubinas, et nonnulli aliquas sibi non metuunt desponsare. Opera Innocent III. p. 558. See also p. 300 and p. 407. The latter cannot be supposed a very common case, after so many prohibitions; the more usual practice was to keep a female in their houses, under some pretence of relationship or servitude, as is still said to be usual in Catholic countries. Du Cange, v. Focaria. A writer of respectable authority asserts that the clergy frequently obtained a bishop's license to cohabit with a mate. Harmer's [Wharton's] Observations on Burnet, p. 11. I find a passage in Nicholas de Clemangis about 1400, quoted in Lewis's Life of Pecock, p. 30. Plerisque in diocesibus, rectores parochiarum ex certo et conducto cum his prælatis pretio, passim et publicè concubinas tenent. This, however, does not amount to a direct license.

[2] Marca, de Concordantiâ, &c., l. vi. c. 2.

[3] Father Paul on Benefices, c. 7.

[4] De Marca, ubi supra. Schmidt, t. iv. p. 173. The form of election of a bishop of Puy, in 1053, runs thus: clerus, populus, et militia elegimus. Vaissette, Hist. de Languedoc. t. ii. Appendix, p. 220. Even Gratian seems to admit in one place that the laity had a sort of share, though no decisive voice, in filling up an episcopal vacancy. Electio clericorum

It does not appear that the early Christian emperors interposed with the freedom of choice any further than to make their own confirmation necessary in the great patriarchal sees, such as Rome and Constantinople, which were frequently the objects of violent competition, and to decide in controverted elections.[1] The Gothic and Lombard kings of Italy followed the same line of conduct.[2] But in the French monarchy a more extensive authority was assumed by the sovereign. Though the practice was subject to some variation, it may be said generally that the Merovingian kings, the line of Charlemagne, and the German emperors of the house of Saxony, conferred bishoprics either by direct nomination, or, as was more regular, by recommendatory letters to the electors.[3] In England also, before the conquest, bishops were appointed in the witenagemot; and even in the reign of William it is said that Lanfranc was raised to the see of Canterbury by consent of parliament.[4] But, independently of this prerogative, which length of time and the tacit sanction of the people have rendered unquestionably legitimate, the sovereign had other means of controlling the election of a bishop. Those estates and honors which compose the temporalities of the see, and without which the naked spiritual privileges would not have tempted an avaricious generation, had chiefly been granted by former kings, and were assimilated to lands held on a beneficiary tenure. As they seemed to partake of the nature of fiefs, they required similar formalities—investiture by the lord, and an oath of fealty by the tenant. Charlemagne is said to have introduced this practice; and, by way of visible symbol, as

Investitures.

est, petitio plebis. Decret. l. i. distinctio 62. And other subsequent passages confirm this.

1 Gibbon, c. 20; St. Marc, Abrégé Chronologique, t. i. p. 7.

2 Fra Paolo on Benefices, c. ix.; Giannone, l. iii. c. 6; l. iv. c. 12; St. Marc, t. i. p. 37.

3 Schmidt, t. i. p. 386; t. ii. p. 245, 487. This interference of the kings was perhaps not quite conformable to their own laws, which only reserved to them the confirmation. Episcopo decedente, says a constitution of Clotaire II. in 615, in loco ipsius, qui a metropolitano ordinari debet, a provincialibus, a clero et populo eligatur: et si persona condigna fuerit, per ordinationem principis ordinetur. Baluz. Capitul. t. i. p. 21. Charlemagne is said to have adhered to this limitation, leaving elections free, and only approving the person, and conferring investiture on him. F. Paul on Benefices, c. xv. But a more direct influence was restored afterwards. Ivon bishop of Chartres, about the year 1100, thus concisely expresses the several parties concurring in the creation of a bishop: eligente clero, suffragante populo, *dono* regis, per manum metropolitani, approbante Romano pontifice. Du Chesne, Script. Rerum Gallicarum, t. iv. p. 174.

4 Lyttelton's Hist. of Henry II. vol. iv. p. 144. But the passage, which he quotes from the Saxon Chronicle, is not found in the best edition.

usual in feudal institutions, to have put the ring and crozier into the hands of the newly consecrated bishop. And this continued for more than two centuries afterwards without exciting any scandal or resistance.[1]

The church has undoubtedly surrendered part of her independence in return for ample endowments and temporal power; nor could any claim be more reasonable than that of feudal superiors to grant the investiture of dependent fiefs. But the fairest right may be sullied by abuse; and the sovereigns, the lay patrons, the prelates of the tenth and eleventh centuries, made their powers of nomination and investiture subservient to the grossest rapacity.[2] According to the ancient canons, a benefice was avoided by any simoniacal payment or stipulation. If these were to be enforced, the church must almost be cleared of its ministers. Either through bribery in places where elections still prevailed, or through corrupt agreements with princes, or at least customary presents to their wives and ministers, a large proportion of the bishops had no valid tenure in their sees. The case was perhaps worse with inferior clerks; in the church of Milan, which was notorious for this corruption, not a single ecclesiastic could stand the test, the archbishop exacting a price for the collation of every benefice.[3]

The bishops of Rome, like those of inferior sees, were regularly elected by the citizens, laymen as well as ecclesiastics. But their consecration was deferred until the popular choice had received the sovereign's sanction. The Romans regularly despatched letters to Constantinople or to the exarchs of Ravenna, praying that their election of a pope might be confirmed. Exceptions, if any, are infrequent while Rome was subject to the eastern empire.[4] This, among other imperial prerogatives, Charlemagne might consider as his own. He possessed the city, especially after his coronation as emperor, in full sovereignty;

Imperial confirmation of popes.

[1] De Marca, p. 416; Giannone, l. vi. c. 7.

[2] Boniface marquis of Tuscany, father of the countess Matilda, and by far the greatest prince in Italy, was flogged before the altar by an abbot for selling benefices. Muratori, ad. ann. 1046. The offence was much more common than the punishment, but the two combined furnish a good specimen of the eleventh century.

[3] St. Marc, t. iii. p. 65, 188, 219, 230, 296, 568; Muratori, A.D. 958, 1057, &c.; Fleury, Hist. Ecclés. t. xiii. p. 73. The sum however appears to have been very small: rather like a fee than a bribe.

[4] Le Blanc, Dissertation sur l'Autorité des Empereurs. This is subjoined to his Traité des Monnoyes; but not in all copies, which makes those that want it less valuable. St. Marc and Muratori, passim.

and even before that event had investigated, as supreme chief, some accusations preferred against the pope Leo III. No vacancy of the papacy took place after Charlemagne became emperor; and it must be confessed that, in the first which happened under Louis the Debonair, Stephen IV. was consecrated in haste without that prince's approbation.[1] But Gregory IV., his successor, waited till his election had been confirmed; and upon the whole the Carlovingian emperors, though less uniformly than their predecessors, retained that mark of sovereignty.[2] But during the disorderly state of Italy which followed the last reigns of Charlemagne's posterity, while the sovereignty and even the name of an emperor were in abeyance, the supreme dignity of Christendom was conferred only by the factious rabble of its capital. Otho the Great, in receiving the imperial crown, took upon him the prerogatives of Charlemagne. There is even extant a decree of Leo VIII., which grants to him and his successors the right of naming future popes. But the authenticity of this instrument is denied by the Italians.[3] It does not appear that the Saxon emperors went to such a length as nomination, except in one instance (that of Gregory V. in 996); but they sometimes, not uniformly, confirmed the election of a pope, according to ancient custom. An explicit right of nomination, was, however, conceded to the emperor Henry III. in 1047, as the only means of rescuing the Roman church from the disgrace and depravity into which it had fallen. Henry appointed two or three very good popes; acting in this against the warnings of a selfish policy, as fatal experience soon proved to his family.[4]

This high prerogative was perhaps not designed to extend beyond Henry himself. But even if it had been transmissible to his successors, the infancy of his son Henry IV., and the factions of that minority, precluded the possibility of its exercise. Nicolas II., in 1059, published a decree which restored the right of election to the Romans, but with a remarkable variation from the original form. The

Decree of Nicolas II.

[1] Muratori, A.D. 817; St. Marc.

[2] Le Blanc; Schmidt, t. ii. p. 186; St. Marc, t. i. p. 387, 393, &c.

[3] St. Marc has defended the authenticity of this instrument in a separate dissertation, t. iv. p. 1167, though admitting some interpolations. Pagi, in Baronium, t. iv. p. 8, seemed to me to have urged some weighty objections: and Muratori, Annali d' Italia, A.D. 962, speaks of it as a gross imposture, in which he probably goes too far. It obtained credit rather early, and is admitted into the Decretum of Gratian. notwithstanding its obvious tendency. p. 211, edit. 1591.

[4] St. Marc; Muratori; Schmidt; Struvius.

cardinal bishops (seven in number, holding sees in the neighborhood of Rome, and consequently suffragans of the pope as patriarch or metropolitan) were to choose the supreme pontiff, with the concurrence first of the cardinal priests and deacons (or ministers of the parish churches of Rome), and afterwards of the laity. Thus elected, the new pope was to be presented for confirmation to Henry, "now king, and hereafter to become emperor," and to such of his successors as should personally obtain that privilege.[1] This decree is the foundation of that celebrated mode of election in a conclave of cardinals which has ever since determined the headship of the church. It was intended not only to exclude the citizens, who had indeed justly forfeited their primitive right, but as far as possible to prepare the way for an absolute emancipation of the papacy from the imperial control; reserving only a precarious and personal concession to the emperors instead of their ancient legal prerogative of confirmation.

Gregory VII. A.D. 1073.

The real author of this decree, and of all other vigorous measures adopted by the popes of that age, whether for the assertion of their independence or the restoration of discipline, was Hildebrand, archdeacon of the church of Rome, by far the most conspicuous person of the eleventh century. Acquiring by his extraordinary qualities an unbounded ascendency over the Italian clergy, they regarded him as their chosen leader and the hope of their common cause. He had been empowered singly to nominate a pope on the part of the Romans after the death of Leo IX., and compelled Henry III. to acquiesce in his choice of Victor II.[2] No man could proceed more fearlessly towards his object than Hildebrand, nor with less attention to conscientious impediments. Though the decree of Nicolas II., his own work, had expressly reserved the right of confirmation of the young king of Germany, yet on the death of that pope Hildebrand procured the election and consecration of Alexander II. without waiting for any authority.[3] During this pontificate he was considered as something greater than the pope, who acted entirely by his counsels. On Alexander's decease Hildebrand, long since the real head of the church,

[1] St. Marc, t. iii. p. 276. The first canon of the third Lateran council makes the consent of two thirds of the college necessary for a pope's election. Labbé, Concilia, t. x. p. 1508.

[2] St. Marc, p. 97.

[3] Id. p. 306.

was raised with enthusiasm to its chief dignity, and assumed the name of Gregory VII.

Notwithstanding the late precedent at the election of Alexander II., it appears that Gregory did not yet consider his plans sufficiently mature to throw off the yoke altogether, but declined to receive consecration until he had obtained the consent of the king of Germany.[1] This moderation was not of long continuance. The situation of Germany speedily afforded him an opportunity of displaying his ambitious views. Henry IV., through a very bad education, was arbitrary and dissolute; the Saxons were engaged in a desperate rebellion; and secret disaffection had spread among the princes to an extent of which the pope was much better aware than the king.[2] He began by excommunicating some of Henry's ministers on pretence of simony, and made it a ground of remonstrance that they were not instantly dismissed. His next step was to publish a decree, or rather to renew one of Alexander II., against lay investitures.[3] The abolition of these was a favorite object of Gregory, and formed an essential part of his general scheme for emancipating the spiritual and subjugating the temporal power. The ring and crosier, it was asserted by the papal advocates, were the emblems of that power which no monarch could bestow; but even if a less offensive symbol were adopted in investitures, the dignity of the church was lowered, and her purity contaminated, when her highest ministers were compelled to solicit the patronage or the approbation of laymen. Though the estates of bishops might, strictly, be of temporal right, yet, as they had been inseparably annexed to their spiritual office, it became just that what was first in dignity and importance should carry with it those accessory parts. And this was more necessary than in former times on account of the notorious traffic which sovereigns made of their usurped nomination to benefices, so that scarcely any prelate sat by their favor whose possession was not invalidated by simony.

His differences with Henry IV.

The contest about investitures, though begun by Gregory VII., did not occupy a very prominent place during his pontificate; its interest being suspended by other more extraordi-

[1] St. Marc, p. 552. He acted, however, as pope, corresponding in that character with bishops of all countries, from the lay of his election. p. 554.

[2] Schmidt; St. Marc. These two are my principal authorities for the contest between the church and the empire.

[3] St. Marc, t. iii. p. 670.

nary and important dissensions between the church and empire. The pope, after tampering some time with the disaffected party in Germany, summoned Henry to appear at Rome and vindicate himself from the charges alleged by his subjects. Such an outrage naturally exasperated a young and passionate monarch. Assembling a number of bishops and other vassals at Worms, he procured a sentence that Gregory should no longer be obeyed as lawful pope. But the time was past for those arbitrary encroachments, or at least high prerogatives, of former emperors. The relations of dependency between church and state were now about to be reversed. Gregory had no sooner received accounts of the proceedings at Worms than he summoned a council in the Lateran palace, and by a solemn sentence not only ex communicated Henry, but deprived him of the kingdoms of Germany and Italy, releasing his subjects from their allegiance, and forbidding them to obey him as sovereign. Thus Gregory VII. obtained the glory of leaving all his predecessors behind, and astonishing mankind by an act of audacity and ambition which the most emulous of his successors could hardly surpass.[1]

The first impulses of Henry's mind on hearing this denunciation were indignation and resentment. But, like other inexperienced and misguided sovereigns, he had formed an erroneous calculation of his own resources. A conspiracy, long prepared, of which the dukes of Suabia and Carinthia were the chiefs, began to manifest itself. Some were alien-

[1] The sentence of Gregory VII. against the emperor Henry was directed, we should always remember, to persons already well disposed to reject his authority. Men are glad to be told that it is their duty to resist a sovereign against whom they are in rebellion, and will not be very scrupulous in examining conclusions which fall in with their inclinations and interests. Allegiance was in those turbulent ages easily thrown off, and the right of resistance was in continual exercise. To the Germans of the eleventh century a prince unfit for Christian communion would easily appear unfit to reign over them; and though Henry had not given much real provocation to the pope, his vices and tyranny might seem to challenge any spiritual censure or temporal chastisement. A nearly contemporary writer combines the two justifications of the rebellious party. Nemo Romanorum pontificem reges a regno deponere posse denegabit, quicunque decreta sanctissimi papæ Gregorii non proscribenda judicabit. Ipse enim vir apostolicus . . . . Præterea, liberi homines Henricum eo pacto sibi præposuerunt in regem, ut electores suos justè judicare et regali providentiâ gubernare satageret, quod pactum ille postea prævaricari et contemnere non cessavit, &c. Ergo, et absque sedis apostolicæ judicio principes eum pro rege meritò refutare possent, cum pactum adimplere contempserit, quod iis pro electione su promiserat; quo non adimpleto, nec rex esse poterat. Vita Greg. VII. in Muratori, Script. Rer. Ital. t. iii. p. 342.

Upon the other hand, the friends and supporters of Henry, though ecclesiastics, protested against this novel stretch of prerogative in the Roman see. Several proofs of this are adduced by Schmidt, t. iii. p. 315.

ated by his vices, and others jealous of his family. The rebellious Saxons took courage; the bishops, intimidated by excommunications, withdrew from his side; and he suddenly found himself almost insulated in the midst of his dominions. In this desertion he had recourse, through panic, to a miserable expedient. He crossed the Alps with the avowed determination of submitting, and seeking absolution from the pope. Gregory was at Canossa, a fortress near Reggio, belonging to his faithful adherent the countess Matilda. It was in a winter of unusual severity. The emperor was admitted, without his guards, into an outer court of the castle; and three successive days remained from morning till evening in a woollen shirt and with naked feet; while Gregory, shut up with the countess, refused to admit him to his presence. On the fourth day he obtained absolution; but only upon condition of appearing on a certain day to learn the pope's decision whether or no he should be restored to his kingdom, until which time he promised not to assume the ensigns of royalty.

A.D. 1077.

This base humiliation, instead of conciliating Henry's adversaries, forfeited the attachment of his friends. In his contest with the pope he had found a zealous support in the principal Lombard cities, among whom the married and simoniacal clergy had great influence.[1] Indignant at his submission to Gregory, whom they affected to consider as an usurper of the papal chair, they now closed their gates against the emperor, and spoke openly of deposing him. In this singular position between opposite dangers, Henry retrod his late steps, and broke off his treaty with the pope; preferring, if he must fall, to fall as the defender rather than the betrayer of his imperial rights. The rebellious princes of Germany chose another king, Rodolph duke of Suabia, on whom Gregory, after some delay, bestowed the crown, with a Latin verse importing that it was given by virtue of the original commission

[1] There had been a kind of civil war at Milan for about twenty years before this time, excited by the intemperate zeal of some partisans who endeavored to execute the papal decrees against irregular clerks by force. The history of these feuds has been written by two contemporaries, Arnulf and Landulf, published in the 4th volume of Muratori's Scriptores Rerum Italicarum; sufficient extracts from which will be found in St. Marc, t. iii. p. 230, &c., and in Muratori's Annals. The Milanese clergy set up a pretence to retain wives, under the authority of their great archbishop, St. Ambrose, who, it seems, has spoken with more indulgence of this practice than most of the fathers. Both Arnulf and Landulf favor the married clerks; and were perhaps themselves of that description. Muratori.

of St. Peter.[1] But the success of this pontiff in his immediate designs was not answerable to his intrepidity. Henry both subdued the German rebellion and carried on the war with so much vigor, or rather so little resistance in, Italy, that he was crowned in Rome by the antipope Guibert, whom he had raised in a council of his partisans to the government of the church instead of Gregory. The latter found an asylum under the protection of Roger Guiscard, at Salerno, where he died an exile. His mantle, however, descended upon his successors, especially Urban II. and Paschal II., who strenuously persevered in the great contest for ecclesiastical independence; the former with a spirit and policy worthy of Gregory VII., the latter with steady but disinterested prejudice.[2] They raised up enemies against Henry IV. out of the bosom of his family, instigating the ambition of two of his sons successively, Conrad and Henry, to mingle in the revolts of Germany. But Rome, under whose auspices the latter had not scrupled to engage in an almost parricidal rebellion, was soon disappointed by his unexpected tenaciousness of that obnoxious prerogative which had occasioned so much of his father's misery. He steadily refused to part with the right of investiture; and the empire was still committed in open hostility with the church for fifteen years of his reign. But Henry V. being stronger in the support of his German vassals than his father had been, none of the popes with whom he was engaged had the boldness to repeat the measures of Gregory VII. At length, each party grown weary of this ruinous contention, a treaty was agreed upon between the emperor and Calixtus II. which put an end by compromise to the question of ecclesiastical investitures. By this compact the emperor resigned forever all pretence to invest bishops by the ring and crosier, and

Dispute about investitures.

Compromised by concordat of Calixtus, A.D. 1122.

[1] Petra dedit Petro, Petrus diadema Rodolpho.

[2] Paschal II. was so conscientious in his abhorrence of investitures, that he actually signed an agreement with Henry V. in 1110, whereby the prelates were to resign all the lands and other possessions which they held in fief of the emperor, on condition of the latter renouncing the right of investiture, which indeed, in such circumstances, would fall of itself. This extraordinary concession, as may be imagined, was not very satisfactory to the cardinals and bishops about Paschal's court, more worldly-minded than himself, nor to those of the emperor's party, whose joint clamor soon put a stop to the treaty. St. Marc, t. iv. p. 976. A letter of Paschal to Anselm (Schmidt, t. iii. p. 304) seems to imply that he thought it better for the church to be without riches than to enjoy them on condition of doing homage to laymen.

recognized the liberty of elections. But in return it was agreed that elections should be made in his presence or that of his officers, and that the new bishop should receive his temporalities from the emperor by the sceptre.[1]

Both parties in the concordat at Worms receded from so much of their pretensions, that we might almost hesitate to determine which is to be considered as victorious. On the one hand, in restoring the freedom of episcopal elections the emperors lost a prerogative of very long standing, and almost necessary to the maintenance of authority over not the least turbulent part of their subjects. And though the form of investiture by the ring and crosier seemed in itself of no importance, yet it had been in effect a collateral security against the election of obnoxious persons. For the emperors detaining this necessary part of the pontificals until they should confer investiture, prevented a hasty consecration of the new bishop, after which, the vacancy being legally filled, it would not be decent for them to withhold the temporalities. But then, on the other hand, they preserved by the concordat their feudal sovereignty over the estates of the church, in defiance of the language which had recently been held by its rulers. Gregory VII. had positively declared, in the Lateran council of 1080, that a bishop or abbot receiving investiture from a layman should not be reckoned as a prelate.[2] The same doctrine had been maintained by all his successors, without any limitation of their censures to the formality of the ring and crosier. But Calixtus II. himself had gone much further, and absolutely prohibited the compelling ecclesiastics to render any service to laymen on account of their benefices.[3] It is evident that such a general immunity from feudal obligations for an order who possessed nearly half the lands in Europe struck at the root of those institutions by which the fabric of society was principally held together. This complete independency had been the aim of Gregory's disciples; and by yielding to the continuance of lay investitures in any shape Calixtus may, in this point of

[1] St. Marc, t. iv. p. 1093; Schmidt, t. iii. p. 178. The latter quotes the Latin words.

[2] St. Marc, t. iv. p. 774. A bishop of Placentia asserts that prelates dishonored their order by putting their hands, which held the body and blood of Christ, between those of impure laymen. p. 956. The same expressions are used by others, and are levelled at the form of feudal homage, which, according to the principles of that age, ought to have been as obnoxious as investiture.

[3] Id. p. 1061, 1067.

view, appear to have relinquished the principal object of contention.[1]

The emperors were not the only sovereigns whose practice of investiture excited the hostility of Rome, although they sustained the principal brunt of the war. A similar contest broke out under the pontificate of Paschal II. with Henry I. of England; for the circumstances of which, as they contain nothing peculiar, I refer to our own historians. It is remarkable that it ended in a compromise not unlike that adjusted at Worms; the king renouncing all sorts of investitures, while the pope consented that the bishop should do homage for his temporalities. This was exactly the custom of France, where an investiture by the ring and crosier is said not to have prevailed;[2] and it answered the main end of sovereigns by keeping up the feudal dependency of ecclesiastical estates. But the kings of Castile were more fortunate than the rest; discreetly yielding to the pride of Rome, they obtained what was essential to their own authority, and have always possessed, by the concession of Urban II., an absolute privilege

[1] Ranke observes that according to the concordat of Worms predominant influence was yielded to the emperor in Germany and to the pope in Italy; an agreement, however, which was not expressed with precision, and which contained the germ of fresh disputes. Hist. of Reform. i. 34. But even if this victory should be assigned to Rome in respect of Germany, it does not seem equally clear as to England. Lingard says of the agreement between Henry I. and Paschal II., — "Upon the whole, the church gained little by this compromise. It might check, but did not abolish, the principal abuse. If Henry surrendered an unnecessary ceremony, he still retained the substance. The right which he assumed of nominating bishops and abbots was left unimpaired." Hist. of Engl. ii. 169. But if this nomination by the crown was so great an abuse, why did the popes concede it to Spain and France? The real truth is, that no mode of choosing bishops is altogether unexceptionable. But, upon the whole, nomination by the crown is likely to work better than any other, even for the religious good of the church. As a means of preserving the connection of the clergy with the state, it is almost indispensable.

Schmidt observes, as to Germany, that the dispute about investitures was not wholly to the advantage of the church; though she seemed to come out successfully, yet it produced a hatred on the part of the laity, and, above all, a determination in the princes and nobility to grant no more lands over which their suzerainty was to be disputed. iii. 269. The emperors retained a good deal — the regale, or possession of the temporalities during a vacancy; the prerogative, on a disputed election, of investing whichever candidate they pleased; above all, perhaps, the recognition of a great principle, that the church was, as to its temporal estate, the subject of the civil magistrate. The feudal element of society was so opposite to the ecclesiastical, that whatever was gained by the former was so much subtracted from the efficacy of the latter. This left an importance to the imperial investiture after the Calixtin concordat, which was not intended probably by the pope. For the words, as quoted by Schmidt (iii. 301), — Habeat imperatoria dignitas electum liber , consecratum canonicè,regaliter per sceptrum sine pretio tamen investire solenniter — imply nothing more than a formality. The emperor is, as it were, commanded to invest the bishop after consecration. But in practice the emperors always conferred the investiture before consecration. Schmidt, iv. 153.

[2] Histoire du Droit public ecclésiastique François, p. 261. I do not fully rely on this authority.

of nomination to bishoprics in their dominions.[1] An early evidence of that indifference of the popes towards the real independence of national churches to which subsequent ages were to lend abundant confirmation.

Introduction of capitular elections.

When the emperors had surrendered their pretensions to interfere in episcopal elections, the primitive mode of collecting the suffrages of clergy and laity in conjunction, or at least of the clergy with the laity's assent and ratification, ought naturally to have revived. But in the twelfth century neither the people, nor even the general body of the diocesan clergy, were considered as worthy to exercise this function. It soon devolved altogether upon the chapters of cathedral churches.[2] The original of these may be traced very high. In the earliest ages we find a college of presbytery consisting of the priests and deacons, assistants as a council of advice, or even a kind of parliament, to their bishops. Parochial divisions, and fixed ministers attached to them, were not established till a later period. But the canons, or cathedral clergy, acquired afterwards a more distinct character. They were subjected by degrees to certain strict observances, little differing, in fact, from those imposed on monastic orders. They lived at a common table, they slept in a common dormitory, their dress and diet were regulated by peculiar laws. But they were distinguished from monks by the right of possessing individual property, which was afterwards extended to the enjoyment of separate prebends or benefices. These strict regulations, chiefly imposed by Louis the Debonair, went into disuse through the relaxation of discipline; nor were they ever effectually restored. Meantime the chapters became extremely rich; and as they monopolized the privilege of electing bishops, it became an object of ambition with noble

[1] F. Paul on Benefices, c. 24; Zurita, Anales de Aragon, t. iv. p. 305. Fleury says that the kings of Spain nominate to bishoprics by virtue of a particular indulgence, renewed by the pope for the life of each prince. Institutions au Droit, t. i. p. 106.

[2] Fra Paolo (Treatise on Benefices, c. 24) says that between 1122 and 1145 it became a rule almost everywhere established that bishops should be chosen by the chapter. Schmidt, however, brings a few instances where the consent of the nobility and other laics is expressed, though perhaps little else than a matter of form. Innocent II. seems to have been the first who declared that whoever had the majority of the chapter in his favor should be deemed duly elected; and this was confirmed by Otho IV. in the capitulation upon his accession. Hist. des Allemands, t. iv. p. 175. Fleury thinks that chapters had not an exclusive election till the end of the twelfth century. The second Lateran council in 1139 represses their attempts to engross it. Institutions au Droit Ecclés. t. i. p. 100.

families to obtain canonries for their younger children, as the surest road to ecclesiastical honors and opulence. Contrary, therefore, to the general policy of the church, persons of inferior birth have been rigidly excluded from these foundations.[1]

General conduct of Gregory VII.

The object of Gregory VII., in attempting to redress those more flagrant abuses which for two centuries had deformed the face of the Latin church, is not incapable, perhaps, of vindication, though no sufficient apology can be offered for the means he employed. But the disinterested love of reformation, to which candor might ascribe the contention against investitures, is belied by the general tenor of his conduct, exhibiting an arrogance without parallel, and an ambition that grasped at universal and unlimited monarchy. He may be called the common enemy of all sovereigns whose dignity as well as independence mortified his infatuated pride. Thus we find him menacing Philip I. of France, who had connived at the pillage of some Italian merchants and pilgrims, not only with an interdict, but a sentence of deposition.[2] Thus too he asserts, as a known historical fact, that the kingdom of Spain had formerly belonged, by special right, to St. Peter; and by virtue of this imprescriptible claim he grants to a certain count de Rouci all territories which he should reconquer from the Moors, to be held in fief from the Holy See by a stipulated rent.[3] A similar pretension he makes to the kingdom of Hungary, and bitterly reproaches its sovereign, Solomon, who had done homage to the emperor, in derogation of St. Peter, his legitimate lord.[4] It was convenient to treat this apostle as a great

[1] Schmidt, t. ii. p. 224, 473; t. iii. p. 281. Encyclopédie art. Chanoine. F. Paul on Benefices, c. 16. Fleury, 8me Discours sur l'Hist. Ecclés.

[2] St. Marc, t. iii. p. 628; Fleury, Hist. Ecclés. t. xiii. p. 281, 284.

[3] The language he employs is worth quoting as a specimen of his style: Non latere vos credimus, regnum Hispaniæ ab antiquo juris sancti Petri fuisse, et adhuc licet diu a paganis sit occupatum, lege tamen justitiæ non evacuatâ, nulli mortalium, sed soli apostolicæ sedi ex æquo pertinere. Quod enim auctore Deo semel in proprietates ecclesiarum justè pervenerit, manente Eo, ab usu quidem, sed ab earum jure, occasione transeuntis temporis, sine legitimâ concessione divelli non poterit. Itaque comes Evalus de Roceio, cujus famam apud vos haud obscuram esse putamus, terram illam ad honorem Sti. Petri ingredi, et a paganorum manibus eripere cupiens, hanc concessionem ab apostolicâ sede obtinuit, ut partem illam, unde paganos suo studio et adjuncto sibi aliorum auxilio expellere possit, sub conditione inter nos factæ pactionis ex parte Sti. Petri possideret. Labbé, Concilia, t. x. p. 10. Three instances occur in the Corps Diplomatique of Dumont, where a duke of Dalmatia (t. i. p. 53), a count of Provence (p. 58), and a count of Barcelona (ibid.), put themselves under the feudal superiority and protection of Gregory VII. The motive was sufficiently obvious.

[4] St. Marc, t. iii. p. 624, 674; Schmidt, p. 73.

feudal suzerain, and the legal principles of that age were dexterously applied to rivet more forcibly the fetters of superstition.[1]

While temporal sovereigns were opposing so inadequate a resistance to a system of usurpation contrary to all precedent and to the common principles of society, it was not to be expected that national churches should persevere in opposing pretensions for which several ages had paved the way. Gregory VII. completed the destruction of their liberties. The principles contained in the decretals of Isidore, hostile as they were to ecclesiastical independence, were set aside as insufficient to establish the absolute monarchy of Rome. By a constitution of Alexander II., during whose pontificate Hildebrand himself was deemed the effectual pope, no bishop in the catholic church was permitted to exercise his functions, until he had received the confirmation of the Holy See:[2] a provision of vast importance, through which, beyond perhaps any other means, Rome has sustained, and still sustains, her temporal influence, as well as her ecclesiastical supremacy. The national churches, long abridged of their liberties by gradual encroachments, now found themselves subject to an undisguised and irresistible despotism. Instead of affording protection to bishops against their metropolitans, under an insidious pretence of which the popes of the ninth century had subverted the authority of the latter, it became the favorite policy of their successors to harass all prelates with citations to Rome.[3] Gregory obliged the metropolitans to attend in person for the pallium.[4] Bishops were summoned even from England and the northern kingdoms to receive the commands of the spiritual monarch. William the Conqueror having made a difficulty about permitting his prelates to obey these citations, Gregory, though in general on good terms with that prince, and treating him with a deference which marks the effect of a firm character in repressing the ebullitions of overbearing pride,[5] complains of this as a persecution unheard of among pagans.[6] The great quarrel between archbishop Anselm and his two sovereigns, William

[1] The character and policy of Gregory VII. are well discussed by Schmidt, t. iii. p. 307.

[2] St. Marc, p. 460.

[3] Schmidt, t. iii. p. 80, 322

[4] Id. t. iv. p. 170.

[5] St. Marc, p. 628, 788; Schmidt, t. iii. p. 82.

[6] St. Marc, t. iv. p. 761; Collier, p. 252

Rufus and Henry I., was originally founded upon a similar refusal to permit his departure for Rome.

Authority of papal legates.

This perpetual control exercised by the popes over ecclesiastical, and in some degree over temporal affairs, was maintained by means of their legates, at once the ambassadors and the lieutenants of the Holy See. Previously to the latter part of the tenth age these had been sent not frequently and upon special occasions. The legatine or vicarial commission had generally been intrusted to some eminent metropolitan of the nation within which it was to be exercised; as the archbishop of Canterbury was perpetual legate in England. But the special commissioners, or legates a latere, suspending the pope's ordinary vicars, took upon themselves an unbounded authority over the national churches, holding councils, promulgating canons, deposing bishops, and issuing interdicts at their discretion. They lived in splendor at the expense of the bishops of the province. This was the more galling to the hierarchy, because simple deacons were often invested with this dignity, which set them above primates. As the sovereigns of France and England acquired more courage, they considerably abridged this prerogative of the Holy See, and resisted the entrance of any legates into their dominions without their consent.[1]

From the time of Gregory VII. no pontiff thought of awaiting the confirmation of the emperor, as in earlier ages, before he was installed in the throne of St. Peter. On the contrary, it was pretended that the emperor was himself to be confirmed by the pope. This had indeed been broached by John VIII. two hundred years before Gregory.[2] It was still a doctrine not calculated for general reception; but the popes availed themselves of every opportunity which the temporizing policy, the negligence or bigotry of sovereigns threw into their hands. Lothaire coming to receive the

[1] De Marca, l. vi. c. 28, 30, 31. Schmidt, t. ii. p. 498; t. iii. p. 312, 320. Hist. du Droit Public Eccl. François, p. 250. Fleury, 4me Discours sur l'Hist. Ecclés. s. 10.

[2] Vide supra. It appears manifest that the scheme of temporal sovereignty was only suspended by the disorders of the Roman See in the tenth century. Peter Damian, a celebrated writer of the age of Hildebrand, and his friend, puts these words into the mouth of Jesus Christ, as addressed to pope Victor II. Ego claves totius universalis ecclesiæ meæ tuis manibus tradidi, et super eam te mihi vicarium posui, quam proprii sanguinis effusione redemi. Et si pauca sunt ista, etiam monarchias addidi: immo sublato rege de medio totius Romani imperii vacantis tibi jura permisi Schmidt, t. iii. p. 78.

imperial crown at Rome, this circumstance was commemorated by a picture in the Lateran palace, in which, and in two Latin verses subscribed, he was represented as doing homage to the pope.[1] When Frederic Barbarossa came upon the same occasion, he omitted to hold the stirrup of Adrian IV., who, in his turn, refused to give him the usual kiss of peace; nor was the contest ended but by the emperor's acquiescence, who was content to follow the precedents of his predecessors. The same Adrian, expostulating with Frederic upon some slight grievance, reminded him of the imperial crown which he had conferred, and declared his willingness to bestow, if possible, still greater benefits. But the phrase employed (majora beneficia) suggested the idea of a fief; and the general insolence which pervaded Adrian's letter confirming this interpretation, a ferment arose among the German princes, in a congress of whom this letter was delivered. "From whom then," one of the legates was rash enough to say, "does the emperor hold his crown, except from the pope?" which so irritated a prince of Wittelsbach, that he was with difficulty prevented from cleaving the priest's head with his sabre.[2] Adrian IV. was the only Englishman that ever sat in the papal chair. It might, perhaps, pass for a favor bestowed on his natural sovereign, when he granted to Henry II. the kingdom of Ireland; yet the language of this donation, wherein he asserts all islands to be the exclusive property of St. Peter, should not have had a very pleasing sound to an insular monarch.

Adrian IV.

I shall not wait to comment on the support given to Becket by Alexander III., which must be familiar to the English reader, nor on his speedy canonization; a reward which the church has always held out to its most active friends, and which may be compared to titles of nobility granted by a temporal sovereign.[3] But the epoch when the spirit of papal usurpation was most strikingly dis-

Innocent III. A.D. 1194-1216.

[1] Rex venit ante fores, jurans prius urbis honores:
Post homo fit papæ, sumit quo dante coronam.
Muratori, Annali, A.D. 1157.

There was a pretext for this artful line. Lothaire had received the estate of Matilda in fief from the pope, with a reversion to Henry the Proud, his son-in-law. Schmidt, p. 349.

[2] Muratori, ubi supra. Schmidt, t iii. p. 393.

[3] The first instance of a solemn papal canonization is that of St. Udalric by John XVI. in 993. However, the metropolitans continued to meddle with this sort of apotheosis till the pontificate of Alexander III., who reserved it, as a choice prerogative, to the Holy See. Art de vérifier les Dates, t. i. p. 247 and 290.

played was the pontificate of Innocent III. In each of the three leading objects which Rome has pursued, independent sovereignty, supremacy over the Christian church, control over the princes of the earth, it was the fortune of this pontiff to conquer. He realized, as we have seen in another place, that fond hope of so many of his predecessors, a dominion over Rome and the central parts of Italy. During his pontificate Constantinople was taken by the Latins; and however he might seem to regret a diversion of the crusaders, which impeded the recovery of the Holy Land, he exulted in the obedience of the new patriarch and the reunion of the Greek church. Never, perhaps, either before or since, was the great eastern schism in so fair a way of being healed; even the kings of Bulgaria and of Armenia acknowledged the supremacy of Innocent, and permitted his interference with their ecclesiastical institutions.

His extraordinary pretensions.

The maxims of Gregory VII. were now matured by more than a hundred years, and the right of trampling upon the necks of kings had been received, at least among churchmen, as an inherent attribute of the papacy. "As the sun and the moon are placed in the firmament" (such is the language of Innocent), "the greater as the light of the day, and the lesser of the night, thus are there two powers in the church — the pontifical, which, as having the charge of souls, is the greater; and the royal, which is the less, and to which the bodies of men only are intrusted."[1] Intoxicated with these conceptions (if we may apply such a word to *successful* ambition), he thought no quarrel of princes beyond the sphere of his jurisdiction. "Though I cannot judge of the right to a fief," said Innocent to the kings of France and England, "yet it is my province to judge where sin is committed, and my duty to prevent all public scandals." Philip Augustus, who had at that time the worse in his war with Richard, acquiesced in this sophism; the latter was more refractory till the papal legate began to menace him with the rigor of the church.[2] But the king of England, as well as his adversary, condescended to obtain

[1] Vita Innocentii Tertii in Muratori, Scriptores Rerum Ital. t. iii. pars i. p. 448. This Life is written by a contemporary. St. Marc, t. v. p. 325. Schmidt, t. iv. p. 227.

[2] Philippus rex Franciæ in manu ejus datâ fide promisit se ad mandatum ipsius pacem vel treugas cum rege Angliæ initurum. Richardus autem rex Angliæ se difficilem ostendebat. Sed cum idem legatus ei *cepit rigorem ecclesiasticum intentare*, saniori ductus consilio acquievit Vita Innocentii Tertii, t. iii. pars i. p. 503.

temporary ends by an impolitic submission to Rome. We have a letter from Innocent to the king of Navarre, directing him, on pain of spiritual censures, to restore some castles which he detained from Richard.[1] And the latter appears to have entertained hopes of recovering his ransom paid to the emperor and duke of Austria, through the pope's interference.[2] By such blind sacrifices of the greater to the less, of the future to the present, the sovereigns of Europe played continually into the hands of their subtle enemy.

Though I am not aware that any pope before Innocent III. had thus announced himself as the general arbiter of differences and conservator of the peace throughout Christendom, yet the scheme had been already formed, and the public mind was in some degree prepared to admit it. Gerohus, a writer who lived early in the twelfth century, published a theory of perpetual pacification, as feasible certainly as some that have been planned in later times. All disputes among princes were to be referred to the pope. If either party refused to obey the sentence of Rome, he was to be excommunicated and deposed. Every Christian sovereign was to attack the refractory delinquent under pain of a similar forfeiture.[3] A project of this nature had not only a magnificence flattering to the ambition of the church, but was calculated to impose upon benevolent minds, sickened by the cupidity and oppression of princes. No control but that of religion appeared sufficient to restrain the abuses of society; while its salutary influence had already been displayed both in the Truce of God, which put the first check on the custom of private war, and more recently in the protection afforded to crusaders against all aggression during the continuance of their engagement. But reasonings from the excesses of liberty in favor of arbitrary government, or from the calamities of national wars in favor of universal monarchy, involve the tacit fallacy, that perfect, or at least superior, wisdom and virtue will be found in the restraining power. The experience of Europe was not such as to authorize so candid an expectation in behalf of the Roman See.

[1] Innocentii Opera (Coloniæ, 1574), p. 124.

[2] Id. p. 134. Innocent actually wrote some letters for this purpose, but without any effect, nor was he probably at all solicitous about it. p. 139 and 141. Nor had he interfered to procure Richard's release from prison: though Eleanor wrote him a letter, in which she asks, "Has not God given you the power to govern nations and kings?" Velly, Hist. de France, t. iii. p. 382.

[3] Schmidt, t. iv. p. 232

There were certainly some instances, where the temporal supremacy of Innocent III., however usurped, may appear to have been exerted beneficially. He directs one of his legates to compel the observance of peace between the kings of Castile and Portugal, if necessary, by excommunication and interdict.[1] He enjoins the king of Aragon to restore his coin, which he had lately debased, and of which great complaint had arisen in his kingdom.[2] Nor do I question his sincerity in these, or in any other cases of interference with civil government. A great mind, such as Innocent III. undoubtedly possessed, though prone to sacrifice every other object to ambition, can never be indifferent to the beauty of social order and the happiness of mankind. But, if we may judge by the correspondence of this remarkable person, his foremost gratification was the display of unbounded power. His letters, especially to ecclesiastics, are full of unprovoked rudeness. As impetuous as Gregory VII., he is unwilling to owe anything to favor; he seems to anticipate denial; heats himself into anger as he proceeds, and, where he commences with solicitation, seldom concludes without a menace.[3] An extensive learning in ecclesiastical law, a close observation of whatever was passing in the world, an unwearied diligence, sustained his fearless ambition.[4] With such a temper, and with such advantages, he was formidable beyond all his predecessors, and perhaps beyond all his successors. On every side the thunder of Rome broke over the heads of princes. A certain Swero is excommunicated for usurping the crown of Norway. A legate, in passing through Hungary, is detained by the king: Innocent writes in tolerably mild terms to this potentate, but fails not to intimate that he might be compelled to prevent his son's accession to the throne. The king of Leon had married his cousin, a princess of Castile.

1 Innocent. Opera, p. 146.

2 p. 378.

3 p. 31, 73, 76, &c. &c.

4 The following instance may illustrate the character of this pope, and his spirit of governing the whole world, as much as those of a more public nature. He writes to the chapter of Pisa that one Rubens, a citizen of that place, had complained to him, that, having mortgaged a house and garden for two hundred and fifty-two pounds, on condition that he might redeem it before a fixed day, within which time he had been unavoidably prevented from raising the money, the creditor had now refused to accept it; and directs them to inquire into the facts, and, if they prove truly stated, to compel the creditor by spiritual censures to restore the premises, reckoning their rent during the time of his mortgage as part of the debt, and to receive the remainder. Id. t. ii. p. 17. It must be admitted that Innocent III. discouraged in general those vexatious and dilatory appeals from inferior ecclesiastical tribunals to the court of Rome, which had gained ground before his time, and especially in the pontificate of Alexander III.

Innocent subjects the kingdom to an interdict. When the clergy of Leon petition him to remove it, because, when they ceased to perform their functions, the laity paid no tithes, and listened to heretical teachers when orthodox mouths were mute, he consented that divine service with closed doors, but not the rites of burial, might be performed.[1] The king at length gave way, and sent back his wife. But a more illustrious victory of the same kind was obtained over Philip Augustus, who, having repudiated Isemburga of Denmark, had contracted another marriage. The conduct of the king, though not without the usual excuse of those times, nearness of blood, was justly condemned; and Innocent did not hesitate to visit his sins upon the people by a general interdict. This, after a short demur from some bishops, was enforced throughout France; the dead lay unburied, and the living were cut off from the offices of religion, till Philip, thus subdued, took back his divorced wife. The submission of such a prince, not feebly superstitious, like his predecessor Robert, nor vexed with seditions, like the emperor Henry IV., but brave, firm, and victorious, is perhaps the proudest trophy in the scutcheon of Rome. Compared with this, the subsequent triumph of Innocent over our pusillanimous John seems cheaply gained, though the surrender of a powerful kingdom into the vassalage of the pope may strike us as a proof of stupendous baseness on one side, and audacity on the other.[2] Yet, under this very pontificate, it was not unparalleled. Peter II., king of Aragon, received at Rome the belt of knighthood and the royal crown from the hands of Innocent III.; he took an oath of perpetual fealty and obedience to him and his successors; he surrendered his kingdom, and accepted it again to be held by an annual tribute, in return for the protection of the Apostolic See.[3] This strange conversion of kingdoms into spiritual fiefs was intended as the price of security from ambitious neighbors, and may be

[1] Innocent. Opera, t. ii. p. 411. Vita Innocent III.

[2] The stipulated annual payment of 1000 marks was seldom made by the kings of England: but one is almost ashamed that it should ever have been so. Henry III. paid it occasionally when he had any object to attain, and even Edward I. for some years; the latest payment on record is in the seventeenth of his reign. After a long discontinuance, it was demanded in the fortieth of Edward III. (1366), but the parliament unanimously declared that John had no right to subject the kingdom to a superior without their consent; which put an end forever to the applications. Prynne's Constitutions, vol. iii.

[3] Zurita, Anales de Aragon, t. i. f 91. This was not forgotten towards the latter part of the same century, when Peter III. was engaged in the Sicilian war, and served as a pretence for the pope's sentence of deprivation.

deemed analogous to the change of alodial into feudal, or more strictly, to that of lay into ecclesiastical tenure, which was frequent during the turbulence of the darker ages.

I have mentioned already that among the new pretensions advanced by the Roman See was that of confirming the election of an emperor. It had however been asserted rather incidentally than in a peremptory manner. But the doubtful elections of Philip and Otho after the death of Henry VI. gave Innocent III. an opportunity of maintaining more positively this pretended right. In a decretal epistle addressed to the duke of Zahringen, the object of which is to direct him to transfer his allegiance from Philip to the other competitor, Innocent, after stating the mode in which a regular election ought to be made, declares the pope's immediate authority to examine, confirm, anoint, crown, and consecrate the elect emperor, provided he shall be worthy; or to reject him if rendered unfit by great crimes, such as sacrilege, heresy, perjury, or persecution of the church; in default of election, to supply the vacancy; or, in the event of equal suffrages, to bestow the empire upon any person at his discretion.[1] The princes of Germany were not much influenced by this hardy assumption, which manifests the temper of Innocent III. and of his court, rather than their power. But Otho IV. at his coronation by the pope signed a capitulation, which cut off several privileges enjoyed by the emperors, even since the concordat of Calixtus, in respect of episcopal elections and investitures.[2]

[1] Decretal. l. i. tit. 6. c. 34, commonly cited Venerabilem. The rubric or synopsis of this epistle asserts the pope's right electum imperatorem examinare, approbare et inungere, consecrare et coronare, si est dignus; vel rejicere si est indignus, ut quia sacrilegus, excommunicatus, tyrannus, fatuus et hæreticus, paganus, perjurus, vel ecclesiæ persecutor. Et electoribus nolentibus eligere, papa supplet. Et data paritate, vocum eligentium, nec accedente majore concordiâ, papa potest gratificari cui vult. The epistle itself is, if possible, more strongly expressed.

[2] Schmidt, t. iv. p. 149, 175.

PART II.

Continual Progress of the Papacy — Canon Law — Mendicant Orders — Dispensing Power — Taxation of the Clergy by the Popes — Encroachments on Rights of Patronage — Mandats, Reserves, &c. — General Disaffection towards the See of Rome in the Thirteenth Century — Progress of Ecclesiastical Jurisdiction — Immunity of the Clergy in Criminal Cases — Restraints imposed upon their Jurisdiction — Upon their Acquisition of Property — Boniface VIII. — His Quarrel with Philip the Fair — Its Termination — Gradual Decline of Papal Authority — Louis of Bavaria — Secession to Avignon and Return to Rome — Conduct of Avignon Popes — Contested Election of Urban and Clement produces the great Schism — Council of Pisa — Constance — Basle — Methods adopted to restrain the Papal Usurpations in England, Germany, and France — Liberties of the Gallican Church — Decline of the Papal Influence in Italy.

Papal authority in the thirteenth century.

THE noonday of papal dominion extends from the pontificate of Innocent III. inclusively to that of Boniface VIII.; or, in other words, through the thirteenth century. Rome inspired during this age all the terror of her ancient name. She was once more the mistress of the world, and kings were her vassals. I have already anticipated the two most conspicuous instances when her temporal ambition displayed itself, both of which are inseparable from the civil history of Italy.[1] In the first of these, her long contention with the house of Suabia, she finally triumphed. After his deposition by the council of Lyons the affairs of Frederic II. went rapidly into decay. With every allowance for the enmity of the Lombards and the jealousies of Germany, it must be confessed that his proscription by Innocent IV. and Alexander IV. was the main cause of the ruin of his family. There is, however, no other instance, to the best of my judgment, where the pretended right of deposing kings has been successfully exercised. Martin IV. absolved the subjects of Peter of Aragon from their allegiance, and transferred his crown to a princ of France; but they did not cease to obey their lawful sovereign. This is the second instance which the thirteenth century presents of interference on the part of the popes in a great temporal quarrel. As feudal lords of Naples and

[1] See above, Chapter III.

Sicily, they had indeed some pretext for engaging in the hostilities between the houses of Anjou and Aragon, as well as for their contest with Frederic II. But the pontiffs of that age, improving upon the system of Innocent III., and sanguine with past success, aspired to render every European kingdom formally dependent upon the see of Rome. Thus Boniface VIII., at the instigation of some emissaries from Scotland, claimed that monarchy as paramount lord, and interposed, though vainly, the sacred panoply of ecclesiastica rights to rescue it from the arms of Edward I.[1]

Canon law.

This general supremacy effected by the Roman church over mankind in the twelfth and thirteenth centuries derived material support from the promulgation of the canon law. The foundation of this jurisprudence is laid in the decrees of councils, and in the rescripts or decretal epistles of popes to questions propounded upon emergent doubts relative to matters of discipline and ecclesiastical economy. As the jurisdiction of the spiritual tribunals increased, and extended to a variety of persons and causes, it became almost necessary to establish an uniform system for the regulation of their decisions. After several minor compilations had appeared, Gratian, an Italian monk, published about the year 1140 his Decretum, or general collection of canons, papal epistles, and sentences of fathers, arranged and digested into titles and chapters, in imitation of the Pandects, which very little before had begun to be studied again with great diligence.[2] This work of Gratian, though it seems rather an extraordinary performance for the age when it appeared, has been censured for notorious incorrectness as well as inconsistency, and especially for the authority given in it to the false decretals of Isidore, and consequently to the papal supremacy. It fell, however, short of what was required in the progress of that usurpation. Gregory IX. caused the five books of Decretals to be published by Raimond de Pennafort in 1234. These consist almost entirely of rescripts issued by the later popes, especially Alexander III., Innocent III., Honorius III., and Gregory himself. They form the most essential part of the canon law, the Decretum of Gratian being comparatively obsolete.

[1] Dalrymple's Annals of Scotland, vol. i. p. 267.

[2] Tiraboschi has fixed on 1140 as the date of its appearance (iii. 343); but others bring it down some years later.

In these books we find a regular and copious system of jurisprudence, derived in a great measure from the civil law, but with considerable deviation, and possibly improvement. Boniface VIII. added a sixth part, thence called the Sext, itself divided into five books, in the nature of a supplement to the other five, of which it follows the arrangement, and composed of decisions promulgated since the pontificate of Gregory IX. New constitutions were subjoined by Clement V. and John XXII., under the name of Clementines and Extravagantes Johannis; and a few more of later pontiffs are included in the body of canon law, arranged as a second supplement after the manner of the Sext, and called Extravagantes Communes.

The study of this code became of course obligatory upon ecclesiastical judges. It produced a new class of legal practitioners, or canonists; of whom a great number added, like their brethren, the civilians, their illustrations and commentaries, for which the obscurity and discordance of many passages, more especially in the Decretum, gave ample scope. From the general analogy of the canon law to that of Justinian, the two systems became, in a remarkable manner, collateral and mutually intertwined, the tribunals governed by either of them borrowing their rules of decision from the other in cases where their peculiar jurisprudence is silent or of dubious interpretation.[1] But the canon law was almost entirely founded upon the legislative authority of the pope; the decretals are in fact but a new arrangement of the bold epistles of the most usurping pontiffs, and especially of Innocent III., with titles or rubrics comprehending the substance of each in the compiler's language. The superiority of ecclesiastical to temporal power, or at least the absolute independence of the former, may be considered as a sort of key-note which regulates every passage in the canon law.[2] It is expressly declared that subjects owe no allegiance to an excommunicated lord, if after admonition he is not reconciled to the church.[3] And the rubric prefixed to the declaration

[1] Duck, De Usu Juris Civilis. l. i. c. 8.

[2] Constitutiones principum ecclesiasticis constitutionibus non præeminent, sed obsequuntur. Decretum, distinct. 10. Statutum generale laicorum ad ecclesias vel ad ecclesiasticas personas, vel eorum bona, in earum præjudicium non extenditur. Decretal. l i. tit. 2, c. 10. Quæcunque a principibus in ordinibus vel in ecclesiasticis rebus decreta inveniuntur, nullius auctoritatis esse monstrantur. Decretum, distinct. 96.

[3] Domino excommunicato manente, subditi fidelitatem non debent; et si longo tempore in e perstiterit, et monitus non pareat ecclesiæ, ab ejus debito

of Frederic II.'s deposition in the council of Lyons asserts that the pope may dethrone the emperor for lawful causes.[1] These rubrics to the decretals are not perhaps of direct authority as part of the law; but they express its sense, so as to be fairly cited instead of it.[2] By means of her new jurisprudence, Rome acquired in every country a powerful body of advocates, who, though many of them were laymen, would, with the usual bigotry of lawyers, defend every pretension or abuse to which their received standard of authority gave sanction.[3]

Next to the canon law I should reckon the institution of the mendicant orders among those circumstances which principally contributed to the aggrandizement of Rome. By the acquisition, and in some respects the enjoyment, or at least ostentation, of immense riches, the ancient monastic orders had forfeited much of the public esteem.[4] Austere principles as to the obligation of evangelical poverty were inculcated by the numerous sectaries of that age, and eagerly received by the people, already much alienated from an established hierarchy. No means appeared so efficacious to counteract this effect as the institution of religious societies strictly debarred from the insidious temptations of wealth. Upon this principle were founded the orders of Mendicant Friars, incapable, by the rules of their foundation, of possessing estates, and maintained only by alms and pious remunerations. Of these the two most celebrated were formed by St. Dominic and St. Francis of Assisi, and established by the authority of Honorius III. in 1216 and 1223. These great reformers, who have produced so extraordinary an effect upon

Mendicant orders.

absolvuntur. Decretal. l. v. tit. 37, c. 18. I must acknowledge that the decretal epistle of Honorius III. scarcely warrants this general proposition of the rubric, though it seems to lead to it.

1 Papa imperatorem deponere potest ex causis legitimis. l. ii. tit. 13, c. 2.

2 If I understand a bull of Gregory XIII., prefixed to his recension of the canon law, he confirms the rubrics or glosses along with the text: but I cannot speak with certainty as to his meaning.

3 For the canon law I have consulted, besides the Corpus Juris Canonici, Tiraboschi, Storia della Litteratura, t. iv. and v.; Giannone, l. xiv. c. 3; l. xix. c. 3; l. xxii. c. 8. Fleury, Institutions au Droit Ecclésiastique, t. i. p. 10, and 5me Discours sur l'Histoire Ecclés. Duck, De Usu Juris Civilis, l. i. c. 8. Schmidt, t. iv. p. 39. F. Paul, Treatise of Benefices, c. 31. I fear that my few citations from the canon law are not made scientifically; the proper mode of reference is to the first word; but the book and title are rather more convenient; and there are not many readers in England who will detect this impropriety.

4 It would be easy to bring evidence from the writings of every successive century to the general viciousness of the regular clergy, whose memory it is sometimes the fashion to treat with respect. See particularly Muratori, Dissert. 65; and Fleury, 8me Discours. The latter observes that their great wealth was the cause of this relaxation in discipline.

mankind, were of very different characters; the one, active and ferocious, had taken a prominent part in the crusade against the unfortunate Albigeois, and was among the first who bore the terrible name of inquisitor; while the other, a harmless enthusiast, pious and sincere, but hardly of sane mind, was much rather accessory to the intellectual than to the moral degradation of his species. Various other mendicant orders were instituted in the thirteenth century; but most of them were soon suppressed, and, besides the two principal, none remain but the Augustin and the Carmelites.[1]

These new preachers were received with astonishing approbation by the laity, whose religious zeal usually depends a good deal upon their opinion of sincerity and disinterestedness in their pastors. And the progress of the Dominican and Franciscan friars in the thirteenth century bears a remarkable analogy to that of our English Methodists. Not deviating from the faith of the church, but professing rather to teach it in greater purity, and to observe her ordinances with greater regularity, while they imputed supineness and corruption to the secular clergy, they drew round their sermons a multitude of such listeners as in all ages are attracted by similar means. They practised all the stratagems of itinerancy, preaching in public streets, and administering the communion on a portable altar. Thirty years after their institution an historian complains that the parish churches were deserted, that none confessed except to these friars, in short, that the regular discipline was subverted.[2] This uncontrolled privilege of performing sacerdotal functions, which their modern antitypes assume for themselves, was conceded to the mendicant orders by the favor of Rome. Aware of the powerful support they might receive in turn, the pontiffs of the thirteenth century accumulated benefits upon the disciples of Francis and Dominic. They were exempted from episcopal authority; they were permitted to preach or hear confessions without leave of the ordinary,[3] to accept of legacies, and to inter in their churches. Such privileges could not be granted without resistance from the other clergy; the bishops

1 Mosheim's Ecclesiastical History; Fleury, 8me Discours; Crevier, Histoire de l'Université de Paris, t. i. p. 318.

2 Matt. Paris, p. 607.

3 Another reason for preferring the friars is given by Archbishop Peckham; quoniam casus episcopales reservati episcopis ab homine, vel a jure, communiter a Deum timentibus episcopis ipsis fratribus committuntur, et non presbyteris, *quorum simplicitas non sufficit aliis dirigendis.* Wilkins, Concilia, t. ii. p. 169

remonstrated, the university of Paris maintained a strenuous opposition; but their reluctance served only to protract the final decision. Boniface VIII. appears to have peremptorily established the privileges and immunities of the mendicant orders in 1295.[1]

It was naturally to be expected that the objects of such extensive favors would repay their benefactors by a more than usual obsequiousness and alacrity in their service. Accordingly the Dominicans and Franciscans vied with each other in magnifying the papal supremacy. Many of these monks became eminent in canon law and scholastic theology. The great lawgiver of the schools, Thomas Aquinas, whose opinions the Dominicans especially treat as almost infallible, went into the exaggerated principles of his age in favor of the see of Rome.[2] And as the professors of those sciences took nearly all the learning and logic of the times to their own share, it was hardly possible to repel their arguments by any direct reasoning. But this partiality of the new monastic orders to the popes must chiefly be understood to apply to the thirteenth century, circumstances occurring in the next which gave in some degree a different complexion to their dispositions in respect of the Holy See.

We should not overlook, among the causes that contributed to the dominion of the popes, their prerogative of dispensing with ecclesiastical ordinances. The most remarkable exercise of this was as to the canonical impediments of matrimony. Such strictness as is prescribed by the Christian religion with respect to divorce was very unpalatable to the barbarous nations. They in fact paid it little regard; under the Merovingian dynasty, even private men put away their wives at pleasure.[3] In many capitularies of Charlemagne we find evidence of the prevailing license of repudiation and even polygamy.[4] The

Papal dispensations of marriage.

[1] Crevier, Hist. de l'Université de Paris, t. i. et t. ii. passim. Fleury, ubi supra. Hist. du Droit Ecclésiastique François, t. i. p. 394, 396, 446. Collier's Ecclesiastical History, vol. i. p. 437, 448, 452. Wood's Antiquities of Oxford, vol. i. p. 376, 480. (Gutch's edition.)

[2] It was maintained by the enemies of the mendicants, especially William St. Amour, that the pope could not give them a privilege to preach or perform the other duties of the parish priests. Thomas Aquinas answered that a bishop might perform any spiritual functions within his diocese, or commit the charge to another instead, and that the pope, being to the whole church what a bishop is to his diocese, might do the same everywhere. Crevier, t. i. p. 474.

[3] Marculfi Formulæ, l. ii. c. 30.

[4] Although a man might not marry again when his wife had taken the veil, he was permitted to do so if she was infected with the leprosy. Compare Capitularia Pippini, A.D. 752 and 755. If a woman conspired to murder her hus

principles which the church inculcated were in appearance the very reverse of this laxity; yet they led indirectly to the same effect. Marriages were forbidden, not merely within the limits which nature, or those inveterate associations which we call nature, have rendered sacred, but as far as the seventh degree of collateral consanguinity, computed from a common ancestor.[1] Not only was affinity, or relationship by marriage, put upon the same footing as that by blood, but a fantastical connection, called spiritual affinity, was invented in order to prohibit marriage between a sponsor and godchild. An union, however innocently contracted, between parties thus circumstanced, might at any time be dissolved, and their subsequent cohabitation forbidden; though their children, I believe, in cases where there had been no knowledge of the impediment, were not illegitimate. One readily apprehends the facilities of abuse to which all this led; and history is full of dissolutions of marriage, obtained by fickle passion or cold-hearted ambition, to which the church has not scrupled to pander on some suggestion of relationship. It is so difficult to conceive, I do not say any reasoning, but any honest superstition, which could have produced those monstrous regulations, that I was at first inclined to suppose them designed to give, by a side-wind, that facility of divorce which a licentious people demanded, but the church could not avowedly grant. This refinement would however be unsupported by facts. The prohibition is very ancient, and was really derived from the ascetic temper which introduced so many other absurdities.[2] It was not until the twelfth century that either this or any other established rules of discipline were sup-

band, he might remarry. Id. A.D. 753. A large proportion of Pepin's laws relate to incestuous connections and divorces. One of Charlemagne seems to imply that polygamy was not unknown even among priests. Si sacerdotes plures uxores habuerint, sacerdotio priventur; quia sæcularibus deteriores sunt. Capitul. A.D. 769. This seems to imply that their marriage with one was allowable, which nevertheless is contradicted by other passages in the Capitularies

1 See the canonical computation explained in St. Marc. t. iii. p. 376. Also in Blackstone's Law Tracts, Treatise on Consanguinity. In the eleventh century an opinion began to gain ground in Italy that third-cousins might marry, being in the seventh degree according to the civil law. Peter Damian, a passionate abettor of Hildebrand and his maxims, treats this with horror, and calls it an heresy. Fleury, t. xiii. p. 152. St. Marc, ubi supra. This opinion was supported by a reference to the Institutes of Justinian; a proof, among several others, how much earlier that book was known than is vulgarly supposed.

2 Gregory I. pronounces matrimony to be unlawful as far as the seventh degree; and even, if I understand his meaning, as long as any relationship could be traced; which seems to have been the maxim of strict theologians, though not absolutely enforced. Du Cange, v. Generatio; Fleury, Hist. Ecclés. t. ix. p. 211.

posed liable to arbitrary dispensation; at least the stricter churchmen had always denied that the pope could infringe canons, nor had he asserted any right to do so.[1] But Innocent III. laid down as a maxim, that out of the plenitude of his power he might lawfully dispense with the law; and accordingly granted, among other instances of this prerogative, dispensations from impediments of marriage to the emperor Otho IV.[2] Similar indulgences were given by his successors, though they did not become usual for some ages. The fourth Lateran council in 1215 removed a great part of the restraint, by permitting marriages beyond the fourth degree, or what we call third-cousins;[3] and dispensations have been made more easy, when it was discovered that they might be converted into a source of profit. They served a more important purpose by rendering it necessary for the princes of Europe, who seldom could marry into one another's houses without transgressing the canonical limits, to keep on good terms with the court of Rome, which, in several instances that have been mentioned, fulminated its censures against sovereigns who lived without permission in what was considered an incestuous union.

Dispensations from promissory oaths.

The dispensing power of the popes was exerted in several cases of a temporal nature, particularly in the legitimation of children, for purposes even of succession. This Innocent III. claimed as an indirect consequence of his right to remove the canonical impediment which bastardy offered to ordination; since it would be monstrous, he says, that one who is legitimate for spiritual functions should continue otherwise in any civil matter.[4] But the most important and mischievous species of dispensations was from the observance of promissory oaths. Two principles are laid down in the decretals — that an oath disadvantageous to the church is not binding; and that one extorted by force was of slight obligation, and might be annulled by ecclesiastical authority.[5] As the first of these

[1] De Marca, l. iii. cc. 7, 8, 14. Schmidt, t. iv. p. 235. Dispensations were originally granted only as to canonical penances, but not prospectively to authorize a breach of discipline. Gratian asserts that the pope is not bound by the canons, in which, Fleury observes, he goes beyond the False Decretals. Septième Discours, p. 291.

[2] Secundum plenitudinem potestatis de jure possumus supra jus dispensare. Schmidt, t. iv. p. 235.

[3] Fleury, Institutions au Droit Ecclésiastique, t. i. p. 296.

[4] Decretal, l. iv. tit. 17, c. 13.

[5] Juramentum contra utilitatem ecclesiasticam præstitum non tenet. Decretal. l. ii. tit. 24, c. 27, et Sext. l. i. tit. 11, c. 1. A juramento per metum extorto ecclesia solet absolvere, et ejus trans-

maxims gave the most unlimited privilege to the popes of breaking all faith of treaties which thwarted their interest or passion, a privilege which they continually exercised,[1] so the second was equally convenient to princes weary of observing engagements towards their subjects or their neighbors. They protested with a bad grace against the absolution of their people from allegiance by an authority to which they did not scruple to repair in order to bolster up their own perjuries. Thus Edward I., the strenuous asserter of his temporal rights, and one of the first who opposed a barrier to the encroachments of the clergy, sought at the hands of Clement V. a dispensation from his oath to observe the great statute against arbitrary taxation.

Encroachments of popes on the freedom of elections,

In all the earlier stages of papal dominion the supreme head of the church had been her guardian and protector; and this beneficent character appeared to receive its consummation in the result of that arduous struggle which restored the ancient practice of free election to ecclesiastical dignities. Not long, however, after this triumph had been obtained, the popes began by little and little to interfere with the regular constitution. Their first step was conformable indeed to the prevailing system of spiritual independency. By the concordat of Calixtus it appears that the decision of contested elections was reserved to the emperor, assisted by the metropolitan

gressores ut peccantes mortaliter non punientur. Eodem lib. et tit. c. 15. The whole of this title in the decretals upon oaths seems to have given the first opening to the lax casuistry of succeeding times.

[1] Take one instance out of many. Piccinino, the famous condottiere of the fifteenth century, had promised not to attack Francis Sforza, at that time engaged against the pope. Eugenius IV. (the same excellent person who had annulled the compatacta with the Hussites, releasing those who had sworn to them, and who afterwards made the king of Hungary break his treaty with Amurath II.) absolves him from this promise, on the express ground that a treaty disadvantageous to the church ought not to be kept. Sismondi, t. ix. p. 196. The church in that age was synonymous with the papal territories in Italy.

It was in conformity to this sweeping principle of ecclesiastical utility that Urban VI. made the following solemn and general declaration against keeping faith with heretics. Attendentes quod hujusmodi confœderationes, colligationes, et ligæ seu conventiones factæ cum hujusmodi hæreticis seu schismaticis postquam tales effecti erant, sunt temerariæ, illicitæ, et ipso jure nullæ (etsi forte ante ipsorum lapsum in schisma, seu hæresin initæ seu factæ fuissent), etiam si forent juramento vel fide datâ firmatæ, aut confirmatione apostolicâ vel quâcunque firmitate aliâ roboratæ, postquam tales, ut præmittitur, sunt effecti. Rymer, t. vii. p. 352.

It was of little consequence that all divines and sound interpreters of canon law maintain that the pope cannot dispense with the divine or moral law, as De Marca tells us, l. iii. c. 15, though he admits that others of less sound judgment assert the contrary, as was common enough, I believe, among the Jesuits at the beginning of the seventeenth century. His power of interpreting the law was of itself a privilege of dispensing with it

and suffragans. In a few cases during the twelfth century this imperial prerogative was exercised, though not altogether undisputed.[1] But it was consonant to the prejudices of that age to deem the supreme pontiff a more natural judge, as in other cases of appeal. The point was early settled in England, where a doubtful election to the archbishopric of York, under Stephen, was referred to Rome, and there kept five years in litigation.[2] Otho IV. surrendered this among other rights of the empire to Innocent III. by his capitulation;[3] and from that pontificate the papal jurisdiction over such controversies became thoroughly recognized. But the real aim of Innocent, and perhaps of some of his predecessors, was to dispose of bishoprics, under pretext of determining contests, as a matter of patronage. So many rules were established, so many formalities required by their constitutions, incorporated afterwards into the canon law, that the court of Rome might easily find means of annulling what had been done by the chapter, and bestowing the see on a favorite candidate.[4] The popes soon assumed not only a right of decision, but of devolution; that is, of supplying the want of election, or the unfitness of the elected, by a nomination of their own.[5] Thus archbishop Langton, if not absolutely nominated, was at least chosen in an invalid and compulsory manner by the order of Innocent III., as we may read in our English historians. And several succeeding archbishops of Canterbury equally owed their promotion to the papal prerogative. Some instances of the same kind occurred in Germany, and it became the constant practice in Naples.[6]

and on rights of patronage.

While the popes were thus artfully depriving the chapters

[1] Schmidt, t. iii. p. 299; t. iv. p. 149. According to the concordat, elections ought to be made in the presence of the emperor or his officers; but the chapters contrived to exclude them by degrees, though not perhaps till the thirteenth century. Compare Schmidt, t. iii. p. 296; t. iv. p 146.

[2] Henry's Hist. of England, vol. v. p. 324. Lyttelton's Henry II., vol. i. p. 356.

[3] Schmidt, t. iv. p. 149. One of these was the *spolium*, or movable estate of a bishop, which the emperor was used to seize upon his decease. p. 154. It was certainly a very *leonine* prerogative; but the popes did not fail, at a subsequent time, to claim it for themselves. Fleury, Institutions au Droit, t. i. p. 425. Lenfant, Concile de Constance, t. ii. p. 130.

[4] F. Paul, c. 30. Schmidt, t. iv. p. 177, 247.

[5] Thus we find it expressed, as captiously as words could be devised, in the decretals, l. i. tit. 6, c. 22. Electus a majori et saniori parte capituli, si est, et erat idoneus tempore electionis, confirmabitur; si autem erit indignus in ordinibus scientiâ vel ætate, et fuit scienter electus, electus a minori parte, si est dignus, confirmabitur.

A person canonically disqualified when presented to the pope for confirmation was said to be *postulatus*, not *electus*.

[6] Giannone, l. xiv. c. 6; l. xix. c. 5.

Mandats.

of their right of election to bishoprics, they interfered in a more arbitrary manner with the collation of inferior benefices. This began, though in so insensible a manner as to deserve no notice but for its consequences, with Adrian IV., who requested some bishops to confer the next benefice that should become vacant on a particular clerk.[1] Alexander III. used to solicit similar favors.[2] These recommendatory letters were called mandats. But though such requests grew more frequent than was acceptable to patrons, they were preferred in moderate language, and could not decently be refused to the apostolic chair. Even Innocent III. seems in general to be aware that he is not asserting a right; though in one instance I have observed his violent temper break out against the chapter of Poitiers, who had made some demur to the appointment of his clerk, and whom he threatens with excommunication and interdict.[3] But, as we find in the history of all usurping governments, time changes anomaly into system, and injury into right; examples beget custom, and custom ripens into law; and the doubtful precedent of one generation becomes the fundamental maxim of another. Honorius III. requested that two prebends in every church might be preserved for the Holy See; but neither the bishops of France nor England, to whom he preferred this petition, were induced to comply with it.[4] Gregory IX. pretended to act generously in limiting himself to a single expectative, or letter directing a particular clerk to be provided with a benefice in every church.[5] But his practice went much further. No country was so intolerably treated by this pope and his successors as England throughout the ignominious reign of Henry III. Her church seemed to have been so richly endowed only as the free pasture of Italian priests, who were placed, by the mandatory letters of Gregory IX. and Innocent IV., in all the best benefices. If we may trust a solemn remonstrance in the name of the whole nation, they drew from England, in the middle of the thirteenth century, sixty or seventy thousand marks every year; a sum far exceeding the royal revenue.[6] This was asserted by the English envoys at the council of Lyons.

[1] St. Marc, t. v. p. 41. Art de vérifier les Dates, t. i. p. 288. Encyclopédie, art. Mandats.

[2] Schmidt, t. iv. p. 239.

[3] Innocent III. Opera, p. 502

[4] Matt. Paris, p. 267. De Marca, l. iv c. 9.

[5] F. Paul on Benefices, c. 30

[6] M. Paris, p. 579, 740.

But the remedy was not to be sought in remonstrances to the court of Rome, which exulted in the success of its encroachments. There was no defect of spirit in the nation to oppose a more adequate resistance; but the weak-minded individual upon the throne sacrificed the public interest sometimes through habitual timidity, sometimes through silly ambition. If England, however, suffered more remarkably, yet other countries were far from being untouched. A German writer about the beginning of the fourteenth century mentions a cathedral where, out of about thirty-five vacancies of prebends that had occurred within twenty years, the regular patron had filled only two.[1] The case was not very different in France, where the continual usurpations of the popes produced the celebrated Pragmatic Sanction of St. Louis. This edict, the authority of which, though probably without cause, has been sometimes disputed, contains three important provisions; namely, that all prelates and other patrons shall enjoy their full rights as to the collation of benefices, according to the canons; that churches shall possess freely their rights of election; and that no tax or pecuniary exaction shall be levied by the pope, without consent of the king and of the national church.[2] We do not find, however, that the

[1] Schmidt, t. vi. p. 104.

[2] Ordonnances des Rois de France, t. i. p. 97. Objections have been made to the authenticity of this edict, and in particular that we do not find the king to have had any previous differences with the see of Rome; on the contrary, he was just indebted to Clement IV. for bestowing the crown of Naples on his brother the count of Provence. Velly has defended it, Hist. de France, t. vi. p. 57; and in the opinion of the learned Benedictine editors of L'Art de vérifier les Dates, t. i. p. 585, cleared up all difficulties as to its genuineness. In fact, however, the Pragmatic Sanction of St. Louis stands by itself, and can only be considered as a protestation against abuses which it was still impossible to suppress.

Of this law, which was published in 1268, Sismondi says, En lisant la pragmatique sanction, on se demande avec étonnement ce qui a pu causer sa prodigieuse célébrité. Elle n'introduit aucun droit nouveau; elle ne change rien à l'organisation ecclésiastique; elle déclare seulement que tous les droits existans seront conservés, que toute la législation canonique soit exécutée. A l'exception de l'article v, sur la levées d'argent de la cour de Rome, elle ne contient rien que cette cour n'eut pu publier elle-même; et quant à cet article, qui paroit seul dirigé contre la chambre apostolique, il n'est pas plus précis que ceux que bien d'autres rois de France, d'Angleterre, et d'Allemagne, avaient déjà promulgués à plusieurs réprises, et toujours sans effet. Hist. des Franc. v. 106. But Sismondi overlooks the fourth article, which enacts that all collations of benefices shall be made according to the maxims of councils and fathers of the church. This was designed to repress the dispensations of the pope; and if the French lawyers had been powerful enough, it would have been successful in that object. He goes on, indeed, himself to say,—Ce qui changea la pragmatique sanction en une barrière puissante contre les usurpations de la cour de Rome, c'est que les légistes s'en emparèrent; ils prirent soin de l'expliquer, de la commenter; plus elle était vague, et plus, entre leurs mains habiles, elle pouvoit recevoir d'extension. Elle suffisait seule pour garantir toutes les libertés du royaume; une fois que les parlemens etoient résolus de ne jamais permettre qu'elle fût violée, tout empiétement de la cour de Rome ou des tribunaux ecclésiasti-

French government acted up to the spirit of this ordinance and the Holy See continued to invade the rights of collation with less ceremony than they had hitherto used. Clement IV. published a bull in 1266, which, after asserting an absolute prerogative of the supreme pontiff to dispose of all preferments, whether vacant or in reversion, confines itself in the enacting words to the reservation of such benefices as belong to persons dying at Rome (vacantes in curiâ).[1] These had for some time been reckoned as a part of the pope's special patronage; and their number, when all causes of importance were drawn to his tribunal, when metropolitans were compelled to seek their pallium in person, and even by a recent constitution exempt abbots were to repair to Rome for confirmation,[2] not to mention the multitude who flocked thither as mere courtiers and hunters after promotion, must have been very considerable. Boniface VIII. repeated this law of Clement IV. in a still more positive tone;[3] and Clement V. laid down as a maxim, that the pope might freely bestow, as universal patron, all ecclesiastical benefices.[4] In order to render these tenable by their Italian courtiers, the canons against pluralities and nonresidence were dispensed with; so that individuals were said to have accumulated fifty or sixty preferments.[5] It was a consequence from this extravagant principle, that the pope might prevent the ordinary collator upon a vacancy; and as this could seldom be done with sufficient expedition in places remote from his court, that he might make reversionary grants during the life of an incumbent, or reserve certain benefices specifically for his own nomination.

Provisions, reserves, &c.

The persons as well as estates of ecclesiastics were secure from arbitrary taxation in all the kingdoms founded upon the ruins of the empire, both by the common liberties of free-

ques, toute levée de deniers ordonnée par elle, toute élection irrégulière, toute excommunication, tout interdit, qui touchoient l'autorité royale ou les droits du sujet, furent dénoncés par les légistes en parlement, comme contraires aux franchises des églises de France, et à la pragmatique sanction. Ainsi s'introduisait l'appel comme d'abus qui réussit seul à contenir la jurisdiction ecclésiastique dans de justes bornes.

1 Sext. Decretal. l. iii. t. iv. c. 2. F. Paul on Benefices, c. 35 This writer thinks the privilege of nominating benefices vacant *in curia* to have been among the first claimed by the popes, even before the usage of mandats. c. 30.

2 Matt. Paris, p. 817.

3 Sext. Decret. l. iii. t. iv. c. 3. He extended the vacancy in curiâ to all places within two days' journey of the papal court.

4 F. Paul, c. 35.

5 Id. c. 33, 34, 35. Schmidt, t. iv. p 104

Papal taxation of the clergy.

men, and more particularly by their own immunities and the horror of sacrilege.[1] Such at least was their legal security, whatever violence might occasionally be practised by tyrannical princes. But this exemption was compensated by annual donatives, probably to a large amount, which the bishops and monasteries were accustomed, and as it were compelled, to make to their sovereigns.[2] They were subject also, generally speaking, to the feudal services and prestations. Henry I. is said to have extorted a sum of money from the English church.[3] But the first eminent instance of a general tax required from the clergy was the famous Saladine tithe; a tenth of all movable estate, imposed by the kings of France and England upon all their subjects, with the consent of their great councils of prelates and barons, to defray the expense of their intended crusade. Yet even this contribution, though called for by the imminent peril of the Holy Land after the capture of Jerusalem, was not paid without reluctance; the clergy doubtless anticipating the future extension of such a precedent.[4] Many years had not elapsed when a new demand was made upon them, but from a different quarter. Innocent III. (the name continually recurs when we trace the commencement of an usurpation) imposed in 1199 upon the whole church a tribute of one fortieth of movable estate, to be paid to his own collectors; but strictly pledging himself that the money should only be applied to the purposes of a crusade.[5] This crusade ended, as is well known, in the capture of Constantinople. But the word had lost much of its original meaning; or rather that meaning had been extended by ambition and bigotry. Gregory IX. preached a crusade against the emperor Frederic, in a quarrel which only concerned his temporal principality; and the church of England was taxed by his authority to carry on this holy war.[6] After some

1 Muratori, Dissert. 70; Schmidt, t. iii. p. 211.

2 Schmidt, t. iii. p. 211. Du Cange, v. Dona.

3 Eadmer, p. 83.

4 Schmidt, t. iv. p. 212. Lyttelton's Henry II., vol. iii. p. 472. Velly, t. iii. p. 316.

5 Innocent, Opera, p. 266.

6 M. Paris, p. 470. It was hardly possible for the clergy to make any effective resistance to the pope, without unraveling a tissue which they had been assiduously weaving. One English prelate distinguished himself in this reign by his strenuous protestation against all abuses of the church. This was Robert Grosstete, bishop of Lincoln, who died in 1253, the most learned Englishman of his time, and the first who had any tincture of Greek literature. Matthew Paris gives him a high character, which he deserved for his learning and integrity; one of his commendations is for keeping

opposition the bishops submitted; and from that time no bounds were set to the rapacity of papal exactions. The usurers of Cahors and Lombardy, residing in London, took up the trade of agency for the pope; and in a few years, he is said, partly by levies of money, partly by the revenues of benefices, to have plundered the kingdom of 950,000 marks; a sum equivalent, perhaps, to not less than fifteen millions sterling at present. Innocent IV., during whose pontificate the tyranny of Rome, if we consider her temporal and spiritual usurpations together, seems to have reached its zenith, hit upon the device of ordering the English prelates to furnish a certain number of men-at-arms to defend the church at their expense. This would soon have been commuted into a standing escuage instead of military service.[1] But the demand was perhaps not complied with, and we do not find it repeated. Henry III.'s pusillanimity would not permit any effectual measures to be adopted; and indeed he sometimes shared in the booty, and was indulged with the produce of taxes imposed upon his own clergy to defray the cost of his projected war against Sicily.[2] A nobler example was set by the kingdom of Scotland: Clement IV. having, in 1267, granted the tithes of its ecclesiastical revenues for one of his mock crusades, king Alexander III., with the concurrence of the church, stood up against this encroachment, and refused the legate permission to enter his dominions.[3] Taxation of the clergy was not so outrageous in other countries; but the popes granted a tithe of benefices to St. Louis for each of his own crusades, and also for the expedition of Charles of Anjou against Manfred.[4] In the council of Lyons, held by Gregory X. in 1274, a general tax in the same proportion was imposed on all the Latin church, for the pretended purpose of carrying on a holy war.[5]

a good table. But Grosstete appears to have been imbued in a great degree with the spirit of his age as to ecclesiastical power, though unwilling to yield it up to the pope: and it is a strange thing to reckon him among the precursors of the Reformation. M. Paris, p. 754. Berington's Literary History of the Middle Ages, p. 378.

1 M. Paris, p. 613. It would be endless to multiply proofs from Matthew Paris, which indeed occur in almost every page. His laudable zeal against papal tyranny, on which some protestant writers have been so pleased to dwell, was a little stimulated by personal feelings for the abbey of St. Alban's; and the same remark is probably applicable to his love of civil liberty.

2 Rymer, t. i. p. 599, &c. The substance of English ecclesiastical history during the reign of Henry III. may be collected from Henry, and still better from Collier.

3 Dalrymple's Annals of Scotland, vol. i. p. 179.

4 Velly, t. iv. p. 343; t. v. p. 343; t. vi. p. 47.

5 Idem, t. vi. p. 308. St. Marc, t. vi p. 347.

Disaffection towards the court of Rome.

These gross invasions of ecclesiastical property, however submissively endured, produced a very general disaffection towards the court of Rome. The reproach of venality and avarice was not indeed cast for the first time upon the sovereign pontiffs; but it had been confined, in earlier ages, to particular instances, not affecting the bulk of the catholic church. But, pillaged upon every slight pretence, without law and without redress, the clergy came to regard their once paternal monarch as an arbitrary oppressor. All writers of the thirteenth and following centuries complain in terms of unmeasured indignation, and seem almost ready to reform the general abuses of the church. They distinguished however clearly enough between the abuses which oppressed them and those which it was their interest to preserve, nor had the least intention of waiving their own immunities and authority. But the laity came to more universal conclusions. A spirit of inveterate hatred grew up among them, not only towards the papal tyranny, but the whole system of ecclesiastical independence. The rich envied and longed to plunder the estates of the superior clergy; the poor learned from the Waldenses and other sectaries to deem such opulence incompatible with the character of evangelical ministers. The itinerant minstrels invented tales to satirize vicious priests, which a predisposed multitude eagerly swallowed. If the thirteenth century was an age of more extravagant ecclesiastical pretensions than any which had preceded, it was certainly one in which the disposition to resist them acquired greater consistence.

Progress of ecclesiastical jurisdiction,

To resist had indeed become strictly necessary, if the temporal governments of Christendom would occupy any better station than that of officers to the hierarchy. I have traced already the first stage of that ecclesiastical jurisdiction, which, through the partial indulgence of sovereigns, especially Justinian and Charlemagne, had become nearly independent of the civil magistrate. Several ages of confusion and anarchy ensued, during which the supreme regal authority was literally suspended in France, and not much respected in some other countries. It is natural to suppose that ecclesiastical jurisdiction, so far as even that was regarded in such barbarous times, would be esteemed the only substitute for coercive law, and the best security against wrong. But I am not aware that it extended itself beyond its former limits till about the beginning of the twelfth century. From that time it rapidly encroached upon the secular tribunals, and seemed to threaten the usurpation of an exclusive supremacy over all persons and causes. The bishops gave the tonsure indiscriminately, in order to swell the list of their subjects. This sign of a clerical state, though below the lowest of their seven degrees of ordination, implying no spiritual office, conferred the privileges and immunities of the profession on all who wore an ecclesiastical habit and had only once been married.[1] Orphans and widows, the stranger and the poor, the pilgrim and the leper, under the appellation of persons in distress (miserabiles personæ), came within the peculiar cognizance and protection of the church; nor could they be sued before any lay tribunal. And the whole body of crusaders, or such as merely took the vow of engaging in a crusade, enjoyed the same clerical privileges.

But where the character of the litigant parties could not, even with this large construction, be brought within their pale, the bishops found a pretext for their jurisdiction in the nature of the dispute. Spiritual causes alone, it was agreed, could appertain to the spiritual tribunal. But the word was indefinite; and according to the interpreters of the twelfth century, the church was always bound to prevent and chastise the commission of sin. By this sweeping maxim, which we have seen Innocent III. apply to vindicate his control over national quarrels, the common differences of individuals, which generally involve some charge of wilful injury, fell into the hands of a religious judge. One is almost surprised to find that it did not extend more universally, and might praise the moderation of the church. Real actions, or suits relating to the property of land, were always the exclusive province of the lay court, even where a clerk was the defendant.[2] But the ecclesiastical tribunals took cognizance of

[1] Clerici qui cum unicis et virginibus contraxerunt, si tonsuram et vestes deferant clericales, privilegium retineant —— præsenti declaramus edicto, hujusmodi clericos conjugatos pro commissis ab iis excessibus vel delictis, trahi non posse criminaliter aut civiliter ad judicium sæculare. Bonifacius Octavus, in Sext. Decretal. l. iii. tit. ii. c. i.

Philip the Bold, however, had subjected these married clerks to taxes, an later ordinances of the French kings rendered them amenable to temporal jurisdiction; from which, in Naples, by various provisions of the Angevin line, they always continued free. Giannone, l. xix. c. 5.

[2] Decretal, l. ii. t. ii. Ordonnances des Rois, t. i. p. 40 (A.D. 1189). In the council of Lambeth in 1261 the bishops

breaches of contract, at least where an oath had been pledged, and of personal trusts.[1] They had not only an exclusive jurisdiction over questions immediately matrimonial, but a concurrent one with the civil magistrate in France, though never in England, over matters incident to the nuptial contract, as claims of marriage portion and of dower.[2] They took the execution of testaments into their hands, on account of the legacies to pious uses which testators were advised to bequeath.[3] In process of time, and under favorable circumstances, they made still greater strides. They pretended a right to supply the defects, the doubts, or the negligence of temporal judges; and invented a class of mixed causes, whereof the lay or ecclesiastical jurisdiction took possession according to priority. Besides this extensive authority in civil disputes, they judged of some offences which naturally belong to the criminal law, as well as of some others which participate of a civil and criminal nature. Such were perjury, sacrilege, usury, incest, and adultery;[4] from the punishment of all which the secular magistrate refrained, at least in England, after they had become the province of a separate jurisdiction. Excommunication still continued the only chastisement which the church could directly inflict. But the bishops acquired a right of having their own prisons for lay offenders,[5] and the monasteries were the appropriate prisons of clerks. Their sentences of excommunication were enforced by the temporal magistrate by imprisonment or sequestration of effects; in some cases by confiscation or death.[6]

claim a right to judge inter clericos suos, vel inter laicos conquerentes et clericos defendentes, in personalibus actionibus super contractibus, aut delictis aut quasi, *i. e.* quasi dilictis. Wilkins, Concilia, t. i. p. 747.

[1] Ordonnances des Rois, p. 319 (A.D. 1290).

[2] Id. p. 40, 121, 220, 319.

[3] Id. p. 319. Glanvil, l. vii. c. 7. Sancho IV. gave the same jurisdiction to the clergy of Castile, Teoria de las Cortes, t. iii. p. 20; and in other respects followed the example of his father, Alfonso X., in favoring their encroachments. The church of Scotland seems to have had nearly the same jurisdiction as that of England. Pinkerton's History of Scotland, vol. i. p. 173.

[4] It was a maxim of the canon, as well as the common law, that no person should be punished twice for the same offence; therefore, if a clerk had been degraded, or a penance imposed on a layman, it was supposed unjust to proceed against him in a temporal court.

[5] Charlemagne is said by Giannone to have permitted the bishops to have prisons of their own. l. vi. c. 7.

[6] Giannone, l. xix. c. 5, t. iii. Schmidt, t. iv. p. 195; t. vi. p. 125. Fleury, 7me Discours, Mém. de l'Acad. des Inscript. t. xxxix. p. 603. Ecclesiastical jurisdiction not having been uniform in different ages and countries, it is difficult without much attention to distinguish its general and permanent attributes from those less completely established. Its description, as given in the Decretals, lib. ii. tit. ii., De foro competenti, does not support the pretensions made by the canonists, nor come up to the sweeping

The clergy did not forget to secure along with this jurisdiction their own absolute exemption from the criminal justice of the state. This, as I have above mentioned, had been conceded to them by Charlemagne; and this privilege was not enjoyed by clerks in England before the conquest; nor do we find it proved by any records long afterwards; though it seems, by what we read about the constitutions of Clarendon, to have grown into use before the reign of Henry II. As to France and Germany, I cannot pretend to say that the law of Charlemagne granting an exemption from ordinary criminal process was ever abrogated. The False Decretals contain some passages in favor of ecclesiastical immunity, which Gratian repeats in his collection.[1] About the middle of the twelfth century the principle obtained general reception, and Innocent III. decided it to be an inalienable right of the clergy, whereof they could not be divested even by their own consent.[2] Much less were any constitutions of princes, or national usages, deemed of force to abrogate such an important privilege.[3] These, by the canon law, were invalid when they affected the rights and liberties of holy church.[4] But the spiritual courts were charged with scandalously neglecting to visit the most atrocious offences of clerks with such punishment as they could inflict. The church could always absolve from her own censures; and confinement in a monastery, the usual sentence upon criminals, was frequently slight and temporary. Several instances are mentioned of heinous outrages that remained nearly unpunished through the shield of ecclesiastical privilege.[5] And as the temporal courts refused their assistance to a rival jurisdiction, the clergy had no redress for their own injuries, and even the murder of a priest at one time, as we are told, was only punishable by excommunication.[6]

and immunity.

definition of ecclesiastical jurisdiction by Boniface VIII. in the Sext. l. iii. tit. xxiii. c. 40, sive ambæ partes hoc voluerint, sive una super causis ecclesiasticis, sive quæ ad forum ecclesiasticum ratione personarum, negotiorum, vel rerum de jure vel de antiquâ consuetudine pertinere noscuntur.

[1] Fleury, 7me Discours.

[2] Id. Institutions au Droit Ecclés. t. ii. p. 8.

[3] In criminalibus causis in nullo casu possunt clerici ab aliquo quàm ab ecclesiastico judice condemnari, etiamsi consuetudo regia habeat ut fures a judicibus sæcularibus judicentur. Decretal. l. i. tit. i. c. 8.

[4] Decret. distinct. 96.

[5] Collier, vol. i. p. 351. It is laid down in the canon laws that a layman cannot be a witness in a criminal case against a clerk. Decretal. l. ii. tit. xx. c. 14.

[6] Lyttelton's Henry II., vol. iii. p. 332. This must be restricted to that period of open hostility between the church and state.

Endeavors made to repress it in England.

Such an incoherent medley of laws and magistrates, upon the symmetrical arrangement of which all social economy mainly depends, could not fail to produce a violent collision. Every sovereign was interested in vindicating the authority of the constitutions which had been formed by his ancestors, or by the people whom he governed. But the first who undertook this arduous work, the first who appeared openly against ecclesiastical tyranny, was our Henry II. The Anglo-Saxon church, not so much connected as some others with Rome, and enjoying a sort of barbarian immunity from the thraldom of canonical discipline, though rich, and highly respected by a devout nation, had never, perhaps, desired the thorough independence upon secular jurisdiction at which the continental hierarchy aimed. William the Conqueror first separated the ecclesiastical from the civil tribunal, and forbade the bishops to judge of spiritual causes in the hundred court.[1] His language is, however, too indefinite to warrant any decisive proposition as to the nature of such causes; probably they had not yet been carried much beyond their legitimate extent. Of clerical exemption from the secular arm we find no earlier notice than in the coronation oath of Stephen; which, though vaguely expressed, may be construed to include it.[2] But I am not certain that the law of England had unequivocally recognized that claim at the time of the constitutions of Clarendon. It was at least an innovation, which the legislature might without scruple or transgression of justice abolish. Henry II., in that famous statute, attempted in three respects to limit the jurisdiction assumed by the church; asserting for his own judges the cognizance of contracts, however confirmed by oath, and of rights of advowson, and also that of offences committed by clerks, whom, as it is gently expressed, after

[1] Ut nullus episcopus vel archidiaconus de legibus episcopalibus amplius in Hundret placita teneant, nec causam quæ ad regimen animarum pertinet, ad judicium sæcularium hominum adducant. Wilkins, Leges Anglo-Saxon. 230.

Before the conquest the bishop and earl sat together in the court of the county or hundred, and, as we may infer from the tenor of this charter, ecclesiastical matters were decided loosely, and rather by the common law than according to the canons. This practice had been already forbidden by some canons enacted under Edgar, id. p. 83, but apparently with little effect. The separation of the civil and ecclesiastical tribunals was not made in Denmark till the reign of Nicholas, who ascended the throne in 1105. Langebek, Script. Rer. Danic. t. iv. p. 380. Others refer the law to St. Canut, about 1080. t. ii. p. 209.

[2] Ecclesiasticarum personarum et omnium clericorum, et rerum eorum justitiam et potestatem, et distributionem honorum ecclesiasticorum, in manu episcoporum esse perhibeo, et confirmo. Wilkins, Leges Anglo-Saxon. p. 310.

conviction or confession the church ought not to protect.[1] These constitutions were the leading subject of difference between the king and Thomas à Becket. Most of them were annulled by the pope, as derogatory to ecclesiastical liberty. It is not improbable, however, that, if Louis VII. had played a more dignified part, the see of Rome, which an existing schism rendered dependent upon the favor of those two monarchs, might have receded in some measure from her pretensions. But France implicitly giving way to the encroachments of ecclesiastical power, it became impossible for Henry completely to withstand them.

The constitutions of Clarendon, however, produced some effect, and in the reign of Henry III. more unremitted and successful efforts began to be made to maintain the independence of temporal government. The judges of the king's court had until that time been themselves principally ecclesiastics, and consequently tender of spiritual privileges.[2] But now, abstaining from the exercise of temporal jurisdiction, in obedience to the strict injunctions of their canons,[3] the clergy gave place to common lawyers, professors of a system very discordant from their own. These soon began to assert the supremacy of their jurisdiction by issuing writs of prohibition whenever the ecclesiastical tribunals passed the boundaries which approved use had established.[4] Little accustomed to such control, the proud hierarchy chafed under the bit; several provincial synods protest against the pretensions of laymen to judge the anointed ministers whom they were bound to obey;[5] the cognizance of rights of patronage and breaches of contract is boldly asserted;[6] but firm and cautious, favored by the nobility, though not much by the king, the judges receded not a step, and ultimately fixed a barrier which the church was forced to respect.[7] In the ensuing reign of Edward I.,

[1] Wilkins, Leges Anglo-Saxon. p. 323; Lyttelton's Henry II.; Collier, &c.

[2] Dugdale's Origines Juridicales, c. 8.

[3] Decretal. l. i. tit. xxxvii. c. 1. Wilkins, Concilia, t. ii. p. 4.

[4] Prynne has produced several extracts from the pipe-rolls of Henry II., where a person has been fined quia placitavit de laico feodo in curiâ christianitatis. And a bishop of Durham is fined five hundred marks quia tenuit placitum *de advocatione cujusdam ecclesiæ* in curiâ christianitatis. Epistle dedicatory to Prynne's Records, vol. iii. Glanvil gives the form of a writ of prohibition to the spiritual court for inquiring de feodo laico; for it had jurisdiction over lands in frankalmoign. This is comformable to the constitutions of Clarendon, and shows that they were still in force. See also Lyttelton's Henry II., vol. iii. p. 97.

[5] Cum judicandi Christos domini nulla sit laicis attributa potestas, apud quos manet necessitas obsequendi. Wilkins, Concilia, t. i. p. 747.

[6] Id. ibid.; et t. ii. p. 90.

[7] Vide Wilkins, Concilia, t. ii. passim.

an archbishop acknowledges the abstract right of the king's bench to issue prohibitions;[1] and the statute entitled Circumspectè agatis, in the thirteenth year of that prince, while by its mode of expression it seems designed to guarantee the actual privileges of spiritual jurisdiction, had a tendency, especially with the disposition of the judges, to preclude the assertion of some which are not therein mentioned. Neither the right of advowson nor any temporal contract is specified in this act as pertaining to the church; and accordingly the temporal courts have ever since maintained an undisputed jurisdiction over them.[2] They succeeded also partially in preventing the impunity of crimes perpetrated by clerks. It was enacted by the statute of Westminster, in 1275, or rather a construction was put upon that act, which is obscurely worded, that clerks indicted for felony should not be delivered to their ordinary until an inquest had been taken of the matter of accusation, and, if they were found guilty, that their real and personal estate should be forfeited to the crown. In later times the clerical privilege was not allowed till the party had pleaded to the indictment, and being duly convict, as is the practice at present.[3]

Less vigorous in France.

The civil magistrates of France did not by any means exert themselves so vigorously for their emancipation. The same or rather worse usurpations existed, and the same complaints were made, under Philip Augustus, St. Louis, and Philip the Bold; but

1 Licet prohibitiones hujusmodi a curiâ christianissimi regis nostri justè proculdubio, ut diximus, concedantur. Id. t. ii. p. 100 and p. 115.

2 The statute Circumspectè agatis, for it is acknowledged as a statute, though not drawn up in the form of one, is founded upon an answer of Edward I. to the prelates who had petitioned for some modification of prohibitions. Collier, always prone to exaggerate church authority, insinuates that the jurisdiction of the spiritual court over breaches of contract, even without oath, is preserved by this statute; but the express words of the king show that none whatever was intended, and the archbishop complains bitterly of it afterwards. Wilkins, Concilia, t. ii. p. 118. Collier's Ecclesiast. History, vol. i. p. 487. So far from having any cognizance of civil contracts not confirmed by oath, to which I am not certain that the church ever pretended in any country, the spiritual court had no jurisdiction at all, even where an oath had intervened, unless there was a deficiency of proof by writing or witnesses. Glanvil, l. x. c. 12; Constitut. Clarendon, art. 15.

3 2 Inst. p. 163. This is not likely to mislead a well-informed reader, but it ought, perhaps, to be mentioned that by the "clerical privilege" we are only to understand what is called benefit of clergy, which in fact is, or rather was till recent alterations of the law since the first edition of this work, no more than the remission of capital punishment for the first conviction of felony, and that not for the clergy alone, but for all culprits alike. They were not called upon at any time, I believe, to prove their claim as clergy, except by reading the *neck-verse* after trial and conviction in the king's court. They were then in strictness to be committed to the ordinary or ecclesiastical superior, which probably was not often done.

the laws of those sovereigns tend much more to confirm than to restrain ecclesiastical encroachments.[1] Some limitations were attempted by the secular courts; and an historian gives us the terms of a confederacy among the French nobles in 1246, binding themselves by oath not to permit the spiritual judges to take cognizance of any matter, except heresy, marriage, and usury.[2] Unfortunately Louis IX. was almost as little disposed as Henry III. to shake off the yoke of ecclesiastical dominion. But other sovereigns in the same period, from various motives, were equally submissive. Frederic II. explicitly adopts the exemption of clerks from criminal as well as civil jurisdiction of seculars.[3] And Alfonso X. introduced the same system in Castile; a kingdom where neither the papal authority nor the independence of the church had obtained any legal recognition until the promulgation of his code, which teems with all the principles of the canon law.[4] It is almost needless to mention that all ecclesiastical powers and privileges were incorporated with the jurisprudence of the kingdom of Naples, which, especially after the accession of the Angevin line, stood in a peculiar relation of dependence upon the Holy See.[5]

Restraints on alienations in mortmain.

The vast acquisitions of landed wealth made for many ages by bishops, chapters, and monasteries, began at length to excite the jealousy of sovereigns. They perceived that, although the prelates might send their stipulated proportion of vassals into the field, yet there could not be that active coöperation which the spirit of feudal tenures required, and that the national arm was palsied by the diminution of military nobles. Again the re-

[1] It seems deducible from a law of Philip Augustus, Ordonnances des Rois, t. i. p. 39, that a clerk convicted of some heinous offences might be capitally punished after degradation; yet a subsequent ordinance, p. 43, renders this doubtful; and the theory of clerical immunity became afterwards more fully established.

[2] Matt. Paris, p. 629.

[3] Statuimus, ut nullus ecclesiasticam personam, in criminali quæstione vel civili, trahere ad judicium sæculare præsumat: Ordonnances des Rois de France, t. i. p. 611, where this edict is recited and approved by Louis Hutin. Philip the Bold had obtained leave from the pope to arrest clerks accused of heinous crimes, on condition of remitting them to the bishop's court for trial. Hist. du Droit Eccl. Franç. t. i. p. 426. A council at Bourges, held in 1276 had so absolutely condemned all interference of the secular power with clerks that the king was obliged to solicit this moderate favor. p. 421.

[4] Marina, Ensayo Historico-Critico sobre las Siete Partidas, c. 320, &c. Hist. du Droit Ecclés. Franç. t. i. p. 442.

[5] Giannone, l. xix. c. v.; l. xx. c. 8. One provision of Robert king of Naples is remarkable: it extends the immunity of clerks to their *concubines*. Ibid.

Villani strongly censures a law made at Florence in 1345, taking away the personal immunity of clerks in criminal cases. Though the state could make such a law, he says, it had no right to do so against the liberties of holy church. l. xii. c. 43.

liefs upon succession, and similar dues upon alienation, incidental to fiefs, were entirely lost when they came into the hands of these undying corporations, to the serious injury of the feudal superior. Nor could it escape reflecting men, during the contest about investitures, that, if the church peremptorily denied the supremacy of the state over her temporal wealth, it was but a just measure of retaliation, or rather self-defence, that the state should restrain her further acquisitions. Prohibitions of gifts in mortmain, though unknown to the lavish devotion of the new kingdoms, had been established by some of the Roman emperors to check the overgrown wealth of the hierarchy.[1] The first attempt at a limitation of this description in modern times was made by Frederic Barbarossa, who, in 1158, enacted that no fief should be transferred, either to the church or otherwise, without the permission of the superior lord. Louis IX. inserted a provision of the same kind in his Establishments.[2] Castile had also laws of a similar tendency.[3] A license from the crown is said to have been necessary in England before the conquest for alienations in mortmain; but however that may be, there seems no reason to imagine that any restraint was put upon them by the common law before Magna Charta; a clause of which statute was construed to prohibit all gifts to religious houses without the consent of the lord of the fee. And by the 7th Edward I. alienations in mortmain are absolutely taken away; though the king might always exercise his prerogative of granting a license, which was not supposed to be affected by the statute.[4]

Boniface VIII.

It must appear, I think, to every careful inquirer that the papal authority, though manifesting outwardly more show of strength every year, had been secretly undermined, and lost a great deal of its hold upon public opinion, before the accession of Boniface VIII., in 1294, to the pontifical throne. The clergy were rendered sullen by demands of money, invasions of the legal right of patronage, and unreasonable partiality to the mendicant orders; a part of the mendicants themselves had begun to

[1] Giannone, l. iii.

[2] Ordonnances des Rois, p. 213. See, too, p. 303 and alibi. Du Cange, v. Manus morta. *Amortissiment*, in Denisart and other French law-books. Fleury, Instit. au Droit, t. i. p. 350.

[3] Marina, Ensayo sobre las Siete Partidas, c. 235.

[4] 2 Inst. p. 74. Blackstone, vol. ii. c. 18.

declaim against the corruptions of the papal court; while the laity, subjects alike and sovereigns, looked upon both the head and the members of the hierarchy with jealousy and dislike. Boniface, full of inordinate arrogance and ambition, and not sufficiently sensible of this gradual change in human opinion, endeavored to strain to a higher pitch the despotic pretensions of former pontiffs. As Gregory VII. appears the most usurping of mankind till we read the history of Innocent III., so Innocent III. is thrown into shade by the superior audacity of Boniface VIII. But independently of the less favorable dispositions of the public, he wanted the most essential quality for an ambitious pope, reputation for integrity. He was suspected of having procured through fraud the resignation of his predecessor Celestine V., and his harsh treatment of that worthy man afterwards seems to justify the reproach. His actions, however, display the intoxication of extreme self-confidence. If we may credit some historians, he appeared at the Jubilee in 1300, a festival successfully instituted by himself to throw lustre around his court and fill his treasury,[1] dressed in imperial habits, with the two swords borne before him, emblems of his temporal as well as spiritual dominion over the earth.[2]

His disputes with the king of England,

It was not long after his elevation to the pontificate before Boniface displayed his temper. The two most powerful sovereigns of Europe, Philip the Fair and Edward I., began at the same moment to attack in a very arbitrary manner the revenues of the church. The English clergy had, by their own voluntary grants, or at least those of the prelates in their name, paid frequent subsidies to the crown from the beginning of the reign of Henry III. They had nearly in effect waived the ancient exemption, and retained only the common privilege of English freemen to tax themselves in a con-

[1] The Jubilee was a centenary commemoration in honor of St. Peter and St. Paul, established by Boniface VIII. on the faith of an imaginary precedent a century before. The period was soon reduced to fifty years, and from thence to twenty-five, as it still continues. The court of Rome, at the next jubilee, will however read with a sigh the description given of that in 1300. Papa innumerabilem pecuniam ab iisdem recepit, quia die et nocte duo clerici stabant ad altare sancti Pauli, tenentes in eorum manibus rastellos, rastellantes pecuniam infinitam. Auctor apud Muratori, Annali d' Italia. Plenary indulgences were granted by Boniface to all who should keep their jubilee at Rome, and I suppose are still to be had on the same terms. Matteo Villani gives a curious account of the throng at Rome in 1350.

[2] Giannone, l. xxi. c. 3. Velly, t. vii. p. 149. I have not observed any good authority referred to for this fact, which is however in the character of Boniface

stitutional manner. But Edward I. came upon them with demands so frequent and exorbitant, that they were compelled to take advantage of a bull issued by Boniface, forbidding them to pay any contribution to the state. The king disregarded every pretext, and, seizing their goods into his hands, with other tyrannical proceedings, ultimately forced them to acquiesce in his extortion. It is remarkable that the pope appears to have been passive throughout this contest of Edward I. with his clergy. But it was far otherwise in France. Philip the Fair had imposed a tax on the ecclesiastical order without their consent, a measure perhaps unprecedented, yet not more odious than the similar exactions of the king of England. Irritated by some previous differences, the pope issued his bull known by the initial words Clericis laicos, absolutely forbidding the clergy of every kingdom to pay, under whatever pretext of voluntary grant, gift, or loan, any sort of tribute to their government without his special permission. Though France was not particularly named, the king understood himself to be intended, and took his revenge by a prohibition to export money from the kingdom. This produced angry remonstrances on the part of Boniface; but the Gallican church adhered so faithfully to the crown, and showed indeed so much willingness to be spoiled of their money, that he could not insist upon the most unreasonable propositions of his bull, and ultimately allowed that the French clergy might assist their sovereign by voluntary contributions, though not by way of tax.

and of France.

For a very few years after these circumstances the pope and king of France appeared reconciled to each other; and the latter even referred his disputes with Edward I. to the arbitration of Boniface, "as a private person, Benedict of Gaeta (his proper name), and not as pontiff;" an almost nugatory precaution against his encroachment upon temporal authority.[1] But a terrible storm broke out in the first year

[1] Walt. Hemingford, p. 150. The award of Boniface, which he expresses himself to make both as pope and Benedict of Gaeta, is published in Rymer, t. ii. p. 819, and is very equitable. Nevertheless, the French historians agreed to charge him with partiality towards Edward, and mention several proofs of it, which do not appear in the bull itself. Previous to its publication it was allowable enough to follow common fame; but Velly has repeated mere falsehoods from Mezeray and Baillet, while he refers to the instrument itself in Rymer, which disproves them. Hist. de France, t. vii. p. 139. M. Gaillard, one of the most candid critics in history that France ever produced, pointed out the error of her common historians in the Mém. de l'Académie des Inscriptions, t. xxxix. p. 642;

of the fourteenth century. A bishop of Pamiers, who had been sent as legate from Boniface with some complaint, displayed so much insolence and such disrespect towards the king, that Philip, considering him as his own subject, was provoked to put him under arrest, with a view to institute a criminal process. Boniface, incensed beyond measure at this violation of ecclesiastical and legatine privileges, published several bulls addressed to the king and clergy of France, charging the former with a variety of offences, some of them not at all concerning the church, and commanding the latter to attend a council which he had summoned to meet at Rome. In one of these instruments, the genuineness of which does not seem liable to much exception, he declares in concise and clear terms that the king was subject to him in temporal as well as spiritual matters. This proposition had not hitherto been explicitly advanced, and it was now too late to advance it. Philip replied by a short letter in the rudest language, and ordered his bulls to be publicly burned at Paris. Determined, however, to show the real strength of his opposition, he summoned representatives from the three orders of his kingdom. This is commonly reckoned the first assembly of the States General. The nobility and commons disclaimed with firmness the temporal authority of the pope, and conveyed their sentiments to Rome through letters addressed to the college of cardinals. The clergy endeavored to steer a middle course, and were reluctant to enter into an engagement not to obey the pope's summons; yet they did not hesitate unequivocally to deny his temporal jurisdiction.

The council, however, opened at Rome; and notwithstanding the king's absolute prohibition, many French prelates held themselves bound to be present. In this assembly Boniface promulgated his famous constitution, denominated Unam sanctam. The church is one body, he therein declares, and has one head. Under its command are two swords, the one spiritual, and the other temporal; that to be used by the supreme pontiff himself; this by kings and knights, by his license and at his will. But the lesser sword must be subject to the greater, and the temporal to the spiritual authority. He concludes by declaring the subjection of every human being to the see of Rome to be an article of necessary faith.[1]

and the editors of L'Art de vérifier les Dates have also rectified it.

[1] Uterque est in potestate ecclesiæ, spiritalis scilicet gladius et materialis

Another bull pronounces all persons of whatever rank obliged to appear when personally cited before the audience or apostolical tribunal at Rome; "since such is our pleasure, who, by divine permission, rule the world." Finally, as the rupture with Philip grew more evidently irreconcilable, and the measures pursued by that monarch more hostile, he not only excommunicated him, but offered the crown of France to the emperor Albert I. This arbitrary transference of kingdoms was, like many other pretensions of that age, an improvement upon the right of deposing excommunicated sovereigns. Gregory VII. would not have denied that a nation, released by his authority from its allegiance, must reënter upon its original right of electing a new sovereign. But Martin IV. had assigned the crown of Aragon to Charles of Valois; the first instance, I think, of such an usurpation of power, but which was defended by the homage of Peter II., who had rendered his kingdom feudally dependent, like Naples, upon the Holy See.[1] Albert felt no eagerness to realize the liberal promises of Boniface; who was on the point of issuing a bull absolving the subjects of Philip from their allegiance, and declaring his forfeiture, when a very unexpected circumstance interrupted all his projects.

It is not surprising, when we consider how unaccustomed men were in those ages to disentangle the artful sophisms, and detect the falsehoods in point of fact, whereon the papal supremacy had been established, that the king of France should not have altogether pursued the course most becoming his dignity and the goodness of his cause. He gave too much the air of a personal quarrel with Boniface to what should have been a resolute opposition to the despotism of Rome.

Sed is quidem pro ecclesiâ, ille vero ab ecclesiâ exercendus: ille sacerdotis, is manu regum ac militum, sed ad nutum et patientiam sacerdotis. Oportet autem gladium esse sub gladio, et temporalem auctoritatem spiritali subjici potestati. Porro subesse Romano pontifici omni humanæ creaturæ declaramus, dicimus, definimus et pronunciamus omnino esse de necessitate fidei. Extravagant. l. i. tit. viii. c. 1.

[1] Innocent IV. had, however, in 1245, appointed one Bolon, brother to Sancho II., king of Portugal, to be a sort of coadjutor in the government of that kingdom, enjoining the barons to honor him as their sovereign, at the same time declaring that he did not intend to deprive the king or his lawful issue, if he should have any, of the kingdom. But this was founded on the request of the Portuguese nobility themselves, who were dissatisfied with Sancho's administration. Sext. Decretal. l. i. tit. viii. c. 2. Art de vérifier les Dates, t. i. p. 778.

Boniface invested James II. of Aragon with the crown of Sardinia, over which, however, the see of Rome had always pretended to a superiority by virtue of the concession (probably spurious) of Louis the Debonair. He promised Frederic king of Sicily the empire of Constantinople, which, I suppose, was not a fief of the Holy See. Giannone, l. xxi. c. 3.

Accordingly, in an assembly of his states at Paris, he preferred virulent charges against the pope, denying him to have been legitimately elected, imputing to him various heresies, and ultimately appealing to a general council and a lawful head of the church. These measures were not very happily planned; and experience had always shown that Europe would not submit to change the common chief of her religion for the purposes of a single sovereign. But Philip succeeded in an attempt apparently more bold and singular. Nogaret, a minister who had taken an active share in all the proceedings against Boniface, was secretly despatched into Italy, and, joining with some of the Colonna family, proscribed as Ghibelins, and rancorously persecuted by the pope, arrested him at Anagnia, a town in the neighborhood of Rome, to which he had gone without guards. This violent action was not, one would imagine, calculated to place the king in an advantageous light; yet it led accidentally to a favorable termination of his dispute. Boniface was soon rescued by the inhabitants of Anagnia; but rage brought on a fever which ended in his death; and the first act of his successor, Benedict XI., was to reconcile the king of France to the Holy See.[1]

The sensible decline of the papacy is to be dated from the pontificate of Boniface VIII., who had strained its authority to a higher pitch than any of his predecessors. There is a spell wrought by uninterrupted good fortune, which captivates men's understanding, and persuades them, against reasoning and analogy, that violent power is immortal and irresistible. The spell is broken by the first change of success. *We* have seen the working and the dissipation of this charm with a rapidity to which the events of former times bear as remote a relation as the gradual processes of nature to her deluges and her volcanoes. In tracing the papal empire over mankind we have no such marked and definite crisis of revolution. But slowly, like the retreat of waters, or the stealthy pace of old age, that extraordinary power over human opinion has been subsiding for five centuries. I have already observed that the symptoms of internal decay may be traced further back. But as the retrocession of the Roman terminus under Adrian gave the first overt proof of decline in the ambitious energies of that empire, so the tacit submission of the suc-

[1] Velly, Hist. de France, t. vii. p. 109-258; Crevier, Hist. de l'Université de Paris, t. ii. p. 170, &c.

cessors of Boniface VIII. to the king of France might have been hailed by Europe as a token that their influence was beginning to abate. Imprisoned, insulted, deprived eventually of life by the violence of Philip, a prince excommunicated, and who had gone all lengths in defying and despising the papal jurisdiction, Boniface had every claim to be avenged by the inheritors of the same spiritual dominion. When Benedict XI. rescinded the bulls of his predecessor, and admitted Philip the Fair to communion, without insisting on any concessions, he acted perhaps prudently, but gave a fatal blow to the temporal authority of Rome.

Removal of papal court to Avignon, A.D. 1305.

Benedict XI. lived but a few months, and his successor Clement V., at the instigation, as is commonly supposed, of the king of France, by whose influence he had been elected, took the extraordinary step of removing the papal chair to Avignon. In this city it remained for more than seventy years; a period which Petrarch and other writers of Italy compare to that of the Babylonish captivity. The majority of the cardinals was always French, and the popes were uniformly of the same nation. Timidly dependent upon the court of France, they neglected the interests and lost the affections of Italy. Rome, forsaken by her sovereign, nearly forgot her allegiance; what remained of papal authority in the ecclesiastical territories was exercised by cardinal legates, little to the honor or advantage of the Holy See. Yet the series of Avignon pontiffs were far from insensible to Italian politics. These occupied, on the contrary, the greater part of their attention. But engaging in them from motives too manifestly selfish, and being regarded as a sort of foreigners from birth and residence, they aggravated that unpopularity and bad reputation which from various other causes attached itself to their court.

Contest of popes with Louis of Bavaria.

Though none of the supreme pontiffs after Boniface VIII. ventured upon such explicit assumptions of a general jurisdiction over sovereigns by divine right as he had made in his controversy with Philip, they maintained one memorable struggle for temporal power against the emperor Louis of Bavaria. Maxims long boldly repeated without contradiction, and engrafted upon the canon law, passed almost for articles of faith among the clergy and those who trusted in them; and in despite of all ancient authorities, Clement V. laid it down that the popes.

having transferred the Roman empire from the Greeks to the Germans, and delegated the right of nominating an emperor to certain electors, still reserved the prerogative of approving the choice, and of receiving from its subject upon his coronation an oath of fealty and obedience.[1] This had a regard to Henry VII., who denied that his oath bore any such interpretation, and whose measures, much to the alarm of the court of Avignon, were directed towards the restoration of his imperial rights in Italy. Among other things, he conferred the rank of vicar of the empire upon Matteo Visconti, lord of Milan. The popes had for some time pretended to possess that vicariate, during a vacancy of the empire; and after Henry's death insisted upon Visconti's surrender of the title. Several circumstances, for which I refer to the political historians of Italy, produced a war between the pope's legate and the Visconti family. The emperor Louis sent assistance to the latter, as heads of the Ghibelin or imperial party. This interference cost him above twenty years of trouble. John XXII., a man as passionate and ambitious as Boniface himself, immediately published a bull in which he asserted the right of administering the empire during its vacancy (even in Germany, as it seems from the generality of his expression), as well as of deciding in a doubtful choice of the electors, to appertain to the Holy See; and commanded Louis to lay down his pretended authority until the supreme jurisdiction should determine upon his election. Louis's election had indeed been questionable; but that controversy was already settled in the field of Muhldorf, where he had obtained a victory over his competitor the duke of Austria nor had the pope ever interfered to appease a civil war during several years that Germany had been internally distracted by the dispute. The emperor, not yielding to this peremptory order, was excommunicated; his vassals were absolved from their oath of fealty, and all treaties of alliance between him and foreign princes annulled. Ger-

A.D. 1323.

[1] Romani principes, &c. . . . . Romano pontifici, a quo approbationem personæ ad imperialis celsitudinis apicem assumendæ, necnon unctionem, consecrationem et imperii coronam accipiunt, sua submittere capita non reputârunt indignum, seque illi et eidem ecclesiæ, quæ a Græcis imperium transtulit in Germanos, et a quâ ad certos eorum principes jus et potestas eligendi regem, in imperatorem postmodum promovendum, pertinet, adstringere vinculo juramenti, &c. Clement. l. ii. t. ix. The terms of the oath, as recited in this constitution, do not warrant the pope's interpretation, but imply only that the emperor shall be the advocate or defender of the church.

many, however, remained firm; and if Louis himself had manifested more decision of mind and uniformity in his conduct, the court of Avignon must have signally failed in a contest from which it did not in fact come out very successful. But while at one time he went intemperate lengths against John XXII., publishing scandalous accusations in an assembly of the citizens of Rome, and causing a Franciscan friar to be chosen in his room, after an irregular sentence of deposition, he was always anxious to negotiate terms of accom modation, to give up his own active partisans, and to make concessions the most derogatory to his independence and dignity. From John indeed he had nothing to expect; but Benedict XII. would gladly have been reconciled, if he had not feared the kings of France and Naples, political adversaries of the emperor, who kept the Avignon popes in a sort of servitude. His successor, Clement VI., inherited the implacable animosity of John XXII. towards Louis, who died without obtaining the absolution he had long abjectly solicited.[1]

Spirit of resistance to papal usurpations.

Though the want of firmness in this emperor's character gave sometimes a momentary triumph to the popes, it is evident that their authority lost ground during the continuance of this struggle. Their right of confirming imperial elections was expressly denied by a diet held at Frankfort in 1338, which established as a fundamental principle that the imperial dignity depended upon God alone, and that whoever should be chosen by a majority of the electors became immediately both king and emperor, with all prerogatives of that station, and did not require the approbation of the pope.[2] This law, confirmed as it was by subsequent usage, emancipated the German empire, which was immediately concerned in opposing the papal claims. But some who were actively engaged in these transactions took more extensive views, and assailed the whole edifice of temporal power which the Roman see had

[1] Schmidt, Hist. des Allemands, t. iv. p. 446–536, seems the best modern authority for this contest between the empire and papacy. See also Struvius, Corp. Hist. German. p. 591.

[2] Quòd imperialis dignitas et potestas immediatè ex solo Deo, et quòd de jure et imperii consuetudine antiquitùs approbatâ postquam aliquis eligitur in imperatorem sive regem ab electoribus imperii concorditer, vel majori parte eorundem, statim ex solâ electione est rex verus et imperator Romanorum censendus et nominandus, et eidem debet ab omnibus imperie subjectis obediri, et administrandi jura imperii, et cætera faciendi, quæ ad imperatorem verum pertinent, plenariam habet potestatem, nec papæ sive sedis apostolicæ aut alicujus alterius approbatione, confirmatione, auctoritate indiget vel censensu. Schmidt, p. 513.

been constructing for more than two centuries. Several men of learning, among whom Dante, Ockham, and Marsilius of Padua are the most conspicuous, investigated the foundations of this superstructure, and exposed their insufficiency.[1] Literature, too long the passive handmaid of spiritual despotism, began to assert her nobler birthright of ministering to liberty and truth. Though the writings of these opponents of Rome are not always reasoned upon very solid principles, they at least taught mankind to scrutinize what had been received with implicit respect, and prepared the way for more philosophical discussions. About this time a new class of enemies had unexpectedly risen up against the rulers of the church. These were a part of the Franciscan order, who had seceded from the main body on account of alleged deviations from the rigor of their primitive rule. Their schism was chiefly founded upon a quibble about the right of property in things consumable, which they maintained to be incompatible with the absolute poverty prescribed to them. This frivolous sophistry was united with the wildest fanatacism; and as John XXII. attempted to repress their follies by a cruel persecution, they proclaimed aloud the corruption of the church, fixed the name of Antichrist upon the papacy, and warmly supported the emperor Louis throughout all his contention with the Holy See.[2]

Rapacity of Avignon popes.

Meanwhile the popes who sat at Avignon continued to invade with surprising rapaciousness the patronage and revenues of the church. The mandats or letters directing a particular clerk to be preferred seem to have given place in a great degree to the more effectual method of appropriating benefices by reservation or provision, which was carried to an enormous extent in the fourteenth century. John XXII., the most insatiate of pontiffs, reserved to himself all the bishoprics in Christendom.[3]

1 Giannone, l. xxii. c. 8. Schmidt, t. vi. p. 152. Dante was dead before these events, but his principles were the same. Ockham had already exerted his talents in the same cause by writing, in behalf of Philip IV., against Boniface, a dialogue between a knight and a clerk on the temporal supremacy of the church. This is published among other tracts of the same class in Goldastus, Monarchia Imperii, p. 13. This dialogue is translated entire in the Songe du Vergier, a more celebrated performance, ascribed to Raoul de Presles under Charles V.

2 The schism of the rigid Franciscans or Fratricelli is one of the most singular parts of ecclesiastical history, and had a material tendency both to depress the temporal authority of the papacy, and to pave the way for the Reformation. It is fully treated by Mosheim, cent. 13 and 14, and by Crevier, Hist. de l'Université de Paris, t. ii. p. 233-264, &c.

3 Fleury, Institutions, &c., t. i. p. 368; F. Paul on Benefices, c. 37.

Benedict XII. assumed the privilege for his own life of disposing of all benefices vacant by cession, deprivation, or translation. Clement VI. naturally thought that his title was equally good with his predecessor's, and continued the same right for his own time; which soon became a permanent rule of the Roman chancery.[1] Hence the appointment of a prelate to a rich bishopric was generally but the first link in a chain of translation which the pope could regulate according to his interest. Another capital innovation was made by John XXII. in the establishment of the famous tax called annates, or first fruits of ecclesiastical benefices, which he imposed for his own benefit. These were one year's value, estimated according to a fixed rate in the books of the Roman chancery, and payable to the papal collectors throughout Europe.[2] Various other devices were invented to obtain money, which these degenerate popes, abandoning the magnificent schemes of their predecessors, were content to seek as their principal object. John XXII. is said to have accumulated an almost incredible treasure, exaggerated perhaps by the ill-will of his contemporaries;[3] but it may be doubted whether even his avarice reflected greater dishonor on the church than the licentious profuseness of Clement VI.[4]

These exactions were too much encouraged by the kings of France, who participated in the plunder, or at least required the mutual assistance of the popes for their own imposts on the clergy. John XXII. obtained leave of Charles the Fair to levy a tenth of ecclesiastical revenues;[5] and Clement VI., in return, granted two tenths to Philip of Valois for the expenses of his war. A similar tax was raised by the same authority towards the ransom of John.[6]

[1] F. Paul, c. 38. Translations of bishops had been made by the authority of the metropolitan till Innocent III. reserved this prerogative to the Holy See. De Marca, l. vi. c. 8.

[2] F. Paul, c. 38; Fleury, p. 424; De Marca, l. vi. c. 10; Pasquier, l. iii. c. 28. The popes had long been in the habit of receiving a pecuniary gratuity when they granted the pallium to an archbishop, though this was reprehended by strict men, and even condemned by themselves. De Marca, ibid. It is noticed as a remarkable thing of Innocent IV. that he gave the pall to a German archbishop without accepting anything. Schmidt, t. iv. p. 172. The original and nature of annates is copiously treated in Lenfant, Concile de Constance, t. ii p. 133.

[3] G. Villani puts this at 25,000,000 of florins, which it is hardly possible to believe. The Italians were credulous enough to listen to any report against the popes of Avignon. l. xi. c. 20. Giannone, l. xxii. c. 8.

[4] For the corruption of morals at Avignon during the secession, see De Sade, Vie de Pétrarque, t. i. p. 70, and several other passages.

[5] Continuator Gul. de Nangis, in Spicilegio d'Achery, t. iii. p. 86, (folio edition.) Ita miseram ecclesiam, says this monk, unus tondet, alter excoriat.

[6] Fleury, Institut. au Droit ecclesiastique, t. ii. p. 245. Villaret, t. ix

These were contributions for national purposes unconnected with religion, which the popes had never before pretended to impose, and which the king might properly have levied with the consent of his clergy, according to the practice of England. But that consent might not always be obtained with ease, and it seemed a more expeditious method to call in the authority of the pope. A manlier spirit was displayed by our ancestors. It was the boast of England to have placed the first legal barrier to the usurpations of Rome, if we except the insulated Pragmatic Sanction of St. Louis, from which the practice of succeeding ages in France entirely deviated. The English barons had, in a letter addressed to Boniface VIII., absolutely disclaimed his temporal supremacy over their crown, which he had attempted to set up by intermeddling in the quarrel of Scotland.[1] This letter, it is remarkable, is nearly coincident in point of time with that of the French nobility; and the two combined may be considered as a joint protestation of both kingdoms, and a testimony to the general sentiment among the superior ranks of the laity. A very few years afterwards, the parliament of Carlisle wrote a strong remonstrance to Clement V. against the system of provisions and other extortions, including that of first fruits, which it was rumored, they say, he was meditating to demand.[2] But the court of Avignon was not to be moved by remonstrances; and the feeble administration of Edward II. gave way to ecclesiastical usurpations at home as well a abroad.[3] His magnanimous son took a bolder line. After complaining ineffectually to Clement VI. of the enormous abuse which reserved almost all English benefices to the pope, and generally for the benefit of aliens,[4] he passed in 1350 the famous statute of provisors. This act, reciting one supposed to have been made at the parliament of Carlisle, which, however, does not appear,[5] and complaining in strong

p. 431. It became a regular practice for the king to obtain the pope's consent to lay a tax on his clergy, though he sometimes applied first to themselves. Garnier, t. xx. p. 141

[1] Rymer, t. ii. p. 373. Collier, vol. i. p. 725.

[2] Rotuli Parliamenti, vol. i. p. 204. This passage, hastily read, has led Collier and other English writers, such as Henry and Blackstone, into the supposition that annates were imposed by Clement V. But the concurrent testimony of foreign authors refers this tax to John XXII. as the canon law also shows. Extravagant. Communes, l. iii. tit. ii. c. 11.

[3] The statute called Articuli cleri, in 1316, was directed rather towards confirming than limiting the clerical immunity in criminal cases.

[4] Collier, p. 546.

[5] It is singular that Sir E. Coke should assert that this act recites and is founded upon the statute 35 E. I., De asportatis religiosorum (2 Inst. 580); whereas there is not the least resemblance in the words, and very little, if any, in the substance. Blackstone, in consequence,

language of the mischief sustained through continual reservations of benefices, enacts that all elections and collations shall be free, according to law, and that, in case any provision or reservation should be made by the court of Rome, the king should for that turn have the collation of such a benefice, if it be of ecclesiatical election or patronage.[1] This devolution to the crown, which seems a little arbitrary, was the only remedy that could be effectual against the connivance and timidity of chapters and spiritual patrons. We cannot assert that a statute so nobly planned was executed with equal steadiness. Sometimes by royal dispensation, sometimes by neglect or evasion, the papal bulls of provision were still obeyed, though fresh laws were enacted to the same effect as the former. It was found on examination in 1367 that some clerks enjoyed more than twenty benefices by the pope's dispensation.[2] And the parliaments both of this and of Richard II.'s reign invariably complain of the disregard shown to the statutes of provisors. This led to other measures, which I shall presently mention.

Return of popes to Rome.

The residence of the popes at Avignon gave very general offence to Europe, and they could not themselves avoid perceiving the disadvantage of absence from their proper diocese, the city of St. Peter, the source of all their claims to sovereign authority. But Rome, so long abandoned, offered but an inhospitable reception: Urban V. returned to Avignon, after a short experiment of the capital; and it was not till 1376 that the promise, often repeated and long delayed, of restoring the papal chair to the metropolis of Christendom, was ultimately fulfilled by Gregory XI. His death, which happened soon afterwards, prevented, it is said, a second flight that he was preparing. This was followed by the great schism, one of the most remarkable events in ecclesiastical history. It is a difficult and by no means an interesting question to determine the validity of that contested election which distracted the Latin church for so many years. All contemporary

Contested election of Urban VI. and Clement VII. A.D. 1377.

mistakes the nature of that act of Edward I., and supposes it to have been made against papal provisions, to which I do not perceive even an allusion. Whether any such statute was really made in the Carlisle parliament of 35 E. I., as is asserted both in 25 E. III. and in the roll of another parliament, 17 E. III. (Rot. Parl. t. ii. p. 144), is hard to decide; and perhaps those who examine this point will have to choose between wilful suppression and wilful interpolation.

[1] 25 E. III. stat. 6.

[2] Collier, p. 568.

testimonies are subject to the suspicion of partiality in a cause where no one was permitted to be neutral. In one fact however there is a common agreement, that the cardinals, of whom the majority were French, having assembled in conclave, for the election of a successor to Gregory XI., were disturbed by a tumultuous populace, who demanded with menaces a Roman, or at least an Italian, pope. This tumult appears to have been sufficiently violent to excuse, and in fact did produce, a considerable degree of intimidation. After some time the cardinals made choice of the archbishop of Bari, a Neapolitan, who assumed the name of Urban VI. His election satisfied the populace, and tranquillity was restored. The cardinals announced their choice to the absent members of their college, and behaved towards Urban as their pope for several weeks. But his uncommon harshness of temper giving them offence, they withdrew to a neighboring town, and, protesting that his election had been compelled by the violence of the Roman populace, annulled the whole proceeding, and chose one of their own number, who took the pontifical name of Clement VII. Such are the leading circumstances which produced the famous schism. Constraint is so destructive of the essence of election, that suffrages given through actual intimidation ought, I think, to be held invalid, even without minutely inquiring whether the degree of illegal force was such as might reasonably overcome the constancy of a firm mind. It is improbable that the free votes of the cardinals would have been bestowed on the archbishop of Bari; and I should not feel much hesitation in pronouncing his election to have been void. But the sacred college unquestionably did not use the earliest opportunity of protesting against the violence they had suffered; and we may infer almost with certainty, that, if Urban's conduct had been more acceptable to that body, the world would have heard little of the transient riot at his election. This however opens a delicate question in jurisprudence; namely, under what circumstances acts, not only irregular, but substantially invalid, are capable of receiving a retroactive confirmation by the acquiescence and acknowledgment of parties concerned to oppose them. And upon this, I conceive, the great problem of legitimacy between Urban and Clement will be found to depend.[1]

[1] Lenfant has collected all the original testimonies on both sides in the first book of his Concile de Pise. No positive decision has ever been made on the subject,

The Great Schism.

Whatever posterity may have judged about the pretensions of these competitors, they at that time shared the obedience of Europe in nearly equal proportions. Urban remained at Rome; Clement resumed the station of Avignon. To the former adhered Italy, the Empire, England, and the nations of the north; the latter retained in his allegiance France, Spain, Scotland, and Sicily. Fortunately for the church, no question of religious faith intermixed itself with this schism; nor did any other impediment to reunion exist than the obstinacy and selfishness of the contending parties. As it was impossible to come to any agreement on the original merits, there seemed to be no means of healing the wound but by the abdication of both popes and a fresh undisputed election. This was the general wish of Europe, but urged with particular zeal by the court of France, and, above all, by the university of Paris, which esteems this period the most honorable in her annals. The cardinals however of neither obedience would recede so far from their party as to suspend the election of a successor upon a vacancy of the pontificate, which would have at least removed one half of the obstacle. The Roman conclave accordingly placed three pontiffs successively, Boniface IX., Innocent VI., and Gregory XII., in the seat of Urban VI.; and the cardinals at Avignon, upon the death of Clement in 1394, elected Benedict XIII. (Peter de Luna), famous for his inflexible obstinacy in prolonging the schism. He repeatedly promised to sacrifice his dignity for the sake of union. But there was no subterfuge to which this crafty pontiff had not recourse in order to avoid compliance with his word, though importuned, threatened, and even besieged in his palace at Avignon. Fatigued by his evasions, France withdrew her obedience, and the Gallican church continued for a few years without acknowledging any supreme head. But this step, which was rather the measure of the university of Paris than of the nation, it seemed advisable to retract; and Benedict was again obeyed, though France continued to urge his resignation. A second subtraction of obedience, or at least declaration of neutrality, was resolved upon, as preparatory to the convocation of a general council. On the

but the Roman popes are numbered in the commonly received list, and those of Avignon are not. The modern Italian writers express no doubt about the legitimacy of Urban; the French at most intimate that Clement's pretensions were not to be wholly rejected.

other hand, those who sat at Rome displayed not less insincerity. Gregory XII. bound himself by oath on his accession to abdicate when it should appear necessary. But while these rivals were loading each other with the mutual reproach of schism, they drew on themselves the suspicion of at least a virtual collusion in order to retain their respective stations. At length the cardinals of both parties, wearied with so much dissimulation, deserted their masters, and summoned a general council to meet at Pisa.[1]

The council assembled at Pisa deposed both Gregory and Benedict, without deciding in any respect as to their pretensions, and elected Alexander V. by its own supreme authority. This authority, however, was not universally recognized; the schism, instead of being healed, became more desperate; for as Spain adhered firmly to Benedict, and Gregory was not without supporters, there were now three contending pontiffs in the church. A general council was still, however, the favorite and indeed the sole remedy; and John XXIII., successor of Alexander V., was reluctantly prevailed upon, or perhaps trepanned, into convoking one to meet at Constance. In this celebrated assembly he was himself deposed; a sentence which he incurred by that tenacious clinging to his dignity, after repeated promises to abdicate, which had already proved fatal to his competitors. The deposition of John, confessedly a legitimate pope, may strike us as an extraordinary measure. But, besides the opportunity it might afford of restoring union, the council found a pretext for this sentence in his enormous vices, which indeed they seem to have taken upon common fame without any judicial process. The true motive, however, of their proceedings against him was a desire to make a signal display of a new system which had rapidly gained ground, and which I may venture to call the whig principles of the catholic church. A great question was at issue, whether the polity of that establishment should be an absolute or an exceedingly limited monarchy. The papal tyranny, long endured and still increasing, had excited an active spirit of reformation which the most distinguished ecclesiastics of France and other countries encouraged. They recurred, as far as their knowledge allowed, to a more primi-

Council of Pisa, A.D. 1409; of Constance, A.D. 1414;

1 Villaret; Lenfant, Concile de Pise; Crevier, Hist de l'Université de Paris, t. iii.

tive discipline than the canon law, and elevated the supremacy of general councils. But in the formation of these they did not scruple to introduce material innovations. The bishops have usually been considered the sole members of ecclesiastical assemblies. At Constance, however, sat and voted not only the chiefs of monasteries, but the ambassadors of all Christian princes, the deputies of universities, with a multitude of inferior theologians, and even doctors of law.[1] These were naturally accessible to the pride of sudden elevation, which enabled them to control the strong, and humiliate the lofty. In addition to this the adversaries of the court of Rome carried another not less important innovation. The Italian bishops, almost universally in the papal interests, were so numerous that, if suffrages had been taken by the head, their preponderance would have impeded any measures of transalpine nations towards reformation. It was determined, therefore, that the council should divide itself into four nations, the Italian, the German, the French, and the English, each with equal rights; and that, every proposition having been separately discussed, the majority of the four should prevail.[2] This revolutionary spirit was very unacceptable to the cardinals, who submitted reluctantly, and with a determination, that did not prove altogether unavailing, to save their papal monarchy by a dexterous policy. They could not, however, prevent the famous resolutions of the fourth and fifth sessions, which declare that the council has received, by divine right, an authority to which every rank, even the papal, is obliged to submit, in matters of faith, in the extirpation of the present schism, and in the reformation of the church both in its head and its members; and that every person, even a pope, who shall obstinately refuse

1 Lenfant, Concile de Constance, t. i. p. 107 (edit. 1727). Crevier, t. iii. p. 405. It was agreed that the ambassadors could not vote upon articles of faith, but only on questions relating to the settlement of the church. But the second order of ecclesiastics were allowed to vote generally.

2 This separation of England, as a co-equal limb of the council, gave great umbrage to the French, who maintained that, like Denmark and Sweden, it ought to have been reckoned along with Germany. The English deputies came down with a profusion of authorities to prove the antiquity of their monarchy, for which they did not fail to put in requisition the immeasurable pedigrees of Ireland. Joseph of Arimathea, who planted Christianity and his stick at Glastonbury, did his best to help the cause. The recent victory of Azincourt, I am inclined to think, had more weight with the council. Lenfant, t. ii. p. 46.

At a time when a very different spirit prevailed, the English bishops under Henry II. and Henry III. had claimed as a right that no more than four of their number should be summoned to a general council. Hoveden, p. 320; Carte, vol. ii. p. 84. This was like boroughs praying to be released from sending members to parliament.

to obey that council, or any other lawfully assembled, is liable to such punishment as shall be necessary.[1] These decrees are the great pillars of that moderate theory with respect to the papal authority which distinguished the Gallican church, and is embraced, I presume, by almost all laymen and the major part of ecclesiastics on this side of the Alps.[2] They embarrass the more popish churchmen, as the Revolution does our English tories; some boldly impugn the authority of the council of Constance, while others chicane upon the interpretation of its decrees. Their practical importance is not, indeed, direct; universal councils exist only in possibility; but the acknowledgment of a possible authority paramount to the see of Rome has contributed, among other means, to check its usurpations.

The purpose for which these general councils had been required, next to that of healing the schism, was the reformation of abuses. All the rapacious exactions, all the scandalous venality of which Europe had complained, while unquestioned pontiffs ruled at Avignon, appeared light in comparison of the practices of both rivals during the schism. Tenths repeatedly levied upon the clergy, annates rigorously exacted and enhanced by new valuations, fees annexed to the complicated formalities of the papal chancery, were the means by which each half of the church was compelled to reimburse its chief for the subtraction of the other's obedience. Boniface IX., one of the Roman line, whose fame is a little worse than that of his antagonists, made a gross traffic of his patronage; selling the privileges of exemption from ordinary jurisdiction, of holding benefices in commendam, and other dispensations invented for the benefit of the Holy See.[3] Nothing had been attempted at Pisa towards reformation. At Constance the majority were ardent and sincere; the representatives of the French, German, and English churches met with a determined and, as we have seen, not always unsuccessful resolution to assert their ecclesiastical liberties. They appointed a committee of reformation, whose recommendations, if carried into effect, would have annihilated almost entirely that artfully constructed machinery by

1 Id. p. 164. Crevier, t. iii. p. 417.

2 This was written in 1816. The present state of opinion among those who belong to the Gallican church has become exceedingly different from what it was in the last two centuries. [1847.]

3 Lenfant, Hist. du Concile de Pise, passim; Crevier; Villaret; Schmidt; Collier.

which Rome had absorbed so much of the revenues and patronage of the church. But men, interested in perpetuating these abuses, especially the cardinals, improved the advantages which a skilful government always enjoys in playing against a popular assembly. They availed themselves of the jealousies arising out of the division of the council into nations, which exterior political circumstances had enhanced. France, then at war with England, whose pretensions to be counted as a fourth nation she had warmly disputed, and not well disposed towards the emperor Sigismund, joined with the Italians against the English and German members of the council in a matter of the utmost importance, the immediate election of a pope before the articles of reformation should be finally concluded. These two nations, in return, united with the Italians to choose the cardinal Colonna, against the advice of the French divines, who objected to any member of the sacred college. The court of Rome were gainers in both questions. Martin V., the new pope, soon evinced his determination to elude any substantial reform. After publishing a few constitutions tending to redress some of the abuses that had arisen during the schism, he contrived to make separate conventions with the several nations, and as soon as possible dissolved the council.[1]

By one of the decrees passed at Constance, another general council was to be assembled in five years, a second at the end of seven more, and from that time a similar representation of the church was to meet every ten years. Martin V. accordingly convoked a council at Pavia, which, on account of the plague, was transferred to Siena; but nothing of importance was transacted by this assembly.[2] That which

of Basle, A.D. 1433.

he summoned seven years afterwards to the city of Basle had very different results. The pope, dying before the meeting of this council, was succeeded by Eugenius IV., who, anticipating the spirit of its discussions, attempted to crush its independence in the outset, by transferring the place of session to an Italian city. No point was reckoned so material in the contest between the popes and reformers as whether a council should sit in Italy or beyond

[1] Lenfant, Concile de Constance. The copiousness as well as impartiality of this work justly renders it an almost exclusive authority. Crevier (Hist. de l'Université de Paris, t. iii.) has given a good sketch of the council, and Schmidt (Hist. des Allemandes, t. v.) is worthy of attention.

[2] Lenfant, Guerre des Hussites, t. i. p. 223.

the Alps. The council of Basle began, as it proceeded, in open enmity to the court of Rome. Eugenius, after several years had elapsed in more or less hostile discussions, exerted his prerogative of removing the assembly to Ferrara, and from thence to Florence. For this he had a specious pretext in the negotiation, then apparently tending to a prosperous issue, for the reunion of the Greek church; a triumph, however transitory, of which his council at Florence obtained the glory. On the other hand, the assembly of Basle, though much weakened by the defection of those who adhered to Eugenius, entered into compacts with the Bohemian insurgents, more essential to the interests of the church than any union with the Greeks, and completed the work begun at Constance by abolishing the annates, the reservations of benefices, and other abuses of papal authority. In this it received the approbation of most princes; but when, provoked by the endeavors of the pope to frustrate its decrees, it proceeded so far as to suspend and even to depose him, neither France nor Germany concurred in the sentence. Even the council of Constance had not absolutely asserted a right of deposing a lawful pope, except in case of heresy, though their conduct towards John could not otherwise be justified.[1] This question indeed of ecclesiastical public law seems to be still undecided. The fathers of Basle acted however with greater intrepidity than discretion, and, not perhaps sensible of the change that was taking place in public opinion, raised Amadeus, a retired duke of Savoy, to the pontifical dignity by the name of Felix V. They thus renewed the schism, and divided the obedience of the catholic church for a few years. The empire, however, as well as France, observed a singular and not very consistent neutrality; respecting Eugenius as a lawful pope, and the assembly at Basle as a general council. England warmly supported Eugenius, and even adhered to his council at Florence; Aragon and some countries of smaller note acknowledged

[1] The council of Basle endeavored to evade this difficulty by declaring Eugenius a relapsed heretic. Lenfant, Guerre des Hussites, t. ii. p. 98. But as the church could discover no heresy in his disagreement with that assembly, the sentence of deposition gained little strength by this previous decision. The bishops were unwilling to take this violent step against Eugenius; but the minor theologians, the democracy of the Catholic church, whose right of suffrage seems rather an anomalous infringement of episcopal authority, pressed it with much heat and rashness. See a curious passage on this subject in a speech of the cardinal of Arles. Lenfant, t. ii. p. 225.

Felix. But the partisans of Basle became every year weaker; and Nicholas V., the successor of Eugenius, found no great difficulty in obtaining the cession of Felix, and terminating this schism. This victory of the court of Rome over the council of Basle nearly counterbalanced the disadvantageous events at Constance, and put an end to the project of fixing permanent limitations upon the head of the church by means of general councils. Though the decree that prescribed the convocation of a council every ten years was still unrepealed, no absolute monarchs have ever more dreaded to meet the representatives of their people, than the Roman pontiffs have abhorred the name of those ecclesiastical synods: once alone, and that with the utmost reluctance, has the catholic church been convoked since the council of Basle; but the famous assembly to which I allude does not fall within the scope of my present undertaking.[1]

It is a natural subject of speculation, what would have been the effects of these universal councils, which were so popular in the fifteenth century, if the decree passed at Constance for their periodical assembly had been regularly observed. Many catholic writers, of the moderate or cisalpine school, have lamented their disuse, and ascribed to it that irreparable breach which the Reformation has made in the fabric of their church. But there is almost an absurdity in conceiving their permanent existence. What chemistry could have kept united such heterogeneous masses, furnished with every principle of mutual repulsion? Even in early times, when councils, though nominally general, were composed of the subjects of the Roman empire, they had been marked by violence and contradiction: what then could have been expected from the delegates of independent kingdoms, whose ecclesiastical polity, whatever may be said of the spiritual unity of the church, had long been far too intimately blended with that of the state to admit of any general control without its assent? Nor, beyond the zeal, unquestionably sincere, which animated their members, especially at Basle, for the abolition of papal abuses, is there anything to praise in their conduct, or to regret in their cessation. The statesman who

[1] There is not, I believe, any sufficient history of the council of Basle. Lenfant designed to write it from the original acts, but, finding his health decline, intermixed some rather imperfect notices of its transactions with his history of the Hussite war, which is commonly quoted under the title of History of the Council of Basle. Schmidt, Crevier, Villaret, are still my other authorities.

dreaded the encroachments of priests upon the civil government, the Christian who panted to see his rights and faith purified from the corruption of ages, found no hope of improvement in these councils. They took upon themselves the pretensions of the popes whom they attempted to supersede. By a decree of the fathers at Constance, all persons, including princes, who should oppose any obstacle to a journey undertaken by the emperor Sigismund, in order to obtain the cession of Benedict, are declared excommunicated, and deprived of their dignities, whether secular or ecclesiastical.[1] Their condemnation of Huss and Jerome of Prague, and the scandalous breach of faith which they induced Sigismund to commit on that occasion, are notorious. But perhaps it is not equally so that this celebrated assembly recognized by a solemn decree the flagitious principle which it had practised, declaring that Huss was unworthy, through his obstinate adherence to heresy, of any privilege; nor ought any faith or promise to be kept with him, by natural, divine, or human law, to the prejudice of the catholic religion.[2] It will be easy to estimate the claims of this congress of theologians to our veneration, and to weigh the retrenchment of a few abuses against the formal sanction of an atrocious maxim.

It was not, however, necessary for any government of tolerable energy to seek the reform of those abuses which affected the independence of national churches, and the integ-

1 Lenfant, t. i. p 439.

2 Nec aliqua sibi fides aut promissio, de jure naturali, divino, et humano, fuerit in prejudicium Catholicæ fidei observanda. Lenfant, t. i. p. 491.

This proposition is the great disgrace of the council in the affair of Huss. But the violation of his safe-conduct being a famous event in ecclesiastical history, and which has been very much disputed with some degree of erroneous statement on both sides, it may be proper to give briefly an impartial summary. 1. Huss came to Constance with a safe-conduct of the emperor very loosely worded, and not directed to any individuals. Lenfant, t. i. p. 59. 2. This pass however was binding upon the emperor himself, and was so considered by him, when he remonstrated against the arrest of Huss. Id. p. 73, 83. 3. It was not binding on the council, who possessed no temporal power, but had a right to decide upon the question of heresy. 4. It is not manifest by what civil authority Huss was arrested, nor can I determine how far the imperial safe-conduct was a legal protection within the city of Constance. 5. Sigismund was persuaded to acquiesce in the capital punishment of Huss, and even to make it his own act (Lenfant, p. 409); by which he manifestly broke his engagement. 6. It is evident that in this he acted by the advice and sanction of the council, who thus became accessory to the guilt of his treachery.

The great moral to be drawn from the story of John Huss's condemnation is, that no breach of faith can be excused by our opinion of ill desert in the party, or by a narrow interpretation of our own engagements. Every capitulation ought to be construed favorably for the weaker side. In such cases it is emphatically true that, if the letter killeth, the spirit should give life.

Gerson, the most eminent theologian of his age, and the coryphæus of the party that opposed the transalpine principles, was deeply concerned in this atrocious business. Crevier, p. 432

rity of their regular discipline, at the hands of a general council. Whatever difficulty there might be in overturning the principles founded on the decretals of Isidore, and sanctioned by the prescription of many centuries, the more flagrant encroachments of papal tyranny were fresh innovations, some within the actual generation, others easily to be traced up, and continually disputed. The principal European nations determined, with different degrees indeed of energy, to make a stand against the despotism of Rome. In this resistance England was not only the first engaged, but the most consistent; her free parliament preventing, as far as the times permitted, that wavering policy to which a court is liable. We have already seen that a foundation was laid in the statute of provisors under Edward III. In the next reign many other measures tending to repress the interference of Rome were adopted, especially the great statute of præmunire, which subjects all persons bringing papal bulls for translation of bishops and other enumerated purposes into the kingdom to the penalties of forfeiture and perpetual imprisonment.[1] This act received, and probably was designed to receive, a larger interpretation than its language appears to warrant. Combined with the statute of provisors, it put a stop to the pope's usurpation of patronage, which had impoverished the church and kingdom of England for nearly two centuries. Several attempts were made to overthrow these enactments; the first parliament of Henry IV. gave a very large power to the king over the statute of provisors, enabling him even to annul it at his pleasure.[2] This, however, does not appear in the statute-book. Henry indeed, like his predecessors, exercised rather largely his prerogative of dispensing with the law against papal provisions; a prerogative which, as to this point, was itself taken away by an act of his own, and another of his son Henry V.[3] But the statute always stood unrepealed; and it is a satisfactory proof of the ecclesiastical supremacy of the legislature that in the concordat made by Martin V. at the council of Constance with the English nation we find no mention of reservation of benefices, of annates, and the other

[1] 16 Ric. II. c. 5.

[2] Rot. Parl. vol. iii. p. 428.

[3] 7 H. IV. c. 8; 3 H. V. c. 4. Martin V. published an angry bull against the "execrable statute" of præmunire; enjoining archbishop Chicheley to procure its repeal. Collier, p. 653. Chicheley did all in his power; but the commons were always inexorable on this head, p. 636; and the archbishop even incurred Martin's resentment by it. Wilkins, Concilia, t. iii. p. 483.

principal grievances of that age;[1] our ancestors disdaining to accept by compromise with the pope any modification or even confirmation of their statute law. They had already restrained another flagrant abuse, the increase of first fruits by Boniface IX.; an act of Henry IV. forbidding any greater sum to be paid on that account than had been formerly accustomed.[2]

Influence of Wicliff's tenets.

It will appear evident to every person acquainted with the contemporary historians, and the proceedings of parliament, that, besides partaking in the general resentment of Europe against the papal court, England was under the influence of a peculiar hostility to the clergy, arising from the dissemination of the principles of Wicliff.[3] All ecclesiastical possessions were marked for spoliation by the system of this reformer; and the house of commons more than once endeavored to carry it into effect, pressing Henry IV. to seize the temporalities of the church for public exigencies.[4] This recommendation, besides its injustice, was not likely to move Henry, whose policy had been to sustain the prelacy against their new adversaries. Ecclesiastical jurisdiction was kept in better control than formerly by the judges of common law, who, through rather a strained construction of the statute of præmunire, extended its penalties to the spiritual courts when they transgressed their limits.[5] The privilege of clergy in criminal cases still remained; but it was acknowledged not to comprehend high treason.[6]

1 Lenfant, t. ii. p. 444.

2 6 H. IV. c. 1.

3 See, among many other passages, the articles exhibited by the Lollards to parliament against the clergy in 1394. Collier gives the substance of them, and they are noticed by Henry; but they are at full length in Wilkins, t. iii. p. 221.

4 Walsingham, p. 371, 379; Rot. Parl. 11 H. IV. vol. iii. p. 645. The remarkable circumstances detailed by Walsingham in the former passage are not corroborated by anything in the records. But as it is unlikely that so particular a narrative should have no foundation, Hume has plausibly conjectured that the roll has been wilfully mutilated. As this suspicion occurs in other instances, it would be desirable to ascertain, by examination of the original rolls, whether they bear any external marks of injury. The mutilators, however, if such there were, have left a great deal. The rolls of Henry IV. and V.'s parliaments are quite full of petitions against the clergy.

5 3 Inst. p. 121; Collier, vol. i. p. 668.

6 2 Inst. p. 634; where several instances of priests executed for coining and other treasons are adduced. And this may also be inferred from 25 E. III. stat. 3, c. 4; and from 4 H. IV. c. 3. Indeed the benefit of clergy has never been taken away by statute from high treason. This renders it improbable that chief justice Gascoyne should, as Carte tells us, vol. ii. p. 664, have refused to try archbishop Scrope for treason, on the ground that no one could lawfully sit in judgment on a bishop for his life. Whether he might have declined to try him as a peer is another question. The pope excommunicated all who were concerned in Scrope's death, and it cost Henry a large sum to obtain absolution. But Boniface IX. was no arbiter of the English law. Edward IV. granted a strange charter to the clergy, not only dispensing with the statutes of præmunire, but absolutely exempting them from temporal jurisdiction in cases of

Germany, as well as England, was disappointed of her hopes of general reformation by the Italian party at Constance; but she did not supply the want of the council's decrees with sufficient decision. A concordat with Martin V. left the pope in possession of too great a part of his recent usurpations.[1] This, however, was repugnant to the spirit of Germany, which called for a more thorough reform with all the national roughness and honesty. The diet of Mentz, during the continuance of the council of Basle, adopted all those regulations hostile to the papal interests which occasioned the deadly quarrel between that assembly and the court of Rome.[2] But the German empire was betrayed by Frederic III., and deceived by an accomplished but profligate statesman, his secretary Æneas Sylvius. Fresh concordats, settled at Aschaffenburg in 1448, nearly upon a footing of those concluded with Martin V., surrendered great part of the independence for which Germany had contended. The pope retained his annates, or at least a sort of tax in their place; and instead of reserving benefices arbitrarily, he obtained the positive right of collation during six alternate months of every year. Episcopal elections were freely restored to the chapters, except in case of translation, when the pope still continued to nominate; as he did also if any person, canonically unfit, were presented to him for confirmation.[3] Such is the concordat of Aschaffenburg, by which the catholic principalities of the empire have always been governed, though reluctantly acquiescing in its disadvantageous provisions. Rome, for the remainder of the fifteenth century, not satisfied with the terms she had imposed, is said to have continually encroached upon the right of election.[4] But she purchased too dearly her triumph over the weakness of Frederic III., and the Hundred Grievances of Germany, presented to Adrian VI. by the diet of Nuremberg in 1522,

Concordats of Aschaffenburg.

treason as well as felony. Wilkins, Concilia, t. iii. p. 583; Collier, p. 678. This, however, being an illegal grant, took no effect, at least after his death.

1 Lenfant, t. ii. p. 428; Schmidt, t. v. p. 131.

2 Schmidt, t. v. p. 221; Lenfant.

3 Schmidt, t. v. p. 250; t. vi. p. 94, &c. He observes that there is three times as much money at present as in the fifteenth century: if therefore the annates are now felt as a burden, what must they have been? p. 113. To this Rome would answer, If the annates were but sufficient for the pope's maintenance at that time, what must they be now?

4 Schmidt, p. 98; Æneas Sylvius, Epist. 369 and 371; and De Moribus Germanorum, p. 1041, 1061. Several little disputes with the pope indicate the spirit that was fermenting in Germany throughout the fifteenth century. But this is the proper subject of a more detailed ecclesiastical history, and should form an introduction to that of the Reformation.

manifested the working of a long-treasured resentment, that had made straight the path before the Saxon reformer.

Papal encroachments on church of Castile.

I have already taken notice that the Castilian church was in the first ages of that monarchy nearly independent of Rome. But after many gradual encroachments the code of laws promulgated by Alfonso X. had incorporated a great part of the decretals, and thus given the papal jurisprudence an authority which it nowhere else possessed in national tribunals.[1] That richly endowed hierarchy was a tempting spoil. The popes filled up its benefices by means of expectatives and reserves with their own Italian dependents. We find the cortes of Palencia in 1388 complaining that strangers are beneficed in Castile, through which the churches are ill supplied, and native scholars cannot be provided, and requesting the king to take such measures in relation to this as the kings of France, Aragon, and Navarre, who do not permit any but natives to hold benefices in their kingdoms. The king answered to this petition that he would use his endeavors to that end.[2] And this is expressed with greater warmth by a cortes of 1473, who declare it to be the custom of all Christian nations that foreigners should not be promoted to benefices, urging the discouragement of native learning, the decay of charity, the bad performance of religious rites, and other evils arising from the non-residence of beneficed priests, and request the king to notify to the court of Rome that no expectative or provision in favor of foreigners can be received in future.[3] This petition seems to have passed into a law; but I am ignorant of the consequences. Spain certainly took an active part in restraining the abuses of pontifical authority at the councils of Constance and Basle; to which I might add the name of Trent, if that assembly were not beyond my province.

Checks on papal authority in France.

France, dissatisfied with the abortive termination of her exertions during the schism, rejected the concordat offered by Martin V., which held out but a promise of imperfect reformation.[4] She suffered in consequence the papal exactions for some years, till the decrees of the council of Basle prompted her to more

[1] Marina, Ensayo Historico-Critico, c. 320, &c.

[2] Id. Teoria de las Cortes, t. iii. p. 126.

[3] Teoria de las Cortes, t. ii. p. 364; Mariana, Hist. Hispan. l. xix. c. 1.

[4] Villaret, t. xv. p. 126.

vigorous efforts for independence, and Charles VII. enacted the famous Pragmatic Sanction of Bourges.[1] This has been deemed a sort of Magna Charta of the Gallican church; for though the law was speedily abrogated, its principle has remained fixed as the basis of ecclesiastical liberties. By the Pragmatic Sanction a general council was declared superior to the pope; elections of bishops were made free from all control; mandats or grants in expectancy, and reservations of benefices, were taken away; first fruits were abolished. This defalcation of wealth, which had now become dearer than power, could not be patiently borne at Rome. Pius II., the same Æneas Sylvius who had sold himself to oppose the council of Basle, in whose service he had been originally distinguished, used every endeavor to procure the repeal of this ordinance. With Charles VII. he had no success; but Louis XI., partly out of blind hatred to his father's memory, partly from a delusive expectation that the pope would support the Angevin faction in Naples, repealed the Pragmatic Sanction.[2] This may be added to other proofs that Louis XI., even according to the measures of worldly wisdom, was not a wise politician. His people judged from better feelings; the parliament of Paris constantly refused to enregister the revocation of that favorite law, and it continued in many respects to be acted upon until the reign of Francis I.[3] At the States General of Tours, in 1484, the inferior clergy, seconded by the two other orders, earnestly requested that the Pragmatic Sanction might be confirmed; but the prelates were timid or corrupt, and the regent Anne was unwilling to risk a quarrel with the Holy See.[4] This unsettled state continued, the Pragmatic Sanction neither quite enforced nor quite repealed, till Francis I., having accommodated the differences of his predecessor with Rome, agreed upon a final concordat with Leo X., the treaty that subsisted for almost three centuries between the papacy and the kingdom of France.[5] Instead of capitular election or papal provision, a new method was devised for filling the vacancies of episcopal sees. The king was to nominate a fit person, whom the

[1] Idem, p. 263; Hist. du Droit Public Ecclés. François, t. ii. p. 234; Fleury, Institutions au Droit; Crevier, t. iv. p. 100; Pasquier, Recherches de la France, l. iii. c. 27.

[2] Villaret, and Garnier, t. xvi.; Crevier, t. iv. p. 256, 274.

[3] Garnier, t. xvi. p. 432; t. xvii. p. 222 et alibi. Crevier, t. iv. p. 318 et alibi.

[4] Garnier, t. xix. p. 216 and 321.

[5] Garnier, t. xxiii. p. 151; Hist. du Droit Public Ecclés. Fr. t. ii. p. 243; Fleury. Institutions au Droit, t. i. p. 107.

pope was to collate. The one obtained an essential patronage, the other preserved his theoretical supremacy. Annates were restored to the pope; a concession of great importance. He gave up his indefinite prerogative of reserving benefices, and received only a small stipulated patronage. This convention met with strenuous opposition in France; the parliament of Paris yielded only to force; the university hardly stopped short of sedition; the zealous Gallicans have ever since deplored it, as a fatal wound to their liberties. There is much exaggeration in this, as far as the relation of the Gallican church to Rome is concerned; but the royal nomination to bishoprics impaired of course the independence of the hierarchy. Whether this prerogative of the crown were upon the whole beneficial to France, is a problem that I cannot affect to solve; in this country there seems little doubt that capitular elections, which the statute of Henry VIII. has reduced to a name, would long since have degenerated into the corruption of close boroughs; but the circumstances of the Gallican establishment may not have been entirely similar, and the question opens a variety of considerations that do not belong to my present subject.

Liberties of the Gallican church.

From the principles established during the schism, and in the Pragmatic Sanction of Bourges, arose the far-famed liberties of the Gallican church, which honorably distinguished her from other members of the Roman communion. These have been referred by French writers to a much earlier era; but except so far as that country participated in the ancient ecclesiastical independence of all Europe, before the papal encroachments had subverted it, I do not see that they can be properly traced above the fifteenth century. Nor had they acquired even at the expiration of that age the precision and consistency which was given in later times by the constant spirit of the parliaments and universities, as well as by the best ecclesiastical authors, with little assistance from the crown, which, except in a few periods of disagreement with Rome, has rather been disposed to restrain the more zealous Gallicans. These liberties, therefore, do not strictly fall within my limits; and it will be sufficient to observe that they depended upon two maxims: one, that the pope does not possess any direct or indirect temporal authority; the other, that his spiritual jurisdiction can only be exercised in conformity with such parts of the canon law as are received by the kingdom of France. Hence the Gallican church rejected a great part of the Sext and Clementines, and paid little regard to modern papal bulls, which in fact obtained validity only by the king's approbation.[1]

Ecclesiastical jurisdiction restrained.

The pontifical usurpations which were thus restrained, affected, at least in their direct operation, rather the church than the state; and temporal governments would only have been half emancipated, if their national hierarchies had preserved their enormous jurisdiction.[2] England, in this also, began the work, and had made a considerable progress, while the mistaken piety or policy of Louis IX. and his successors had laid France open to vast encroachments. The first method adopted in order to check them was rude enough; by seizing the bishop's effects when he exceeded his jurisdiction.[3] This jurisdiction, according to the construction of churchmen, became perpetually larger: even the reforming council of Constance give an enumeration of ecclesiastical causes far beyond the limits acknowledged in England, or perhaps in France.[4] But the parliament of Paris, instituted in 1304, gradually established a paramount authority over ecclesiastical as well as civil tribunals. Their progress was indeed very slow. At a famous assembly in 1329, before Philip of Valois, his advocate-general, Peter de Cugnieres, pronounced a long harangue

1 Fleury, Institutions au Droit, t. ii. p. 226, &c., and Discours sur les Libertés de l'Eglise Gallicane. The last editors of this dissertation go far beyond Fleury, and perhaps reach the utmost point in limiting the papal authority which a sincere member of that communion can attain. See notes, p. 417 and 445.

2 It ought always to be remembered that *ecclesiastical*, and not merely *papal*, encroachments are what civil governments and the laity in general have had to resist; a point which some very zealous opposers of Rome have been willing to keep out of sight. The latter arose out of the former, and perhaps were in some respects less objectionable. But the true enemy is what are called High-church principles; be they maintained by a pope, a bishop, or a presbyter. Thus archbishop Stratford writes to Edward III.: Duo sunt, quibus principaliter regitur mundus, sacra pontificalis auctoritas, et regalis ordinata potestas: in quibus est pondus tanto gravius et sublimius sacerdotum, quanto et de regibus illi in divino reddituri sunt examine rationem; et ideo scire debet regia celsitudo ex illorum vos dependere judicio, non illos ad vestram dirigi posse voluntatem. Wilkins, Concilia, t. ii. p. 663. This amazing impudence towards such a prince as Edward did not succeed; but it is interesting to follow the track of the star which was now rather receding, though still fierce.

3 De Marca, De Concordantiâ, l. iv. c. 18.

4 De Marca, De Concordantiâ, l. iv. c. 15; Lenfant, Conc. de Constance, t. ii. p. 331. De Marca, l. iv. c. 15, gives us passages from one Durandus about 1309, complaining that the lay judges invaded ecclesiastical jurisdiction, and reckoning the cases subject to the latter, under which he includes feudal and criminal causes in some circumstances, and also those in which the temporal judges are in doubt; si quid ambiguum inter judices sæculares oriatur.

against the excesses of spiritual jurisdiction. This is a curious illustration of that branch of legal and ecclesiastical history. It was answered at large by some bishops, and the king did not venture to take any active measures at that time.[1] Several regulations were, however, made in the fourteenth century, which took away the ecclesiastical cognizance of adultery, of the execution of testaments, and other causes which had been claimed by the clergy.[2] Their immunity in criminal matters was straitened by the introduction of priviledged cases, to which it did not extend; such as treason, murder, robbery, and other heinous offences.[3] The parliament began to exercise a judicial control over episcopal courts. It was not, however, till the beginning of the sixteenth century, according to the best writers, that it devised its famous form of procedure, the "appeal because of abuse."[4] This, in the course of time, and through the decline of ecclesiastical power, not only proved an effectual barrier against encroachments of spiritual jurisdiction, but drew back again to the lay court the greater part of those causes which by prescription, and indeed by law, had appertained to a different cognizance. Thus testamentary, and even, in a great degree, matrimonial causes were decided by the parliament; and in many other matters that body, being the judge of its own competence, narrowed, by means of the appeal because of abuse, the boundaries of the opposite jurisdiction.[5] This remedial process appears to have been more extensively applied than our English writ of prohibition. The latter merely restrains the interference of the ecclesiastical courts in matters which the law has not committed to them. But the parliament of Paris considered itself, I apprehend, as conservator of the liberties and discipline of the Gallican church; and interposed the appeal because of abuse, whenever the spiritual court, even in its proper province, transgressed the canonical rules by which it ought to be governed.[6]

[1] Velly, t. viii. p. 234; Fleury, Institutions, t. ii. p. 12; Hist. du Droit Ecclés. Franç. t. ii. p. 86.

[2] Villaret, t. xi. p. 182.

[3] Fleury, Institutions au Droit, t. ii. p. 138. In the famous case of Balue, a bishop and cardinal, whom Louis XI. detected in a treasonable intrigue, it was contended by the king that he had a right to punish him capitally. Du Clos, Vie de Louis XI. t. i. p. 422; Garnier, Hist. de France, t. xvii. p. 330. Balue was confined for many years in a small iron cage, which till lately was shown in the castle of Loches.

[4] Pasquier, l. iii. c. 33; Hist. du Droit Ecclés. François, t. ii. p. 119; Fleury, Institutions au Droit Ecclés François, t. ii. p. 221; De Marca, De Concordantiâ Sacerdotii et Imperii, l. iv. c. 19. The last author seems to carry it rather higher.

[5] Fleury, Institutions, t. ii. p. 42, &c.

[6] De Marca, De Concordantiâ, l. iv. c. 9; Fleury, t. ii. p. 224. In Spain, even now, says De Marca, bishops or clerks

Decline of papal influence in Italy.

While the bishops of Rome were losing their general influence over Europe, they did not gain more estimation in Italy. It is indeed a problem of some difficulty, whether they derived any substantial advantage from their temporal principality. For the last three centuries it has certainly been conducive to the maintenance of their spiritual supremacy, which, in the complicated relations of policy, might have been endangered by their becoming the subjects of any particular sovereign. But I doubt whether their real authority over Christendom in the middle ages was not better preserved by a state of nominal dependence upon the empire, without much effective control on one side, or many temptations to worldly ambition on the other. That covetousness of temporal sway which, having long prompted their measures of usurpation and forgery, seemed, from the time of Innocent III. and Nicholas III., to reap its gratification, impaired the more essential parts of the papal authority. In the fourteenth and fifteenth centuries the popes degraded their character by too much anxiety about the politics of Italy. The veil woven by religious awe was rent asunder, and the features of ordinary ambition appeared without disguise. For it was no longer that magnificent and original system of spiritual power which made Gregory VII., even in exile, a rival of the emperor, which held forth redress where the law could not protect, and punishment where it could not chastise, which fell in sometimes with superstitious feeling, and sometimes with political interest. Many might believe that the pope could depose a schismatic prince, who were disgusted at his attacking an unoffending neighbor. As the cupidity of the clergy in regard to worldly estate had lowered their character everywhere, so the similar conduct of their head undermined the respect felt for him in Italy. The censures of the church, those excommunications and interdicts which had made Europe tremble, became gradually despicable as well as odious when they were lavished in every squabble for territory which the pope was pleased to make his own.[1] Even the crusades, which had already been tried

not obeying royal mandates that inhibit the excesses of ecclesiastical courts are expelled from the kingdom and deprived of the rights of denizenship.

[1] In 1290 Pisa was put under an interdict for having conferred the signiory on the count of Montefeltro; and he was ordered, on pain of excommunication, to lay down the government within a month. Muratori ad ann. A curious style for the pope to adopt towards a free city! Six years before the Venetians had been interdicted because they would not allow their galleys to be hired by the king of Naples. But it would be almost endless to quote every instance.

against the heretics of Languedoc, were now preached against all who espoused a different party from the Roman see in the quarrels of Italy. Such were those directed at Frederic II., at Manfred, and at Matteo Visconti, accompanied by the usual bribery, indulgences, and remission of sins. The papal interdicts of the fourteenth century wore a different complexion from those of former times. Though tremendous to the imagination, they had hitherto been confined to spiritual effects, or to such as were connected with religion, as the prohibition of marriage and sepulture. But Clement V., on account of an attack made by the Venetians upon Ferrara in 1309, proclaimed the whole people infamous, and incapable for three generations of any office, their goods, in every part of the world, subject to confiscation, and every Venetian, wherever he might be found, liable to be reduced into slavery.[1] A bull in the same terms was published by Gregory XI. in 1376 against the Florentines.

From the termination of the schism, as the popes found their ambition thwarted beyond the Alps, it was diverted more and more towards schemes of temporal sovereignty. In these we do not perceive that consistent policy which remarkably actuated their conduct as supreme heads of the church. Men generally advanced in years, and born of noble Italian families, made the papacy subservient to the elevation of their kindred, or to the interests of a local faction. For such ends they mingled in the dark conspiracies of that bad age, distinguished only by the more scandalous turpitude of their vices from the petty tyrants and intriguers with whom they were engaged. In the latter part of the fifteenth century, when all favorable prejudices were worn away, those who occupied the most conspicuous station in Europe disgraced their name by more notorious profligacy than could be paralleled in the darkest age that had preceded; and at the moment beyond which this work is not carried, the invasion of Italy by Charles VIII., I must leave the pontifical throne in the possession of Alexander VI.

It has been my object in the present chapter to bring within the compass of a few hours' perusal the substance of a great and interesting branch of history; not certainly with such extensive reach of learning as the subject might require,

[1] Muratori.

but from sources of unquestioned credibility. Unconscious of any partialities that could give an oblique bias to my mind, I have not been very solicitous to avoid offence where offence is so easily taken. Yet there is one misinterpretation of my meaning which I would gladly obviate. I have not designed, in exhibiting without disguise the usurpations of Rome during the middle ages, to furnish materials for unjust prejudice or unfounded distrust. It is an advantageous circumstance for the philosophical inquirer into the history of ecclesiastical dominion, that, as it spreads itself over the vast extent of fifteen centuries, the dependence of events upon general causes, rather than on transitory combinations or the character of individuals, is made more evident, and the future more probably foretold from a consideration of the past, than we are apt to find in political history. Five centuries have now elapsed, during every one of which the authority of the Roman see has successively declined. Slowly and silently receding from their claims to temporal power, the pontiffs hardly protect their dilapidated citadel from the revolutionary concussions of modern times, the rapacity of governments, and the growing averseness to ecclesiastical influence. But if, thus bearded by unmannerly and threatening innovation, they should occasionally forget that cautious policy which necessity has prescribed, if they should attempt (an unavailing expedient!) to revive institutions which can be no longer operative, or principles that have died away, their defensive efforts will not be unnatural, nor ought to excite either indignation or alarm. A calm, comprehensive study of ecclesiastical history, not in such scraps and fragments as the ordinary partisans of our ephemeral literature obtrude upon us, is perhaps the best antidote to extravagant apprehensions. Those who know what Rome has once been are best able to appreciate what she is; those who have seen the thunderbolt in the hands of the Gregories and the Innocents will hardly be intimidated at the sallies of decrepitude, the impotent dart of Priam amidst the crackling ruins of Troy.[1]

[1] It is again to be remembered that this paragraph was written in 1816.

NOTES TO CHAPTER VII.

NOTE I. Page 142.

THIS grant is recorded in two charters differing materially from each other; the first transcribed in Ingulfus's History of Croyland, and dated at Winchester on the Nones of November, 855; the second extant in two chartularies, and bearing date at Wilton, April 22, 854. This is marked by Mr. Kemble as spurious (Codex Ang.-Sax. Diplom. ii. 52); and the authority of Ingulfus is not sufficient to support the first. The fact, however, that Ethelwolf made some great and general donation to the church rests on the authority of Asser, whom later writers have principally copied. His words are,—"Eodem quoque anno [855] Adelwolfus venerabilis, rex Occidentalium Saxonum, decimam totius regni sui partem ab omni regali servitio et tributo liberavit, et in sempiterno grafio in cruce Christi, pro redemptione animæ suæ et antecessorum suorum, Uni et Trino Deo immolavit." (Gale, XV. Script. iii. 156.)

It is really difficult to infer anything from such a passage; but whatever the writer may have meant, or whatever truth there may be in his story, it seems impossible to strain his words into a grant of tithes. The charter in Ingulfus rather leads to suppose, but that in the Codex Diplomaticus decisively proves, that the grant conveyed a tenth part of the land, and not of its produce. Sir F. Palgrave, by quoting only the latter charter, renders Selden's Hypothesis, that the general right to tithes dates from this concession of Ethelwolf, even more untenable than it is. Certainly the charter copied by Ingulfus, which Sir F. Palgrave passes in silence, does grant "decimam partem bonorum;" that is, I presume, of chattels, which, as far as it goes, implies a tithe; while the words applicable to land are so obscure and apparently corrupt, that Selden might be warranted in giving them the like construction. Both charters probably are spurious; but there may have been an extensive grant to the church, not only of immunity from the *trinoda necessitas*, which they express, but of actual possessions. Since, however, it must have been impracticable to endow the church with a tenth part of appropriated lands, it might possibly be conjectured that she took a tenth part of the produce, either as a composition, or until means should be found of putting her in possession of the soil. And although, according to the notions of those times, the actual property might be more desirable, it is plain to us that a tithe of the produce was of much greater value than the same proportion of the land itself.

NOTE II. Page 153.

TWO living writers of the Roman Catholic communion, Dr. Milner, in his History of Winchester, and Dr. Lingard, in his Antiquities of the Anglo-Saxon Church, contend that Elgiva, whom some protestant historians are willing to represent as the queen of Edwy, was but his mistress; and seem inclined to justify the conduct of Odo and Dunstan towards this unfortunate couple. They are unquestionably so far right, that few, if any, of those writers who have been quoted as authorities in respect of this story speak of the lady as a queen or lawful wife. I must therefore strongly reprobate the conduct of Dr. Henry, who, calling Elgiva queen, and asserting that she was married, refers, at the bottom of his page, to William of Malmsbury and other chroniclers, who give a totally opposite account; especially as he does not intimate, by a single expression, that the nature of her connection with the king was equivocal. Such a practice, when it proceeds, as I fear it did in this instance, not from oversight, but from prejudice, is a glaring violation of historical integrity, and tends to render the use of references, that great improvement of modern history, a sort of fraud upon the reader. The subject, since the first publication of these volumes, has been discussed by Dr. Lingard in his histories both of England and of the Anglo-Saxon Church, by the Edinburgh reviewer of that history, vol. xlii. (Mr. Allen), and by other late writers. Mr. Allen has also given a short dissertation on the subject, in the second edition of his Inquiry into the

Royal Prerogative, posthumously published. It must ever be impossible, unless unknown documents are brought to light, to clear up all the facts of this litigated story. But though some protestant writers, as I have said, in maintaining the matrimonial connection of Edwy and Elgiva, quote authorities who give a different color to it, there is a presumption of the marriage from a passage of the Saxon Chronicle, A.D. 958 (wanting in Gibson's edition, but discovered by Mr. Turner, and now restored to its place by Mr. Petrie), which distinctly says that archbishop Odo separated Edwy the king and Elgiva because they were too nearly related. It is therefore highly probable that she was queen, though Dr. Lingard seems to hesitate. This passage was written as early as any other which we have on the subject, and in a more placid and truthful tone.

The royalty, however, of Elgiva will be out of all possible doubt, if we can depend on a document, being a reference to a charter, in the Cotton library (Claudius, B. vi.), wherein she appears as a witness. Turner says of this,— "Had the charter even been forged, the monks would have taken care that the names appended were correct." This Dr. Lingard inexcusably calls "confessing that the instrument is of very doubtful authenticity."

The Edinburgh reviewer, who had seen the manuscript, believes it genuine, and gives an account of it. Mr. Kemble has printed it without mark of spuriousness. (Cod. Diplom. vol. v. p. 378.) In this document we have the names of Ælfgifu, the king's wife, and of Æthelgifu, the king's wife's mother. The signatures are merely recited, so that the document itself cannot be properly styled a charter; but we are only concerned with the testimony it bears to the existence of the queen Elgiva and her mother.

If this charter, thus recited, is established, we advance a step, so as to prove the existence of a mother and daughter, bearing nearly the same names, and such names as apparently imply royal blood, the latter being married to Edwy. This would tend to corroborate the coronation story, divesting it of the gross exaggerations of the monkish biographers and their followers. It might be supposed that the young king, little more than a boy, retired from the drunken revelry of his courtiers to converse, and perhaps romp, with his cousin and her mother; that Dunstan audaciously broke in upon him, and forced him back to the banquet; that both he and the ladies resented this insolence as it deserved, and drove the monk into exile; and that the marriage took place.

It is more difficult to deal with the story originally related by the biographer of Odo, that after his marriage Edwy carried off a woman with whom he lived, and whom Odo seized and sent out of the kingdom. This lady is called by Eadmer una de præscriptis mulieribus; whence Dr. Lingard assumes her to have been Ethelgiva, the queen's mother. This was in his History of England (i. 517); but in the second edition of the Antiquities of the Anglo-Saxon Church he is far less confident than either in the first edition of that work or in his History. In fact, he plainly confesses that nothing can be clearly made out beyond the circumstances of the coronation.

Although the writers before the conquest do not bear witness to the cruelties exercised on some woman connected with the king, either as queen or mistress, at Gloucester, yet the subsequent authorities of Eadmer, Osbern, and Malmsbury may lead us to believe that there was truth in the main facts, though we cannot be certain that the person so treated was the queen Elgiva. If indeed their accounts are accurate, it seems at first that they do not agree with their predecessors; for they represent the lady as being in the king's company up to his flight from the insurgents:—"Regem cum adultera fugitantem persequi non desistunt." But though we read in the Saxon Chronicle that Odo divorced Edwy and Elgiva, we are not sure that they submitted to the sentence. It is therefore possible that she was with him in this disastrous flight, and, having fallen into the hands of the pursuers, was put to death at Gloucester. True it is that her proximity of blood to the king would not warrant Osbern to call her *adultera;* but bad names cost nothing. Malmsbury's words look more like it, if we might supply something, "proximè cognatam invadens uxorem [cujusdam?] ejus forma deperibat;" but as they stand in his text, they defy my scanty knowledge of the Latin tongue. On the whole, however, no reliance is to be placed on very passionate and late authorities. What is manifest alone is, that a young king was persecuted and dethroned by the insolence of monkery exciting a superstitious people against him.

NOTE III. Page 153.

I AM induced, by further study, to modify what is said in the text with respect to the well-known passages in Irenæus and Cyprian. The former assigns, indeed, a considerable weight to the *Church* of Rome, simply as testimony to apostolical teaching; but this is plainly not limited to the bishop of that city, nor is he personally mentioned. It is therefore an argument, and no slight one, against the pretended supremacy rather than the contrary.

The authority of Cyprian is not, perhaps, much more to the purpose. For the only words in his treatise De Unitate Ecclesiæ which assert any authority in the chair of St. Peter, or indeed connect Rome with Peter at all, are interpolations, not found in the best manuscripts or in the oldest editions. They are printed within brackets in the best modern ones. (See James on Corruptions of Scripture in the Church of Rome, 1612.) True it is, however, that, in his Epistle to Cornelius bishop of Rome, Cyprian speaks of "Petri cathedram, atque ecclesiam principalem unde unitas sacerdotalis exorta est." (Epist. lix. in edit. Lip. 1838; lv. in Baluze and others.) And in another he exhorts Stephen, successor of Cornelius, to write a letter to the bishops of Gaul, that they should depose Marcian of Arles for adhering to the Novatian heresy. (Epist. lxviii. or lxvii.) This is said to be found in very few manuscripts. Yet it seems too long, and not sufficiently to the purpose, for a popish forgery. All bishops of the catholic church assumed a right of interference with each other by admonition; and it is not entirely clear from the language that Cyprian meant anything more authoritative; though I incline, on the whole, to believe that, when on good terms with the see of Rome, he recognized in her a kind of primacy derived from that of St. Peter.

The case, nevertheless, became very different when she was no longer of his mind. In a nice question which arose, during the pontificate of this very Stephen, as to the rebaptism of those to whom the rite had been administered by heretics, the bishop of Rome took the negative side; while Cyprian, with the utmost vehemence, maintained the contrary. Then we find no more honeyed phrases about the principal church and the succession to Peter, but a very different style: "Cur in tantum Stephani, fratris nostri, obstinatio dura prorupit?" (Epist. lxxiv.) And a correspondent of Cyprian, doubtless a bishop, Firmilianus by name, uses more violent language:—"Audacia et insolentia ejus—aperta et manifesta Stephani stultitia—de episcopatûs sui loco gloriatur, et se successionem Petri tenere contendit." (Epist. lxxv.) Cyprian proceeded to summon a council of the African bishops, who met, seventy-eight in number, at Carthage. They all agreed to condemn heretical baptism as absolutely invalid. Cyprian addressed them, requesting that they would use full liberty, not without a manifest reflection on the pretensions of Rome:—"Neque enim quisquam nostrûm episcopum se esse episcoporum constituit, aut tyrannico terrore ad obsequendi necessitatem collegas suos adigit, quando habeat omnis episcopus pro licentia libertatis et potestatis suæ arbitrium proprium, tamque judicari ab alio non possit, quam nec ipse potest alterum judicare." We have here an allusion to what Tertullian had called *horrenda vox*, "episcopus episcoporum;" manifestly intimating that the see of Rome had begun to assert a superiority and right of control, by the beginning of the third century, but at the same time that it was not generally endured. Probably the notion of their superior authority, as witnesses of the faith, grew up in the Church of Rome very early; and when Victor, towards the end of the second century, excommunicated the churches of Asia for a difference as to the time of keeping Easter, we see the germination of that usurpation, that tyranny, that uncharitableness, which reached its culminating point in the centre of the mediæval period.

CHAPTER VIII.

THE CONSTITUTIONAL HISTORY OF ENGLAND.

PART I.

The Anglo-Saxon Constitution — Sketch of Anglo-Saxon History — Succession to the Crown — Orders of Men — Thanes and Ceorls — Witenagemot — Judicial System — Division into Hundreds — County Court — Trial by Jury — Its Antiquity investigated — Law of Frank-Pledge — Its several Stages — Question of Feudal Tenures before the Conquest.

No unbiassed observer, who derives pleasure from the welfare of his species, can fail to consider the long and uninterruptedly increasing prosperity of England as the most beautiful phenomenon in the history of mankind. Climates more propitious may impart more largely the mere enjoyments of existence; but in no other region have the benefits that political institutions can confer been diffused over so extended a population; nor have any people so well reconciled the discordant elements of wealth, order, and liberty. These advantages are surely not owing to the soil of this island, nor to the latitude in which it is placed, but to the spirit of its laws, from which, through various means, the characteristic independence and industriousness of our nation have been derived. The constitution, therefore, of England must be to inquisitive men of all countries, far more to ourselves, an object of superior interest; distinguished especially, as it is, from all free governments of powerful nations which history has recorded, by its manifesting, after the lapse of several centuries, not merely no symptom of irretrievable decay, but a more expansive energy. Comparing long periods of time, it may be justly asserted that the administration of government has progressively become more equitable, and the privileges of the subject more secure; and, though it would be both presumptuous and unwise to express an unlimited confidence as to the durability of liberties which owe their greatest security to the constant suspicion of the people, yet, if we calmly reflect on the present aspect of this country, it will probably appear that whatever perils may threaten our constitution are rather from circumstances altogether unconnected with it than from any intrinsic defects of its own. It will be the object of the ensuing chapter to trace the gradual formation of this system of government. Such an investigation, impartially conducted, will detect errors diametrically opposite; those intended to impose on the populace, which, on account of their palpable absurdity and the ill faith with which they are usually proposed, I have seldom thought it worth while directly to repel; and those which better informed persons are apt to entertain, caught from transient reading and the misrepresentations of late historians, but easily refuted by the genuine testimony of ancient times.

Sketch of Anglo-Saxon history.

The seven very unequal kingdoms of the Saxon Heptarchy, formed successively out of the countries wrested from the Britons, were originally independent of each other. Several times, however, a powerful sovereign acquired a preponderating influence over his neighbors, marked perhaps by the payment of tribute. Seven are enumerated by Bede as having thus reigned over the whole of Britain; an expression which must be very loosely interpreted.[1] Three kingdoms became at length predominant — those of Wessex, Mercia, and Northumberland. The first rendered tributary the small estates of the South-East, and the second that of the Eastern Angles. But Egbert king of Wessex not only incorporated with his own monarchy the dependent kingdoms of Kent and Essex, but obtained an acknowledgment of his superiority from Mercia and Northumberland; the latter of which, though the most extensive of any Anglo-Saxon state, was too much weakened by its internal divisions to offer any resistance.[2] Still, however, the kingdoms of Mercia, East Anglia, and Northumberland remained under their ancient line of sovereigns; nor did either Egbert or his five immediate successors assume the title of any other crown than Wessex.[3]

The destruction of those minor states was reserved for a different enemy. About the end of the eighth century the

[1] [NOTE I.]

[2] Chronicon Saxonicum, p. 70.

[3] Alfred denominates himself in his will Occidentalium Saxorum rex; and Asserius never gives him any other name. But his son Edward the Elder takes the title of Rex Anglorum on his coins. Vid. Numismata Anglo-Saxon. in Hickes's Thesaurus, vol. ii.

northern pirates began to ravage the coast of England. Scandinavia exhibited in that age a very singular condition of society. Her population, continually redundant in those barren regions which gave it birth, was cast out in search of plunder upon the ocean. Those who loved riot rather than famine embarked in large armaments under chiefs of legitimate authority as well as approved valor. Such were the Sea-kings, renowned in the stories of the North: the younger branches, commonly, of royal families, who inherited, as it were, the sea for their patrimony. Without any territory but on the bosom of the waves, without any dwelling but their ships, these princely pirates were obeyed by numerous subjects, and intimidated mighty nations.[1] Their invasions of England became continually more formidable: and, as their confidence increased, they began first to winter, and ultimately to form permanent settlements in the country. By their command of the sea, it was easy for them to harass every part of an island presenting such an extent of coast as Britain; the Saxons, after a brave resistance, gradually gave way, and were on the brink of the same servitude or extermination which their own arms had already brought upon the ancient possessors.

From this imminent peril, after the three dependent kingdoms, Mercia, Northumberland, and East Anglia, had been overwhelmed, it was the glory of Alfred to rescue the Anglo-Saxon monarchy. Nothing less than the appearance of a hero so undesponding, so enterprising, and so just, could have prevented the entire conquest of England. Yet he never subdued the Danes, nor became master of the whole kingdom. The Thames, the Lea, the Ouse, and the Roman road called Watling Street, determined the limits of Alfred's dominion.[2] To the north-east of this boundary were spread the invaders, still denominated the *armies* of East Anglia and Northumberland;[3] a name terribly expressive of foreign conquerors, who retained their warlike confederacy, without melting into the mass of their subject population. Three able and active sovereigns, Edward, Athelstan, and Edmund the successors of Alfred, pursued the course of victory, and

[1] For these Vikings, or Sea-kings, a new and interesting subject, I would refer to Mr. Turner's History of the Anglo-Saxons, in which valuable work almost every particular that can illustrate our early annals will be found.

[2] Wilkins, Leges Anglo-Saxon. p. 47; Chron. Saxon. p. 99.

[3] Chronicon Saxon. passim.

not only rendered the English monarchy coextensive with the present limits of England, but asserted at least a supremacy over the bordering nations.[1] Yet even Edgar, the most powerful of the Anglo-Saxon kings, did not venture to interfere with the legal customs of his Danish subjects.[2]

Under this prince, whose rare fortune as well as judicious conduct procured him the surname of Peaceable, the kingdom appears to have reached its zenith of prosperity. But his premature death changed the scene. The minority and feeble character of Ethelred II. provoked fresh incursions of our enemies beyond the German Sea. A long series of disasters, and the inexplicable treason of those to whom the public safety was intrusted, overthrew the Saxon line, and established Canute of Denmark upon the throne.

The character of the Scandinavian nations was in some measure changed from what it had been during their first invasions. They had embraced the Christian faith; they were consolidated into great kingdoms; they had lost some of that predatory and ferocious spirit which a religion invented, as it seemed, for pirates had stimulated. Those, too, who had long been settled in England became gradually more assimilated to the natives, whose laws and language were not radically different from their own. Hence the accession of a Danish line of kings produced neither any evil nor any sensible change of polity. But the English still outnumbered their conquerors, and eagerly returned, when an opportunity arrived, to the ancient stock. Edward the Confessor, notwithstanding his Norman favorites, was endeared by the mildness of his character to the English nation, and subsequent miseries gave a kind of posthumous credit to a reign not eminent either for good fortune or wise government.

Succession to the crown.

In a stage of civilization so little advanced as that of the Anglo-Saxons, and under circumstances of such incessant peril, the fortunes of a nation chiefly depend upon the wisdom and valor of its sovereigns. No free people, therefore, would intrust their safety to blind chance, and permit an uniform observance of hereditary succession to prevail against strong public expediency. Accordingly,

[1] [NOTE II.]

[2] Wilkins, Leges Anglo-Saxon. p. 83. In 1064, after a revolt of the Northumbrians, Edward the Confessor renewed the laws of Canute. Chronic. Saxon. It seems now to be ascertained, by the comparison of dialects, that the inhabitants from the Humber, or at least the Tyne, to the Firth of Forth, were chiefly Danes.

the Saxons, like most other European nations, while they limited the inheritance of the crown exclusively to one royal family, were not very scrupulous about its devolution upon the nearest heir. It is an unwarranted assertion of Carte, that the rule of the Anglo-Saxon monarchy was "lineal agnatic succession, the blood of the second son having no right until the extinction of that of the eldest."[1] Unquestionably the eldest son of the last king, being of full age, and not manifestly incompetent, was his natural and probable successor; nor is it perhaps certain that he always waited for an election to take upon himself the rights of sovereignty, although the ceremony of coronation, according to the ancient form, appears to imply its necessity. But the public security in those times was thought incompatible with a minor king; and the artificial substitution of a regency, which stricter notions of hereditary right have introduced, had never occurred to so rude a people. Thus, not to mention those instances which the obscure times of the Heptarchy exhibit, Ethelred I., as some say, but certainly Alfred, excluded the progeny of their elder brother from the throne.[2] Alfred, in his testament, dilates upon his own title, which he builds upon a triple foundation, the will of his father, the compact of his brother Ethelred, and the consent of the West Saxon nobility.[3] A similar objection to the government of an infant seems to have rendered Athelstan, notwithstanding his reputed illegitimacy, the public choice upon the death of Edward the Elder. Thus, too, the sons of Edmund I. were postponed to their uncle Edred, and, again, preferred to his issue. And happy might it have been for England if this exclusion of infants had always obtained. But upon the death of Edgar the royal family wanted some prince of mature years to prevent the crown from resting upon the head of a child;[4] and hence the minorities of Edward II. and Ethelred II. led to misfortunes which overwhelmed for a time both the house of Cerdic and the English nation.

The Anglo-Saxon monarchy, during its earlier period,

[1] Vol. i. p. 365. Blackstone has labored to prove the same proposition; but his knowledge of English history was rather superficial.

[2] Chronicon Saxon. p. 99. Hume says that Ethelwold, who attempted to raise an insurrection against Edward the Elder, was son of Ethelbert. The Saxon Chronicle only calls him the king's cousin; which he would be as the son of Ethelred.

[3] Spelman, Vita Alfredi, Appendix.

[4] According to the historian of Ramsey, a sort of interregnum took place on Edgar's death; his son's birth not being thought sufficient to give him a clear right during infancy. 3 Gale, XV Script. p. 413.

Influence of provincial governors.

seems to have suffered but little from that insubordination among the superior nobility which ended in dismembering the empire of Charlemagne. Such kings as Alfred and Athelstan were not likely to permit it. And the English counties, each under its own alderman, were not of a size to encourage the usurpations of their governors. But when the whole kingdom was subdued, there arose, unfortunately, a fashion of intrusting great provinces to the administration of a single earl. Notwithstanding their union, Mercia, Northumberland, and East Anglia were regarded in some degree as distinct parts of the monarchy. A difference of laws, though probably but slight, kept up this separation. Alfred governed Mercia by the hands of a nobleman who had married his daughter Ethelfleda; and that lady after her husband's death held the reins with a masculine energy till her own, when her brother Edward took the province into his immediate command.[1] But from the era of Edward II.'s succession the provincial governors began to overpower the royal authority, as they had done upon the continent. England under this prince was not far removed from the condition of France under Charles the Bald. In the time of Edward the Confessor the whole kingdom seems to have been divided among five earls,[2] three of whom were Godwin and his sons Harold and Tostig. It cannot be wondered at that the royal line was soon supplanted by the most powerful and popular of these leaders, a prince well worthy to have founded a new dynasty, if his eminent qualities had not yielded to those of a still more illustrious enemy.

Distribution into thanes and ceorls.

There were but two denominations of persons above the class of servitude, Thanes and Ceorls; the owners and the cultivators of land, or rather perhaps, as a more accurate distinction, the gentry and the inferior people. Among all the northern nations, as is well known, the weregild, or compensation for murder, was the standard measure of the gradations of society. In the Anglo-Saxon laws we find two ranks of freeholders; the first, called King's Thanes, whose lives were valued at 1200 shillings; the second

[1] Chronicon Saxon.

[2] The word earl (eorl) meant originally a man of noble birth, as opposed to the ceorl. It was not a title of office till the eleventh century, when it was used as synonymous to alderman, for a governor of a county or province. After the conquest it superseded altogether the more ancient title. Selden's Titles of Honor, vol. iii. p. 638 (edit. Wilkins), and Anglo-Saxon writings *passim*.

of inferior degree, whose composition was half that sum.[1] That of a ceorl was 200 shillings. The nature of this distinction between royal and lesser thanes is very obscure; and I shall have something more to say of it presently. However, the thanes in general, or Anglo-Saxon gentry, must have been very numerous. A law of Ethelred directs the sheriff to take twelve of the chief thanes in every hundred, as his assessors on the bench of justice.[2] And from Domesday Book we may collect that they had formed a pretty large class, at least in some counties, under Edward the Confessor.[3]

Condition of the ceorls.

The composition for the life of a ceorl was, as has been said, 200 shillings. If this proportion to the value of a thane points out the subordination of ranks, it certainly does not exhibit the lower freemen in a state of complete abasement. The ceorl was not bound, at least universally, to the land which he cultivated;[4] he was occasionally called upon to bear arms for the public safety;[5] he was protected against personal injuries, or trespasses on his land;[6] he was capable of property, and of the privileges which it conferred. If he came to possess five hydes of land (or about 600 acres), with a church and mansion of his own, he was entitled to the name and rights of a thane.[7] And if by owning five hydes of land he became a thane, it is plain that he might possess a less quantity without reaching that rank. There were, therefore, ceorls with land of their own, and ceorls without land of their own; ceorls who might commend themselves to what lord they pleased, and ceorls who could not quit the land on which they lived, owing various services to the lord of the manor, but always freemen, and capable of becoming gentlemen.[8]

1 Wilkins, p. 40, 43, 64, 72, 101.

2 Id. p. 117.

3 Domesday Book having been compiled by different sets of commissioners, their language has sometimes varied in describing the same class of persons. The *liberi homines*, of whom we find continual mention in some counties, were perhaps not different from the *thaini*, who occur in other places. But this subject is very obscure; and a clear apprehension of the classes of society mentioned in Domesday seems at present unattainable.

4 Leges Alfredi, c. 33, in Wilkins. This text is not unequivocal; and I confess that a law of Ina (c. 39) has rather a contrary appearance. But the condition of all ceorls need not be supposed to have been the same; and in the latter period this can be shown to have been subject to much diversity.

5 Leges Inæ, c. 51, ibid.

6 Leges Alfredi, c. 31, 35.

7 Leges Athelstani, ibid. p. 70, 71.

8 It is said in the Introduction to the Supplementary Records of Domesday, which I quote from Cooper's Account of Public Records (i. 223), that the word *commendatio* is confined to the three counties in the second volume of Domesday, except that it occurs twice in the Inquisitio Eliensis for Cambridgeshire. But, if this particular word does not occur, we have the sense, in "ire cum terra ubi voluerit," or "quærere dominum

Some might be inclined to suspect that the ceorls were sliding more and more towards a state of servitude before the conquest.[1] The natural tendency of such times of rapine, with the analogy of a similar change in France, leads to this conjecture. But there seems to be no proof of it; and the passages which recognize the capacity of a ceorl to become a thane are found in the later period of Anglo-Saxon law. Nor can it be shown, as I apprehend, by any authority earlier than that of Glanvil, whose treatise was written about 1180, that the peasantry of England were reduced to that extreme debasement which our law-books call villenage; a condition which left them no civil rights with respect to their lord. For, by the laws of William the Conqueror, there was still a composition fixed for the murder of a villein or ceorl, the strongest proof of his being, as it was called, law-worthy, and possessing a rank, however subordinate, in political society. And this composition was due to his kindred, not to the lord.[2] Indeed, it seems positively declared in another passage that the cultivators, though bound to remain upon the land, were only subject to certain services.[3] Again, the treatise denominated the Laws of Henry I., which, though not deserving that appellation, must be considered as a contemporary document, expressly mentions the twyhinder or villein as a freeman.[4] Nobody can doubt that the *villani* and *bordarii* of Domesday Book, who are always distinguished from the serfs of the demesne, were the ceorls of Anglo-Saxon law. And I presume that the socmen, who so frequently occur in that record, though far more in some counties than in others, were ceorls more fortunate than the rest, who by purchase had acquired freeholds, or by prescription and the indulgence of their lords had obtained such a property in the outlands allotted to them that they could not be removed, and in many instances might dispose of them at pleasure. They are the root of a noble plant, the free socage tenants, or English yeomanry, whose independence has stamped with peculiar features both our constitution and our national character.[5]

Beneath the ceorls in political estimation were the con

ubi voluerit," which meet our eyes perpetually in the first volume of Domesday. The difference of phrases in this record must, in great measure, be attributed to that of the persons employed.

1 If the laws that bear the name of William are, as is generally supposed, those of his predecessor Edward, they were already annexed to the soil. p. 225.

2 Wilkins, p. 221.

3 Id. p. 225.

4 Leges, Henr. I. c. 70 and 76, in Wilkins.

5 [NOTE III.]

British natives.

quered natives of Britain. In a war so long and so obstinately maintained as that of the Britons against their invaders, it is natural to conclude that in a great part of the country the original inhabitants were almost extirpated, and that the remainder were reduced into servitude. This, till lately, has been the concurrent opinion of our antiquaries; and, with some qualification, I do not see why it should not still be received.[1] In every kingdom of the continent which was formed by the northern nations out of the Roman empire, the Latin language preserved its superiority, and has much more been corrupted through ignorance and want of a standard, than intermingled with their original idiom. But our own language is, and has been from the earliest times after the Saxon conquest, essentially Teutonic, and of the most obvious affinity to those dialects which are spoken in Denmark and Lower Saxony. With such as are extravagant enough to controvert so evident a truth it is idle to contend; and those who believe great part of our language to be borrowed from the Welsh may doubtless infer that great part of our population is derived from the same source.[2] If we look through the subsisting Anglo-Saxon records, there is not very frequent mention of British subjects. But some undoubtedly there were in a state of freedom, and possessed of landed estate. A Welshman (that is, a Briton) who held

[1] [NOTE IV.]

[2] It is but just to mention a partial exception, according to a considerable authority, to what has been said in the text as to the absence of British roots in the English language; though it can but slightly affect the general proposition. Mr. Kemble remarks the number of minute distinctions, in describing the local features of a country, which abound in the Anglo-Saxon charters, and the difficulties which occur in their explanation. One of these relates to the language itself. "It cannot be doubtful that local names, and those devoted to distinguish the natural features of a country, possess an inherent vitality, which even the urgency of conquest is frequently unable to destroy. A race is rarely so entirely removed as not to form an integral, although subordinate, part of the new state based upon its ruins; and in the case where the cultivator continues to be occupied with the soil, a change of master will not necessarily lead to the abandonment of the names by which the land itself, and the instruments or processes of labor are designated. On the contrary, the conquering race are apt to adopt these names from the conquered; and thus, after the lapse of twelve centuries and innumerable civil convulsions, the principal words of the class described yet prevail in the language of our people, and partially in our literature. Many, then, of the words which we seek in vain in the Anglo-Saxon dictionaries, are, in fact, to be sought in those of the Cymri, from whose practice they were adopted by the victorious Saxons, in all parts of the country; and they are not Anglo-Saxon, but Welsh (*i. e.* foreign, Wylisc), very frequently unmodified either in meaning or pronunciation." Preface to Codex Diplom. vol. iii. p. 15. Though this bears intrinsic marks of probability, it is yet remarkable that, in a long list of descriptive words which immediately follows, there are not six for which Mr. Kemble suggests a Cambrian root: and of these some, such as *comb*, a valley, belong to parts of England where the British long kept their ground

five hydes was raised, like a ceorl, to the dignity of thane.[1] In the composition, however, for their lives, and consequently in their rank in society, they were inferior to the meanest Saxon freemen. The slaves, who were frequently the objects of legislation, rather for the purpose of ascertaining their punishment than of securing their rights, may be presumed, at least in early times, to have been part of the conquered Britons. For though his own crimes, or the tyranny of others, might possibly reduce a Saxon ceorl to this condition,[2] it is inconceivable that the lowest of those who won England with their swords should in the establishment of the new kingdoms have been left destitute of personal liberty.

Slaves.

The great council by which an Anglo-Saxon king was guided in all the main acts of government bore the appellation of Witenagemot, or the assembly of the wise men. All their laws express the assent of this council; and there are instances where grants made without its concurrence have been revoked. It was composed of prelates and abbots, of the aldermen of shires, and, as it is generally expressed, of the noble and wise men of the kingdom.[3] Whether the lesser thanes, or inferior proprietors of lands, were entitled to a place in the national council, as they certainly were in the shiregemot, or county-court, is not easily to be decided. Many writers have concluded, from a passage in the History of Ely, that no one, however nobly born, could sit in the witenagemot, so late at least as the reign of Edward the Confessor, unless he possessed forty hydes of land, or about five thousand acres.[4] But the passage in question does not unequivocally relate to the witenagemot; and being vaguely worded by an ignorant monk, who perhaps had never gone beyond his fens, ought not to be assumed as an incontrovertible testimony. Certainly so very high a qualification cannot be supposed to have been requisite in the kingdoms of the Heptarchy; nor do we find any collateral evidence to confirm the hypothesis. If, however, all the body of thanes or freeholders were admissible to the witenagemot, it is unlikely that the privilege should have been fully exercised. Very few, I believe, at present imagine that there

The Witenagemot.

1 Leges Inæ, p. 18; Leg. Athelst. p. 71.
2 Leges Inæ, c. 24.
3 Leges Anglo-Saxon. In Wilkins, passim.
4 Quoniam ille quadraginta hydarum terræ dominium minimè obtineret, licet nobilis esset, inter proceres tunc numerari non potuit. 3 Gale, p. 513.

was any representative system in that age; much less that the ceorls or inferior freemen had the smallest share in the deliberations of the national assembly. Every argument which a spirit of controversy once pressed into this service has long since been victoriously refuted.[1]

Judicial power.

It has been justly remarked by Hume, that, among a people who lived in so simple a manner as these Anglo-Saxons, the judicial power is always of more consequence than the legislative. The liberties of these Anglo-Saxon thanes were chiefly secured, next to their swords and their free spirits, by the inestimable right of deciding civil and criminal suits in their own county-court; an institution which, having survived the conquest, and contributed in no small degree to fix the liberties of England upon a broad and popular basis, by limiting the feudal aristocracy, deserves attention in following the history of the British constitution.

Division into counties, hundreds, and tythings.

The division of the kingdom into counties, and of these into hundreds and decennaries, for the purpose of administering justice, was not peculiar to England. In the early laws of France and Lombardy frequent mention is made of the hundred-court, and now and then of those petty village-magistrates who in England were called tything-men. It has been usual to ascribe the establishment of this system among our Saxon ancestors to Alfred, upon the authority of Ingulfus, a writer contemporary with the conquest. But neither the biographer of Alfred, Asserius, nor the existing laws of that prince, bear testimony to the fact. With respect indeed to the division of counties, and their government by aldermen and sheriffs, it is certain that both existed long before his time;[2] and the utmost that can be supposed is, that he might in some instances have ascertained an unsettled boundary. There does not seem to

1 [NOTE V.]

2 Counties, as well as the alderman who presided over them, are mentioned in the laws of Ina, c. 36.

For the division of counties, which were not always formed in the same age, nor on the same plan, see Palgrave, i. 116. We do not know much about the inland counties in general; those on the coasts are in general larger, and are mentioned in history. All we can say is, that they all existed at the conquest as at present. The hundred is supposed by Sir H. Ellis, on the authority of an ancient record, to have consisted of an hundred hydes of land, cultivated and waste taken together. Introduction to Domesday, i. 185. But this implies equality of size, which is evidently not the case. A passage in the Dialogus de Scaccario (p. 31) is conclusive:—Hyda a primitiva institutione in centum acris constat: hundredus est ex hydarum aliquot centenariis, sed non determinatis; quidam enim ex pluribus, quidam ex paucioribus hydis constat.

be equal evidence as to the antiquity of the minor divisions. Hundreds, I think, are first mentioned in a law of Edgar, and tythings in one of Canute.[1] But as Alfred, it must be remembered, was never master of more than half the kingdom, the complete distribution of England into these districts cannot, upon any supposition, be referred to him.

There is, indeed, a circumstance observable in this division which seems to indicate that it could not have taken place at one time, nor upon one system; I mean the extreme inequality of hundreds in different parts of England. Whether the name be conceived to refer to the number of free families, or of landholders, or of petty vills, forming so many associations of mutual assurance or frank-pledge, one can hardly doubt that, when the term was first applied, a hundred of one or other of these were comprised, at an average reckoning, within the district. But it is impossible to reconcile the varying size of hundreds to any single hypothesis. The county of Sussex contains sixty-five, that of Dorset forty-three; while Yorkshire has only twenty-six, and Lancashire but six. No difference of population, though the south of England was undoubtedly far the best peopled, can be conceived to account for so prodigious a disparity. I know of no better solution than that the divisions of the north, properly called wapentakes,[2] were planned upon a different system, and obtained the denomination of hundreds incorrectly after the union of all England under a single sovereign.

Assuming, therefore, the name and partition of hundreds to have originated in the southern counties, it will rather, I think, appear probable that they contained only an hundred free families, including the ceorls as well as their landlords. If we suppose none but the latter to have been numbered, we should find six thousand thanes in Kent, and six thousand five hundred in Sussex; a reckoning totally inconsistent with any probable estimate.[3] But though we have little direct testimony as to the population of those times, there is one passage which falls in very sufficiently with the former supposition. Bede says that the kingdom of the South Saxons, comprehending Surrey as well as Sussex, contained seven

[1] Wilkins, pp. 87, 136. The former, however, refers to them as an ancient institution: quæratur centuriæ conventus, sicut antea institutum erat.

[2] Leges Edwardi Confess. c. 33.

[3] It would be easy to mention particular hundreds in these counties so small as to render this supposition quite ridiculous.

thousand families. The county of Sussex alone is divided into sixty-five hundreds, which comes at least close enough to prove that free families, rather than proprietors, were the subject of that numeration. And this is the interpretation of Du Cange and Muratori as to the Centenæ and Decaniæ of their own ancient laws.

I cannot but feel some doubt, notwithstanding a passage in the laws ascribed to Edward the Confessor,[1] whether the tything-man ever possessed any judicial magistracy over his small district. He was, more probably, little different from a petty constable, as is now the case, I believe, wherever that denomination of office is preserved. The court of the hundred was held, as on the continent, by its own centenarius, or hundred-man, more often called alderman, and, in the Norman times, bailiff or constable, but under the sheriff's writ. It is, in the language of the law, the sheriff's tourn and leet. And in the Anglo-Saxon age it was a court of justice for suitors within the hundred, though it could not execute its process beyond that limit. It also punished small offences, and was intrusted with the "view of frank-pledge," and the maintenance of the great police of mutual surety. In some cases, that is, when the hundred was competent to render judgment, it seems that the county-court could only exercise an appellant jurisdiction for denial of right in the lower tribunal. But in course of time the former and more celebrated court, being composed of far more conspicuous judges, and held before the bishop and the earl, became the real arbiter of important suits; and the court-leet fell almost entirely into disuse as a civil jurisdiction, contenting itself with punishing petty offences and keeping up a local police.[2] It was, however, to the county-court that an English freeman chiefly looked for the maintenance of his civil rights. In this assembly, held twice in the year by the bishop and the alderman,[3] or, in his absence, the sheriff, the oath of allegiance was administered to all freemen, breaches of the peace were inquired into, crimes were investigated,

County-court.

[1] Leges Edwardi Confess. p. 203. Nothing, as far as I know, confirms this passage, which hardly tallies with what the genuine Anglo-Saxon documents contain as to the judicial arrangements of that period.

[2] [NOTE VI.]

[3] The alderman was the highest rank after the royal family, to which he sometimes belonged. Every county had its alderman; but the name is not applied in written documents to magistrates of boroughs before the conquest. Palgrave, ii. 350. He thinks, however, that London had aldermen from time immemorial. After the conquest the title seems to have become appropriated to municipal magistrates.

and claims were determined. I assign all these functions to the county-court upon the supposition that no other subsisted during the Saxon times, and that the separation of the sheriff's tourn for criminal jurisdiction had nōt yet taken place; which, however, I cannot pretend to determine.[1]

Suit in the county-court.

A very ancient Saxon instrument, recording a suit in the county-court under the reign of Canute, has been published by Hickes, and may be deemed worthy of a literal translation in this place. "It is made known by this writing that in the shiregemot (county-court) held at Agelnothes-stane (Aylston in Herefordshire) in the reign of Canute there sat Athelstan the bishop, and Ranig the alderman, and Edwin his son, and Leofwin Wulfig's son; and Thurkil the White and Tofig came there on the king's business; and there were Bryning the sheriff, and Athelweard of Frome, and Leofwin of Frome, and Goodric of Stoke, and all the thanes of Herefordshire. Then came to the mote Edwin son of Enneawne, and sued his mother for some lands, called Weolintun and Cyrdeslea. Then the bishop asked who would answer for his mother. Then answered Thurkil the White, and said that he would, if he knew the facts, which he did not. Then were seen in the mote three thanes, that belonged to Feligly (Fawley, five miles from Aylston), Leofwin of Frome, Ægelwig the Red, and Thinsig Stægthman; and they went to her, and inquired what she had to say about the lands which her son claimed. She said that she had no land which belonged to him, and fell into a noble passion against her son, and, calling for Leofleda her kinswoman, the wife of Thurkil, thus spake to her before them: 'This is Leofleda my kinswoman, to whom I give my lands, money, clothes, and whatever I possess after my life:' and this said, she thus spake to the thanes: 'Behave like thanes, and declare my message to all the good men in the mote, and tell them to whom I have given my lands and all my possessions, and nothing to my son;' and bade them be witnesses to this. And thus they did, rode to the mote, and told all the good men what she had enjoined them. Then Thurkil the White addressed the mote, and requested all the thanes to let his wife have the lands which her kinswoman had given her; and thus they did, and Thurkil rode

[1] This point is obscure; but I do not perceive that the Anglo-Saxon laws distinguish the civil from the criminal tribunal.

to the church of St. Ethelbert, with the leave and witness of all the people, and had this inserted in a book in the church." [1]

It may be presumed from the appeal made to the thanes present at the county-court, and is confirmed by other ancient authorities,[2] that all of them, and they alone, to the exclusion of inferior freemen, were the judges of civil controversies. The latter indeed were called upon to attend its meetings, or, in the language of our present law, were suitors to the court, and it was penal to be absent. But this was on account of other duties, the oath of allegiance which they were to take, or the frank-pledges into which they were to enter, not in order to exercise any judicial power; unless we conceive that the disputes of the ceorls were decided by judges of their own rank. It is more important to remark the crude state of legal process and inquiry which this instrument denotes. Without any regular method of instituting or conducting causes, the county-court seems to have had nothing to recommend it but, what indeed is no trifling matter, its security from corruption and tyranny; and in the practical jurisprudence of our Saxon ancestors, even at the beginning of the eleventh century, we perceive no advance of civility and skill from the state of their own savage progenitors on the banks of the Elbe. No appeal could be made to the royal tribunal, unless justice was denied in the county-court.[3] This was the great constitutional judicature in all questions of civil right. In another instrument, published by Hickes, of the age of Ethelred II., the tenant of lands which were claimed in the king's court refused to submit to the decree of that tribunal, without a regular trial in the county; which was accordingly granted.[4] There were, however, royal judges, who, either by way of appeal from the lower courts, or in excepted cases, formed a paramount judicature; but

1 Hickes, Dissertatio Epistolaris, p. 4, in Thesaurus Antiquitatum Septentrion, vol. iii. "Before the Conquest," says Gurdon (on Courts-Baron, p. 589), "grants were enrolled in the shire-book in public shire-mote, after proclamation made for any to come in that could claim the lands conveyed; and this was as irreversible as the modern fine with proclamations, or recovery." This may be so; but the county-court has at least long ceased to be a court of record; and one would ask for proof of the assertion. The book kept in the church of St Ethelbert, wherein Thurkil is said to have inserted the proceedings of the county-court, may or may not have been a public record.

2 Id. p. 3. Leges Henr. Primi, c 29.

3 Leges Eadgari, p. 77; Canuti, p. 136; Henrici Primi, c. 34. I quote the latter freely as Anglo-Saxon, though posterior to the conquest; their spirit being perfectly of the former period.

4 Dissertatio Epistolaris, p. 5.

how their court was composed under the Anglo-Saxon sovereigns I do not pretend to assert.[1]

Trial by jury.

It had been a prevailing opinion that trial by jury may be referred to the Anglo-Saxon age, and common tradition has ascribed it to the wisdom of Alfred. In such an historical deduction of the English government as I have attempted, an institution so peculiarly characteristic deserves every attention to its origin; and I shall, therefore, produce the evidence which has been supposed to bear upon this most eminent part of our judicial system. The first text of the Saxon laws which may appear to have such a meaning is in those of Alfred. "If any one accuse a king's thane of homicide, if he dare to purge himself (ladian), let him do it along with twelve king's thanes." "If any one accuse a thane of less rank (læssa maga) than a king's thane, let him purge himself along with eleven of his equals, and one king's thane."[2] This law, which Nicholson contends to mean nothing but trial by jury, has been referred by Hickes to that ancient usage of compurgation, where the accused sustained his own oath by those of a number of his friends, who pledged their knowledge, or at least their belief, of his innocence.[3]

In the canons of the Northumbrian clergy we read as follows: "If a king's thane deny this (the practice of heathen superstitions), let twelve be appointed for him, and let him take twelve of his kindred (or equals, *maga*) and twelve British strangers; and if he fail, then let him pay for his breach of law twelve half-marcs: If a landholder (or lesser thane) deny the charge, let as many of his equals and as many strangers be taken as for a royal thane; and if he fail, let him pay six half-marcs: If a ceorl deny it, let as many of his equals and as many strangers be taken for him as for the others; and if he fail, let him pay twelve oræ for his breach of law."[4] It is difficult at first sight to imagine that these

1 Madox, History of the Exchequer, p. 65 will not admit the existence of any court analogous to the Curia Regis before the conquest; all pleas being determined in the county. There are, however, several instances of decisions before the king; and in some cases it seems that the witenagemot had a judicial authority. Leges Canuti, p. 135, 136; Hist. Eliensis, p. 469; Chron. Sax. p. 169. In the Leges Henr. I. c. 10, the limits of the royal and local jurisdictions are defined, as to criminal matters, and seem to have been little changed since the reign of Canute, p. 135 [1818]. [NOTE VII.]

2 Leges Alfredi, p. 47.

3 Nicholson, Prefatio ad Leges Anglo-Saxon.; Wilkinsii, p. 10; Hickes, Dissertatio Epistolaris.

4 Wilkins, p. 100.

thirty-six so selected were merely compurgators, since it seems absurd that the judge should name indifferent persons, who without inquiry were to make oath of a party's innocence. Some have therefore conceived that, in this and other instances where compurgators are mentioned, they were virtually jurors, who, before attesting the facts, were to inform their consciences by investigating them. There are however passages in the Saxon laws nearly parallel to that just quoted, which seem incompatible with this interpretation. Thus, by a law of Athelstan, if any one claimed a stray ox as his own, five of his neighbors were to be assigned, of whom one was to maintain the claimant's oath.[1] Perhaps the principle of these regulations, and indeed of the whole law of compurgation, is to be found in that stress laid upon general character which pervades the Anglo-Saxon jurisprudence. A man of ill reputation was compelled to undergo a triple ordeal, in cases where a single one sufficed for persons of credit; a provision rather inconsistent with the trust in a miraculous interposition of Providence which was the basis of that superstition. And the law of frank-pledge proceeded upon the maxim that the best guarantee of every man's obedience to the government was to be sought in the confidence of his neighbors. Hence, while some compurgators were to be chosen by the sheriff, to avoid partiality and collusion, it was still intended that they should be residents of the vicinage, witnesses of the defendant's previous life, and competent to estimate the probability of his exculpatory oath. For the British strangers, in the canon quoted above, were certainly the original natives, more intermingled with their conquerors, probably, in the provinces north of the Humber than elsewhere, and still denominated strangers, as the distinction of races was not done away.

If in this instance we do not feel ourselves warranted to infer the existence of trial by jury, still less shall we find even an analogy to it in an article of the treaty between England and Wales during the reign of Ethelred II. "Twelve persons skilled in the law, six English and six Welsh, shall instruct the natives of each country, on pain of forfeiting their possessions, if, except through ignorance, they give false information."[2] This is obviously but a regulation intended to settle disputes among the Welsh and English, to

[1] Leges Athelstani, p. 58

[2] Leges Ethelredi, p. 125.

which their ignorance of each other's customs might give rise.

By a law of the same prince, a court was to be held in every wapentake, where the sheriff and twelve principal thanes should swear that they would neither acquit any criminal nor convict any innocent person.[1] It seems more probable that these thanes were permanent assessors to the sheriff, like the scabini so frequently mentioned in the early laws of France and Italy, than jurors indiscriminately selected. This passage, however, is stronger than those which have been already adduced; and it may be thought, perhaps, with justice, that at least the seeds of our present form of trial are discoverable in it. In the History of Ely we twice read of pleas held before twenty-four judges in the court of Cambridge; which seems to have been formed out of several neighboring hundreds.[2]

But the nearest approach to a regular jury which has been preserved in our scanty memorials of the Anglo-Saxon age occurs in the history of the monastery of Ramsey. A controversy relating to lands between that society and a certain nobleman was brought into the county-court, when each party was heard in his own behalf. After this commencement, on account probably of the length and difficulty of the investigation, it was referred by the court to thirty-six thanes, equally chosen by both sides.[3] And here we begin to perceive the manner in which those tumultuous assemblies, the mixed body of freeholders in their county-court, slid gradually into a more steady and more diligent tribunal. But this was not the work of a single age. In the Conqueror's reign we find a proceeding very similar to the case of Ramsey, in which the suit has been commenced in the county-court, before it was found expedient to remit it to a select body of freeholders. In the reign of William Rufus, and down to that of Henry II., when the trial of writs of right by the grand assize was introduced, Hickes has discovered other instances of the original usage.[4] The language of Domesday Book lends some confirmation to its existence at the time of that survey; and even our common legal expression of trial by the country seems to be derived from a period when the form was literally popular.

[1] Leges Ethelredi, p. 117.

[2] Hist. Eliensis, in Gale's Scriptores iii. p. 471 and 478.

[3] Hist. Ramsey, id. p. 415.

[4] Hickesii Dissertatio Epistolaris, p. 33, 36.

In comparing the various passages which I have quoted it is impossible not to be struck with the preference given to twelve, or some multiple of it, in fixing the number either of judges or compurgators. This was not peculiar to England. Spelman has produced several instances of it in the early German laws. And that number seems to have been regarded with equal veneration in Scandinavia.[1] It is very immaterial from what caprice or superstition this predilection arose. But its general prevalence shows that, in searching for the origin of trial by jury, we cannot rely for a moment upon any analogy which the mere number affords. I am induced to make this observation, because some of the pas sages which have been alleged by eminent men for the purpose of establishing the existence of that institution before the conquest seem to have little else to support them.[2]

Law of frank-pledge.

There is certainly no part of the Anglo-Saxon polity which has attracted so much the notice of modern times as the law of frank-pledge, or mutual responsibility of the members of a tything for each other's abiding the course of justice. This, like the distribution of hundreds and tythings themselves, and like trial by jury, has been generally attributed to Alfred; and of this, I suspect, we must also deprive him. It is not surprising that the great services of Alfred to his people in peace and in war should have led posterity to ascribe every institution, of which the beginning was obscure, to his contrivance, till his fame has become almost as fabulous in legislation as that of Arthur in arms. The English nation redeemed from servitude, and their name from extinction; the lamp of learning refreshed, when scarce a glimmer was visible; the watchful observance of justice and public order; these are the genuine praises of Alfred, and entitle him to the rank he has always held in men's esteem, as the best and greatest of English kings. But of his legislation there is little that can be asserted with sufficient evidence; the laws of his time that remain are neither numerous nor particularly interesting; and a loose report of late writers is not sufficient to prove that he compiled a dom-boc, or general code for the government of his kingdom.

An ingenious and philosophical writer has endeavored to

[1] Spelman's Glossary, voc. Jurata; Du Cange, voc. Nembda; Edinb. Review, vol. xxxi. p. 115 — a most learned and elaborate essay.

[2] [NOTE VIII.]

found the law of frank-pledge upon one of those general principles to which he always loves to recur. "If we look upon a tything," he says, "as regularly composed of ten families, this branch of its police will appear in the highest degree artificial and singular; but if we consider that society as of the same extent with a town or village, we shall find that such a regulation is conformable to the general usage of barbarous nations, and is founded upon their common notions of justice."[1] A variety of instances are then brought forward, drawn from the customs of almost every part of the world, wherein the inhabitants of a district have been made answerable for crimes and injuries imputed to one of them. But none of these fully resemble the Saxon institution of which we are treating. They relate either to the right of reprisals, exercised with respect to the subjects of foreign countries, or to the indemnification exacted from the district, as in our modern statutes which give an action in certain cases of felony against the hundred, for crimes which its internal police was supposed capable of preventing. In the Irish custom, indeed, which bound the head of a sept to bring forward every one of his kindred who should be charged with any heinous crime, we certainly perceive a strong analogy to the Saxon law, not as it latterly subsisted, but under one of its prior modifications. For I think that something of a gradual progression may be traced to the history of this famous police, by following the indications afforded by those laws through which alone we become acquainted with its existence.

The Saxons brought with them from their original forests at least as much roughness as any of the nations which overturned the Roman empire; and their long struggle with the Britons could not contribute to polish their manners. The royal authority was weak; and little had been learned of that regular system of government which the Franks and Lombards had acquired from the provincial Romans, among whom they were mingled. No people were so much addicted to robbery, to riotous frays, and to feuds arising out of family revenge, as the Anglo-Saxons. Their statutes are filled with complaints that the public peace was openly violated, and with penalties which seem by their repetition to have been disregarded. The vengeance taken by the kindred of a murdered man was a sacred right, which no law ventured to

[1] Millar on the English Government, vol. i. p. 189

forbid, though it was limited by those which established a composition, and by those which protected the family of the murderer from their resentment. Even the author of the laws ascribed to the Confessor speaks of this family warfare, where the composition had not been paid, as perfectly lawful.[1] But the law of composition tended probably to increase the number of crimes. Though the sums imposed were sometimes heavy, men paid them with the help of their relations, or entered into voluntary associations, the purposes whereof might often be laudable, but which were certainly susceptible of this kind of abuse. And many led a life of rapine, forming large parties of ruffians, who committed murder and robbery with little dread of punishment.

Against this disorderly condition of society, the wisdom of our English kings, with the assistance of their great councils, was employed in devising remedies, which ultimately grew up into a peculiar system. No man could leave the shire to which he belonged without the permission of its alderman.[2] No man could be without a lord, on whom he depended; though he might quit his present patron, it was under the condition of engaging himself to another. If he failed in this, his kindred were bound to present him in the county-court, and to name a lord for him themselves. Unless this were done, he might be seized by any one who met him as a robber.[3] Hence, notwithstanding the personal liberty of the peasants, it was not very practicable for one of them to quit his place of residence. A stranger guest could not be received more than two nights as such; on the third the host became responsible for his inmate's conduct.[4]

The peculiar system of frank-pledges seems to have passed through the following very gradual stages. At first an accused person was obliged to find bail for standing his trial.[5] At a subsequent period his relations were called upon to become sureties for payment of the composition and other fines to which he was liable.[6] They were even subject to be imprisoned until payment was made, and this imprisonment was commutable for a certain sum of money. The next stage

[1] Parentibus occisi fiat emendatio, vel guerra eorum portetur. Wilkins, p. 199. This, like many other parts of that spurious treatise, appears to have been taken from some older laws, or at least traditions. I do not conceive that this private revenge was tolerated by law after the conquest.

[2] Leges Alfredi, c. 33.

[3] Leges Athelstani, p. 56.

[4] Leges Edwardi Confess. p. 202.

[5] Leges Lotharii [regis Cantii], p 8.

[6] Leges Edwardi Senioris, p. 53.

was to make persons already convicted, or of suspicious repute, give sureties for their future behavior.[1] It is not till the reign of Edgar that we find the first general law, which places every man in the condition of the guilty or suspected, and compels him to find a surety, who shall be responsible for his appearance when judicially summoned.[2] This is perpetually repeated and enforced in later statutes, during his reign and that of Ethelred. Finally, the laws of Canute declare the necessity of belonging to some hundred and tything, as well as of providing sureties;[3] and it may, perhaps, be inferred that the custom of rendering every member of a tything answerable for the appearance of all the rest, as it existed after the conquest, is as old as the reign of this Danish monarch.

It is by no means an accurate notion which the writer to whom I have already adverted has conceived that "the members of every tything were responsible for the conduct of one another; and that the society, or their leader, might be prosecuted and compelled to make reparation for an injury committed by any individual." Upon this false apprehension of the nature of frank-pledges the whole of his analogical reasoning is founded. It is indeed an error very current in popular treatises, and which might plead the authority of some whose professional learning should have saved them from so obvious a misstatement. But in fact the members of a tything were no more than perpetual bail for each other. "The greatest security of the public order (says the laws ascribed to the Confessor) is that every man must bind himself to one of those societies which the English in general call freeborgs, and the people of Yorkshire ten men's tale."[4] This consisted in the responsibility of ten men, each for the other, throughout every village in the kingdom; so that, if one of the ten committed any fault, the nine should produce him in justice; where he should make reparation by his own property or by personal punishment. If he fled from justice, a mode was provided according to which the tything might clear themselves from participation in his crime or escape; in default of such exculpation, and the malefactor's estate proving deficient, they were compelled to make good the penalty. And it is equally manifest, from every other passage in which

1 Leges Athelstani, p. 57, c. 6, 7, 8

2 Leges Eadgari, p. 78.

3 Leges Canuti, p. 137.

4 Leges Edwardi, in Wilkins, p. 201.

mention is made of this ancient institution, that the obligation of the tything was merely that of permanent bail, responsible only indirectly for the good behavior of their members.

Every freeman above the age of twelve years was required to be enrolled in some tything.[1] In order to enforce this essential part of police, the courts of the tourn and leet were erected, or rather perhaps separated from that of the county. The periodical meetings of these, whose duty it was to inquire into the state of tythings, whence they were called the view of frank-pledge, are regulated in Magna Charta. But this custom, which seems to have been in full vigor when Bracton wrote, and is enforced by a statute of Edward II., gradually died away in succeeding times.[2] According to the laws ascribed to the Confessor, which are perhaps of insufficient authority to fix the existence of any usage before the Conquest, lords who possessed a baronial jurisdiction were permitted to keep their military tenants and the servants of their household under their own peculiar frank-pledge.[3] Nor was any freeholder, in the age of Bracton, bound to be enrolled in a tything.[4]

Feudal tenures, whether known before the Conquest.

It remains only, before we conclude this sketch of the Anglo-Saxon system, to consider the once famous question respecting the establishment of feudal tenures in England before the Conquest. The position asserted by Sir Henry Spelman in his

[1] Leges Canuti, p. 136.

[2] Stat. 18 E. II. Traces of the actual view of frank-pledge appear in Cornwall as late as the 10th of Henry VI. Rot. Parliam. vol. iv. p. 403. And indeed Selden tells us (Janus Anglorum, t. ii. p. 993) that it was not quite obsolete in his time. The form may, for aught I know, be kept up in some parts of England at this day. For some reason which I cannot explain, the distribution by tens was changed into one by dozens. Briton, c. 29, and Stat. 18 E. II.

[3] p. 202.

[4] Sir F Palgrave, who does not admit the application of some of the laws cited in the text, says: "At some period, towards the close of the Anglo-Saxon monarchy, the free-pledge was certainly established in the greater part of Wessex and Mercia, though, even there, some special exceptions existed. The system was developed between the accession of Canute and the demise of the Conqueror; and it is not improbable but that the Normans completed what the Danes had begun." Vol. ii. p. 123

It is very remarkable that there is no appearance of the frank-pledge in that part of England which had formed the kingdom of Northumberland. Vol. i. p. 202. This indeed contradicts a passage, quoted in the text from the laws of Edward the Confessor, which Sir F. P. suspects to be interpolated. But we find a presentment by the county of Westmoreland in 20 Ed. I.:—Comitatus recordatur quod nulla Englescheria presentatur in comitatu isto, nec murdrum, nec est aliqua decenna nec visus franciplegii nec manupastus in comitatu isto, nec unquam fuit in partibus borealibus citra Trentam. Ibidem. "It is impossible to speak positively to a negative proposition; and in the vast mass of these most valuable records, all of which are still unindexed, some entry relating to the collective frank-pledge may be concealed. Yet, from their general tenor, I doubt whether any will be discovered." The immense knowledge of records possessed by Sir F. P. gives the highest weight to his judgment.

Glossary, that lands were not held feudally before that period, having been denied by the Irish judges in the great case of tenures, he was compelled to draw up his treatise on Feuds, in which it is more fully maintained. Several other writers, especially Hickes, Madox, and Sir Martin Wright, have taken the same side. But names equally respectable might be thrown into the opposite scale; and I think the prevailing bias of modern antiquaries is in favor of at least a modified affirmative as to this question.

Lands are commonly supposed to have been divided, among the Anglo-Saxons, into bocland and folkland. The former was held in full propriety, and might be conveyed by boc or written grant; the latter was occupied by the common people, yielding rent or other service, and perhaps without any estate in the land, but at the pleasure of the owner. These two species of tenure might be compared to freehold and copyhold, if the latter had retained its original dependence upon the will of the lord.[1] Bocland was devisable by will; it was equally shared among the children; it was capable of being entailed by the person under whose grant it was originally taken; and in case of a treacherous or cowardly desertion from the army it was forfeited to the crown.[2] But a different theory, at least as to the nature of folkland, has lately been maintained by writers of very great authority.[3]

It is an improbable, and even extravagant supposition, that all these hereditary estates of the Anglo-Saxon freeholders were originally parcels of the royal demesne, and consequently that the king was once the sole proprietor in his kingdom. Whatever partitions were made upon the conquest of a British province, we may be sure that the shares of the army were coeval with those of the general. The great mass of Saxon property could not have been held by actual beneficiary grants from the crown. However, the royal demesnes were undoubtedly very extensive. They continued to be so, even in the time of the Confessor, after

1 This supposition may plead the great authorities of Somner and Lye, the Anglo-Saxon lexicographers, and appears to me far more probable than the theory of Sir John Dalrymple, in his Essay on Feudal Property, or that of the author of a discourse on the Bocland and Folkland of the Saxons, 1775, whose name, I think, was Ibbetson. The first of these supposes bocland to have been feudal, and folkland alodial; the second takes folkland for feudal. I cannot satisfy myself whether thainland and reveland, which occur sometimes in Domesday Book, merely correspond with the other two denominations.

2 Wilkins, p. 43, 145. The latter law is copied from one of Charlemagne's Capitularies. Baluze, p. 767.

3 [NOTE IX.]

the donations of his predecessors. And several instruments granting lands to individuals, besides those in favor of the church, are extant. These are generally couched in that style of full and unconditional conveyance which is observable in all such charters of the same age upon the continent. Some exceptions, however, occur; the lands bequeathed by Alfred to certain of his nobles were to return to his family in default of male heirs; and Hickes is of opinion that the royal consent, which seems to have been required for the testamentary disposition of some estates, was necessary on account of their beneficiary tenure.[1]

All the freehold lands of England, except some of those belonging to the church, were subject to three great public burdens: military service in the king's expeditions, or at least in defensive war,[2] the repair of bridges, and that of royal fortresses. These obligations, and especially the first, have been sometimes thought to denote a feudal tenure. There is, however, a confusion into which we may fall by not sufficiently discriminating the rights of a king as chief lord of his vassals, and as sovereign of his subjects. In every country the supreme power is entitled to use the arm of each citizen in the public defence. The usage of all nations agrees with common reason in establishing this great principle. There is nothing therefore peculiarly feudal in this military service of landholders; it was due from the alodial proprietors upon the continent; it was derived from their German ancestors; it had been fixed, probably, by the legislatures of the Heptarchy upon the first settlement in Britain.

It is material, however, to observe that a thane forfeited his hereditary freehold by misconduct in battle: a penalty more severe than was inflicted upon alodial proprietors on the continent. We even find in the earliest Saxon laws that the sithcundman, who seems to have corresponded to the inferior thane of later times, forfeited his land by neglect of attendance in war; for which an alodialist in France would only have paid his heribannum, or penalty.[3] Nevertheless, as the

1 Dissertatio Epistolaris, p. 60.

2 This duty is by some expressed rata expeditio; by others, hostis propulsio, which seems to make no small difference. But, unfortunately, most of the military service which an Anglo-Saxon freeholder had to render was of the latter kind.

3 Leges Inæ, p. 23; Du Cange, voc. Heribannum. By the laws of Canute, p. 135, a fine only was imposed for this offence.

policy of different states may enforce the duties of subjects by more or less severe sanctions, I do not know that a law of forfeiture in such cases is to be considered as positively implying a feudal tenure.

But a much stronger presumption is afforded by passages that indicate a mutual relation of lord and vassal among the free proprietors. The most powerful subjects have not a natural right to the service of other freemen. But in the laws enacted during the Heptarchy we find that the sithcundman, or petty gentleman, might be dependent on a superior lord.[1] This is more distinctly expressed in some ecclesiastical canons, apparently of the tenth century, which distinguish the king's thane from the landholder, who depended upon a lord.[2] Other proofs of this might be brought from the Anglo-Saxon laws.[3] It is not, however, sufficient to prove a mutual relation between the higher and lower order of gentry, in order to establish the existence of feudal tenures. For this relation was often personal, as I have mentioned more fully in another place, and bore the name of commendation. And no nation was so rigorous as the English in compelling every man, from the king's thane to the ceorl, to place himself under a lawful superior. Hence the question is not to be hastily decided on the credit of a few passages that express this gradation of dependence; feudal vassalage, the object of our inquiry, being of a *real*, not a *personal* nature, and resulting entirely from the tenure of particular lands. But it is not unlikely that the personal relation of client, if I may use that word, might in a multitude of cases be changed into that of vassal. And certainly many of the motives which operated in France to produce a very general commutation of alodial into feudal tenure might have a similar influence in England, where the disorderly condition of society made it the interest of every man to obtain the protection of some potent lord.

The word thane corresponds in its derivation to vassal; and the latter term is used by Asserius, the contemporary biographer of Alfred, in speaking of the nobles of that prince.[4]

1 Leges Inæ, p. 10, 23.

2 Wilkins, p. 101.

3 p. 71, 144, 145.

4 Alfredus cum paucis suis nobilibus et etiam cum quibusdam militibus et Vassallis. p. 166. Nobiles Vassali Sumertunensis pagi, p. 167. Yet Hickes objects to the authenticity of a charter ascribed to Edgar, because it contains the word Vassallus, "quam à Nortmannis Angli habuerunt." Dissertatio Epistol. p. 7.

The word *vassallus* occurs not only in the suspicious charter of Cenulf, quoted

In their attendance, too, upon the royal court, and the fidelity which was expected from them, the king's thanes seem exactly to have resembled that class of followers who, under different appellations, were the guards as well as courtiers of the Frank and Lombard sovereigns. But I have remarked that the word thane is not applied to the whole body of gentry in the more ancient laws, where the word *eorl* is opposed to the *ceorl* or roturier, and that of *sithcundman*[1] to the royal thane. It would be too much to infer, from the extension of this latter word to a large class of persons, that we should interpret it with a close attention to etymology, a very uncertain guide in almost all investigations.

For the age immediately preceding the Norman invasion we cannot have recourse to a better authority than Domesday Book. That incomparable record contains the names of every tenant, and the conditions of his tenure, under the Confessor, as well as at the time of its compilation, and seems to give little countenance to the notion that a radical change in the system of our laws had been effected during the interval. In almost every page we meet with tenants either of the crown or of other lords, denominated thanes, freeholders (liberi homines), or socagers (socmanni). Some of these, it is stated, might sell their lands to whom they pleased; others were restricted from alienation. Some, as it is expressed, might go with their lands whither they would; by which I understand the right of commending themselves to any patron of their choice. These of course could not be feudal tenants in any proper notion of that term. Others could not depart from the lord whom they served; not, certainly, that they were personally bound to the soil, but that, so long as they retained it, the seigniory of the superior could not be defeated.[2] But I

in a subsequent note, but in one A.D. 952 (Codex Diplomat. ii. 303), to which I was led by Mr. Spence (Equitable Jurisdiction, p. 44), who quotes another from p. 323, which is probably a misprint; but I have found one of Edgar, A.D. 967. Cod. Diplomat. iii. 11. I think that Mr. Spence, in the ninth and tenth chapters of his learned work, has too much blended the Anglo-Saxon *man* of a lord with the continental vassal; which is a *petitio principii*. Certainly the word was of rare use in England; and the authenticity of Asserius, whom I have quoted as a contemporary biographer of Alfred, which is the common opinion, has been called in question by Mr. Wright, who refers that Life to the age of the Conquest. Archæologia, vol xxix.

1 Wilkins, p. 3, 7, 23, &c.

2 It sometimes weakens a proposition, which is capable of innumerable proofs, to take a very few at random; yet the following casual specimens will illustrate the common language of Domesday Book.

Hæc tria maneria tenuit Ulveva tempore regis Edwardi et potuit ire cum terrâ quò volebat. p. 85.

Toti emit eam T. R. E. (temp. regis Edwardi) de ecclesiâ Malmsburiensi ad ætatem trium hominum; et infra hunc

am not aware that military service is specified in any instance to be due from one of these tenants; though it is difficult to speak as to a negative proposition of this kind with any confidence.

No direct evidence appears as to the ceremony of homage or the oath of fealty before the Conquest. The feudal exaction of aid in certain prescribed cases seems to have been unknown. Still less could those of wardship and marriage prevail, which were no general parts of the great feudal system. The English lawyers, through an imperfect acquaintance with the history of feuds upon the continent, have treated these unjust innovations as if they had formed essential parts of the system, and sprung naturally from the relation between lord and vassal. And, with reference to the present question, Sir Henry Spelman has certainly laid too much stress upon them in concluding that feudal tenures did not exist among the Anglo-Saxons, because their lands were not in ward, nor their persons sold in marriage. But I cannot equally concur with this eminent person in denying the existence of reliefs during the same period. If the heriot, which is first mentioned in the time of Edgar[1] (though it may probably have been an established custom long before), were not identical with the relief, it bore at least a very strong analogy to it. A charter of Ethelred's interprets one word by the other.[2] In the laws of William, which reënact those of Canute concerning heriots, the term relief is employed as synonymous.[3] Though the heriot was in later times paid in chattels, the relief in money, it is equally true that originally the law fixed a sum of money in certain cases for the heriot, and a chattel for the relief. And the most plausible distinction alleged by Spelman, that the heriot is by law due from the personal estate, but the relief from the heir, seems hardly applicable to that remote age, when the law of succession as to real and personal estate was not different.

It has been shown in another place how the right of ter-

terminum poterat ire cum eâ ad quem vellet dominum. p. 72.

Tres Angli tenuerunt Darneford T. R. E. et non poterant ab ecclesiâ separari. Duo ex iis reddebant v. solidos, et tertius serviebat sicut Thainus. p. 68.

Has terras qui tenuerunt T. R. E. quò voluerunt ire poterunt, præter unum Seric vocatum, qui in Ragendal tenuit iii carucatas terræ; sed non poterat cum eâ alicubi recedere. p. 235.

1 Selden's Works, vol. ii. p. 1620.

2 Hist. Ramseiens. p. 430.

3 Leges Canuti, p. 144; Leges Gulielmi, p. 223.

ritorial jurisdiction was generally, and at last inseparably, connected with feudal tenure. Of this right we meet frequent instances in the laws and records of the Anglo-Saxons, though not in those of an early date. A charter of Edred grants to the monastery of Croyland, soc, sac, toll team, and infangthef: words which generally went together in the description of these privileges, and signify the right of holding a court to which all freemen of the territory should repair, of deciding pleas therein, as well as of imposing amercements according to law, of taking tolls upon the sale of goods, and of punishing capitally a thief taken in the fact within the limits of the manor.[1] Another charter from the Confessor grants to the abbey of Ramsey similar rights over all who were suitors to the sheriff's court, subject to military service, and capable of landed possessions; that is, as I conceive, all who were not in servitude.[2] By a law of Ethelred, none but the king could have jurisdiction over a royal thane.[3] And Domesday Book is full of decisive proofs that the English lords had their courts wherein they rendered justice to their suitors, like the continental nobility: privileges which are noticed with great precision in that record, as part of the statistical survey. For the right of jurisdiction at a time when punishments were almost wholly pecuniary was a matter of property, and sought from motives of rapacity as well as pride.

Whether therefore the law of feudal tenures can be said to have existed in England before the Conquest must be left to every reader's determination. Perhaps any attempt to decide it positively would end in a verbal dispute. In tracing the history of every political institution, three things are to be considered, the principle, the form, and the name. The

1 Ingulfus, p. 35. I do not pretend to assert the authenticity of these charters, which at all events are nearly as old as the Conquest. Hicks calls most of them in question. Dissert. Epist. p. 66. But some later antiquaries seem to have been more favorable. Archæologia, vol. xviii. p. 49; Nouveau Traité de Diplomatique, t. i. p. 348.

2 Hist. Ramsey, p. 454.

3 p. 118. This is the earliest allusion, if I am not mistaken, to territorial jurisdiction in the Saxon laws. Probably it was not frequent till near the end of the tenth century.

Mr. Kemble is of opinion that the words granting territorial jurisdiction do not occur in any genuine charter before the Confessor. Codex Diplom. i. 43. They are of constant occurrence in those of the first Norman reigns. But the Normans did not understand them, and the words are often misspelled. He thinks, therefore, that the rights were older than the Conquest, and accounts for the rare mention of them by the somewhat unsatisfactory supposition that they were so inherent in the possession of land as not to require particular notice. See Spence, Equit. Juris. pp. 64, 68

last will probably not be found in any genuine Anglo-Saxon record.[1] Of the form or the peculiar ceremonies and incidents of a regular fief, there is some, though not much, appearance. But those who reflect upon the dependence in which free and even noble tenants held their estates of other subjects, and upon the privileges of territorial jurisdiction, will, I think, perceive much of the intrinsic character of the feudal relation, though in a less mature and systematic shape than it assumed after the Norman conquest.[2]

1 Feodum twice occurs in the testament of Alfred; but it does not appear to be used in its proper sense, nor do I apprehend that instrument to have been originally written in Latin. It was much more consonant to Alfred's practice to employ his own language.

2 It will probably be never disputed again that lands were granted by a military tenure before the Conquest. Thus, besides the proofs in the text, in the laws of Canute (c. 78): — "And the man who shall flee from his lord or from his comrade by reason of his cowardice, be it in the shipfyrd, be it in the landfyrd, let him forfeit all he owns, and his own life; and let the lord seize his possessions, and his land which he previously gave him; and if he have bôcland, let that go into the king's hands." Ancient Laws, p. 180. And we read of lands called *hlafordsgifu*, lord's gift. Leges Ethelred I., Ancient Laws, p. 125. But these were not always feudal, or even hereditary; they were what was called on the continent præstariæ, granted for life or for a certain term; and this, as it appears to me, may have been the proper meaning of the term læn-lands.

But the general tenure of lands was still alodial. Taini lex est, says a curious document on the rights, that is obligations, of different ranks, published by Mr. Thorpe, — ut sit dignus rectitudine testamenti sui (*his boc-rightes wyrthe*, that is, perhaps, bound to the duties implied by the deed which creates his estates), — et ut ita faciat pro terrâ suâ, scilicet expeditionem *burhbotam* et *brigbotam*. Et de multis terris majus *landirectum* exsurgit ad bannum regis, &c. p. 185. Here we find the well-known *trinoda necessitas* of alodial land, with other contingent liabilities imposed by grant or usage.*

We may probably not err very much in supposing that the state of tenures in England under Canute or the Confessor was a good deal like those in France under Charlemagne or Charles the Bald,— an alodial trunk with numerous branches of feudal benefice grafted into it. But the conversion of the one mode of tenure into the other, so frequent in France, does not appear by evidence to have prevailed on this side of the channel.

I will only add here that Mr. Spence, an authority of great weight, maintains a more complete establishment of the feudal polity before the Conquest than I have

* Mr. Kemble has printed a charter of Cenulf king of Mercia to the abbey of Abingdon, in 820, without the asterisk of spuriousness (Codex Diplom. i. 269); and it is quoted by Sir F. Palgrave (vol. i. p. 159) in proof of military tenures. The expression, however, expeditionem cum duodecim *vassallis*, et totidem *scutis* exerceant, seems not a little against its authenticity. The former has observed that the testamentary documents before the Conquest, made by men who were under a superior lord, contain a clause of great interest; namely, an earnest prayer to the lord that he will permit the will to stand according to the disposition of the testator, coupled not unfrequently with a legacy to him on condition of his so doing, or to some person of influence about him for intercession on the testator's behalf. And hence he infers that, "as no man supplicates for that which he is of his own right entitled to enjoy, it appears as if these great vassals of the crown had not the power of disposing of their lands and chattels but as the king might permit; and, in the strict construction of the bond between the king and them, all that they gained in his service must be taken to fall into his hands after their death." Introduction to Cod. Dip. p. 111. This inference seems hardly borne out by the premises: a man might sometimes be reduced to supplicate a superior for that which he had a right to enjoy.

done. p. 48. This is a subject on which it is hard to lay down a definite line. But I must protest against my learned friend's derivation of the feudal system from "the aristocratic principle that prevailed in the Roman dominions while the republic endured, and which was incorporated with the principles of despotism introduced during the empire." It is because the aristocratic principle could not be incorporated with that of despotism, that I conceive the feudal system to have been incapable of development, whatever inchoate rudiments of it may be traced, until a powerful territorial aristocracy had rendered despotism no longer possible. [1847.]

PART II.

THE ANGLO-NORMAN CONSTITUTION.

The Anglo-Norman Constitution — Causes of the Conquest — Policy and Character of William — his Tyranny — Introduction of Feudal Services — Difference between the Feudal Governments of France and England — Causes of the great Power of the first Norman Kings — Arbitrary Character of their Government — Great Council — Resistance of the Barons to John — Magna Charta — its principal Articles — Reign of Henry III. — The Constitution acquires a more liberal Character — Judicial System of the Anglo-Normans — Curia Regis, Exchequer, &c. — Establishment of the Common Law — its Effect in fixing the Constitution — Remarks on the Limitation of Aristocratical Privileges in England.

Conquest of England by William.

IT is deemed by William of Malmsbury an extraordinary work of Providence that the English should have given up all for lost after the battle of Hastings, where only a small though brave army had perished.[1] It was indeed the conquest of a great kingdom by the prince of a single province, an event not easily paralleled, where the vanquished were little, if at all, less courageous than their enemies, and where no domestic factions exposed the country to an invader. Yet William was so advantageously situated, that his success seems neither unaccountable nor any matter of discredit to the English nation. The heir of the house of Cerdic had been already set aside at the election of Harold; and his youth, joined to a mediocrity of understanding which excited neither esteem nor fear,[2] gave no encouragement to the scheme of placing him upon the throne in those moments of imminent peril which followed the battle of Hastings. England was peculiarly destitute of great men. The weak reigns of Ethelred and Edward had rendered the government a mere oligarchy, and reduced the

[1] Malmsbury, p. 53. And Henry of Huntingdon says emphatically, Millesimo et sexagesimo sexto anno gratiæ, perfecit dominator Deus de gente Anglorum quod diu cogitaverat. Genti namque Normannorum asperæ et callidæ tradidit eos ad exterminandum. p. 210.

[2] Edgar, after one or two ineffectual attempts to recover the kingdom, was treated by William with a kindness which could only have proceeded from contempt of his understanding; for he was not wanting in courage. He became the intimate friend of Robert duke of Normandy, whose fortunes, as well as character, much resembled his own.

nobility into the state of retainers to a few leading houses, the representatives of which were every way unequal to meet such an enemy as the duke of Normandy. If indeed the concurrent testimony of historians does not exaggerate his forces, it may be doubted whether England possessed military resources sufficient to have resisted so numerous and well-appointed an army.[1]

This forlorn state of the country induced, if it did not justify, the measure of tendering the crown to William, which he had a pretext or title to claim, arising from the intentions, perhaps the promise, perhaps even the testament of Edward, which had more weight in those times than it deserved, and was at least better than the naked title of conquest. And this, supported by an oath exactly similar to that taken by the Anglo-Saxon kings, and by the assent of the multitude, English as well as Normans, on the day of his coronation, gave as much appearance of a regular succession as the circumstances of the times would permit. Those who yielded to such circumstances could not foresee, and were unwilling to anticipate,

[1] It has been suggested, in the second Report of a Committee of the Lords' House on the Dignity of a Peer, to which I shall have much recourse in the following pages,* that "the facility with which the Conquest had been achieved seems to have been, in part, the consequence of defects in the Saxon institutions, and of the want of a military force similar to that which had then been established in Normandy, and in some other parts of the continent of Europe. The adventurers in the army of William were of those countries in which such a military establishment had prevailed." p. 24. It cannot be said, I think, that there were any manifest defects in the Saxon institutions, so far as related to the defence of the country against invasion. It was part of the *trinoda necessitas*, to which all alodial landholders were bound. Nor is it quite accurate to speak of a military force then established in Normandy, or anywhere else. We apply these words to a permanent body always under arms. This was no attribute of feudal tenure, however the frequency of war, general or private, may have inured the tenants by military service to a more habitual discipline than the thanes of England ever knew. The adventurers in William's army were from various countries, and most of them, doubtless, had served before, but whether as hired mercenaries or no we have probably not sufficient means of determining. The practice of hiring troops does not attract the notice of historians, I believe, in so early an age. We need not, however, resort to this conjecture, since history sufficiently explains the success of William.

* This Report I generally quote from that printed in 1819; but in 1829 it was reprinted with corrections. It has been said that these were occasioned by the strictures of Mr. Allen, in the 35th volume of the Edinburgh Review, not more remarkable for their learning and acuteness than their severity on the Report. The corrections, I apprehend, are chiefly confined to errors of names, dates, and others of a similar kind, which no doubt had been copiously pointed out. But it has not appeared to me that the Lords' Committee have altered, in any considerable degree, the positions upon which the reviewer animadverts. It was hardly, indeed, to be expected that the supposed compiler of the Report, the late Lord Redesdale, having taken up his own line of opinion, would abandon it on the suggestions of one whose comments, though extremely able, and often, in the eyes of many, well founded, are certainly not couched in the most conciliatory or respectful language

the bitterness of that servitude which William and his Norman followers were to bring upon their country.

The commencement of his administration was tolerably equitable. Though many confiscations took place, in order to gratify the Norman army, yet the mass of property was left in the hands of its former possessors. Offices of high trust were bestowed upon Englishmen, even upon those whose family renown might have raised the most aspiring thoughts.[1] But partly through the insolence and injustice of William's Norman vassals, partly through the suspiciousness natural to a man conscious of having overturned the national government, his yoke soon became more heavy. The English were oppressed; they rebelled, were subdued, and oppressed again. All their risings were without concert, and desperate; they wanted men fit to head them, and fortresses to sustain their revolt.[2] After a very few years they sank in despair, and yielded for a century to the indignities of a comparatively small body of strangers without a single tumult. So possible is it for a nation to be kept in permanent servitude, even without losing its reputation for individual courage, or its desire of freedom![3]

His conduct at first moderate.

It becomes more tyrannical.

The tyranny of William displayed less of passion or inso-

[1] Ordericus Vitalis, p. 520 (in Du Chesne, Hist. Norm. Script.).

[2] Ordericus notices the want of castles in England as one reason why rebellions were easily quelled. p. 511. Failing in their attempts at a generous resistance, the English endeavored to get rid of their enemies by assassination, to which many Normans became victims. William therefore enacted that in every case of *murder*, which strictly meant the killing of any one by an unknown hand, the hundred should be liable in a fine, unless they could prove the person murdered to be an Englishman. This was tried by an inquest, upon what was called a presentment of Englishry. But from the reign of Henry II., the two nations having been very much intermingled, this inquiry, as we learn from the Dialogue de Scaccario, p. 26, ceased; and in every case of a freeman murdered by persons unknown the hundred was fined. See however Bracton, l. iii. c. 15.

[3] The brave resistance of Hereward in the fens of Lincoln and Cambridge is well told by M. Thierry, from Ingulfus and Gaimar. Conquête d'Anglet. par les Normands, vol. ii. p. 168. Turner had given it in some detail from the former. Hereward ultimately made his peace with William, and recovered his estate. According to Ingulfus, he died peaceably, and was buried at Croyland; according to Gaimar, he was assassinated in his house by some Normans. The latter account is confirmed by an early chronicler, from whom an extract is given by Mr. Wright. A more detailed memoir of Hereward (De Gestis Herewardi Saxonis) is found in the chartulary of Swaffham Abbey, now preserved in Peterborough Cathedral, and said to be as old as the twelfth century. Mr. Wright published it in 1838, from a copy in the library of Trinity College, Cambridge. If the author is to be believed, he had conversed with some companions of Hereward. But such testimony is often feigned by the mediæval semiromancers. Though the writer appears to affect a different origin, he is too full of Anglo-Saxon sympathies to be disguised; and in fact, he has evidently borrowed greatly from exaggerated legends, perhaps metrical, current among the English, as to the early life of Hereward, to which Ingulfus, or whoever personated him, cursorily alludes.

lence than of that indifference about human suffering which distinguishes a cold and far-sighted statesman. Impressed by the frequent risings of the English at the commencement of his reign, and by the recollection, as one historian observes, that the mild government of Canute had only ended in the expulsion of the Danish line,[1] he formed the scheme of riveting such fetters upon the conquered nation, that all resistance should become impracticable. Those who had obtained honorable offices were successively deprived of them; even the bishops and abbots of English birth were deposed; [2] a stretch of power very singular in that age. Morcar, one of the most illustrious English, suffered perpetual imprisonment. Waltheoff, a man of equally conspicuous birth, lost his head upon a scaffold by a very harsh if not iniquitous sentence. It was so rare in those times to inflict judicially any capital punishment upon persons of such rank, that his death seems to have produced more indignation and despair in England than any single circumstance. The name of Englishman was turned into a reproach. None of that race for a hundred years were raised to any dignity in the state or church.[3] Their language

1 Malmsbury, p. 104.

2 Hoveden, p. 453. This was done with the concurrence and sanction of the pope, Alexander II., so that the stretch of power was by Rome rather than by William. It must pass for a gross violation of ecclesiastical as well as of national rights, and Lanfranc cannot be reckoned, notwithstanding his distinguished name, as any better than an intrusive bishop. He showed his arrogant scorn of the English nation in another and rather a singular manner. They were excessively proud of their national saints, some of whom were little known, and whose barbarous names disgusted Italian ears. Angli inter quos vivimus, said the foreign priests, quosdam sibi instituerunt sanctos, quorum incerta sunt merita. This might be true enough; but the same measure should have been meted to others. Thierry, vol. ii. p. 158, edit. 1830. The Norman bishops, and the primate especially, set themselves to disparage, and in fact to dispossess, St. Aldhelm, St. Elfig, and, for aught we know, St. Swithin, St. Werburg, St. Ebb, and St. Alphage: names, it must be owned,

> "That would have made Quintilian stare and gasp."

We may judge what the eminent native of Pavia thought of such a hagiology. The English church found herself, as it were, with an attainted peerage. But the calender withstood these innovations.

Mr. Turner, in his usual spirit of panegyric, says,—"He (William) made important changes among the English clergy; he caused Stigand and others to be deposed, and he filled their places with men from Normandy and France, who were distinguished by the characters of piety, decorous morals, and a love of literature. This measure was an important addition to the civilization of the island," &c. Hist. of England, vol. i. p. 104. Admitting this to be partly true, though he would have found by no means so favorable an account of the Norman prelates in Ordericus Vitalis, if he had read a few pages beyond the passages to which he refers, is it consonant to historical justice that a violent act, like the deposition of almost all the Anglo-Saxon hierarchy, should be spoken of in a tone of praise, which the whole tenor of the paragraph conveys?

3 Becket is said to have been the firs Englishman who reached any consider able dignity. Lord Lyttelton's Hist. of Henry II. vol. ii. p. 22. And Eadmer declares that Henry I. would not place a single Englishman at the head of a monastery. Si Anglus erat, nulla virtus, ut honore aliquo dignus judicaretur, eum poterat adjuvare. p. 110.

and the characters in which it was written were rejected as barbarous; in all schools, if we trust an authority often quoted, children were taught French, and the laws were administered in no other tongue.[1] It is well known that this use of French in all legal proceedings lasted till the reign of Edward III. Several English nobles, desperate of the fortunes of their country, sought refuge in the court of Constantinople, and approved their valor in the wars of Alexius against another Norman conqueror, scarcely less celebrated than their own Robert Guiscard. Under the name of Varangians, those true and faithful supporters of the Byzantine empire preserved to its dissolution their ancient Saxon idiom.[2]

An extensive spoliation of property accompanied these revolutions. It appears by the great national survey of Domesday Book, completed near the close of the Conqueror's reign,[3] that the tenants in capite of the crown were generally

1 Ingulfus, p. 61. Tantum tunc Anglicos abominati sunt, ut quantocunque merito pollerent, de dignitatibus repellebantur; et multo minus habiles alienigenæ de quâcunque aliâ natione, quæ sub cœlo est, extitissent, gratanter assumerentur. Ipsum etiam idioma tantum abhorrebant, quod leges terræ, statutaque Anglicorum regum linguâ Gallicâ tractarentur; et pueris etiam in scholis principia literarum grammatica Gallicè, ac non Anglicè traderentur; modus etiam scribendi Anglicus omitteretur, et modus Gallicus in chartis et in libris omnibus admitteretur.

But the passage in Ingulfus, quoted in support of this position, has been placed by Sir F. Palgrave among the proofs that we have a forgery of the fourteenth century in that historian, the facts being in absolute contradiction to him. "Before the reign of Henry III. we cannot discover a deed or law drawn or composed in French. Instead of prohibiting the English language, it was employed by the Conqueror and his successors in their charters until the reign of Henry II., when it was superseded, not by the French, but by the Latin language, which had been gradually gaining or rather regaining ground." Edinb. Rev. xxxiv. 262. "The Latin language had given way in a great measure, from the time of Canute, to the vernacular Anglo-Saxon. Several charters in the latter language occur before; but for fifty years ending with the Conquest, out of 254 (published in the fourth volume of the Codex Diplomaticus), 137 are in Anglo-Saxon, and only 117 in Latin." Kemble's Preface, p. 6.

If I have rightly translated, in the text of Ingulfus, leges *tractarentur* by *administered*, the falsehood is manifest; since the laws were administered in the county and hundred courts, and certainly not there in French. I really do not perceive how this passage could have been written by Ingulfus, who must have known the truth; at all events, his testimony must be worth little on any subject, if he could so palpably misrepresent a matter of public notoriety. The supposition of entire forgery is one which we should not admit without full proof; but, in this instance, there are perhaps fewer difficulties on this side than on that of authenticity.

2 Gibbon, vol. x. p. 223. No writer, except perhaps the Saxon Chronicler, is so full of William's tyranny as Ordericus Vitalis. See particularly p. 507, 512, 514, 521, 523, in Du Chesne, Hist. Norm. Script. Ordericus was an Englishman, but passed at ten years old, A.D. 1084, into Normandy, where he became professed in the monastery of Eu. Ibid. p. 924.

3 The regularity of the course adopted when this record was compiled is very remarkable; and affords a satisfactory proof that the business of the government was well conducted, and with much less rudeness than is usually supposed. The commissioners were furnished with interrogatories, upon which they examined the jurors of the shire and hundred, and also such other witnesses as they thought expedient.

Hic subscribitur inquisicio terrarum quomodo Barones Reges inquirunt, videlicet, per sacramentum vicecomitis Sciræ

foreigners. Undoubtedly there were a few left in almost every county who still enjoyed the estates which they held under Edward the Confessor, free from any superiority but that of the crown, and were denominated, as in former times, the king's thanes.[1] Cospatric, son perhaps of one of that name who had possessed the earldom of Northumberland, held forty-one manors in Yorkshire, though many of them are stated in Domesday to be waste. But inferior freeholders were much less disturbed in their estates than the higher class. Brady maintains that the English had suffered universally a deprivation of their lands. But the valuable labors of Sir Henry Ellis, in presenting us with a complete analysis of Domesday Book, afford an opportunity, by his list of mesne tenants at the time of the survey, to form some approximation to the relative numbers of English and foreigners holding manors under the immediate vassals of the crown. The baptismal names (there are rarely any others) are not always conclusive; but, on the whole, we learn by a little practice to distinguish the Norman from the Anglo-Saxon. It would be manifest, by running the eye over some pages of this list, how considerably mistaken is the supposition that few of English birth held entire manors. Though I will not now affirm or deny that they were a majority, they form a large proportion of nearly 8000 *mesne* tenants,[2] who are summed up by the diligence of Sir Henry Ellis. And we may presume that they were in a very much greater proportion among the "liberi homines," who held lands, subject only to free services, seldom or never very burdensome. It may be added that

et omnium Baronum et eorum Francigenarum et tocius centuriatus — presbiteri præpositi VI villani uniuscujusque villæ [sic].— Deinde quomodo vocatur mansio, quis tenuit eam tempore Regis *Edwardi*, quis modo tenet, quot hidæ, quot carrucatæ in domino quot homines, quot villani, quot cotarii, quot servi, quot liberi homines, quot sochemanni, quantum silvæ, quantum prati, quot pascuorum, quot molidenæ, quot piscinæ, quantum est additum vel ablatum, quantum valebat totum simul; et quantum modo; quantum ibi quisque liber homo vel sochemanus habuit vel habet. Hoc totum tripliciter, scilicet tempore Regis *Ædwardi;* et quando Rex *Willielmus* dedit; et quomodo sit modo, et si plus potest haberi quam habeatur. Isti homines juraverunt (then follow the names). Inquisitio Eliensis, p. 497. Palgrave, ii. 444.

[1] Brady, whose unfairness always keeps pace with his ability, pretends that all these were menial officers of the king's household. But notwithstanding the difficulty of disproving these gratuitous suppositions, it is pretty certain that many of the English proprietors in Domesday could not have been of this description. See p. 99, 153, 218, 219, and other places. The question, however, was not worth a battle, though it makes a figure in the controversy of Normans and Anti-Normans, between Dugdale and Brady on the one side, and Tyrrell, Petyt, and Attwood on the other.

[2] Ellis's Introduction to Domesday, vol. ii. p. 811. "The tenants in capite, including ecclesiastical corporations, amounted scarcely to 1400; the under-tenants were 7871."

many Normans, as we learn from history, married English heiresses, rendered so frequently, no doubt, by the violent deaths of their fathers and brothers, but still transmitting ancient rights, as well as native blood, to their posterity.

This might induce us to suspect that, great as the spoliation must appear in modern times, and almost completely as the nation was excluded from civil power in the commonwealth, there is some exaggeration in the language of those writers who represent them as universally reduced to a state of penury and servitude. And this suspicion may be in some degree just. Yet these writers, and especially the most English in feeling of them all, M. Thierry, are warranted by the language of contemporary authorities. An important passage in the Dialogus de Scaccario, written towards the end of Henry III.'s reign, tends greatly to diminish the favorable impression which the Saxon names of so many mesne tenants in Domesday Book would create. If we may trust Gervase of Tilbury, author of this little treatise, the estates of those who had borne arms against William were alone confiscated; though the others were subjected to the feudal superiority of a Norman lord. But when these lords abused their power to dispossess the native tenants, a clamor was raised by the English, and complaint made to the king; by whom it was ordered (if we rightly understand a passage not devoid of obscurity) that the tenant might make a bargain with his lord, so as to secure himself in possession; but that none of the English should have any right of succession, a fresh agreement with the lord being required on every change of tenancy. The Latin words will be found below.[1] This, as here expressed,

[1] Post regni conquisitionem, post justam rebellium subversionem, cum rex ipse regisque proceres loca nova perlustrarent, facta est inquisitio diligens, qui fuerunt qui contra regem in bello dimicantes per fugam se salvaverant. His omnibus et item hæredibus eorum qui in bello occubuerant, spes omnis terrarum et fundorum atque redituum quos ante possederant, præclusa est; magnum namque reputabant frui vitæ beneficio sub inimicis. Verum qui vocati ad bellum necdum convenerant, vel familiaribus vel quibuslibet necessariis occupati negotiis non interfuerant, cum tractu temporis devotis obsequiis gratiam dominorum possedissent sine spe successionis, filii tantum pro voluptate [sic. voluntate?] tamen dominorum possidere cœperunt succedente vero tempore cum dominis suis odiosi passim a possessionibus pellerentur, nec esset qui ablatis restituerit, communis indigenarum ad regem pervenit querimonia, quasi sic omnibus exosi et rebus spoliatis ad alienigenas transire cogerentur. Communicato tantum super his consilio, decretum est, ut quod a dominis suis exigentibus meritis interveniente pactione legitima poterant obtinere, illis inviolabilis jure concederentur; cæterum autem nomine successionis a temporibus subactæ gentis nihil sibi vindicarent. . . . Sic igitur quisquis de gente subacta fundos vel aliquid hujusmodi possidet, non quod ratione successionis deberi sibi videbatur, adeptus est; sed quod solummodo meritis suis exigentibus, vel aliqua pactione interveniente, obtinuit. Dial. de Scaccario, c. 10.

suggests something like an uncertain relief at the lord's will, and paints the condition of the English tenant as wretchedly dependent. But an instrument published by Spelman, and which will be found in Wilkins, Leg. Ang. Sax. p. 287, gives a more favorable view, and asserts that William permitted those who had taken no part against him to retain their lands; though it appears by the very same record that the Normans did not much regard the royal precept.

But whatever may have been the legal condition of the English mesne tenant, by knight-service or socage, (for the case of villeins is of course not here considered,) during the first two Norman reigns, it seems evident that he was protected by the charter of Henry I. in the hereditary possession of his lands, subject only to a "lawful and just relief towards his lord." For this charter is addressed to all the liege men of the crown, "French and English;" and purports to abolish all the evil customs by which the kingdom had been oppressed, extending to the tenants of the barons as well as those of the crown. We cannot reasonably construe the language in the Dialogue of the Exchequer, as if in that late age the English tenant had no estate of fee-simple. If this had been the case, there could not have been the difficulty, which he mentions in another place, of distinguishing among freemen or freeholders (liberi homines) the Norman blood from the Englishman, which frequent intermarriage had produced. He must, we are led to think, either have copied some other writer, or made a careless and faulty statement of his own. But, at the present, we are only considering the state of the English in the reign of the Conqueror. And here we have, on the one hand, a manifest proof from the Domesday record that they retained the usufruct, in a very great measure, of the land; and on the other, the strong testimony of contemporary historians to the spoliation and oppression which they endured. It seems on the whole most probable that, notwithstanding innumerable acts of tyranny, and a general exposure to contumely and insolence, they did in fact possess what they are recorded to have possessed by the Norman Commissioners of 1085.

The vast extent of the Norman estates in capite is apt to deceive us. In reading of a baron who held forty or fifty or one hundred manors, we are prone to fancy his wealth something like what a similar estate would produce at this day.

But if we look at the next words, we shall continually find that some one else held of him; and this was a holding by knight's service, subject to feudal incidents no doubt, but not leaving the seigniory very lucrative, or giving any right of possessory ownership over the land. The real possessions of the tenant of a manor, whether holding in chief or not, consisted in the demesne lands, the produce of which he obtained without cost by the labor of the villeins, and in whatever other payments they might be bound to make in money or kind. It will be remembered, what has been more than once inculcated, that at this time the villani and bordarii, that is, ceorls, were not like the villeins of Bracton and Littleton, destitute of rights in their property; their condition was tending to the lower stage, and with a Norman lord they were in much danger of oppression; but they were "law-worthy," they had a civil *status* (to pass from one technical style to another), for a century after the Conquest.

Yet I would not extenuate the calamities of this great revolution, true though it be that much good was brought out of them, and that we owe no trifling part of what inspires self-esteem to the Norman element of our population and our polity. England passed under the yoke; she endured the arrogance of foreign conquerors; her children, even though their loss in revenue may have been exaggerated, and still it was enormous, became a lower race, not called to the councils of their sovereign, not sharing his trust or his bounty. They were in a far different condition from the provincial Romans after the conquest of Gaul, even if, which is hardly possible to determine, their actual deprivation of lands should have been less extensive. For not only they did not for several reigns occupy the honorable stations which sometimes fell to the lot of the Roman subject of Clovis or Alaric, but they had a great deal more freedom and importance to lose. Nor had they a protecting church to mitigate barbarous superiority; their bishops were degraded and in exile; the footstep of the invader was at their altars; their monasteries were plundered, and the native monks insulted. Rome herself looked with little favor on a church which had preserved some measure of independence. Strange contrast to the triumphant episcopate of the Merovingian kings![1]

[1] The oppression of the English during the first reigns after the Conquest is fully described by the Norman historians themselves, as well as by the Saxon

Devastation of Yorkshire and New Forest.

Besides the severities exercised upon the English after every insurrection, two instances of William's unsparing cruelty are well known, the devastation of Yorkshire and of the New Forest. In the former, which had the tyrant's plea, necessity, for its pretext, an invasion being threatened from Denmark, the whole country between the Tyne and the Humber was laid so desolate, that for nine years afterwards there was not an inhabited village, and hardly an inhabitant, left; the wasting of this district having been followed by a famine, which swept away the whole population.[1] That of the New Forest though undoubtedly less calamitous in its effects, seems even more monstrous from the frivolousness of the cause.[2] He afforested several other tracts. And these favorite demesnes of the Norman kings were protected by a system of iniquitous and cruel regulations, called the Forest Laws, which it became afterwards a great object with the assertors of liberty to correct. The penalty for killing a stag or a boar was loss of eyes; for William loved the great game, says the Saxon Chronicle, as if he had been their father.[3]

A more general proof of the ruinous oppression of William the Conqueror may be deduced from the comparative condi-

Chronicle. Their testimonies are well collected by M. Thierry, in the second volume of his valuable history.

[1] Malmsbury, p. 103; Hoveden, p. 451; Orderic. Vitalis, p. 514. The desolation of Yorkshire continued in Malmsbury's time, sixty or seventy years afterwards; nudum omnium solum usque ad hoc etiam tempus.

[2] Malmsbury, p. 111.

[3] Chron. Saxon. p. 191. M. Thierry conjectures that these severe regulations had a deeper motive than the mere preservation of game, and were intended to prevent the English from assembling in arms on pretence of the chase. Vol. ii. p. 257. But perhaps this is not necessary. We know that a disproportionate severity has often guarded the beasts and birds of chase from depredation.

Allen admits (Edinburgh Rev. xxvi. 355) that the forest-laws seem to have been enacted by the king's sole authority; or, as we may rather say, that they were considered as a part of his prerogative. The royal forests were protected by extraordinary penalties even before the Conquest. "The royal forests were part of the demesne of the crown. They were not included in the territorial divisions of the kingdom, civil or ecclesiastical, nor governed by the ordinary courts of law, but were set apart for the recreation and diversion of the king, as waste lands, which he might use and dispose of at pleasure." "Forestæ," says Sir Henry Spelman, "nec villas propriè accepere, nec parochias, nec de corpore alicujus comitatûs vel episcopatûs habitæ sunt, sed extraneum quiddam et feris datum, ferino jure, non civili, non municipali fruebantur; regem in omnibus agnoscentes dominum unicum et ex arbitrio disponentem." Mr. Allen quotes afterwards a passage from the 'Dialogus de Scaccario,' which indicates the peculiarity of the forest-laws. "Forestarum ratio, pœna quoque vel absolutio delinquentium in eas, sive pecuniaria fuerit sive corporalis, seorsim ab aliis regni judiciis secernitur, et solius regis arbitrio, vel cujuslibet familiaris ad hoc specialiter deputati subjicitur. Legibus quidem propriis subsistit; quas non communi regni jure, sed voluntaria principum institutione subnixas dicunt." The forests were, to use a word in rather an opposite sense to the usual, an oasis of despotism in the midst of the old common law

Proofs of depopulation from Domesday Book.

tion of the English towns in the reign of Edward the Confessor, and at the compilation of Domesday. At the former epoch there were in York 1607 inhabited houses, at the latter 967; at the former there were in Oxford 721, at the latter 243; of 172 houses in Dorchester, 100 were destroyed; of 243 in Derby, 103; of 487 in Chester, 205. Some other towns had suffered less, but scarcely any one fails to exhibit marks of a decayed population. As to the relative numbers of the peasantry and value of lands at these two periods, it would not be easy to assert anything without a laborious examination of Domesday Book.[1]

Domains of the crown.

The demesne lands of the crown, extensive and scattered over every county, were abundantly sufficient to support its dignity and magnificence;[2] and William, far from wasting this revenue by prodigal grants, took care to let them at the highest rate to farm, little caring how much the cultivators were racked by his tenants.[3] Yet his exactions, both feudal and in the way of tallage from his burgesses and the tenants of his vassals, were almost as violent as his confiscations. No source of income was neglected by him, or indeed by his successors, however trifling, unjust, or unreasonable.

Riches of the Conqueror.

His revenues, if we could trust Ordericus Vitalis, amounted to 1060*l.* a day. This, in mere weight of silver, would be equal to nearly 1,200,000*l.* a year at present. But the arithmetical statements of these writers are not implicitly to be relied upon. He left at his death a treasure of 60,000*l*, which, in conformity to his dying request, his successor distributed among the church and poor of the kingdom, as a feeble expiation of the crimes by which it had been accumulated;[4] an act of disinterestedness which seems to prove that Rufus, amidst all his vices, was not destitute of better feelings than historians have ascribed to him. It might appear that William had little use for his extorted wealth. By the feudal constitution, as established during his reign, he commanded the service of a vast army

[1] The population recorded in Domesday is about 283,000; which, in round numbers, allowing for women and children, may be called about a million. Ellis's Introduction to Domesday, vol. ii. p. 511.

[2] They consisted of 1422 manors. Lyttelton's Henry II. vol. ii. p. 288.

[3] Chron. Saxon. p. 188.

[4] Huntingdon, p. 371. Ordericus Vitalis puts a long penitential speech into William's mouth on his death-bed. p. 66. Though this may be his invention, yet facts seem to show the compunction of the tyrant's conscience.

at its own expense, either for domestic or continental warfare. But this was not sufficient for his purpose; like other tyrants, he put greater trust in mercenary obedience. Some of his predecessors had kept bodies of Danish troops in pay; partly to be secure against their hostility, partly from the convenience of a regular army, and the love which princes bear to it. But William carried this to a much greater length. He had always stipendiary soldiers at his command. Indeed his army at the Conquest could not have been swollen to such numbers by any other means. They were drawn, by the allurement of high pay, not from France and Brittany alone, but Flanders, Germany, and even Spain. When Canute of Denmark threatened an invasion in 1085, William, too conscious of his own tyranny to use the arms of his English subjects, collected a mercenary force so vast, that men wondered, says the Saxon Chronicler, how the country could maintain it. This he quartered upon the people, according to the proportion of their estates.[1]

His mercenary troops.

Whatever may be thought of the Anglo-Saxon tenures, it is certain that those of the feudal system were thoroughly established in England under the Conqueror. It has been observed, in another part of this work, that the rights, or feudal incidents, of wardship and marriage were more common in England and Normandy than in the rest of France. They certainly did not exist in the former before the Conquest; but whether they were ancient customs of the latter cannot be ascertained, unless we had more incontestable records of its early jurisprudence. For the Great Customary of Normandy is a compilation as late as the reign of Richard Cœur-de-Lion, when the laws of England might have passed into a country so long and intimately connected with it. But there appears reason to think that the seizure of the lands in wardship, the selling of the heiress in marriage, were originally deemed rather acts of violence than conformable to law. For Henry I.'s charter expressly promises that the mother, or next of kin, shall have the custody of the lands as well as person of the heir.[2] And as the charter of Henry II. refers to and confirms that of his

Feudal system established.

[1] Chron. Saxon. p. 185; Ingulfus, p. 79.

[2] Terræ et liberorum custos erit sive uxor, sive alius propinquorum, qui justus esse debebit; et præcipio ut barones mei similiter se contineant ergà filios vel filias vel uxores hominum meorum. Leges Anglo-Saxonicæ, p. 234.

grandfather, it seems to follow that what is called guardianship in chivalry had not yet been established. At least it is not till the assize of Clarendon, confirmed at Northampton in 1176,[1] that the custody of the heir is clearly reserved to the lord. With respect to the right of consenting to the marriage of a female vassal, it seems to have been, as I have elsewhere observed, pretty general in feudal tenures. But the sale of her person in marriage, or the exaction of a sum of money in lieu of this scandalous tyranny, was only the law of England, and was not perhaps fully authorized as such till the statute of Merton in 1236.

One innovation made by William upon the feudal law is very deserving of attention. By the leading principle of feuds, an oath of fealty was due from the vassal to the lord of whom he immediately held his land, and to no other. The king of France, long after this period, had no feudal and scarcely any royal authority over the tenants of his own vassals. But William received at Salisbury, in 1085, the fealty of all landholders in England, both those who held in chief, and their tenants;[2] thus breaking in upon the feudal compact in its most essential attribute, the exclusive dependence of a vassal upon his lord. And this may be reckoned among the several causes which prevented the continental notions of independence upon the crown from ever taking root among the English aristocracy.

Preservation of public peace.

The best measure of William was the establishment of public peace. He permitted no rapine but his own. The feuds of private revenge, the lawlessness of robbery, were repressed. A girl laden with gold, if we believe some ancient writers, might have passed safely through the kingdom.[3] But this was the tranquillity of an imperious and vigilant despotism, the degree of which may be measured by these effects, in which no improvement of civilization had any share. There is assuredly nothing to wonder

1 Leges Anglo-Saxonicæ, p. 330.

2 Chron. Saxon. p. 187. The oath of allegiance or fealty, for they were in spirit the same, had been due to the king before the Conquest; we find it among the laws of Edmund. Allen's Inquiry, p. 68. It was not, therefore, likely that William would surrender such a tie upon his subjects. But it had also been usual in France under Charlemagne, and perhaps later.

3 Chron. Saxon. p. 190; M. Paris, p. 10. I will not omit one other circumstance, apparently praiseworthy, which Odericus mentions of William, that he tried to learn English, in order to render justice by understanding every man's complaint, but failed on account of his advanced age. p. 520. This was in the early part of his reign, before the reluctance of the English to submit had exasperated his disposition.

at in the detestation with which the English long regarded the memory of this tyrant.[1] Some advantages undoubtedly, in the course of human affairs, eventually sprang from the Norman conquest. The invaders, though without perhaps any intrinsic superiority in social virtues over the native English, degraded and barbarous as these are represented to us, had at least that exterior polish of courteous and chivalric manners, and that taste for refinement and magnificence, which serve to elevate a people from mere savage rudeness. Their buildings, sacred as well as domestic, became more substantial and elegant. The learning of the clergy, the only class to whom that word could at all be applicable, became infinitely more respectable in a short time after the Conquest. And though this may by some be ascribed to the general improvements of Europe in that point during the twelfth century, yet I think it was partly owing to the more free intercourse with France, and the closer dependence upon Rome, which that revolution produced. This circumstance was, however, of no great moment to the English of those times, whose happiness could hardly be effected by the theological reputation of Lanfranc and Anselm. Perhaps the chief benefit which the natives of that generation derived from the government of William and his successors, next to that of a more vigilant police, was the security they found from invasion on the side of Denmark and Norway. The high reputation of the Conqueror and his sons, with the regular organization of a feudal militia, deterred those predatory armies which had brought such repeated calamity on England in former times.

Difference between the feudal policy in England and France.

The system of feudal policy, though derived to England from a French source, bore a very different appearance in the two countries. France, for about two centuries after the house of Capet had usurped the throne of Charlemagne's posterity, could hardly be deemed a regular confederacy, much less an entire monarchy. But in England a government, feudal indeed in its form, but arbitrary in its exercise, not only maintained subordination, but almost extinguished liberty. Several causes seem to have conspired towards this radical difference. In the first place, a kingdom comparatively small is much more easily kept under control than one of vast extent. And

[1] W. Malmsb. Præf. ad l. iii.

the fiefs of Anglo-Norman barons after the Conquest were far less considerable, even relatively to the size of the two countries, than those of France. The earl of Chester held, indeed, almost all that county;[1] the earl of Shrewsbury, nearly the whole of Salop. But these domains bore no comparison with the dukedom of Guienne, or the county of Toulouse. In general, the lordships of William's barons, whether this were owing to policy or accident, were exceedingly dispersed. Robert earl of Moreton, for example, the most richly endowed of his followers, enjoyed 248 manors in Cornwall, 54 in Sussex, 196 in Yorkshire, 99 in Northamptonshire, besides many in other counties.[2] Estates so disjoined, however immense in their aggregate, were ill calculated for supporting a rebellion. It is observed by Madox that the knight's fees of almost every barony were scattered over various counties.

In the next place, these baronial fiefs were held under an actual derivation from the crown. The great vassals of France had usurped their dominions before the accession of Hugh Capet, and barely submitted to his nominal sovereignty. They never intended to yield the feudal tributes of relief and aid, nor did some of them even acknowledge the supremacy of his royal jurisdiction. But the Conqueror and his successors imposed what conditions they would upon a set of barons who owed all to their grants; and as mankind's notions of right are generally founded upon prescription, these peers grew accustomed to endure many burdens, reluctantly indeed, but without that feeling of injury which would have resisted an attempt to impose them upon the vassals of the French crown. For the same reasons the barons of England were regularly summoned to the great council, and by their attendance in it, and concurrence in the measures which were there resolved upon, a compactness and unity of interest was given to the monarchy which was entirely wanting in that of France.

We may add to the circumstances that rendered the crown powerful during the first century after the Conquest, an

[1] This was, upon the whole, more like a great French fief than any English earldom. Hugh de Abrincis, nephew of William I., had barons of his own, one of whom held forty-six and another thirty manors. Chester was first called a county-palatine under Henry II.; but it previously possessed all regalian rights of jurisdiction. After the forfeitures of the house of Montgomery, it acquired all the country between the Mersey and Ribble. Several eminent men inherited the earldom; but upon the death of the most distinguished, Ranulf, in 1232, it fell into a female line, and soon escheated to the crown. Dugdale's Baronage, p. 45 Lyttelton's Henry II., vol. ii. p. 218.

[2] Dugdale's Baronage, p. 25.

Hatred of English to Normans.

extreme antipathy of the native English towards their invaders. Both William Rufus and Henry I. made use of the former to strengthen themselves against the attempts of their brother Robert; though they forgot their promises to the English after attaining their object.[1] A fact mentioned by Ordericus Vitalis illustrates the advantage which the government found in this national animosity. During the siege of Bridgenorth, a town belonging to Robert de Belesme, one of the most turbulent and powerful of the Norman barons, by Henry I. in 1102, the rest of the nobility deliberated together, and came to the conclusion that if the king could expel so distinguished a subject, he would be able to treat them all as his servants. They endeavored therefore to bring about a treaty; but the English part of Henry's army, hating Robert de Belesme as a Norman, urged the king to proceed with the siege; which he did, and took the castle.[2]

Tyranny of the Norman government.

Unrestrained, therefore, comparatively speaking, by the aristocratic principles which influenced other feudal countries, the administration acquired a tone of rigor and arbitrariness under William the Conqueror, which, though sometimes perhaps a little mitigated, did not cease during a century and a half. For the first three reigns we must have recourse to historians; whose language, though vague, and perhaps exaggerated, is too uniform and impressive to leave a doubt of the tyrannical character of the government. The intolerable exactions of tribute, the rapine of purveyance, the iniquity of royal courts, are continually in their mouths. "God sees the wretched people," says the Saxon Chronicler, "most unjustly oppressed; first they are despoiled of their possessions, then butchered. This was a grievous year (1124). Whoever had any property lost it by heavy taxes and unjust decrees."[3] The same ancient chronicle, which appears to have been continued from time to time in the abbey of Peterborough, frequently utters similar notes of lamentation.

From the reign of Stephen, the miseries of which are not to my immediate purpose, so far as they proceeded from

[1] W. Malmsbury, p. 120 et 156. R. Hoveden, p. 461. Chron. Saxon. p. 194.

[2] Du Chesne, Script. Norman. p. 807.

[3] Chron. Saxon. p. 228. Non facile potest narrari miseria, says Roger de Hoveden, quam sustinuit illo tempore [circ. ann. 1103] terra Anglorum propter regias exactiones. p. 470.

Its exactions.

anarchy and intestine war,[1] we are able to trace the character of government by existing records.[2] These, digested by the industrious Madox into his History of the Exchequer, gives us far more insight into the spirit of the constitution, if we may use such a word, than all our monkish chronicles. It was not a sanguinary despotism. Henry II. was a prince of remarkable clemency; and none of the Conqueror's successors were as grossly tyrannical as himself. But the system of rapacious extortion from their subjects prevailed to a degree which we should rather expect to find among eastern slaves than that high-spirited race of Normandy whose renown then filled Europe and Asia. The right of wardship was abused by selling the heir and his land to the highest bidder. That of marriage was carried to a still grosser excess. The kings of France indeed claimed the prerogative of forbidding the marriage of their vassals' daughters to such persons as they thought unfriendly or dangerous to themselves; but I am not aware that they ever compelled them to marry, much less that they turned this attribute of sovereignty into a means of revenue. But in England, women and even men, simply as tenants in chief, and not as wards, fined to the crown for leave to marry whom they would, or not to be compelled to marry any other.[3] Towns not only fined for original grants of franchises, but for repeated confirmations. The Jews paid exorbitant sums for every common right of mankind, for protection, for justice. In return they were sustained against their Christian debtors in demands of usury, which superstition and tyranny rendered enormous.[4] Men fined for the king's good-will; or that he would remit his anger; or to have his mediation with their adversaries. Many fines seem as it were imposed in sport, if we look to the cause; though

[1] The following simple picture of that reign from the Saxon Chronicle may be worth inserting. "The nobles and bishops built castles, and filled them with devilish and wicked men, and oppressed the people, cruelly torturing men for their money. They imposed taxes upon towns, and, when they had exhausted them of everything, set them on fire. You might travel a day, and not find one man living in a town, nor any land in cultivation. Never did the country suffer greater evils. If two or three men were seen riding up to a town, all its inhabitants left it, taking them for plunderers. And this lasted, growing worse and worse, throughout Stephen's reign. Men said openly that Christ and his saints were asleep." p. 239.

[2] The earliest record in the Pipe-office is that which Madox, in conformity to the usage of others, cites by the name of Magnum Rotulum quinto Stephani. But in a particular dissertation, subjoined to his History of the Exchequer, he inclines, though not decisively, to refer this record to the reign of Henry I.

[3] Madox, c. 10.

[4] Id. c. 7.

their extent, and the solemnity with which they were recorded, prove the humor to have been differently relished by the two parties. Thus the bishop of Winchester paid a tun of good wine for not reminding the king (John) to give a girdle to the countess of Albemarle; and Robert de Vaux five best palfreys, that the same king might hold his peace about Henry Pinel's wife. Another paid four marks for leave to eat (pro licentiâ comedendi). But of all the abuses which deformed the Anglo-Norman government, none was so flagitious as the sale of judicial redress. The king, we are often told, is the fountain of justice; but in those ages it was one which gold alone could unseal. Men fined to have right done them; to sue in a certain court; to implead a certain person; to have restitution of land which they had recovered at law.[1] From the sale of that justice which every citizen has a right to demand, it was an easy transition to withhold or deny it. Fines were received for the king's help against the adverse suitor; that is, for perversion of justice, or for delay. Sometimes they were paid by opposite parties, and, of course, for opposite ends. These were called counterfines; but the money was sometimes, or as Lord Lyttelton thinks invariably, returned to the unsuccessful suitor.[2]

General taxes.

Among a people imperfectly civilized the most outrageous injustice towards individuals may pass without the slightest notice, while in matters affecting the community the powers of government are exceedingly controlled. It becomes therefore an important question what prerogative these Norman king's were used to exercise in raising money and in general legislation. By the prevailing feudal customs the lord was entitled to demand a pecuniary aid of his vassals in certain cases. These were, in England, to make his eldest son a knight, to marry his eldest daughter, and to ransom himself from captivity. Accordingly, when such circumstances occurred, aids were levied by the crown upon its tenants, at the rate of a mark or a pound for every knight's fee.[3] These aids, being strictly due in the prescribed cases,

[1] Madox, c. 12 and 13.

[2] The most opposite instances of these exactions are well selected from Madox by Hume, Appendix II.; upon which account I have gone less into detail than would otherwise have been necessary.

[3] The *reasonable aid* was fixed by the statute of Westminster I., 3 Edw. I., c. 36, at twenty shillings for every knight's fee, and as much for every 20*l*. value of land held by socage. The aid pour faire fitz chevalier might be raised when he entered into his fifteenth year; pour fille marier, when she reached the age of seven.

were taken without requiring the consent of parliament. Escuage, which was a commutation for the personal service of military tenants in war, having rather the appearance of an indulgence than an imposition, might reasonably be levied by the king.[1] It was not till the charter of John that escuage became a parliamentary assessment; the custom of commuting service having then grown general, and the rate of commutation being variable.

None but military tenants could be liable for escuage; but the inferior subjects of the crown were oppressed by tallages. The demesne lands of the king and all royal towns were liable to tallage; an imposition far more rigorous and irregular than those which fell upon the gentry. Tallages were continually raised upon different towns during all the Norman reigns without the consent of parliament, which neither represented them nor cared for their interests. The itinerant justices in their circuit usually set this tax. Sometimes the tallage was assessed in gross upon a town, and collected by the burgesses; sometimes individually at the judgment of the justices. There was an appeal from an excessive assessment to the barons of the exchequer. Inferior lords might tallage their own tenants and demesne towns, though not, it seems, without the king's permission.[3] Customs upon the import and export of merchandise, of which the prisage of wine, that is, a right of taking two casks out of each vessel, seems the most material, were immemorially exacted by the crown. There is no appearance that these originated with parliament.[4] Another tax, extending to all the lands of the kingdom, was Danegeld, the ship-money of those times. This name had been originally given to the tax imposed under Ethelred II., in order to raise a tribute exacted by the Danes. It was afterwards applied to a permanent contribution for the public defence against the same enemies. But after the Conquest this tax is said to have been only

1 Fit interdum, ut imminente vel insurgente in regnum hostium machinatione, decernat rex de singulis feodis militum summam aliquam solvi, marcam scilicet, vel libram unam; unde militibus stipendia vel donativa succedant. Mavult enim princeps stipendiarios quàm domesticos bellicis exponere casibus. Hæc itaque summa, quia nomine scutorum solvitur, scutagium nominatur. Dialogus de Scaccario, ad finem. Madox, Hist. Exchequer, p. 25 (edit. in folio).

2 The tenant in capite was entitled to be reimbursed what would have been his escuage by his vassals even if he performed personal service. Madox, c. 16.

3 For the important subject of tallages, see Madox, c. 17.

4 Madox, c. 18. Hale's Treatise on the Customs in Hargrave's Tracts, vol. i. p. 116.

occasionally required; and the latest instance on record of its payment is in the 20th of Henry II. Its imposition appears to have been at the king's discretion.[1]

Right of legislation.

The right of general legislation was undoubtedly placed in the king, conjointly with his great council,[2] or, if the expression be thought more proper, with their advice. So little opposition was found in these assemblies by the early Norman kings, that they gratified their own love of pomp, as well as the pride of their barons, by consulting them in every important business. But the limits o legislative power were extremely indefinite. New laws, lik new taxes, affecting the community, required the sanction of that assembly which was supposed to represent it; but there was no security for individuals against acts of prerogative, which we should justly consider as most tyrannical. Henry II., the best of these monarchs, banished from England the relations and friends of Becket, to the number of four hundred. At another time he sent over from Normandy an injunction, that all the kindred of those who obeyed a papal interdict should be banished, and their estates confiscated.[3]

Laws and charters of Norman kings.

The statutes of those reigns do not exhibit to us many provisions calculated to maintain public liberty on a broad and general foundation. And although the laws then enacted have not all been preserved, yet it is unlikely that any of an extensively remedial nature should have left no trace of their existence. We find, however, what has sometimes been called the Magna Charta of William the Conqueror, published by Wilkins from a document of considerable authority.[4] We will, enjoin, and grant, says the king, that all freemen of our kingdom shall enjoy their lands in peace, free from all tallage, and from every unjust exaction, so that nothing but their service lawfully due to us shall be demanded at their hands.[5] The laws

[1] Henr. Huntingdon, l. v. p. 205. Dialogus de Scaccario, c. 11. Madox, c. 17. Lyttelton's Henry II. vol. ii. p. 170.

[2] Glanvil, Prologus ad Tractatum de Consuetud.

[3] Hoveden, p. 496. Lyttelton, vol. ii. p. 530. The latter says that this edict must have been framed by the king with the advice and assent of his council. But if he means his great council, I cannot suppose that all the barons and tenants in capite could have been duly summoned to a council held beyond seas. Some English barons might doubtless have been with the king, as at Verneuil in 1176, where a mixed assembly of English and French enacted laws for both countries. Benedict. Abbas apud Hume. So at Northampton, in 1165 several Norman barons voted; nor is any notice taken of this as irregular. Fitz Stephen, ibid. So unfixed, or rather unformed, were all constitutional principles. [NOTE X.]

[4] [NOTE XI.]

[5] Volumus etiam, ac firmiter præcipi-

of the Conqueror, found in Hoveden, are wholly different from those in Ingulfus, and are suspected not to have escaped considerable interpolation.[1] It is remarkable that no reference is made to this concession of William the Conqueror in any subsequent charter. A charter of Henry I., the authenticity of which is undisputed, though it contains nothing specially expressed but a remission of unreasonable reliefs, wardships, and other feudal burdens,[2] proceeds to declare that he gives his subjects the laws of Edward the Confessor, with the emendations made by his father with consent of his barons.[3] The charter of Stephen not only confirms that of his predecessor, but adds, in fuller terms than Henry had used, an express concession of the laws and customs of Edward.[4] Henry II. is silent about these, although he repeats the confirmation of his grandfather's charter.[5] The people however had begun to look back to a more ancient standard of law. The Norman conquest, and all that ensued upon it, had endeared the memory of their Saxon government. Its disorders were forgotten, or, rather, were less odious to a rude nation, than the coercive justice by which they were afterwards restrained.[6] Hence it became the favorite cry to

mus et concedimus, ut omnes liberi homines totius monarchiæ prædicti regni nostri habeant et teneant terras suas et possessiones suas benè, et in pace, liberè ab omni exactione injustâ, et ab omni tallagio, ita quod nihil ab iis exigatur vel capiatur, nisi servitium suum liberum, quod de jure nobis facere debent, et facere tenentur; et prout statutum est iis, et illis a nobis datum et concessum jure hæreditario in perpetuum per commune concilium totius regni nostri prædicti.

1 Selden, ad Eadmerum. Hody (Treatise on Convocations, p. 249) infers from the great alterations visible on the face of these laws that they were altered from the French original by Glanvil.

2 Wilkins, p. 234. The accession of Henry inspired hopes into the English nation which were not well realized. His marriage with Matilda, "of the rightful English kin," is mentioned with apparent pleasure by the Saxon Chronicler under the year 1100. And in a fragment of a Latin treatise on the English laws, praising them with a genuine feeling, and probably written in the earlier part of Henry's reign, the author extols his behavior towards the people, in contrast with that of preceding times, and bears explicit testimony to the confirmation and amendment of Edward's laws by the Conqueror and by the reigning king—Qui non solum legem regis Eadwardi nobis reddidit, quam omni gaudiorum delectatione suscepimus, sed beati patris ejus emendationibus roboratam propriis institutionibus honestavit. See Cooper on Public Records (vol. ii. p. 423), in which very useful collection the whole fragment (for the first time in England) is published from a Cottonian manuscript. Henry ceased not, according to the Saxon Chronicle, to lay on many tributes. But it is reasonable to suppose that tallages on towns and on his demesne tenants, at that time legal, were reckoned among them.

3 A great impression is said to have been made on the barons confederated against John by the production of Henry I.'s charter, whereof they had been ignorant. Matt. Paris, p. 212. But this could hardly have been the existing charter, for reasons alleged by Blackstone. Introduction to Magna Charta, p. 6.

4 Wilkins, Leges Anglo-Saxon. p. 310

5 Id. p. 318.

6 The Saxon Chronicler complains of a witenagemot, as he calls it, or assizes, held at Leicester in 1124, where forty-four thieves were hanged, a greater num-

demand the laws of Edward the Confessor; and the Normans themselves, as they grew dissatisfied with the royal administration, fell into these English sentiments.[1] But what these laws were, or more properly, perhaps, these customs subsisting in the Confessor's age, was not very distinctly understood.[2] So far, however, was clear, that the rigorous feudal servitude, the weighty tributes upon poorer freemen, had never prevailed before the Conquest. In claiming the laws of Edward the Confessor, our ancestors meant but the redress of grievances, which tradition told them had not always existed.

Richard I.'s chancellor deposed by the barons

It is highly probable, independently of the evidence supplied by the charters of Henry I. and his two successors, that a sense of oppression had long been stimulating the subjects of so arbitrary a government, before they gave any demonstrations of it sufficiently palpable to find a place in history. But there are certainly no instances of rebellion, or even, as far as we know, of a constitutional resistance in parliament, down to the reign of Richard I. The revolt of the earls of Leicester and Norfolk against Henry II., which endangered his throne and comprehended his children with a large part of his barons, appears not to have been founded even upon the pretext of public grievances. Under Richard I. something more of a national spirit began to show itself. For the king having left his chancellor William Longchamp joint regent and justiciary with the bishop of Durham during his crusade, the foolish insolence of the former, who excluded his coadjutor

ber than was ever before known; it was said that many suffered unjustly, p. 228. Mr. Turner translates this differently; but, as I conceive, without attending to the spirit of the context. Hist. of Engl. vol. i. p. 174.

1 The distinction between the two nations was pretty well obliterated at the end of Henry II.'s reign, as we learn from the Dialogue on the Exchequer, then written: jam cohabitantibus Anglicis et Normannis, et alterutrûm uxores ducentibus vel nubentibus, sic permixtæ sunt nationes, ut vix discerni possit hodie, de liberis loquor, quis Anglicus, quis Normannus sit genere; exceptis duntaxat ascriptitiis qui villani dicuntur, quibus non est liberum obstantibus dominis suis a sui status conditione discedere. Eapropter pene quicunque sic hodie occisus reperitur, ut murdrum punitur, exceptis his quibus certa sunt ut diximus servilis conditionis indicia. p. 26. [NOTE XII.]

2 Non quas tulit, sed quas observaverit, says William of Malmsbury, concerning the Confessor's laws. Those bearing his name in Lambard and Wilkins are evidently spurious, though it may not be easy to fix upon the time when they were forged. Those found in Ingulfus, in the French language, are genuine, though translated from Latin, and were confirmed by William the Conqueror. Neither of these collections, however, can be thought to have any relation to the civil liberty of the subject. It has been deemed more rational to suppose that these longings for Edward's laws were rather meant for a mild administration of government, free from unjust Norman innovations, than any written and definitive system.

from any share in the administration, provoked every one of the nobility. A convention of these, the king's brother placing himself at their head, passed a sentence of removal and banishment upon the chancellor. Though there might be reason to conceive that this would not be unpleasing to the king, who was already apprised how much Longchamp had abused his trust, it was a remarkable assumption of power by that assembly, and the earliest authority for a leading principle of our constitution, the responsibility of ministers to parliament.

Magna Charta.

In the succeeding reign of John all the rapacious exactions usual to these Norman kings were not only redoubled, but mingled with other outrages of tyranny still more intolerable.[1] These too were to be endured at the hands of a prince utterly contemptible for his folly and cowardice. One is surprised at the forbearance displayed by the barons, till they took up arms at length in that confederacy which ended in establishing the Great Charter of Liberties. As this was the first effort towards a legal government, so is it beyond comparison the most important event in our history, except that Revolution without which its benefits would have been rapidly annihilated. The constitution of England has indeed no single date from which its duration is to be reckoned. The institutions of positive law, the far more important changes which time has wrought in the order of society, during six hundred years subsequent to the Great Charter, have undoubtedly lessened its direct application to our present circumstances. But it is still the keystone of English liberty. All that has since been obtained is little more than as confirmation or commentary; and if every subsequent law were to be swept away, there would still remain the bold features that distinguish a free from a despotic monarchy. It has been lately the fashion to depreciate the value of Magna Charta, as if it had sprung from the private ambition of a few selfish barons, and redressed only some feudal abuses. It is indeed of little importance by what motives those who obtained it were guided. The real characters of men most distinguished in the transactions of that time are not easily determined at present. Yet if we bring

1 In 1207 John took a seventh of the movables of lay and spiritual persons, cunctis murmurantibus, sed contradicere non audentibus. Matt. Paris, p. 186, ed. 1684. But his insults upon the nobility in debauching their wives and daughters were, as usually happens, the most exasperating provocation

these ungrateful suspicions to the test, they prove destitute of all reasonable foundation. An equal distribution of civil rights to all classes of freemen forms the peculiar beauty of the charter. In this just solicitude for the people, and in the moderation which infringed upon no essential prerogative of the monarchy, we may perceive a liberality and patriotism very unlike the selfishness which is sometimes rashly imputed to those ancient barons. And, as far as we are guided by historical testimony, two great men, the pillars of our church and state, may be considered as entitled beyond the rest to the glory of this monument; Stephen Langton, archbishop of Canterbury, and William earl of Pembroke. To their temperate zeal for a legal government, England was indebted during that critical period for the two greatest blessings that patriotic statesmen could confer; the establishment of civil liberty upon an immovable basis, and the preservation of national independence under the ancient line of sovereigns, which rasher men were about to exchange for the dominion of France.

By the Magna Charta of John, reliefs were limited to a certain sum according to the rank of the tenant, the waste committed by guardians in chivalry restrained, the disparagement in matrimony of female wards forbidden, and widows secured from compulsory marriage. These regulations, extending to the sub-vassals of the crown, redressed the worst grievances of every military tenant in England. The franchises of the city of London and of all towns and boroughs were declared inviolable. The freedom of commerce was guaranteed to alien merchants. The Court of Common Pleas, instead of following the king's person, was fixed at Westminster. The tyranny exercised in the neighborhood of royal forests met with some check, which was further enforced by the Charter of Forests under Henry III.

But the essential clauses of Magna Charta are those which protect the personal liberty and property of all freemen, by giving security from arbitrary imprisonment and arbitrary spoliation. "No freeman (says the 29th chapter of Henry III.'s charter, which, as the existing law, I quote in preference to that of John, the variations not being very material) shall be taken or imprisoned, or be disseized of his freehold, or liberties, or free customs, or be outlawed, or exiled, or any otherwise destroyed; nor will we pass upon him, nor send upon him, but by lawful judgment of his peers, or by the law of the land.[1] We will sell to no man, we will not deny or delay to any man, justice or right." It is obvious that these words, interpreted by any honest court of law, convey an ample security for the two main rights of civil society. From the era, therefore, of king John's charter, it must have been a clear principle of our constitution that no man can be detained in prison without trial. Whether courts of justice framed the writ of Habeas Corpus in conformity to the spirit of this clause, or found it already in their register, it became from that era the right of every subject to demand it. That writ, rendered more actively remedial by the statute of Charles II., but founded upon the broad basis of Magna Charta, is the principal bulwark of English liberty; and if ever temporary circumstances, or the doubtful plea of political necessity, shall lead men to look on its denial with apathy, the most distinguishing characteristic of our constitution will be effaced.

As the clause recited above protects the subject from any absolute spoliation of his freehold rights, so others restrain the excessive amercements which had an almost equally ruinous operation. The magnitude of his offence, by the 14th clause of Henry III.'s charter, must be the measure of his fine; and in every case the *contenement* (a word expressive of chattels necessary to each man's station, as the arms of a gentleman, the merchandise of a trader, the plough and wagons of a peasant) was exempted from seizure. A provision was made in the charter of John that no aid or escuage should be imposed, except in the three feudal cases of aid, without consent of parliament. And this was extended to aids paid by the city of London. But the clause was omitted in the

[1] Nisi per legale judicium parium suorum, *vel* per legem terræ. Several explanations have been offered of the alternative clause, which some have referred to judgment by default or demurrer—others to the process of attachment for contempt. Certainly there are many legal procedures besides trial by jury, through which a party's goods or person may be taken. But one may doubt whether these were in contemplation of the framers of Magna Charta. In an entry of the charter of 1217 by a contemporary hand, preserved in a book in the town-clerk's office in London, called Liber Custumarum et Regum antiquorum, a various reading, *et* per legem terræ, occurs. Blackstone's Charters, p. 42. And the word *vel* is so frequently used for *et*, that I am not wholly free from a suspicion that it was so intended in this place. The meaning will be that no person shall be disseized, &c., except upon a lawful cause of action or indictment found by the verdict of a jury. This really seems as good as any of the disjunctive interpretations, but I do not offer it with much confidence.

But perhaps the best sense of the disjunctive will be perceived by remembering that judicium parium was generally opposed to the combat or the ordeal, which were equally *lex terræ*.

three charters granted by Henry III., though parliament seem to have acted upon it in most part of his reign. It had, however, no reference to tallages imposed upon towns without their consent. Fourscore years were yet to elapse before the great principle of parliamentary taxation was explicitly and absolutely recognized.

A law which enacts that justice shall neither be sold, denied, nor delayed, stamps with infamy that government under which it had become necessary. But from the time of the charter, according to Madox, the disgraceful perversions of right, which are upon record in the rolls of the exchequer, became less frequent.[1]

State of the constitution under Henry III.

From this era a new soul was infused into the people of England. Her liberties, at the best long in abeyance, became a tangible possession, and those indefinite aspirations for the laws of Edward the Confessor were changed into a steady regard for the Great Charter. Pass but from the history of Roger de Hoveden to that of Matthew Paris, from the second Henry to the third, and judge whether the victorious struggle had not excited an energy of public spirit to which the nation was before a stranger. The strong man, in the sublime language of Milton, was aroused from sleep, and shook his invincible locks. Tyranny, indeed, and injustice will, by all historians not absolutely servile, be noted with moral reprobation; but never shall we find in the English writers of the twelfth century that assertion of positive and national rights which distinguishes those of the next age, and particularly the monk of St. Alban's. From his prolix history we may collect three material propositions as to the state of the English constitution during the long reign of Henry III.; a prince to whom the epithet of worthless seems best applicable; and who, without committing any flagrant crimes, was at once insincere, ill-judging, and pusillanimous. The intervention of such a reign was a very fortunate circumstance for public liberty, which might possibly have been crushed in its infancy if an Edward had immediately succeeded to the throne of John.

1. The Great Charter was always considered as a fundamental law. But yet it was supposed to acquire additional security by frequent confirmation. This it received, with

[1] Hist. of Exchequer, c. 12

some not inconsiderable variation, in the first, second, and ninth years of Henry's reign. The last of these is in our present statute-book, and has never received any alterations; but Sir E. Coke reckons thirty-two instances wherein it has been solemnly ratified. Several of these were during the reign of Henry III., and were invariably purchased by the grant of a subsidy.[1] This prudent accommodation of parliament to the circumstances of their age not only made the law itself appear more inviolable, but established that correspondence between supply and redress which for some centuries was the balance-spring of our constitution. The charter, indeed, was often grossly violated by their administration. Even Hubert de Burgh, of whom history speaks more favorably than of Henry's later favorites, though a faithful servant of the crown, seems, as is too often the case with such men, to have thought the king's honor and interest concerned in maintaining an unlimited prerogative.[2] The government was, however, much worse administered after his fall. From the great difficulty of compelling the king to observe the boundaries of law, the English clergy, to whom we are much indebted for their zeal in behalf of liberty during this reign, devised means of binding his conscience and terrifying his imagination by religious sanctions. The solemn excommunication, accompanied with the most awful threats, pronounced against the violators of Magna Charta, is well known from our common histories. The king was a party to this ceremony, and swore to observe the charter. But Henry III., though a very devout person, had his own notions as to the validity of an oath that affected his power, and indeed passed his life in a series of perjuries. According to the creed of that age, a papal dispensation might annul any prior engagement; and he was generally on sufficiently good terms with Rome to obtain such an indulgence.

2. Though the prohibition of levying aids or escuages without consent of parliament had been omitted in all Henry's charters, yet neither one nor the other seem in fact to have been exacted at discretion throughout his reign. On the contrary, the barons frequently refused the aids, or rather subsidies, which his prodigality was always demanding. Indeed it would probably have been impossible for the king,

1 Matt. Paris, p. 272

2 Id. p. 284

however frugal, stripped as he was of so many lucrative though oppressive prerogatives by the Great Charter, to support the expenditure of government from his own resources. Tallages on his demesnes, and especially on the rich and ill-affected city of London, he imposed without scruple; but it does not appear that he ever pretended to a right of general taxation. We may therefore take it for granted that the clause in John's charter, though not expressly renewed, was still considered as of binding force. The king was often put to great inconvenience by the refusal of supply; and at one time was reduced to sell his plate and jewels, which the citizens of London buying, he was provoked to exclaim with envious spite against their riches, which he had not been able to exhaust.[1]

3. The power of granting money must of course imply the power of withholding it; yet this has sometimes been little more than a nominal privilege. But in this reign the English parliament exercised their right of refusal, or, what was much better, of conditional assent. Great discontent was expressed at the demand of a subsidy in 1237; and the king alleging that he had expended a great deal of money on his sister's marriage with the emperor, and also upon his own, the barons answered that he had not taken their advice in those affairs, nor ought they to share the punishment of acts of imprudence they had not committed.[2] In 1241, a subsidy having been demanded for the war in Poitou, the barons drew up a remonstrance, enumerating all the grants they had made on former occasions, but always on condition that the imposition should not be turned into precedent. Their last subsidy, it appears, had been paid into the hands of four barons, who were to expend it at their discretion for the benefit of the king and kingdom;[3] an early instance of parliamentary control over public expenditure. On a similar demand in 1244 the king was answered by complaints against the violation of the charter, the waste of former subsidies, and the maladministration of his servants.[4] Finally the barons positively refused any money; and he extorted 1500

[1] M. Paris, p. 650.

[2] Quod hæc omnia sine consilio fidelium suorum facerat, nec debuerant esse pœnæ participes, qui fuerant a culpâ immunes. p. 367.

[3] M. Paris, p. 515.

[4] Id. p. 563, 572. Matthew Paris's language is particularly uncourtly: rex cum instantissimè, ne dicam impudentissimè, auxilium pecuniare ab iis iterum postularet, toties læsi et illusi, contradixerunt ei unanimiter et uno ore in facie.

marks from the city of London. Some years afterwards they declared their readiness to burden themselves more than ever if they could secure the observance of the charter; and requested that the justiciary, chancellor, and treasurer might be appointed with consent of parliament, according, as they asserted, to ancient custom, and might hold their offices during good behavior.[1]

Forty years of mutual dissatisfaction had elapsed, when a signal act of Henry's improvidence brought on a crisis which endangered his throne. Innocent IV., out of mere animosity against the family of Frederic II., left no means untried to raise up a competitor for the crown of Naples, which Manfred had occupied. Richard earl of Cornwall having been prudent enough to decline this speculation, the pope offered to support Henry's second son, prince Edmund. Tempted by such a prospect, the silly king involved himself in irretrievable embarrassments by prosecuting an enterprise which could not possibly be advantageous to England, and upon which he entered without the advice of his parliament. Destitute himself of money, he was compelled to throw the expense of this new crusade upon the pope; but the assistance of Rome was never gratuitous, and Henry actually pledged his kingdom for the money which she might expend in a war for her advantage and his own.[2] He did not even want the effrontery to tell parliament in 1257, introducing his son Edmund as king of Sicily, that they were bound for the repayment of 14,000 marks with interest. The pope had also, in furtherance of the Neapolitan project, conferred upon Henry the tithes of all benefices in England, as well as the first fruits of such as should be vacant.[3] Such a concession drew upon the king the implacable resentment of his clergy, already complaining of the cowardice or connivance that had

[1] De communi consilio regni, sicut ab antiquo consuetum et justum. p. 778. This was not so great an encroachment as it may appear. Ralph de Neville, bishop of Chichester, had been made chancellor in 1223, assensu totius regni; itaque scilicet ut non deponeretur ab ejus sigilli custodi nisi totius regni ordinante consensu et consilio. p. 266. Accordingly, the king demanding the great seal from him in 1236, he refused to give it up, alleging that, having received it in the general council of the kingdom, he could not resign it without the same authority. p. 363. And the parliament of 1248 complained that the king had not followed the steps of his predecessors in appointing these three great officers by their consent. p. 646. What had been in fact the practice of former kings I do not know; but it is not likely to have been such as they represent. Henry, however, had named the archbishop of York to the regency of the kingdom during his absence beyond seas in 1242, de consilio omnium comitum et baronum nostrorum et omnium fidelium nostrorum. Rymer, t. i. p. 400

[2] Id. p. 771.

[3] p. 813

during all his reign exposed them to the shameless exactions of Rome. Henry had now indeed cause to regret his precipitancy. Alexander IV., the reigning pontiff, threatened him not only with a revocation of the grant to his son, but with an excommunication and general interdict, if the money advanced on his account should not be immediately repaid,[1] and a Roman agent explained the demand to a parliament assembled in London. The sum required was so enormous, we are told, that it struck all the hearers with astonishment and horror. The nobility of the realm were indignant to think that one man's supine folly should thus bring them to ruin.[2] Who can deny that measures beyond the ordinary course of the constitution were necessary to control so prodigal and injudicious a sovereign? Accordingly the barons insisted that twenty-four persons should be nominated, half by the king and half by themselves, to reform the state of the kingdom. These were appointed on the meeting of the parliament at Oxford, after a prorogation.

The seven years that followed are a revolutionary period, the events of which we do not find satisfactorily explained by the historians of the time.[3] A king divested of prerogatives by his people soon appears even to themselves an injured party. And, as the baronial oligarchy acted with that arbitrary temper which is never pardoned in a government that has an air of usurpation about it, the royalists began to gain ground, chiefly through the defection of some who had joined in the original limitations imposed on the crown, usually called the provisions of Oxford. An ambitious man, confident in his talents and popularity, ventured to display too marked a superiority above his fellows in the same cause. But neither his character nor the battles of Lewes and Evesham fall strictly within the limits of a constitutional history. It is however important to observe, that, even in the moment of success, Henry III. did not presume to revoke any part of the Great Charter. His victory had been

[1] Rymer, t. i. p. 632. This inauspicious negotiation for Sicily, which is not altogether unlike that of James I. about the Spanish match, in its folly, bad success, and the dissatisfaction it occasioned at home, receives a good deal of illustration from documents in Rymer's collection.

[2] Quantitas pecuniæ ad tantam ascendit summam, ut stuporem simul et horrorem in auribus generaret audientium. Doluit igitur nobilitas regni, se unius hominis ita confundi supinâ simplicitate. M. Paris, p. 827.

[3] The best account of the provisions of Oxford in 1260 and the circumstances connected with them is found in the Burton Annals. 2 Gale, XV Scriptores, p. 407. Many of these provisions were afterwards enacted in the statute of Marlebridge.

achieved by the arms of the English nobility, who had, generally speaking, concurred in the former measures against his government, and whose opposition to the earl of Leicester's usurpation was compatible with a steady attachment to constitutional liberty.[1]

Limitations of the prerogative proved from Bracton.

The opinions of eminent lawyers are undoubtedly, where legislative or judicial authorities fail, the best evidence that can be adduced in constitutional history. It will therefore be satisfactory to select a few passages from Bracton, himself a judge at the end of Henry III.'s reign, by which the limitations of prerogative by law will clearly appear to have been fully established. "The king," says he, "must not be subject to any man, but to God and the law; for the law makes him king. Let the king therefore give to the law what the law gives to him, dominion and power; for there is no king where will, and not law, bears rule."[2] "The king (in another place) can do nothing on earth, being the minister of God, but what he can do by law; nor is what is said (in the Pandects) any objection, that whatever the prince pleases shall be law; because by the words that follow in that text it appears to design not any mere will of the prince, but that which is established by the advice of his councillors, the king giving his authority, and deliberation being had upon it."[3] This passage is undoubtedly a misrepresentation of the famous lex regia, which has ever been interpreted to convey the unlimited power of the people to their emperors.[4] But the very circumstance of so perverted a gloss put upon this text is a proof that no other doctrine could be admitted in the law of England. In another passage Bracton reckons as superior to the king, "not only God and the law, by which he is made king, but his court of earls and barons; for the former (comites) are so styled as associates of the king, and whoever has an associate has a master;[5] so that, if the king were without a bridle, that is, the law, they ought to put a bridle upon him."[6] Several other passages in Bracton might be

[1] The Earl of Gloucester, whose personal quarrel with Montfort had overthrown the baronial oligarchy, wrote to the king in 1267, ut provisiones Oxoniæ teneri faciat per regnum suum, et ut promissa sibi apud Evesham de facto compleret. Matt. Paris, p. 850.

[2] l. i. c. 8.

[3] l. iii. c. 9. These words are nearly copied from Glanvil's introduction to his treatise.

[4] See Selden ad Fletam, p. 1046.

[5] This means, I suppose, that he who acts with the consent of others must be in some degree restrained by them; but it is ill expressed.

[6] l. ii. c. 16.

produced to the same import; but these are sufficient to demonstrate the important fact that, however extensive or even indefinite might be the royal prerogative in the days of Henry III., the law was already its superior, itself but made part of the law, and was incompetent to overthrow it.[1] It is true that in this very reign the practice of dispensing with statutes by a non-obstante was introduced, in imitation of the papal dispensations.[2] But this prerogative could only be exerted within certain limits, and, however pernicious it may be justly thought, was, when thus understood and defined, not, strictly speaking, incompatible with the legislative sovereignty of parliament.

The King's Court.

In conformity with the system of France and other feudal countries, there was one standing council, which assisted the kings of England in the collection and management of their revenue, the administration of justice to suitors, and the despatch of all public business. This was styled the King's Court, and held in his palace, or wherever he was personally present. It was composed of the great officers; the chief justiciary,[3] the chancellor, the constable,

1 Allen has pointed out that the king might have been sued in his own courts, like one of his subjects, until the reign of Edward I., who introduced the method of suing by petition of right; and in the Year Book of Edward III. one of the judges says that he has seen a writ beginning—*Præcipe Henry regi Angliæ.* Bracton, however, expressly asserts the contrary, as Mr. Allen owns, so that we may reckon this rather doubtful. Bracton has some remarkable words which I have omitted to quote: after he has broadly asserted that the king has no superior but God, and that no remedy can be had by law against him, he proceeds: Nisi sit qui dicat, quod universitas regni et baronagium suum hoc facere debeant et possint in curia ipsius regis. By *curia* we must here understand parliament, and not the law-courts.

2 M. Paris, p. 701.

3 The chief justiciary was the greatest subject in England. Besides presiding in the king's court and in the Exchequer, he was originally, by virtue of his office, the regent of the kingdom during the absence of the sovereign, which, till the loss of Normandy, occurred very frequently. Writs, at such times, ran in his name, and were tested by him. Madox, Hist. of Exchequer. p. 16. His appointment upon these temporary occasions was expressed, ad custodiendum loco nostro terram nostram Angliæ et pacem regni nostri; and all persons were enjoined to obey him tanquam justitiario nostro. Rymer, t. i. p. 181. Sometimes, however, the king issued his own writ de ultra mare. The first time when the dignity of this office was impaired was at the death of John, when the justiciary, Hubert de Burgh, being besieged in Dover Castle, those who proclaimed Henry III. at Gloucester constituted the earl of Pembroke governor of the king and kingdom, Hubert still retaining his office. This is erroneously stated by Matthew Paris, who has misled Spelman in his Glossary; but the truth appears from Hubert's answer to the articles of charge against him, and from a record in Madox's Hist. of Exch c. 21, note A. wherein the earl of Pembroke is named rector regis et regni, and Hubert de Burgh justiciary. In 1241 the archbishop of York was appointed to the regency during Henry's absence in Poitou, without the title of justiciary. Rymer, t. i. p. 410. Still the office was so considerable that the barons who met in the Oxford parliament of 1258 insisted that the justiciary should be annually chosen with their approbation. But the subsequent successes of Henry prevented this being established, and Edward I. discontinued the office altogether.

marshal, chamberlain, steward, and treasurer, with any others whom the king might appoint. Of this great court there was, as it seems, from the beginning, a particular branch, in which all matters relating to the revenue were exclusively transacted. This, though composed of the same persons, yet, being held in a different part of the palace, and for different business, was distinguished from the king's court by the name of the Exchequer; a separation which became complete when civil pleas were decided and judgments recorded in this second court.[1]

The Court of Exchequer.

It is probable that in the age next after the Conquest few causes in which the crown had no interest were carried before the royal tribunals; every man finding a readier course of justice in the manor or county to which he belonged.[2] But by degrees this supreme jurisdiction became more familiar; and, as it seemed less liable to partiality or intimidation than the provincial courts, suitors grew willing to submit to its expensiveness and inconvenience. It was obviously the interest of the king's court to give such equity and steadiness to its decisions as might encourage this disposition Nothing could be more advantageous to the king's authority, nor, what perhaps was more immediately regarded, to his revenue, since a fine was always paid for leave to plead in his court, or to remove thither a cause commenced below. But because few, comparatively speaking, could have recourse to so distant a tribunal as that of the king's court, and perhaps also on account of the attachment which the English felt to their ancient right of trial by the neighboring freeholders, Henry II. established itinerant justices to decide civil and criminal pleas within each county.[3] This excellent institution is referred by some to the twenty-second year of that prince; but Madox traces it several years higher.[4] We have owed to it the uniformity

Institution of justices of assize.

[1] For much information about the Curia Regis, and especially this branch of it, the student of our constitutional history should have recourse to Madox's History of the Exchequer, and to the Dialogus de Scaccario, written in the time of Henry II. by Richard bishop of Ely, though commonly ascribed to Gervase of Tilbury. This treatise he will find subjoined to Madox's work. [NOTE XIII.]

[2] Omnis causa terminetur comitatu, vel hundredo, vel halimoto socam habentium. Leges Henr. I. c. 9.

[3] Dialogus de Scaccario, p. 38.

[4] Hist. of Exchequer, c. iii. Lord Lyttelton thinks that this institution may have been adopted in imitation of Louis VI., who half a century before had introduced a similar regulation in his domains. Hist. of Henry II. vol. ii. p. 206. Justices in eyre, or, as we now call them, of assize, were sometimes commissioned in the reign of Henry I

of our common law, which would otherwise have been split, like that of France, into a multitude of local customs; and we still owe to it the assurance, which is felt by the poorest and most remote inhabitant of England, that his right is weighed by the same incorrupt and acute understanding upon which the decision of the highest questions is reposed. The justices of assize seem originally to have gone their circuits annually; and as part of their duty was to set tallages upon royal towns, and superintend the collection of the revenue, we may be certain that there could be no long interval. This annual visitation was expressly confirmed by the twelfth section of Magna Charta, which provides also that no assize of novel disseizin, or mort d'ancestor, should be taken except in the shire where the lands in controversy lay. Hence this clause stood opposed on the one hand to the encroachments of the king's court, which might otherwise, by drawing pleas of land to itself, have defeated the suitor's right to a jury from the vicinage; and on the other, to those of the feudal aristocracy, who hated any interference of the crown to chastise their violations of law, or control their own jurisdiction. Accordingly, while the confederacy of barons against Henry III. was in its full power, an attempt was made to prevent the regular circuits of the judges.[1]

The court of Common Pleas.

Long after the separation of the exchequer from the king's court, another branch was detached for the decision of private suits. This had its beginning, in Madox's opinion, as early as the reign of Richard I.[2] But it was completely established by Magna Charta. "Common Pleas," it is said in the fourteenth clause, "shall not follow our court, but be held in some certain place." Thus was formed the Court of Common Bench at Westminster, with full, and, strictly speaking, exclusive jurisdiction over all civil disputes, where neither the king's interest, nor any matter

Hardy's Introduction to Close Rolls. They do not appear to have gone their circuits regularly before 22 Hen. II. (1176.)

[1] Justiciarii regis Angliæ, qui dicuntur itineris, missi Herfordiam pro suo exequendo officio repelluntur, allegantibus his qui regi adversabantur, ipsos contrà formam provisionum Oxoniæ nuper factarum venisse. Chron. Nic. Trivet. A.D. 1260. I forget where I found this quotation.

[2] Hist of Exchequer, c. 19. Justices of the bench are mentioned several years before Magna Charta. But Madox thinks the chief justiciary of England might preside in the two courts, as well as in the exchequer. After the erection of the Common Bench the style of the superior court began to alter. It ceased by degrees to be called the king's court. Pleas were said to be held coram rege, or coram rege ubicunque fuerit. And thus the court of king's bench was formed out of the remains of the ancient curia regis.

savoring of a criminal nature, was concerned. For of such disputes neither the court of king's bench, nor that of exchequer, can take cognizance, except by means of a legal fiction, which, in the one case, supposes an act of force, and, in the other, a debt to the crown.

Origin of the Common Law.

The principal officers of state, who had originally been effective members of the king's court, began to withdraw from it, after this separation into three courts of justice, and left their places to regular lawyers though the treasurer and chancellor of the exchequer have still seats on the equity side of that court, a vestige of its ancient constitution. It would indeed have been difficult for men bred in camps or palaces to fulfil the ordinary functions of judicature under such a system of law as had grown up in England. The rules of legal decision, among a rude people, are always very simple; not serving much to guide, far less to control, the feelings of natural equity. Such were those which prevailed among the Anglo-Saxons; requiring no subtler intellect, or deeper learning, than the earl or sheriff at the head of his county-court might be expected to possess. But a great change was wrought in about a century after the Conquest. Our English lawyers, prone to magnify the antiquity, like the other merits of their system, are apt to carry up the date of the common law, till, like the pedigree of an illustrious family, it loses itself in the obscurity of ancient time. Even Sir Matthew Hale does not hesitate to say that its origin is as undiscoverable as that of the Nile. But though some features of the common law may be distinguishable in Saxon times, while our limited knowledge prevents us from assigning many of its peculiarities to any determinable period, yet the general character and most essential parts of the system were of much later growth. The laws of the Anglo-Saxon kings, Madox truly observes, are as different from those collected by Glanvil as the laws of two different nations. The pecuniary compositions for crimes, especially for homicide, which run through the Anglo-Saxon code down to the laws ascribed to Henry I.,[1] are not mentioned by Glanvil. Death seems to have been the regular punishment of murder, as well as robbery. Though the investigation by means of ordeal was not disused in his time,[2]

1 C. 70.

2 A citizen of London, suspected of murder, having failed in the ordeal of cold water, was hanged by order of Henry

yet trial by combat, of which we find no instance before the Conquest, was evidently preferred. Under the Saxon government, suits appear to have commenced, even before the king, by verbal or written complaint; at least, no trace remains of the original writ, the foundation of our civil procedure.[1] The descent of lands before the Conquest was according to the custom of gavelkind, or equal partition among the children;[2] in the age of Henry I. the eldest son took the principal fief to his own share;[3] in that of Glanvil he inherited all the lands held by knight service; but the descent of socage lands depended on the particular custom of the estate. By the Saxon laws, upon the death of the son without issue, the father inherited;[4] by our common law, he is absolutely, and in every case, excluded. Lands were, in general, devisable by testament before the Conquest; but not in the time of Henry II., except by particular custom. These are sufficient samples of the differences between our Saxon and Norman jurisprudence; but the distinct character of the two will strike more forcibly every one who peruses successively the laws published by Wilkins, and the treatise ascribed to Glanvil. The former resemble the barbaric codes of the continent, and the capitularies of Charlemagne and his family, minute to an excess in apportioning punishments, but sparing and indefinite in treating of civil rights; while the other, copious, discriminating, and technical, displays the characteristics, as well as unfolds the principles, of English law. It is difficult to assert anything decisively as to the period between the Conquest and the reign of Henry II., which presents fewer materials for legal history than the preceding age; but the treatise denominated the Laws of Henry I., compiled at the soonest about the end of Stephen's reign,[5] bears so much of a Saxon character, that I should be inclined to ascribe our present common law to a date, so far as it is capable of any date, not much antecedent to the publication of Glanvil.[6] At

II., though he offered 500 marks to save his life. Hoveden, p. 566. It appears as if the ordeal were permitted to persons already convicted by the verdict of a jury. If they escaped in this purgation, yet, in cases of murder, they were banished the realm. Wilkins, Leges Anglo-Saxon, p. 330. Ordeals were abolished about the beginning of Henry III.'s reign.

[1] Hickes, Dissert. Epistol. p. 8.

[2] Leges Gulielmi, p. 225.

[3] Leges Henr. I. c. 70.

[4] Ibid.

[5] The Decretum of Gratian is quoted in this treatise, which was not published in Italy till 1151.

[6] Madox, Hist. of Exch. p. 122, edit. 1711. Lord Lyttelton, vol. ii. p. 267, has given reasons for supposing that Glanvil was not the author of this treatise, but some clerk under his direction.

the same time, since no kind of evidence attests any sudden and radical change in the jurisprudence of England, the question must be considered as left in great obscurity. Perhaps it might be reasonable to conjecture that the treatise called Leges Henrici Primi contains the ancient usages still prevailing in the inferior jurisdictions, and that of Glanvil the rules established by the Norman lawyers of the king's court, which would of course acquire a general recognition and efficacy, in consequence of the institution of justices holding their assizes periodically throughout the country.

Character and defects of the English law.

The capacity of deciding legal controversies was now only to be found in men who had devoted themselves to that peculiar study; and a race of such men arose, whose eagerness and even enthusiasm in the profession of the law were stimulated by the self-complacency of intellectual dexterity in threading its intricate and thorny mazes. The Normans are noted in their own country for a shrewd and litigious temper, which may have given a character to our courts of justice in early times. Something too of that excessive subtlety, and that preference of technical to rational principles, which runs through our system, may be imputed to the scholastic philosophy, which was in vogue during the same period, and is marked by the same features. But we have just reason to boast of the leading causes of these defects; an adherence to fixed rules, and a jealousy of judicial discretion, which have in no country, I believe, been carried to such a length. Hence precedents of adjudged cases, becoming authorities for the future, have been constantly noted, and form indeed almost the sole ground of argument in questions of mere law. But these authorities being frequently unreasonable and inconsistent, partly from the infirmity of all human reason, partly from the imperfect manner in which a number of unwarranted and incorrect reporters have handed them down, later judges grew anxious to elude by impalpable distinctions what they did not venture to overturn. In some instances this evasive skill has been applied to acts of the legislature. Those who are moderately conversant with the history of our law will easily trace other circumstances that have coöperated in producing that technical and subtle system which regulates the course of real property. For as that formed almost the whole of our ancient jurisprudence, it is there that we must seek its original character. But much of the same spirit pervades every part of the law. No tribunals of a civilized people ever borrowed so little, even of illustration, from the writings of philosophers, or from the institutions of other countries. Hence law has been studied, in general, rather as an art than a science, with more solicitude to know its rules and distinctions than to perceive their application to that for which all rules of law ought to have been established, the maintenance of public and private rights. Nor is there any reading more jejune and unprofitable to a philosophical mind than that of our ancient law-books. Later times have introduced other inconveniences, till the vast extent and multiplicity of our laws have become a practical evil of serious importance, and an evil which, between the timidity of the legislature on the one hand, and the selfish views of practitioners on the other, is likely to reach, in no long period, an intolerable excess. Deterred by an interested clamor against innovation from abrogating what is useless, simplifying what is complex, or determining what is doubtful, and always more inclined to stave off an immediate difficulty by some patchwork scheme of modifications and suspensions than to consult for posterity in the comprehensive spirit of legal philosophy, we accumulate statute upon statute, and precedent upon precedent, till no industry can acquire, nor any intellect digest, the mass of learning that grows upon the panting student; and our jurisprudence seems not unlikely to be simplified in the worst and least honorable manner, a tacit agreement of ignorance among its professors. Much indeed has already gone into desuetude within the last century, and is known only as an occult science by a small number of adepts. We are thus gradually approaching the crisis of a necessary reformation, when our laws, like those of Rome, must be cast into the crucible. It would be a disgrace to the nineteenth century, if England could not find her Tribonian.[1]

[1] Whitelocke, just after the Restoration, complains that "*Now* the volume of our statutes is grown or swelled to a great bigness." The volume! What would he have said to the monstrous birth of a volume triennially, filled with laws professing to be the deliberate work of the legislature, which every subject is supposed to read, remember, and understand! The excellent sense of the following sentences from the same passage may well excuse me for quoting them, and, perhaps, in this age of bigoted averseness to innovation, I have need of some apology for what I have ventured to say in the text. "I remember the opinion of a wise and learned statesman and lawyer (the chancellor Oxenstiern), that multiplicity of written laws do but distract the judges, and render the law less certain; that where the law sets due and clear bounds betwixt the prerogative royal and the rights of the people, and gives remedy in private causes, there needs no more laws to be increased; for thereby litigation will be increased likewise. It

This establishment of a legal system, which must be considered as complete at the end of Henry III.'s reign, when the unwritten usages of the common law as well as the forms and precedents of the courts were digested into the great work of Bracton, might, in some respects, conduce to the security of public freedom. For, however highly the prerogative might be strained, it was incorporated with the law, and treated with the same distinguished and argumentative subtlety as every other part of it. Whatever things, therefore, it was asserted that the king might do, it was a necessary implication that there were other things which he could not do; else it were vain to specify the former. It is not meant to press this too far; since undoubtedly the bias of lawyers towards the prerogative was sometimes too discernible. But the sweeping maxims of absolute power, which servile judges and churchmen taught the Tudor and Stuart princes, seem to have made no progress under the Plantagenet line.

Hereditary right of the crown established.

Whatever may be thought of the effect which the study of the law had upon the rights of the subject, it conduced materially to the security of good order by ascertaining the hereditary succession of the crown. Five kings out of seven that followed William the Conqueror were usurpers, according at least to modern notions. Of these, Stephen alone encountered any serious opposition upon that ground; and with respect to him, it must be remembered that all the barons, himself included, had solemnly sworn to maintain the succession of Matilda. Henry II. procured a parliamentary settlement of the crown upon his eldest and second sons; a strong presumption that their hereditary right was not absolutely secure.[1] A mixed notion of right and choice in fact prevailed as to the succession of every European monarchy. The coronation oath and the form of popular consent then required were considered as more material, at least to perfect a title, than we deem them at present. They gave seizin, as it were, of the crown, and, in cases of disputed pretensions, had a sort of judicial efficacy.

were a work worthy of a parliament, and cannot be done otherwise, to cause a review of all our statutes, to repeal such as they shall judge inconvenient to remain in force; to confirm those which they shall think fit to stand, and those several statutes which are confused, some repugnant to others, many touching the same matters, to be reduced into certainty, all of one subject into one statute, that perspicuity and clearness may appear in our written laws, which at this day few students or sages can find in them." Whitelocke's Commentary on Parliamentary Writ, vol. i. p. 409.

[1] Lyttelton, vol. ii. p. 14.

The Chronicle of Dunstable says, concerning Richard I., that he was "elevated to the throne by hereditary right, after a solemn election by the clergy and people:"[1] words that indicate the current principles of that age. It is to be observed, however, that Richard took upon him the exercise of royal prerogatives without waiting for his coronation.[2] The succession of John has certainly passed in modern times for an usurpation. I do not find that it was considered as such by his own contemporaries on this side of the Channel. The question of inheritance between an uncle and the son of his deceased elder brother was yet unsettled, as we learn from Glanvil, even in private succession.[3] In the case of sovereignties, which were sometimes contended to require different rules from ordinary patrimonies, it was, and continued long to be, the most uncertain point in public law. John's pretensions to the crown might therefore be such as the English were justified in admitting, especially as his reversionary title seems to have been acknowledged in the reign of his brother Richard.[4] If indeed we may place reliance on Matthew Paris, archbishop Hubert, on this occasion, declared in the most explicit terms that the crown was elective, giving even to the blood royal no other preference than their merit might challenge.[5] Carte rejects this as a fiction of the historian; and it is certainly a strain far beyond the constitution, which, both before and after the Conquest, had invariably limited the throne to one royal stock, though not strictly to its nearest branch. In a charter of the first year of his reign, John calls himself king, "by hereditary right, and through the consent and favor of the church and people."[6]

It is deserving of remark, that, during the rebellions against this prince and his son Henry III., not a syllable was breathed in favor of Eleanor, Arthur's sister, who, if the present rules of succession had been established, was the undoubted heiress of his right. The barons chose rather to call in the aid of Louis, with scarcely a shade of title, though with much better means of maintaining himself. One should think that men whose fathers had been in the field for Matilda could make no difficulty about female succession. But I doubt

1 Lyttelton, vol. ii. p. 42. Hæreditario jure promovendus in regnum, post cleri et populi solennem electionem.

2 Gul. Neubrigensis, l. iv. c. 1.

3 Glanvil, l. vii. c. 3.

4 Hoveden, p. 702.

5 p. 165.

6 Jure hæreditario, et mediante tam cleri et populi consensu et favore. Gurdon on Parliaments, p. 139

whether, notwithstanding that precedent, the crown of England was universally acknowledged to be capable of descending to a female heir. Great averseness had been shown by the nobility of Henry I. to his proposal of settling the kingdom on his daughter.[1] And from a remarkable passage which I shall produce in a note, it appears that even in the reign of Edward III. the succession was supposed to be con fined to the male line.[2]

At length, about the middle of the thirteenth century, the lawyers applied to the crown the same strict principles of descent which regulate a private inheritance. Edward I. was proclaimed immediately upon his father's death, though absent in Sicily. Something however of the old principle may be traced in this proclamation, issued in his name by the guardians of the realm, where he asserts the crown of England "to have devolved upon him by hereditary succession and the will of his nobles."[3] These last words were omitted in the proclamation of Edward II.;[4] since whose time the crown has been absolutely hereditary. The coronation oath, and the recognition of the people at that solemnity, are formalities which convey no right either to the sovereign or the people, though they may testify the duties of each.[5]

English gentry destitute of exclusive privileges.

I cannot conclude the present chapter without observing one most prominent and characteristic distinction between the constitution of England and that of every other country in Europe; I mean its refusal of civil privileges to the lower nobility, or those

[1] Lyttelton, vol. i. p. 162.

[2] This is intimated by the treaty made in 1339 for a marriage between the eldest son of Edward III. and the duke of Brabant's daughter. Edward therein promises that, if his son should die before him, leaving male issue, he will procure the consent of his barons, nobles, and cities (that is, of parliament; nobles here meaning knights, if the word has any distinct sense), for such issue to inherit the kingdom; and if he die leaving a daughter only, Edward or his heir shall make such provision for her as belongs to the daughter of a king. Rymer, t. v. p. 114. It may be inferred from this instrument that, in Edward's intention, if not by the constitution, the Salic law was to regulate the succession of the English crown. This law, it must be remembered, he was compelled to admit in his claim on the kingdom of France, though with a certain modification which gave a pretext of title to himself.

[3] Ad nos regni gubernaculum successione hæreditariâ, ac procerum regni voluntate, et fidelitate nobis præstitâ sit devolutum. Brady (History of England, vol. ii. Appendix, p. 1) expounds procerum voluntate to mean willingness, not will; as much as to say, they acted readily and without command. But in all probability it was intended to save the usual form of consent.

[4] Rymer, t. iii. p. 1. Walsingham, however, asserts that Edward II. ascended the throne non tam jure hæreditario quàm unanimi assensu procerum et magnatum. p. 95. Perhaps we should omit the word *non*, and he might intend to say that the king had not only his hereditary title, but the free consent of his barons.

[5] [NOTE XIV.]

whom we denominate the gentry. In France, in Spain, in Germany, wherever in short we look, the appellations of nobleman and gentleman have been strictly synonymous. Those entitled to bear them by descent, by tenure of land, by office or royal creation, have formed a class distinguished by privileges inherent in their blood from ordinary freemen. Marriage with noble families, or the purchase of military fiefs, or the participation of many civil offices, were, more or less, interdicted to the commons of France and the empire. Of these restrictions, nothing, or next to nothing, was ever known in England. The law has never taken notice of gentlemen.[1] From the reign of Henry III. at least, the legal equality of all ranks below the peerage was, to every essential purpose, as complete as at present. Compare two writers nearly contemporary, Bracton with Beaumanoir, and mark how the customs of England are distinguishable in this respect. The Frenchman ranges the people under three divisions, the noble, the free, and the servile; our countryman has no generic class, but freedom and villenage.[2] No restraint seems ever to have lain upon marriage; nor have the children even of a peer been ever deemed to lose any privilege by his union with a commoner. The purchase of lands held by knight-service was always open to all freemen. A few privileges indeed were confined to those who had received knighthood.[3] But, upon the whole, there was a virtual equality of rights among all the commoners of England. What is most particular is, that the peerage itself imparts no privilege except to its actual possessor. In every other country the descendants of nobles cannot but themselves be noble, because their nobility is the immediate consequence of their birth. But though we commonly say that the blood of

[1] It is hardly worth while, even for the sake of obviating cavils, to notice as an exception the statute of 23 H. VI. c. 14, prohibiting the election of any who were not born gentlemen for knights of the shire. Much less should I have thought of noticing, if it had not been suggested as an objection, the provision of the statute of Merton, that guardians in chivalry shall not marry their wards to villeins or burgesses, to their disparagement. Wherever the distinctions of rank and property are felt in the customs of society, such marriages will be deemed unequal; and it was to obviate the tyranny of feudal superiors who compelled their wards to accept a mean alliance, or to forfeit its price, that this provision of the statute was made. But this does not affect the proposition I had maintained as to the *legal* equality of commoners, any more than a report of a Master in Chancery at the present day, that a proposed marriage for a ward of the court was unequal to what her station in society appeared to claim, would invalidate the same proposition.

[2] Beaumanoir, c. 45. Bracton, l. i. c. 6.

[3] See for these, Selden's Titles of Honor vol. iii. p. 806.

a peer is ennobled, yet this expression seems hardly accurate, and fitter for heralds than lawyers; since in truth nothing confers nobility but the actual descent of a peerage. The sons of peers, as we well know, are commoners, and totally destitute of any legal right beyond a barren precedence.

There is no part, perhaps, of our constitution so admirable as this equality of civil rights; this *isonomia*, which the philosophers of ancient Greece only hoped to find in democratical government.[1] From the beginning our law has been no respecter of persons. It screens not the gentleman of ancient lineage from the judgment of an ordinary jury, nor from ignominious punishment. It confers not, it never did confer, those unjust immunities from public burdens, which the superior orders arrogated to themselves upon the continent. Thus, while the privileges of our peers, as hereditary legislators of a free people, are incomparably more valuable and dignified in their nature, they are far less invidious in their exercise than those of any other nobility in Europe. It is, I am firmly persuaded, to this peculiarly democratical character of the English monarchy, that we are indebted for its long permanence, its regular improvement, and its present vigor. It is a singular, a providential circumstance, that, in an age when the gradual march of civilization and commerce was so little foreseen, our ancestors, deviating from the usages of neighboring countries, should, as if deliberately, have guarded against that expansive force which, in bursting through obstacles improvidently opposed, has scattered havoc over Europe.

Causes of the eqality among freemen in England.

This tendency to civil equality in the English law may, I think, be ascribed to several concurrent causes. In the first place the feudal institutions were far less military in England than upon the continent. From the time of Henry II. the escuage, or pecuniary commutation for personal service, became almost universal. The armies of our kings were composed of hired troops, great part of whom certainly were knights and gentlemen, but who, serving for pay, and not by virtue of their birth or tenure, preserved nothing of the feudal character. It was

[1] *Πλῆθος ἄρχον, πρῶτον μὲν οὔνομα κάλλιστον ἔχει, ἰσονομίαν*, says the advocate of democracy, in the discussion of forms of government which Herodotus (Thalia, c. 80) has put into the mouths of three Persian satraps, after the murder of Smerdis; a scene conceived in the spirit of Corneille.

not, however, so much for the ends of national as of private warfare, that the relation of lord and vassal was contrived. The right which every baron in France possessed of redressing his own wrongs and those of his tenants by arms rendered their connection strictly military. But we read very little of private wars in England. Notwithstanding some passages in Glanvil, which certainly appear to admit their legality, it is not easy to reconcile this with the general tenor of our laws.[1] They must always have been a breach of the king's peace, which our Saxon lawgivers were perpetually striving to preserve, and which the Conqueror and his sons more effectually maintained.[2] Nor can we trace many instances (some we perhaps may) of actual hostilities among the nobility of England after the Conquest, except during such an anarchy as the reign of Stephen or the minority of Henry III. Acts of outrage and spoliation were indeed very frequent. The statute of Marlebridge, soon after the baronial wars of Henry III., speaks of the disseizins that had taken place during the late disturbances;[3] and thirty-five verdicts are said to have been given at one court of assize against Foulkes de Breauté, a notorious partisan, who commanded some foreign mercenaries at the beginning of the same reign;[4] but these are faint resemblances of that wide-spreading devastation which the nobles of France and Germany were entitled to carry among their neighbors. The most prominent instance perhaps of what may be deemed a private war arose out of a contention between the earls of Gloucester and Hereford, in the reign of Edward I., during which acts of extraordinary violence were perpetrated; but, far from its having passed for lawful, these powerful nobles were both committed to prison, and paid heavy fines.[5] Thus the tenure of knight-service was not in effect much more peculiarly connected with the pro-

[1] I have modified this passage in consequence of the just animadversion of a periodical critic. In the first edition I had stated too strongly the difference which I still believe to have existed between the customs of England and other feudal countries in respect of private warfare. [Note XV.]

[2] The penalties imposed on breaches of the peace, in Wilkins's Anglo-Saxon Laws, are too numerous to be particularly inserted. One remarkable passage in Domesday appears, by mentioning a legal custom of private feuds in an individual manor, and there only among Welshmen, to afford an inference that it was an anomaly. In the royal manor of Archenfeld in Herefordshire, if one Welshman kills another, it was a custom for the relations of the slain to assemble and plunder the murderer and his kindred, and burn their houses, until the corpse should be interred, which was to take place by noon on the morrow of his death. Of this plunder the king had a third part, and the rest they kept for themselves p. 179.

[3] Stat. 52 H. III.

[4] Matt. Paris, p. 271.

[5] Rot. Parl. vol. i. p. 70.

fession of arms than that of socage. There was nothing in the former condition to generate that high self-estimation which military habits inspire. On the contrary, the burdensome incidents of tenure in chivalry rendered socage the more advantageous, though less honorable of the two.

In the next place, we must ascribe a good deal of efficacy to the old Saxon principles that survived the conquest of William and infused themselves into our common law. A respectable class of free socagers, having, in general, full rights of alienating their lands, and holding them probably at a small certain rent from the lord of the manor, frequently occur in Domesday Book. Though, as I have already observed, these were derived from the superior and more fortunate Anglo-Saxon ceorls, they were perfectly exempt from all marks of villenage both as to their persons and estates. Most have derived their name from the Saxon *soc*, which signifies a franchise, especially one of jurisdiction,[1] and they undoubtedly were suitors to the court-baron of the lord, to whose *soc*, or right of justice, they belonged. They were consequently judges in civil causes, determined before the manorial tribunal.[2] Such privileges set them greatly above the roturiers or

1 It now appears strange to me that I could ever have given the preference to Bracton's derivation of *socage* from *soc de charue*. The word sokeman, which occurs so often in Domesday, is continually coupled with *soca*, a franchise or right of jurisdiction belonging to the lord, whose tenant or rather suitor, the sokeman is described to be. *Soc* is an idle and improbable etymology; especially as at the time when sokeman was most in use there was hardly a word of a French root in the language. *Soc* is plainly derived from *seco*, and therefore cannot pass for a Teutonic word.

I once thought the etymology of Bracton and Lyttelton curiously illustrated by a passage in Blomefield's Hist. of Norfolk, vol. iii. p. 538 (folio). In the manor of Cawston a man with a brazen hand holding a ploughshare was carried before the steward as a sign that it was held by socage of the duchy of Lancaster.

2 The feudal courts, if under that name we include those of landholders having grants of soc, sac, infangthef, &c., from the crown, had originally a jurisdiction exclusive of the county and hundred. The Laws of Henry I., a treatise of great authority as a contemporary exposition of the law of England in the middle of the twelfth century, just before the great though silent revolution which brought in the Norman jurisprudence, bear abundant witness to the territorial courts, collateral to and independent of those of the sheriff. Other proofs are easily furnished for a later period. Vide Chron. Jocelyn de Brakelonde, *et alia.*

It is nevertheless true that territorial jurisdiction was never so extensive as in governments of a more aristocratical character, either in criminal or civil cases. 1. In the laws ascribed to Henry I. it is said that all great offences could only be tried in the king's court, or by his commission. c. 10. Glanvil distinguishes the criminal pleas, which could only be determined before the king's judges, from those which belong to the sheriff. Treason, murder, robbery, and rape were of the former class; theft of the latter. l. xiv. The criminal jurisdiction of the sheriff is entirely taken away by Magna Charta c. 17. Sir E. Coke says the territorial franchises of infangthief and outfangthief "had some continuance afterwards, but either by this act, or per desuetudinem for inconvenience, these franchises within manors are antiquated and gone." 2 Inst. p. 31. The statute hardly seems to reach them; and they were certainly both claimed and exercised as late as the

censiers of France. They were all Englishmen, and their tenure strictly English; which seems to have given it credit in the eyes of our lawyers, when the name of Englishman was affected even by those of Norman descent, and the laws of Edward the Confessor became the universal demand. Certainly Glanvil, and still more Bracton, treat the tenure in free socage with great respect. And we have reason to think that this class of freeholders was very numerous even before the reign of Edward I.

But, lastly, the change which took place in the constitution of parliament consummated the degradation, if we must use the word, of the lower nobility: I mean, not so much their attendance by representation instead of personal summons, as their election by the whole body of freeholders, and their separation, along with citizens and burgesses, from the house of peers. These changes will fall under consideration in the following chapter.

reign of Edward I. Blomefield mentions two instances, both in 1285, where executions for felony took place by the sentence of a court-baron. In these cases the lord's privilege was called in question at the assizes, by which means we learn the transaction; it is very probable that similar executions occurred in manors where the jurisdiction was not disputed. Hist. of Norfolk, vol. i. p. 313; vol. iii. p. 50. Felonies are now cognizable in the greater part of boroughs; though it is usual, except in the most considerable places, to remit such as are not within benefit of clergy to the justices of gaol delivery on their circuit. This jurisdiction, however, is given, or presumed to be given, by special charter, and perfectly distinct from that which was feudal and territorial. Of the latter some vestiges appear to remain in particular liberties, as for example the Soke of Peterborough; but most, if not all, of these local franchises have fallen, by right or custom, into the hands of justices of the peace. A territorial privilege somewhat analogous to criminal jurisdiction, but considerably more oppressive, was that of private gaols. At the parliament of Merton, 1237, the lords requested to have their own prison for trespasses upon their parks and ponds, which the king refused. Stat. Merton, c. 11. But several lords enjoyed this as a particular franchise; which is saved by the statute 5 H. IV. c. 10, directing justices of the peace to imprison no man, except in the common gaol. 2. The civil jurisdiction of the court-baron was rendered insignificant, not only by its limitation in personal suits to debts or damages not exceeding forty shillings, but by the writs of *tolt* and *pone*, which at once removed a suit for lands, in any state of its progress before judgment, into the county court or that of the king. The statute of Marlebridge took away all appellant jurisdiction of the superior lord, for false judgment in the manorial court of his tenant, and thus aimed another blow at the feudal connection. 52 H. III. c. 19. 3. The lords of the counties palatine of Chester and Durham, and the Royal franchise of Ely, had not only a capital jurisdiction in criminal cases, but an exclusive cognizance of civil suits; the former still is retained by the bishops of Durham and Ely, though much shorn of its ancient extent by an act of Henry VIII. (27 H. VIII. c. 24), and administered by the king's justices of assize; the bishops or their deputies being put only on the footing of ordinary justices of the peace. Id. s. 20.

NOTES TO CHAPTER VIII.

(PARTS I. AND II.)

NOTE I. Page 256.

THESE seven princes enumerated by Bede have been called Bretwaldas, and they have, by late historians, been advanced to higher importance and to a different kind of power than, as it appears to me, there is any sufficient ground to bestow on them. But as I have gone more fully into this subject in a paper published in the 32d volume of the 'Archæologia,' I shall content myself with giving the most material parts of what will there be found.

Bede is the original witness for the seven monarchs who before his time had enjoyed a preponderance over the Anglo-Saxons south of the Humber: — "Qui cunctis australibus gentis Anglorum provinciis, quæ Humbræ fluvio et contiguis ei terminis sequestrantur a Borealibus, imperârunt." (Hist. Eccl. lib. ii. c. 5.) The four first-named had no authority over Northumbria; but the last three being sovereigns of that kingdom, their sway would include the whole of England.

The Saxon Chronicle, under the reign of Egbert, says that he was the eighth who had a dominion over Britain; using the remarkable word Bretwalda, which is found nowhere else. This, by its root *waldan*, a Saxon verb, to rule (whence our word *wield*), implies a ruler of Britain or the Britons. The Chronicle then copies the enumeration of the other seven in Bede, with a little abridgment. The kings mentioned by Bede are Ælli or Ella, founder of the kingdom of the South-Saxons, about 477; Ceaulin, of Wessex, after the interval of nearly a century; Ethelbert, of Kent, the first Christian king; Redwald, of East Anglia; after him three Northumbrian kings in succession, Edwin, Oswald, Oswin. We have, therefore, sufficient testimony that before the middle of the seventh century four kings, from four Anglo-Saxon kingdoms, had, at intervals of time, become superior to the rest; excepting, however, the Northumbrians, whom Bede distinguishes, and whose subjection to a southern prince does not appear at all probable. None, therefore, of these could well have been called Bretwalda, or ruler of the Britons, while not even his own countrymen were wholly under his sway.

We now come to three Northumbrian kings, Edwin, Oswald, and Oswin, who ruled, in Bede's language, with greater power than the preceding, over all the inhabitants of Britain, both English and British, with the sole exception of the men of Kent. This he reports in another place with respect to Edwin, the first Northumbrian convert to Christianity; whose worldly power, he says, increased so much that, what no English sovereign had done before, he extended his dominion to the furthest bounds of Britain, whether inhabited by English or by Britons. (Hist. Eccl. lib. ii. c. 9.) Dr. Lingard has pointed out a remarkable confirmation of this testimony of Bede in a Life of St. Columba, published by the Bollandists. He names Cuminius, a contemporary writer, as the author of this Life; but I find that these writers give several reasons for doubting whether it be his. The words are as follow:—"Oswaldum regem, in procinctu belli castra metatum, et in papilione supra pulvillum dormientem allocutus est, et ad bellum procedere jussit. Processit et secuta est victoria; reversusque postea totius Britanniæ imperator ordinatus a Deo, et tota incredula gens baptizata est." (Acta Sanctorum, Jun. 23.) This passage, on account of the uncertainty of the author's age, might not appear sufficient. But this anonymous Life of Columba is chiefly taken from that by Adamnan, written about 700; and in that Life we find the important expression about Oswald—"totius Britanniæ imperator ordinatus a Deo." We have, therefore, here probably a distinct recognition of the Saxon word Bretwalda; for what else could answer to emperor of Britain? And, as far as I know, it is the only one that exists. It seems more likely that Adamnan refers to a distinct title bestowed on Oswald by his subjects, than that he means to assert as a fact that he truly ruled over all Britain. This is not very credible, notwithstanding the language of Bede, who loves to amplify the power of favorite monarchs. For though it may be admitted that these Northumbrian kings enjoyed at times a preponderance over the other Anglo-Saxon principalities, we know that both Edwin and Oswald lost their lives in great defeats by Penda of Mercia. Nor were the Strathcluyd Britons in any permanent subjection. The name of Bretwalda, as applied to these three kings, though not so absurd as to make it incredible that they assumed it, asserts an untruth.

It is, however, at all events plain from history that they obtained their superiority by force; and we may probably believe the same of the four earlier kings enumerated by Bede. An elective dignity, such as is now sometimes supposed, cannot be presumed in the absence of every semblance of evidence, and against manifest probability. What appearance do we find of a federal union among the kites and crows, as Milton calls them, of the Heptarchy? What but the law of the strongest could have kept these rapacious and restless warriors from tearing the vitals of their common country? The influence of Christianity in effecting a comparative civilization, and producing a sense of political as well as religious unity, had not yet been felt.

Mercia took the place of Northumberland as the leading kingdom of the Heptarchy in the eighth century. Even before Bede brought his Ecclesiastical History to a close, in 731, Ethelbald of Mercia had become paramount over the southern kingdoms; certainly more so than any of the first four who are called by the Saxon Chronicler Bretwaldas. "Et hæ omnes provinciæ cæteræque australes ad confinium usque Hymbræ fluminis cum suis quæque regibus, Merciorum regi Ethelbaldo subjectæ sunt." (Hist. Eccl. v. 23.) In a charter of Ethelbald he styles himself—"non solum Mercensium sed et universarum provinciarum quæ communi vocabulo dicuntur Suthangli divina largiente gratia rex." (Codex Ang.-Sax. Diplom. i. 96; vide etiam 100, 107.) Offa, his successor, retained great part of this ascendency, and in his charters sometimes styles himself "rex Anglorum," sometimes "rex Merciorum simulque aliarum circumquaque nationum." (Ib. 162, 166, 167, *et alibi.*) It is impossible to define the subordination of the southern kingdoms, but we cannot reasonably imagine it to have been less than they paid in the sixth century to Ceaulin and Ethelbert. Yet to these potent sovereigns the Saxon Chronicle does not give the name Bretwalda, nor a place in the list of British rulers. It copies Bede in this passage servilely, without regard to events which had occurred since the termination of his history.

I am, however, inclined to believe, combining the passage Adamnan with this less explicitly worded of the Saxon Chronicle, that the three Northumbrian kings, having been victorious in war and paramount over the minor kingdoms, were really designated, at least among their own subjects, by the name Bretwalda, or ruler of Britain, and totius Britanniæ imperator. The assumption of so pompous a title is characteristic of the vaunting tone which continued to increase down to the Conquest. We may, therefore, admit as probable that Oswald of Northumbria in the seventh century, as well as his father Edwin and his son Oswin, took the appellation of Bretwalda to indicate the supremacy they had obtained, not only over Mercia and the other kingdoms of their countrymen, but, by dint of successful invasions, over the Strathcluyd Britons and the Scots beyond the Forth. I still entertain the greatest doubts, to say no more, whether this title was ever applied to any but these Northumbrian kings. It would have been manifestly ridiculous, too ridiculous, one would think, even for Anglo-Saxon grandiloquence, to confer it on the first four in Bede's list; and if it expressed an acknowledged supremacy over the whole nation, why was it never assumed in the eighth century?

We do not derive much additional information from later historians. Florence of Worcester, who usually copies the Saxon Chronicle, merely in this instance transcribes the text of Bede with more exactness than that had done; he neither repeats nor translates the word Bretwalda. Henry of Huntingdon, after repeating the passage in Bede, adds Egbert to the seven kings therein mentioned, calling him "rex et monarcha totius Britanniæ," doubtless as a translation of the word Bretwalda in the Saxon Chronicle; subjoining the names of Alfred and Edgar as ninth and tenth in the list. Egbert, he says, was eighth of ten kings remarkble for their bravery and power (fortissimorum) who have reigned in England. It is strange that Edward the Elder, Athelstan and Edred are passed over.

Rapin was the first who broached the theory of an elective Bretwalda, possessing a sort of monarchical supremacy in the constitution of the Heptarchy; something like, as he says, the dignity of stadtholder of the Netherlands. It was taken up in later times by Turner, Lingard, Palgrave, and Lappenberg. But for this there is certainly no evidence whatever; nor do I perceive in it anything but the very reverse of probability, especially in the earlier instances. With what we read in Bede we may be content, confirmed as with respect to a Northumbrian sovereign it appears to be by the Life of Columba; and the plain history will be no more than this — that four princes from among the southern Anglo-Saxon kingdoms, at different times obtained, probably by force, a superiority over the rest; that afterwards three Northumbrian kings united a similar supremacy with the government of their own dominions; and that, having been successful in reducing the Britons of the north and also the Scots into subjection, they assumed the title of Bretwalda, or ruler of Britain. This title was not taken by any later kings, though some in the eighth century were very powerful in England; nor did it attract much attention, since we find the word only once employed by an historian, and never in a charter. The consequence I should draw is, that too great prominence has been given to the appellation, and undue inferences sometimes derived from it, by the eminent writers above mentioned.

NOTE II. Page 258.

The reduction of all England under a single sovereign was accomplished by Edward the Elder, who may, therefore, be reckoned the founder of our monarchy more justly than Egbert. The five Danish towns, as they were called, Leicester, Lincoln, Stamford, Derby, and Nottingham, had been brought under the obedience of his gallant sister Æthelfleda, to whom Alfred had intrusted the viceroyalty of Mercia. Edward himself subdued the Danes of East Anglia and Northumberland. In 922 "the kings of the North Welsh sought him to be their lord." And in 924 "chose him for father and lord, the king of the Scots and the whole nation of the Scots, and Regnald, and the son of Eadulf, and all those who dwell in Northumberland, as well English as Danes and Northmen and others, and also the king of the Strathcluyd Britons, and all the Strathcluyd Britons." (Sax. Chronicle.)

Edward died next year; of his son Æthelstan it is said

that "he ruled all the kings who were in this island; first, Howel king of West Welsh, and Constantine king of the Scots, and Uwen king of the Gwentian (Silurian) people, and Ealdrad son of Ealdalf of Bamborough, and they confirmed the peace by pledge and by oaths at the place which is called Earnot, on the fourth of the Ides of July; and they renounced all idolatry, and after that submitted to him in peace." (Id. A.D. 926.)

From this time a striking change is remarkable in the style of our kings. Edward, of whom we have no extan charters after these great submissions of the native princes calls himself only Angul-Saxonum rex. But in those of Athelstan, such as are reputed genuine (for the tone is still more pompous in some marked by Mr. Kemble with an asterisk), we meet, as early as 927, with "totius Britanniæ monarchus, rex, rector, or basileus;" "totius Britanniæ solio sublimatus;" and other phrases of *insular* sovereignty. (Codex Diplom. vol. ii. *passim;* vol. v. 198.) What has been attributed to the imaginary Bretwaldas, belonged truly to the kings of the tenth century. And the grandiloquence of their titles is sometimes almost ridiculous. They affected particularly that of Basileus as something more imperial than king, and less easily understood. Edwy and Edgar are remarkable for this pomp, which shows itself also in the spurious charters of older kings. But Edmund and Edred with more truth and simplicity had generally denominated themselves "rex Anglorum, cæterorumque in circuitu persistentium gubernator et rector." (Codex Diplom. vol. ii. *passim.*) An expression which was retained sometimes by Edgar. And though these exceedingly pompous phrases seem to have become less frequent in the next century, we find "totius Albionis rex," and equivalent terms, in all the charters of Edward the Confessor.[1]

But looking from these charters, where our kings asserted what they pleased, to the actual truth, it may be inquired whether Wales and Scotland were really subject, and in what degree, to the self-styled Basileus at Winchester. This is a debatable land, which, as merely historical antiquities are far

[1] "As a general rule it may be observed that before the tenth century the proem is comparatively simple; that about that time the influence of the Byzantine court began to be felt; and that from the latter half of that century pedantry and absurdity struggle for the mastery." Kemble's Introduction to vol. ii. p. x.

from being the object of this work, I shall leave to national prejudice or philosophical impartiality. Edgar, it may be mentioned, in a celebrated charter, dated in 964, asserts his conquest of Dublin and great part of Ireland: — "Mihi autem concessit propitia divinitas cum Anglorum imperio omnia regna insularum oceani cum suis ferocissimis regibus usque Norwegiam, maximamque partem Hiberniæ cum suâ nobilissimâ civitate Dublinia Anglorum regno subjugare; quos etiam omnes meis imperiis colla subdere, Dei favente gratiâ, coegi." (Codex Diplom. ii. 404.) No historian mentions any conquest or even expedition of this kind. Sir Francis Palgrave (ii. 258) thinks the charter "does not contain any expression which can give rise to suspicion; and its tenor is entirely consistent with history:" meaning, I presume, that the silence of history is no contradiction. Mr. Kemble, however, marks it with an asterisk. I will mention here that an excellent summary of Anglo-Saxon history, from the earliest times to the Conquest, has been drawn up by Sir F. Palgrave, in the second volume of the Rise and Progress of the English Commonwealth.

NOTE III. Page 262.

The proper division of freemen was into eorls and ceorls: ge eorle — ge ceorle; ge eorlische — ge ceorlische; occur in several Anglo-Saxon texts. The division corresponds to the phrase "gentle and simple" of later times. Palgrave (p. 11) agrees with this. Yet in another place (vol. ii. p. 352) he says, "It certainly designated a person of noble race. This is the form in which it is employed in the laws of Ethelbert. The earl and the churl are put in opposition to each other as the two extremes of society." I cannot assent to this; the second thoughts of my learned friend I like less than the first. It seems like saying men and women are the extremes of humanity, or odd and even of number. What was in the middle?[1] Mr. Kemble, in his Glossary to Beowulf, explains eorl by *vir fortis, pugil vir;* and proceeds thus: — "*Eorl* is not a title, as with us, any more than *beorn* . . . We

[1] An earlier writer has fallen into the same mistake, which should be corrected, as the equivocal meaning of the word eorl might easily deceive the reader. "Ceorls, or cyrlise men, are opposed, as the lowest description of freemen, to eorls, as the highest of the nobility." Heywood "On Ranks among the Anglo Saxons," p. 278.

may safely look upon the origin of earl, as a title of rank, to be the same as that of the *comites*, who, according to Tacitus, especially attached themselves to any distinguished chief. That these *fideles* became under a warlike prince something more important than the early constitution of our tribes contemplated, is natural, and is moreover proved by history, and they laid the foundations of that system which recognizes the king as the fountain of honor. In the later Anglo-Saxon constitution, ealdorman was a prince, a governor of a country or small kingdom, *sub-regulus;* he was a constitutional officer; the earl was not an officer at all, though afterwards the government of counties came to be intrusted to him; at first, if he had a *beneficium* or feud at all, it was a horse, or rings, or arms; afterwards lands. This appears constantly in Beowulf, and requires no further remark." A speech indeed ascribed to Withred king of Kent, in 696, by the Saxon Chronicle, would prove earls to have been superior to aldermen in that early age. But the forgery seems too gross to impose on any one. Ceorl, in Beowulf, is a man, *vir;* it is sometimes a husband; a woman is said *ceorlian, i. e.* viro se adjungere.

Dr. Lingard has clearly apprehended, and that long before Mr. Kemble's publication, the *distributive* character of the words eorl and ceorl. "Among the Anglo-Saxons the free population was divided into the eorl and ceorl, the man of noble and ignoble descent;" and he well observes that "by not attending to this meaning of the word eorl, and rendering it earl, or rather *comes,* the translators of the Saxon laws have made several passages unintelligible." (Hist. of England, i. 468.) Mr. Thorpe has not, as I conceive, explained the word as accurately or perspicuously as Mr. Kemble. He says, in his Glossary to Ancient English Laws, — "Eorl, comes, satelles principis. This is the prose definition of the word; in Anglo-Saxon and Old Saxon poetry it signifies man, though generally applied to one of consideration on account of his rank or valor. Its etymon is unknown, one deriving it from Old Norse, *ar,* minister, satelles; another from *jara,* prœlium. (See B. Hald. voc. Jarl, and the Gloss. to Sœmund, by Edda, t. i. p. 597.) This title, which seems introduced by the Jutes of Kent, occurs frequently in the laws of the kings of that district, the first mention of it being in Ethelbert, 13. Its more general use among us dates from the later Scandinavian invasions; and though originally only a title of honor, it became in later times one of office, nearly supplanting the older and more Saxon one of ealdorman." The editor does not here particularly advert to the use of the word in opposition to ceorl. That a word merely expressing man may become appropriate to men of dignity appears from *bar* and *baro;* and something analogous is seen in the Latin *vir.* Lappenberg (vol. ii. p. 13) says,—"The title of eorl occurs in early times among the laws of the Kentish kings, but became more general only in the Danish times, and is probably of old Jutish origin." This is a confusion of words: in the laws of the Kentish kings, eorl means only *ingenuus*, or, if we please, *nobilis;* in the Danish times it was *comes*, as has just been pointed out.

Such was the eorl, and such the ceorl, of our forefathers —one a gentleman, the other a yeoman, but both freemen. We are liable to be misled by the new meaning which from the tenth century was attached to the former word, as well as by the inveterate prejudice that nobility of birth must carry with it something of privilege above the most perfect freedom. But we do not appreciate highly enough the value of the latter in a semi-barbarous society. The eorlcundman was generally, though not necessarily, a freeholder; he might, unless restrained by special tenure, depart from or alienate his land; he was, if a freeholder, a judge in the county court: he might marry, or become a priest, at his discretion; his oath weighed heavily in compurgation; above all, his life was valued at a high composition; we add, of course, the general respect which attaches itself to the birth and position of a gentleman. Two classes indeed there were, both "eorlcund," or of gentle birth, and so called in opposition to ceorls, but in a relative subordination. Sir F. Palgrave has pointed out the distinction in a passage which I shall extract:—

"The whole scheme of the Anglo-Saxon law is founded upon the presumption that every freeman, not being a 'hlaford,' was attached to a superior, to whom he was bound by fealty, and from whom he could claim a legal protection or warranty, when accused of any transgression or crime. If, therefore, the 'eorlcund' individual did not possess the real property which, either from its tenure or its extent, was such as to constitute a lordship, he was then ranked in the very numerous class whose members, in Wessex and its dependent states, were originally known by the name of 'sithcundmen,' an appellation which we may paraphrase by the heraldic expression, 'gentle by birth and blood.'[1] This term of sithcundman, however, was only in use in the earlier periods. After the reign of Alfred it is lost; and the most comprehensive and significant denomination given to this class is that of 'sixhœndmen,' indicating their position between the highest and lowest law-worthy classes of society. Other designations were derived from their services and tenures. Radechnights, and lesser thanes, seem to be included in this rank, and to which, in many instances, the general name of sokemen was applied. But, however designated, the sithcundman, or sixhœndman, appears in every instance in the same relative position in the community — classed amongst the nobility, whenever the eorl and the ceorl are placed in direct opposition to each other; always considered below the territorial aristocracy, and yet distinguished from the villainage by the important right of selecting his hlaford at his will and pleasure. By common right the 'sixhœndman' was not to be annexed to the glebe. To use the expressions employed by the compilers of Domesday, he could 'go with his land wheresoever he chose,' or, leaving his land, he might 'commend' himself to any hlaford who would accept of his fealty." (Vol. i. p. 14.)[2]

It may be pointed out, however, which Sir F. P. has here forgotten to observe, that the distinction of weregild between the twelfhynd and syxhynd was abolished by a treaty between Alfred and Guthrum. (Thorpe's Ancient Laws, p. 66.) This indeed affects only the reciprocity of law between English and Danes. Yet it is certain that from that time we rarely find mention of the intermediate rank between the twelfhynd, or superior thane, and the twyhynd or ceorl. The sithcundman, it would seem, was from henceforth rated at the same composition as his lord; yet there is one apparent exception (I have not observed any other) in the laws of Henry I. It is said here (C. 76), — "Liberi alii twyhyndi, alii syxhyndi, alii twelfhyndi. Twyhyndus homo dicitur, cujus wera est 22 solidorum, qui faciunt 4 libras. Twelfhyndus est homo plene nobilis, id est, thainus, cujus wera est 1200 solidorum,

[1] Is not the word sithcundman properly descriptive of his dependence on a lord, from the Saxon verb *sithian*, to follow?

[2] This right of choosing a lord at pleasure, so little feudal, seems not indisputable enough to warrant so general a proposition. The conditions of tenure in the eleventh century, whatever they may once have been, had become exceedingly various.

qui faciunt libras 25." It is remarkable that, though the syxhyndman is named at first, nothing more is said of him, and the twelfhyndman is defined to be a thane. It appears from several passages that the laws recorded in this treatise are chiefly those of the West Saxons, which differed in some respects from those of Mercia, Kent, and the Danish counties. With regard to the word sithcund, it does occur once or twice in the laws of Edward the Elder. It might be supposed that the Danes had retained the principle of equality among all of gentle birth, common, as we read in Grimm, to the northern nations, which the distinction brought in by the kings of Kent between two classes of eorls or thanes seemed to contravene. We shall have occasion, however, to quote a passage from the laws of Canute, which indicates a similar distinction of rank among the Danes themselves, whatever might be the rule as to composition for life.

The influence of Danish connections produced another great change in the nomenclature of ranks. *Eorl* lost its general sense of good birth and became an official title, for the most part equivalent to alderman, the governor of a shire or district. It is used in this sense, for the first time, in the laws of Edward the Elder. Yet it had not wholly lost its primary meaning, since we find *eorlish* and *ceorlish* opposed, as distributive appellations, in one of Athelstan. (Id. p. 96.) It is said in a sort of compilation, entitled, "On Oaths, Weregilds, and Ranks," subjoined to the laws of Edward the Elder, but bearing no date, that "It was whilom in the laws of the English . . . . that, if a thane thrived so that he became an eorl, then was he henceforth of eorl-right worthy." (Ancient Laws, p. 81.[1]) But this passage is wanting in one manuscript, though not in the oldest, and we find, just before it, the old distributive opposition of eorl and ceorl. It is certainly a remarkable exception to the common use of the word eorl in any age, and has led Mr. Thorpe to suppose that the rank of earl could be obtained by landed wealth. The learned editor thinks that "these pieces cannot have had a later origin than the period in which they here stand. Some of them are probably much earlier" (p. 76). But the mention of the "Danish law," in

[1] The references are to the folio edition of 'Ancient Laws and Institutes of England,' 1840, as published by the Record Commission. I fear this may cause some trouble to those who possess the octavo edition, which is much more common.

p. 79, seems much against an earlier date; and this is so mentioned as to make us think that the Danes were then in subjection. In the time of Edgar eorl had fully acquired its secondary meaning; in its original sense it seems to have been replaced by thane. Certain it is that we find thane opposed to ceorl in the later period of Anglo-Saxon monuments, as eorl is in the earlier—as if the law knew no other broad line of demarcation among laymen, saving always the official dignities and the royal family.[1] And the distinction between the greater and the lesser thanes was not lost, though they were put on a level as to composition. Thus, in the Forest Laws of Canute:—"Sint jam deinceps quattuor ex liberalioribus hominibus qui habent salvas suas consuetudines, quos Angli thegnes appellant, in qualibet regni mei provincia constituti. Sint sub quolibet eorum quattuor ex mediocribus hominibus, quos Angli lesthegenes nuncupant, Dani vero yoongmen vocant, locati." (Ancient Laws, p. 183.) Meantime the composition for an earl, whether we confine that word to office or suppose that it extended to the wealthiest landholders, was far higher in the later period than that for a thane, as was also his heriot when that came into use. The heriot of the king's thane was above that of what was called a medial thane, or mesne vassal, the sithcundman, or syxhynder, as I apprehend, of an earlier style.

In the laws of the continental Saxons we find the rank corresponding to the *eorlcunde* of our own country, denominated *edelingi* or noble, as opposed to the *frilingi* or ordinary freemen. This appellation was not lost in England, and was perhaps sometimes applied to nobles; but we find it generally reserved for the royal family.[2] *Ethel* or noble, sometimes contracted, forms, as is well known, the peculiar prefix to the names of our Anglo-Saxon royal house. And the word *atheling* was used, not as in Germany for a noble, but a prince; and his composition was not only above that of a thane, but of an alderman. He ranked as an archbishop in this respect, the alderman as a bishop. (Leges

1 "That the thane, at least originally, was a military follower, a holder by military service, seems certain; though in later times the rank seems to have been enjoyed by all great landholders, as the natural concomitant of possession to a certain value. By Mercian law, he appears as a 'twelfhynde' man, his 'wer' being 1200 shillings. That this dignity ceased from being exclusively of a military character is evident from numerous passages in the laws, where thanes are mentioned in a judicial capacity, and as civil officers." Thorpe's Glossary to Ancient Laws, voc. Thegen.

2 Thorpe's Glossary.

Ethelredi, p. 141.) It is necessary to mention this, lest, in speaking of the words *eorl* and *ceorl* as originally distributive, I should seem to have forgotten the distinctive superiority of the royal family. But whether this had always been the case I am not prepared to determine. The aim of the later kings, I mean after Alfred, was to carry the monarchical principle as high as the temper of the nation would permit. Hence they prefer to the name of king, which was associated in all the Germanic nations with a limited power, the more indefinite appellations of imperator and basileus. And the latter of these they borrowed from the Byzantine court, liking it rather better than the other, not merely out of the pompous affectation characteristic of their style in that period, but because, being less intelligible, it served to strike more awe, and also probably because the title of western emperor seemed to be already appropriated in Germany. It was natural that they would endeavor to enhance the superiority of all athelings above the surrounding nobility.

A learned German writer, who distributes freemen into but two classes, considers the *ceorl* of the Anglo-Saxon laws as corresponding to the *ingenuus*, and the *thrall* or *esne*, that is, slave, to the *lidus* of the continent. "*Adelingus* und *liber*, *nobilis* und *ingenuus*, *edelingus* und *frilingus*, *jarl* und *karl*, stehen hier immer als Stand der freien dem der unfreien, dem *servus*, *litus*, *lazzus*, *thrall* entgegen." (Grimm, Deutsche Rechts-Alterthümer, Göttingen, 1828, p. 226 *et alibi*.) *Ceorl*, however, he owns to have "etwas befremdendes," something peculiar. "Der Sinn ist bald *mas*, bald *liber*; allein *colonus*, *rusticus*, *ignobilis*; die Mitte zwischen *nobilis* und *servus*."

It does not appear from the continental laws that the *litus*, or *lidus*, was strictly a slave, but rather a cultivator of the earth for a master, something like the Roman *colonus*, though of inferior estimation.[1] No slave had a composition due to

[1] Mr. Spence remarks (Equitable Jurisdiction, p. 51) — "In the condition of the ceorls we observe one of the many striking examples of the adaptation of the German to the Roman institutions — the ceorls and servile cultivators or *adscriptitii* in England, as well as in the continental states, exactly corresponded with the *coloni* and *inquilini* of the Roman provinces." Yet he immediately subjoins — "The condition of the rural slaves of the Germans nearly resembled that of the Roman *coloni* and Anglo-Saxon ceorls," quoting Tacitus, c. 21. But did the Germans at that time adapt their institutions to those of the Romans? Do we not rather see here an illustration of what appears to me the true theory, that similarity of laws and customs may often be traced to natural causes in the state of society rather than to imitation? My notion is, that the Germans, through principles of common sympathy among the same tribe, the Romans, through memory of republican institutions carried on into the empire, repudiated the

his kindred by law; the price of his life was paid to his lord. By some of the barbaric laws, one third of the composition for a *lidus* went to the kindred; the remainder was the lord's share. This indicates something above the Anglo-Saxon *theow* or slave, and yet considerably below the ceorl. The word, indeed, has been puzzling to continental antiquaries and if, in deference to the authorities of Gothofred and Grimm, we find the *lidi* in the barbaric *læti* of the Roman empire, we cannot think these at least to have been slaves, though they may have become *coloni*. But I am not quite convinced of the identity resting on a slight resemblance of name.

The ceorl, or *villanus*, as we find him afterwards called in Domesday, was not generally an independent freeholder; but his condition was not always alike. He might acquire land, and if he did this to the extent of five hydes, he became a thane.[1] He required no enfranchisement for this; his own industry might make him a gentleman. This was not the case, at least not so easily, in France. It appears by the will of Alfred, published in 1788, that certain ceorls might choose their own lord; and the text of his law above quoted furnishes some ground for supposing that he extended the privilege to all. The editor of his will says — "All ceorls by the Saxon constitution might choose such man for their landlord as they would" (p. 26). But even though we should think that so high a privilege was conferred by Alfred on the whole class, it is almost certain that they did not continue to enjoy it.

personal servitude of citizens, while they maintained very strict obligations of prædial tenure; and thus the *coloni* of the lower empire on the one hand, the *lidi* and ceorls on the other, were neither absolutely free nor merely slaves.

"In the Lex Frisiorum," says Sir F. Palgrave, in one of his excellent contributions to the Edinburgh Review (xxxii. 16), we find the usual distinctions of *nobilis*, *liber*, and *litus*. The rank of the Teutonic *litus* has been much discussed; he appears to have been a villein, owing many services to his lord, but above the class of slaves." The word villein, it should be remembered, bore several senses: the *litus* was below a Saxon ceorl, but he was also above the villein of Bracton and Littleton.

1 This is not in the laws of Athelstan, to which I have referred in p. 363, nor in any regular statute, but in a kind of brief summary of law, printed by Wilkins and Thorpe. But I think that Sir Francis Palgrave treats this too slightly when he calls it a "traditionary notice of an unknown writer, who says, 'Whilom it was the law of England;' leaving it doubtful whether it were so still, or had been at any definite time." (Edinb. Rev. xxxiv. 263.) Though this phrase is once used, it is said also expressly: — "If a ceorl be enriched to that degree that he have five hydes of land, and any one slay him, let him be paid for with 2000 thrymsas." Thorpe, p. 79. This, a few sentences before, is named as the composition for a thane in the Danelage. And, indeed, though no king's name appears, I have little doubt that these are real statutes, collected probably by some one who has inserted a little of his own.

In the Anglo-Saxon charters the Latin words for the cultivators are "manentes" or "casati." Their number is generally mentioned; and sometimes it is the sole description of land, except its title. The French word *manant* is evidently derived from *manentes*. There seems more difficulty about *casati*, which is sometimes used for persons in a state of servitude, sometimes even for vassals (Du Cange). In our charters it does not bear the latter meaning. (See Codex Diplomaticus, *passim*. Spence on Equitable Jurisdiction, p. 50.)

But when we turn over the pages of Domesday Book, a record of the state of Anglo-Saxon orders of society under Edward the Confessor, we find another kind of difficulty. New denominations spring up, evidently distinguishable, yet such as no information communicated either in that survey or in any other document enables us definitively and certainly to distinguish. Nothing runs more uniformly through the legal documents antecedent to thê Conquest than the broad division of freemen into eorls, afterwards called thanes, and ceorls. In Domesday, which enumerates, as I need hardly say, the inhabitants of every manor, specifying their ranks, not only at the epoch of the survey itself, about 1085, but as they were in the time of king Edward, we find abundant mention of the thanes, generally indeed, but not always in reference to the last-named period. But the word ceorl never occurs. This is immaterial, for by the name *villani* we have upwards of 108,000. And this word is frequently used in the first Anglo-Norman reigns as the equivalent of ceorl. No one ought to doubt that they expressed the same persons. But we find also a very numerous class, above 82,000, styled *bordarii;* a word unknown, I apprehend, to any other public document, certainly not used in the laws anterior to the Conquest. They must, however, have been also ceorls, distinguished by some legal difference, some peculiarity of service or tenure, well understood at the time. A small number are denominated coscetz, or cosceti; a word which does in fact appear in one Anglo-Saxon document. There are also several minor denominations in Domesday, all of which, as they do not denote slaves, and certainly not thanes, must have been varieties of the ceorl kind. The most frequent of these appellations is "cotarii."

But, besides these peasants, there are two appellations

which it is less easy, though it would be more important, to define. These are the *liberi homines* and the *socmanni*. Of the former Sir Henry Ellis, to whose indefatigable diligence we owe the only real analysis of Domesday Book that has been given, has counted up about 12,300; of the latter, about 23,000; forming together about one eighth of the whole population, that is, of male adults. This, it must be understood, was at the time of the survey; but there is no appearance, as far as I have observed, that any material difference in the proportion of these respective classes, or of those below them, had taken place. The confiscation fell on the principal tenants. It is remarkable that in Norfolk alone we have 4487 *liberi homines* and 4588 socmen — the whole enumerated population being 27,087. But in Suffolk, out of a population of 20,491, we find 7470 *liberi homines*, with 1060 socmen. Thus these two counties contained almost all the *liberi homines* of the kingdom. In Lincolnshire, on the other hand, where 11,504 are returned as socmen, the word *liber homo* does not occur. These Lincolnshire socmen are not, as usual in other counties, mentioned among occupiers of the demesne lands, but mingled with the villeins and bordars; sometimes not standing first in the enumeration, so as to show that, in one country, they were both a more numerous and more subordinate class than in the rest of the realm.[1]

The concise distinction between what we should call freehold and copyhold is made by the forms of entering each manor throughout Domesday Book. *Liberi homines* invariably, and socmen I believe, except in Lincolnshire, occupied the one, *villani* and *bordarii* the other. Hence *liberum tenementum* and *villenagium*. What then, in Anglo-Saxon language, was the *kind* of the two former classes? They belong, it will be observed, almost wholly to the Danish counties; not one of either denomination appears in Wessex, as will be seen by reference to Sir H. Ellis's abstract. Were they thanes or ceorls, or a class distinct from both? What was their *were*? We cannot think that a poor cultivator of a few acres, though of his own land, was estimated at 1200

[1] Socmen are returned in not a few instances as sub-tenants of whole manors, but only in Cambridgeshire and some neighboring counties. Ellis's Introd. to Domesday, ii. 389. But this could, it seems, have only originated in the phraseology of different commissioners; for the counties in which we find socmen so much elevated had not belonged to the same Anglo-Saxon kingdom; some were East-Anglian, some Mercian, some probably, as Hertfordshire, of either the Kent or Wessex law.

shillings, like a royal thane. The intermediate composition of the sixhyndman would be a convenient guess; but unfortunately this seems not to have existed in the Danelage. We gain no great light from the laws of Edward the Confessor, which fix the *manbote*, or fine, to the lord for a man slain, regulated according to the *were* due to his children. Manbote, in Danelage, "de villano et de sokemanno 12 oras; de liberis hominibus, tres marcas" (c. 12). Thus, in the Danish counties, of which Lincolnshire was one, the socman was estimated like a *villanus*, and much lower than a *liber homo*. The ora is said to have been one eighth of a mark, consequently the *liber homo's* manbote was double that of the villein or socman. If this bore a fixed ratio to the *were*, we have a new and unheard-of rank who might be called fourhyndmen. But such a distinction is never met with. It would not in itself be improbable that the *liberi homines* who occupied freehold lands, and owed no prædial service, should be raised in the composition for their lives above common ceorls. But in these inquiries new difficulties are always springing forth.

We must upon the whole, I conceive, take the socmen for twyhyndi, for ceorls more fortunate than the rest, who had acquired some freehold land, or to whose ancestors possibly it had been allotted in the original settlement. It indicates a remarkable variety in the condition of these East-Anglian counties, Norfolk and Suffolk, and a more diffused freedom in their inhabitants. The population, it must strike us, was greatly higher, relatively to their size, than in any other part of England; and the multitude of small manors and of parish churches, which still continue, bespeaks this progress. The socmen, as well as the *liberi homines*, in whose condition there may have been little difference, except in Lincolnshire, where we have seen that, for whatever cause, those denominated socmen were little, if at all, better than the *villani*, were all *commended;* they had all some lord, though bearing to him a relation neither of fief nor of villenage; they could in general, though with some exceptions, alienate their lands at pleasure; it has been thought that they might pay some small rent in acknowledgment of commendation; but the one class undoubtedly, and probably the other, were freeholders in every legal sense of the word, holding by that ancient and respectable tenure, free and common socage, or in a manner at least analogous to it. Though socmen are chiefly mentioned in the Danelage, other obscure denominations of occupiers occur in Wessex and Mercia, which seem to have denoted a similar class. But the style of Domesday is so concise, and so far from uniform, that we are very liable to be deceived in our conjectural inferences from it.

It may be remarked here that many of our modern writers draw too unfavorable a picture of the condition of the Anglo-Saxon ceorl. Few indeed fall into the capital mistake of Mr. Sharon Turner, by speaking of him as legally in servitude, like the villein of Bracton's age. But we often find a tendency to consider him as in a very uncomfortable condition, little caring "to what lion's paw be might fall," as Bolingbroke said in 1745, and treated by his lord as a miserable dependant. Half a century since, in the days of Sir William Jones, Granville Sharp, and Major Cartwright, the Anglo-Saxon constitution was built on universal suffrage; every man in his tything a partaker of sovereignty, and sending from his rood of land an annual representative to the witenagemot. Such a theory could not stand the first glimmerings of historical knowledge in a mind tolerably sound. But while we absolutely deny political privileges of this kind to the ceorl, we need not assert his life to have been miserable. He had very definite legal rights, and acknowledged capacities of acquiring more; that he was sometimes exposed to oppression is probable enough; but, in reality, the records of all kinds that have descended to us do not speak in such strong language of this as we may read in those of the continent. We have no insurrection of the ceorls, no outrages by themselves, no atrocious punishment by their masters, as in Normandy. Perhaps we are a little too much struck by their obligation to reside on the lands which they cultivated; the term *ascriptus glebæ* denotes, in our apprehension, an ignoble servitude. It is, of course, inconsistent with our modern equality of rights; but we are to remember that he who deserted his land, and consequently his lord, did so in order to become a thief. *Hlafordles* men, of whom we read so much, were invariably of this character. What else, indeed, could he become? Children have an idle play, to count buttons, and say, — Gentleman, apothecary, ploughman, thief. Now this, if we consider the second as representative of burgesses in towns, is actually a distributive enumeration, setting aside the clergy of the Anglo-Saxon population; a thane, a burgess, a ceorl, a hlafordles man; that is, a man without land, lord, or law, who lived upon what he could take. For the sake of protecting the honest ceorl from such men, as well as of protecting the lord in what, if property be regarded at all, must be protected, his rights to services legally due, it was necessary to restrain the cultivator from quitting his land. Exceptions to this might occur, as we find among the *liberi homines* and others in Domesday; but it was the general rule. We might also ask whether a lessee for years at present is not in one sense *ascriptus glebæ?* It is true that he may go wherever he will, and, if he continue to pay his rent and perform his covenants, no more can be said. But if he does not this, the law will follow his person, and, though it cannot force him to return, will make it by no means his interest to desert the premises. Such remedies as the law now furnishes were not in the power of the Saxon landlord; but all that any lord could desire was to have the services performed, or to receive a compensation for them.

NOTE IV. Page 263.

THOSE who treat this opinion as chimerical, and seem to suppose that a very large portion of the people of England, during the Anglo-Saxon period, must have been of British descent, do not, I think, sufficiently consider — first, the exterminating character of barbarous warfare, not here confined, as in Gaul, to a single and easy conquest, but protracted for two centuries with the most obstinate resistance of the natives; secondly, the facilities which the possessions of the Welsh and Cumbrian Britons gave to their countrymen for retreat; and thirdly, the natural increase of population among the Saxons, especially when settled in a country already reduced into a state of culture. Nor can the successive migrations from Germany and Norway be shown to have been insignificant. Nothing can be scantier than our historical materials for the fifth and sixth centuries. We cannot also but observe that the silence of the Anglo-Saxon records, at a later time, as to Welsh inhabitants, except in a few passages, affords a presumption that they were not very considerable. Yet these passages, three or four in number (I do not include those which obviously relate to the independent Welsh, whether

Cambrian or Cumbrian), repel the hypothesis that they may have been wholly overlooked and confounded with the ceorls. Their composition was less than that of the ceorl in Wessex and Northumbria; would not this have been mentioned in Kent if they had been found there?

It is by no means unimportant in this question that we find no mention of bishops or churches remaining in the parts of England occupied by the Saxons before their conversion. If a large part of the population was British, though in subjection, what religion did they profess? If it is said that the worshippers of Thor persecuted the Christian priesthood, why have we no records of it in hagiology? Is it conceivable that all alike, priests and people, of that ancient church, pusillanimously relinquished their faith? Sir F. Palgrave indeed meets this difficulty by supposing that the doctrines of Christianity were never cordially embraced by the British tribes, nor had become the national religion. (Engl. Commonwealth, i. 154.) Perhaps this was in some measure the case, though it must be received with much limitation: for the retention of heathen superstitions was not incompatible in that age with a cordial faith; but it will not account for the disappearance of the original clergy in the English kingdoms. Their persecution, which I do not deny, though we have no evidence of it, would be part of the exterminating system; they fled before it into the safe quarters of Wales. And to obtain the free exercise of their religion was probably an additional motive with the nation to seek liberty where it was to be found.

It must have struck every one who has looked into Domesday Book that we find for the most part the same manors, the same parishes, and known by the same names, as in the present age. England had been as completely appropriated by Anglo-Saxon thanes as it was by the Normans who supplanted them. This, indeed, only carries us back to the eleventh century. But in all charters with which the excellent Codex Diplomaticus supplies us we find the boundaries assigned; and these, if they do not establish the identity of manors as well as Domesday Book, give us at least a great number of local names, which subsist, of course with the usual changes of language, to this day. If British names of places occur, it is rarely, and in the border counties, or in Cornwall. No one travelling through England would discover that any people had ever inhabited it before the Saxons, save so far as the mighty Rome has left traces of her empire in some enduring walls, and a few names that betray the colonial city, the Londinium, the Camalodunum, the Lindum. And these names show that the Saxons did not systematically innovate, but often left the appellations of places where they found them given. Their own favorite terminations were *ton* and *by;* both words denoting a village or township, like *ville* in French.[1] In each of these there gradually rose a church, and the ecclesiastical division for the most part corresponds to the civil; though to this, as is well known, there are frequent exceptions. The central point of every township or manor was its lord, the thane to whose court the socagers and ceorls did service; we may believe this to have been so from the days of the Heptarchy, as it was in those of the Confessor.

The *servi* enumerated in Domesday Book are above 25,000, or nearly one eleventh part of the whole. These seem generally to have been domestic slaves, and partly employed in tending the lord's cattle or swine, as Gurth, whom we all remember, the δῖος ὑφορβὸς of the thane Cedric, in Ivanhoe. They are never mentioned as occupiers of land, and have nothing to do with the villeins of later times. A genuine Saxon, as I have said, could only become a slave by his own or his forefather's default, in not paying a weregild, or some legal offence; and of these there might have been many. The few slaves whose names Mr. Turner has collected from Hickes and other authorities appear to be all Anglo-Saxon. (Hist. of Anglo-Saxons, vol. iii. p. 92.) Several others are mentioned in charters quoted by Mr. Wright in the 30th volume of the "Archæologia," p. 220. But the higher proportion which *servi* bore to *villani* and *bordarii*, that is, free ceorls, in the western counties, those in Gloucestershire being almost one third, may naturally induce us to suspect that many were

[1] The word *tun* denotes originally any enclosure. "But its more usual, though restricted sense, is that of a dwelling, a homestead, the house and inland; all, in short, that is surrounded and bounded by a hedge or fence. It is thus capable of being used to express what we mean by the word *town*, viz., a large collection of dwellings; or, like the Scottish town, even a solitary farm-house. It is very remarkable that the largest proportion of the names of places among the Anglo-Saxons should have been formed with this word, while upon the continent of Europe it is never used for such a purpose. In the first two volumes of the Codex Diplomaticus, Dr. Lee computes the proportion of local names compounded with *tun* at one eighth of the whole number; a ratio which unavoidably leads us to the conclusion, that enclosures were as much favored by the Anglo-Saxons as they were avoided by their German brethren beyond the sea." Preface to Kemble's Codex Diplom. vol. iii. p. xxxix.

of British origin; and these might be sometimes in prædial servitude. All inference, however, from the sentence in Domesday, as to the particular state of the enumerated inhabitants, must be conjecturally proposed.

NOTE V. Page 265.

The constituent parts of the witenagemot cannot be certainly determined, though few parts of the Anglo-Saxon polity are more important. A modern writer espouses the more popular theory. "There is no reason extant for doubting that every thane had the right of appearing and voting in the witenagemot, not only of his shire, but of the whole kingdom, without however being bound to personal attendance, the absent being considered as tacitly assenting to the resolutions of those present." (Lappenberg, Hist. of England, vol. ii. p. 317.) Palgrave on the other hand, adheres to the testimony of the Historia Eliensis, that forty hydes of land were a necessary qualification; which of course would have excluded all but very wealthy thanes. He observes, and I believe with much justice, that "proceres terræ" is a common designation of those who composed a *curia regis* synonymous, as he conceives, with the witenagemot. Mr. Thorpe ingeniously conjectures that "inter proceres terræ enumerari" was to have the rank of an earl; on the ground that five hydes of land was a qualification for a common thane, whose heriot, by the laws of Canute, was to that of an earl as one to eight. (Ancient Laws of Anglo-Saxons, p. 81.) Mr. Spence supposes the rank annexed to forty hydes to have been that of king's thane. (Inquiry into Laws of Europe, p. 311.) But they were too numerous for so high a qualification.

Mr. Thorpe explains the word witenagemot thus:—"The supreme council of the nation, or meeting of the witan, This assembly was summoned by the king; and its members, besides the archbishop or archbishops, were the bishops, aldermen, duces, eorls, thanes, abbots, priests, and even deacons. In this assembly, laws, both secular and ecclesiastical, were promulgated and repealed; and charters of grants made by the king confirmed and ratified. Whether this assembly met by royal summons, or by usage at stated periods, is a point of doubt." (Glossary to Ancient Laws.)

This is not remarkably explicit: aldermen are distinguished from earls, and *duces*, an equivocal word, from both;[1] and the important difficulty is slurred over by a general description, thanes. But what thanes? remains to be inquired.

The charters of all Anglo-Saxon sovereigns are attested, not only by bishops and abbots, but by laymen, described, if by any Saxon appellation, as aldermen, or as thanes. Their number is not very considerable; and some appear hence to have inferred that only the superior or royal thanes were present in the witenagemot. But, as the signatures of the whole body could not be required to attest a charter, this is far too precarious an inference. Few, however, probably, are found to believe that the lower thanes flocked to the national council, whatever their rights may have been; and if we have no sufficient proof that any such privileges had been recognized in law or exercised in fact, if we are rather led to consider the sithcundman, or sixhynder, as dependent merely on his lord, in something very analogous to a feudal relation, we may reasonably doubt the strong position which Lappenberg, though following so many of our own antiquaries, has laid down. Probably the traditions of the Teutonic democracy led to the insertion of the assent of the people in some of the Anglo-Saxon laws. But it is done in such a manner as to produce a suspicion that no substantial share in legislation had been reserved to them. Thus, in the preamble of the laws of Withrœd, about 696, we read. "The great men decreed, with the suffrages of all, these dooms." Ina's laws are enacted "with all my ealdormen, and the most distinguished witan of my people." Alfred has consulted his "witan." And this is the uniform word in all later laws in Anglo-Saxon. Canute's, in Latin, run — "Cum consilio primariorum meorum." We have not a hint of any numerous or popular body in the Anglo-Saxon code.

Sir F. Palgrave (i. 637) supposes that the laws enacted in the witenagemot were not valid till accepted by the legisla-

[1] *Dux* appears to be sometimes used in the subscription of charters for *thane*, more commonly for alderman. Thane is generally, in Latin, *minister*. Codex Diplomat. *passim*. Some have supposed *dux* to signify, at least occasionally, a peculiar dignity, called, in Anglo-Saxon, Heretoch (herzog, *Germ.*). This word frequently occurs in the later period. Mr. Thorpe says, — "This title, among the Anglo-Saxons, was, as it implies, given originally to the leader of an army; but in the latter days of the monarchy it seems to have become hereditary in the families of those on whom the government of the provinces formed out of the kingdoms of the Heptarchy were bestowed, and was sometimes used synonymously with those of ealdorman and eorl." Glossary, voc. Heretoga.

tures of the different kingdoms. This seems a paradox, *though* supported with his usual learning and ingenuity. He admits that Edgar "speaks in the tone of prerogative, and directs his statutes to be observed and transmitted by writ to the aldermen of the other subordinate states." (p. 638.) But I must say that this is not very exact. The words in Thorpe's translation are,—"And let many writings be written concerning these things, and sent both to Ælfere, alderman, and to Æthelwine, alderman, and let them [send] in every direction, that this ordinance be known to the poor and rich." (p. 118.) "And yet," Sir F. P. proceeds, "in defiance of this positive injunction, the laws of Edgar were not accepted in Mercia till the reign of Canute the Dane." For this, however, he cites no authority, and I do not find it in the Anglo-Saxon laws. Edgar says,—"And I will that secular rights stand among the Danes with as good laws as they best may choose. But with the English, let that stand which I and my witan have added to the dooms of my forefathers, for the behoof of all the people. Let this ordinance, nevertheless, be common to all the people, whether English, Danes, or Britons, on every side of my dominion." (Thorpe's Ancient Laws, p. 116.) But what does this prove as to *Mercia?* The inference is, that Edgar, when he thought any particular statute necessary for the public weal, enforced it on all his subjects, but did not generally meddle with the Danish usages.

"The laws of the glorious Athelstan had no effect in Kent, the dependent appanage of his crown, until sanctioned by the witan of the shire." It is certainly true that we find a letter addressed to the king in the name of "episcopi tui de Kancia, et omnes Cantescyre thaini, comites et villani," thanking him "quod nobis de pace nostra præcipere voluisti et de commodo nostro quærere et consulere, quia magnum inde nobis est opus divitibus et pauperibus." But the whole tenor of this letter, which relates to the laws enacted at the witenagemot, or "grand synod" of Greatanlea (supposed near Andover), though it expresses approbation of those laws, and repeats some of them with slight variations, does not, in my judgment, amount to a distinct enactment of them; and the final words are not very legislative. "Precamur, Domine, misericordiam tuam, si in hoc scripto alterutrum est vel nimis vel minus, ut hoc emendari jubeas secundum velle tuum. Et nos devote parati sumus ad omnia quæ nobis præcipere velis quæ unquam aliquatenus implere valeamus." (p. 91.)

It is, moreover, an objection to considering this as a formal enactment by the witan of the shire, that it runs in the names of "thaini, comites et villani." Can it be maintained that the ceorls ever formed an integrant element of the legislature in the kingdom of Kent? It may be alleged that their name was inserted, though they had not been formally consenting parties, as we find in some parliamentary grants of money much later. But this would be an arbitrary conjecture, and the terms "omnes thaini," &c., are very large. By *comites* we are to understand, not earls, who in that age would not have been spoken of distinctly from thanes, at least in the plural number, nor postponed to them, but thanes of the second order, sithcundmen, sixhynder. Alfred translates "comes" by "gesith," and the meaning is nearly the same.

In the next year we have a very peremptory declaration of the exclusive rights of the king and his witan. "Athelstan, king, makes known that I have learned that our 'frith' (peace) is worse kept than is pleasing to me, or as at Greatanlea was ordained, and my witan say that I have too long borne with it. Now, I have decreed, with the witan who were with me at Exeter at midwinter, that they [the frithbreakers] shall all be ready, themselves and with wives and property, and with all things, to go whither I will (unless from thenceforth they shall desist), on this condition, that they never come again to the country. And if they shall ever again be found in the country, that they be as guilty as he who may be taken with stolen goods (handhabbende)."

Sir Francis Palgrave, a strenuous advocate for the antiquity of municipal privileges, contends for aldermen, elected by the people in boroughs, sitting and assenting among the king's witan. (Edinb. Rev. xxvi. 26.) "Their seats in the witenagemot were connected as inseparably with their office as their duties in the folkmote. Nor is there any reason for denying to the aldermen of the boroughs the rights and rank possessed by the aldermen of the hundreds; and they, in all cases, were equally elected by the commons." The passage is worthy of consideration, like everything which comes from this ingenious and deeply read author. But we must be staggered by the absence of all proof, and particularly by the fact that we do not find aldermen of towns, so described, among the witnesses of any royal charter. Yet it is possible that such a privilege was confined to the superior thanes, which weakens the inference. We cannot pretend, I think, to deny, in so obscure an inquiry, that some eminent inhabitants (I would here avoid the ambiguous word citizens) of London, or even other cities, might occasionally be present in the witenagemot. But were not these, as we may confidently assume, of the rank of thane? The position in my text is, that ceorls or inferior freemen had no share in the deliberations of that assembly. Nor would these aldermen, if actually present, have been chosen by the court-leet for that special purpose, but as regular magistrates. "Of this great council," Sir F. P. says in another place (Edinb. Rev. xxxiv. 336), "as constituted anterior to the Conquest, we know little more than the name." The greater room, consequently, for hypothesis. In a later work, as has been seen above, Sir F. P. adopts the notion that forty hydes of land were the necessary qualification for a seat in the witenagemot. This is almost inevitably inconsistent with the presence, as by right, of aldermen elected by boroughs. We must conclude, therefore, that he has abandoned that hypothesis. Neither of the two is satisfactory to my judgment.

NOTE VI. Page 267.

The hundred-court, and indeed the hundred itself, do not appear in our Anglo-Saxon code before the reign of Edgar, whose regulations concerning the former are rather full. But we should be too hasty in concluding that it was then first established. Nothing in the language of those laws implies it. A theory has been developed in a very brilliant and learned article of the Edinburgh Review for 1822 (xxxvi. 287), justly ascribed to Sir F. Palgrave, which deduces the hundred from the *hærad* of the Scandinavian kingdoms, the integral unit of the Scandinavian commonwealths. "The Gothic commonwealth is not an unit of which the smaller bodies politic are fractions. They are the units, and the commonwealth is the multiple. Every Gothic monarchy is in the nature of a confederation. It is composed of towns, townships, shires, bailiwicks, burghs, earldoms, dukedoms, all in a certain degree strangers to each other, and separated in jurisdiction. Their magistrates, therefore, in theory at least, ought not to emanate from the sovereign. . . . . The strength of the state ascends from region to region. The representative form of government, adopted by no nation but the Gothic tribes, and originally common to them all, necessarily resulted from this federative system, in which the sovereign was compelled to treat the component members as possessing a several authority."

The hundred was as much, according to Palgrave, the organic germ of the Anglo-Saxon commonwealth, as the hærad was of the Scandinavian. Thus, the leet, held every month, and composed of the tythingmen or head-boroughs, representing the inhabitants, were both the inquest and the jury, possessing jurisdiction, as he conceives, in all cases civil, criminal, and ecclesiastical, though this was restrained after the Conquest. William forbade the bishop or archdeacon to sit there; and by the 17th section of Magna Charta no pleas of the crown could be held before the sheriff, the constable, the coroner, or other bailiff (inferior officer) of the crown. This was intended to secure for the prisoner, on charges of felony, a trial before the king's justices on their circuits; and, from this time, if not earlier, the hundred-court was reduced to insignificance. That, indeed, of the county, retaining its civil jurisdiction, as it still does in name, continued longer in force. In the reign of Henry I., or when the customal (as Sir F. Palgrave denominates what are usually called his laws) was compiled (which in fact was a very little later), all of the highest rank were bound to attend at it. And though the extended jurisdiction of the *curia regis* soon cramped its energy, we are justified in saying that the proceedings before the justices of assize were nearly the same in effect as those before the shiremote. The same suitors were called to attend, and the same duties were performed by them, though under different presidents. The grand jury, it may be remarked, still corresponds, in a considerable degree, to the higher class of landholders bound to attendance in the county-court of the Saxon and Norman periods.

I must request the reader to turn, if he is not already acquainted with it, to this original disquisition in the Edinburgh Review. The analogies between the Scandinavian and Anglo-Saxon institutions are too striking to be disregarded, though some conclusions may have been drawn from them to which we cannot thoroughly agree. If it is alleged that we do not find in the ancient customs of Germany that peculiar scale of society which ascends from the hundred, as a monad of self-government, to the collective unity of a royal commonwealth, it may be replied that we trace the essential principle in the *pagus*, or *gau*, of Tacitus, though perhaps there might be nothing numerical in that territorial direction; that we have, in fact, the centenary distribution under peculiar magistrates in the old continental laws and other documents; and that a large proportion of the inhabitants of England, ultimately coalescing with the rest, so far at least as to acknowledge a common sovereign, came from the very birthplace of Scandinavian institutions. In the Danelage we might expect more traces of a northern policy than in the south and west; and perhaps they may be found.[1] Yet we are not to disregard the effect of countervailing agencies, or the evidence of our own records, which attest, as I must think, a far greater unity of power, and a more paramount authority in the crown, throughout the period which we denominate Anglo-Saxon, than, according to the scheme of a Scandinavian commonwealth sketched in the Edinburgh Review, could be attributed to that very ancient and rude state of society. And there is a question that might naturally be asked, how it happens that, if the division by hundreds and the court of the hundred were parts so essential of the Anglo-Saxon commonwealth that all its unity is derived from them, we do not find any mention of either in the numerous laws and other documents which remain before the reign of Edgar in the middle of the tenth century. But I am far from supposing that hundreds did not exist in a much earlier period.

NOTE VII. Page 270.

"The judicial functions of the Anglo-Saxon monarchs were of a twofold nature; the ordinary authority which the king exercised, like the inferior territorial judges, differing, perhaps, in degree, though the same in kind; and the prerogative supremacy, pervading all the tribunals of the people, and which was to be called into action when they were un-

[1] Vide Leges Ethelredi.

able or unwilling to afford redress. The jurisdiction which he exercised over his own thanes was similar to the authority of any other hlaford; it resulted from the peculiar and immediate relation of the vassal to the superior. Offences committed in the fyrd or army were punished by the king, in his capacity of military commander of the people. He could condemn the criminal, and decree the forfeiture of his property, without the intervention of any other judge or tribunal. Furthermore, the rights which the king had over all men, though slightly differing in "Danelage" from the prerogative which he possessed in Wessex and Mercia, allowed him to take cognizance of almost every offence accompanied by violence and rapine; and amongst these "pleas of the crown" we find the terms, so familiar to the Scottish lawyer and antiquary, of "hamsoken" and "flemen firth," or the crimes of invading the peaceful dwelling, and harboring the outlawed fugitive. (Rise and Progress of Engl. Commonwealth, vol. i. p. 282.)

Edgar was renowned for his strict execution of justice. "Twice in every year, in the winter and in the spring, he made the circuit of his dominions, protecting the lowly, rigidly examining the judgments of the powerful in each province, and avenging all violations of the law." (Id. p. 286.) He infers from some expressions in the history of Ramsey (Gale, iii. 441) — "cum more assueto rex Cnuto regni fines peragraret" — that these judicial eyres continued to be held. It is not at all improbable that such a king as Canute would revive the practice of Edgar; but it was usual in all the Teutonic nations for the king, once after his accession, to make the circuit of his realm. Proofs of this are given by Grimm, p. 237.

In this royal court the sovereign was at least assisted by his "witan," both ecclesiastic and secular. Their consent was probably indispensable; but the monarchical element of Anglo-Saxon polity had become so vigorous in the tenth and eleventh centuries, that we can hardly apply the old Teutonic principle expressed by Grimm. "All judicial power was exercised by the assembly of freemen, under the presidence of an elective or hereditary superior." (Deutsche Rechts-Alterth. p. 749.) This was the case in the county-court, and perhaps had once been so in the court of the king.

The analogies of the Anglo-Saxon monarchy to that of

France during the same period, though not uniformly to be traced, are very striking. The regular jurisdiction over the king's domanial tenants, that over the vassals of the crown, that which was exercised on denial of justice by the lower tribunals, meet us in the two first dynasties of France, and in the early reigns of the third. But they were checked in that country by the feudal privileges, or assumptions of privilege, which rendered many kings of these three races almost impotent to maintain any authority. Edgar and Canute, or even less active princes, had never to contend with the feudal aristocracy. They legislated for the realm; they wielded its entire force; they maintained, not always thoroughly, but in right and endeavor they failed not to maintain, the public peace. The scheme of the Anglo-Saxon commonwealth was better than the feudal; it preserved more of the Teutonic character, it gave more to the common freeman as well as to the king. The love of Utopian romance, and the bias in favor of a democratic origin for our constitution, have led many to overstate the freedom of the Saxon commonwealth; or rather, perhaps, to look less for that freedom where it is really best to be found, in the administration of justice, than in representative councils, which authentic records do not confirm. But in comparison to France or Italy, perhaps to Germany, with the exception of a few districts which had preserved their original customs, we may reckon the Anglo-Saxon polity, at the time when we know most of it, from Alfred to the Conquest, rude and defective as it must certainly appear when tried by the standard of modern ages, not quite unworthy of those affectionate recollections which long continued to attach themselves to its name.

The most important part, perhaps, of the jurisdiction exercised by the Anglo-Saxon kings, as by those of France, was *ob defectum justitiæ*, where redress could not be obtained from an inferior tribunal, a case of not unusual occurrence in those ages. It forms, as has been shown in the second chapter, a conspicuous feature in that feudal jurisprudence which we trace in the establishments of St. Louis, and in Beaumanoir. Nothing could have a more decided tendency to create and strengthen a spirit of loyalty towards the crown, a trust in its power and paternal goodness. "The sources of ordinary jurisdiction," says Sir F. Palgrave, "however extensive, were less important than the powers assigned to the king as the lord and leader of his people; and by which he remedied the defects of the legislation of the state, speaking when the law was silent, and adding new vigor to its administration. It was to the royal authority that the suitor had recourse when he could not obtain 'right at home,' though this appeal was not to be had until he had thrice 'demanded right' in the hundred. If the letter of the law was grievous or burdensome, the alleviation was to be sought only from the king.[1] All these doctrines are to be discerned in the practice of the subsequent ages; in this place it is only necessary to remark that the principle of law which denied the king's help in civil suits, until an endeavor had first been made to obtain redress in the inferior courts, became the leading allegation in the 'Writ of Right Close;' this prerogative process being founded upon the default of the lord's court, and issued lest the king should hear any more complaints of want of justice. And the alleviation of 'the heavy law' is the primary source of the authority delegated by the king to his council, and afterwards assumed by his chancery and chancellor, and from whence our courts of equity are derived." (Rise and Progress of English Commonwealth, vol. i. p. 203.) I hesitate about this last position; the "heavy law" seems to have been the legal fine or penalty for an offence. (Leges Edgar. *ubi suprà.*)

That there was a select council of the Anglo-Saxon kings, distinct from the witenagemot, and in constant attendance upon them, notwithstanding the opinion of Madox and of Allen (Edinb. Rev. xxxv. 8), appears to be indubitable. "From the numerous charters granted by the kings to the church, and to their vassals, which are dated from the different royal vills or manors wherein they resided in their progresses through their dominions, it would appear that there were always a certain number of the optimates in attendance on the king, or ready to obey his summons, to act as his council when circumstances required it. This may have been what afterwards appears as the select council." (Spence's Equitable Jurisdict. p. 72.) The charters published by Mr. Kembler in the Codex Ang.-Sax. Diplomaticus are attested by those whom we may suppose to have been the members of this council, with the exception of some, which, by the

[1] Edgar II. 2; Canute II. 16; Ethelred, 17.

number of witnesses and the importance of the matter, were probably granted in the witenagemot.

The jurisdiction of the king is illustrated by the laws of Edgar. "Now this is the secular ordinance which I will that it be held. This then is just what I will; that every man be worthy of folk-right, as well poor as rich; and that righteous dooms be judged to him; and let there be that remission in the 'bot' as may be becoming before God and tolerable before the world. And let no man apply to the king in any suit, unless he at home may not be worthy of law, or cannot obtain law. If the law be too heavy, let him seek a mitigation of it from the king; and for any *botworthy* crime let no man forfeit more than his 'wer.'" (Thorpe's Ancient Laws, p. 112.) *Bot* is explained in the glossary, "amends, atonement, compensation, indemnification."

This law seems not to include appeals of false judgment, in the feudal phrase. But they naturally come within the spirit of the provision; and "injustum judicium" is named in Leges Henr. Primi, c. 10, among the exclusive pleas of the crown. It does not seem clear to me, as Palgrave assumes, that the disputes of royal thanes with each other came before the king's court. Is there any ground for supposing that they were exempt from the jurisdiction of the county-court? Doubtless, when powerful men were at enmity, no petty court could effectively determine their quarrel, or prevent them from having recourse to arms; such suits would fall naturally into the king's own hands. But the jurisdiction might not be exclusively his; nor would it extend, as of course, to every royal thane; some of whom might be amenable, without much difficulty, to the local courts. It is said in the seventh chapter of the laws of Henry I., which are Anglo-Saxon in substance, concerning the business to be transacted in the county-court, where bishops, earls, and others, as well as "barons and vavassors," that is, king's thanes and inferior thanes in the older language of the law, were bound to be present, — "Agantur itaque primo debita verè Christianitatis jure; secundo regis placita; postremo causæ singulorum dignis satisfactionibus expleantur." The notion that the king's thanes resorted to his court, as to that of their lord or common superior, is merely grounded on feudal principles; but the great constitutional theory of jurisdiction in Anglo-

Saxon times, as Sir F. Palgrave is well aware, was not feudal, but primitive Teutonic.

"The witenagemot," says Allen, "was not only the king's legislative assembly, but his supreme court of judicature." (Edinb. Rev. xxxv. 9; referring for proofs to Turner's History of the Anglo-Saxons.) Nothing can be less questionable than that civil as well as criminal jurisdiction fell within the province of this assembly. But this does not prove that there was not also a less numerous body, constantly accessible, following the king's person, and though not, perhaps, always competent in practice to determine the quarrels of the most powerful, ready to dispose of the complaints which might come before it from the hundred or county courts for delay of justice or manifest wrong. Sir F. Palgrave's arguments for the existence of such a tribunal before the Conquest, founded on the general spirit and analogy of the monarchy, are of the greatest weight. But Mr. Allen had acquired too much a habit of looking at the popular side of the constitution, and, catching at every passage which proved our early kings to have been limited in their prerogative, did not quite attend enough to the opposite scale.

NOTE VIII. Page 273.

Though the following note relates to a period subsequent to the Conquest, yet, as no better opportunity will occur for following up the very interesting inquiry into the origin and progress of trial by jury, I shall place here what appears most worthy of the reader's attention. And, before we proceed, let me observe that the twelve thanes, mentioned in the law of Ethelred, quoted in the text (p. 270), appear to have been clearly analogous to our grand juries. Their duties were to present offenders; they corresponded to the scabini or échevins of the foreign laws. Palgrave has, with his usual clearness, distinguished both compurgators, such as were previously mentioned in the text, and these thanes from real jurors. "Trial by compurgators offers many resemblances to a jury; for the dubious suspicion that fell upon the culprit might often be decided by their knowledge of his general conduct and conversation, or of some fact or circumstance which convinced them of his innocence. The thanes or échevins may equally be confounded with a jury; since the floating, customary, unwritten law of the country was a fact to be ascertained from their belief and knowledge, and, unlike the suitors, they were sworn to the due discharge of their duty. Still, each class will be found to have some peculiar distinction. Virtually elected by the community, the échevins constituted a permanent magistracy, and their duty extended beyond the mere decision of a contested question; but the jurors, when they were traversers, or triers of the issue, were elected by the king's officers, and impanelled for that time and turn. The juror deposed to facts, the compurgator pledged his faith." (English Commonw. i. 248).

In the Anglo-Saxon laws we find no trace of the trial of offences by the judgment, properly so called, of peers, though civil suits were determined in the county court. The party accused by the twelve thanes, on their presentment, or perhaps by a single person, was to sustain his oath of innocence by that of compurgators or by some mode of ordeal. It has been generally doubted whether trial by combat were known before the Conquest; and distinct proofs of it seem to be wanting. Palgrave, however, thinks it rather probable that, in questions affecting rights in land, it may sometimes have been resorted to (p. 224). But let us now come to trial by jury, both in civil and criminal proceedings, as it slowly grew up in the Norman and later periods, erasing from our minds all prejudices about its English original, except in the form already mentioned of the grand inquest for presentment of offenders, and in that which the passage quoted in the text from the History of Ramsey furnishes — the reference of a suit already commenced, by consent of both parties, to a select number of sworn arbitrators. It is to be observed that the thirty-six thanes were to be upon oath, and consequently came very near to a jury.

The period between the Conquest and the reign of Henry II. is one in which the two nations, not yet blended by the effects of intermarriage, and retaining the pride of superiority on the one hand, the jealousy of a depressed but not vanquished spirit on the other, did not altogether fall into a common law. Thus we find in a law of the Conqueror, that, while the Englishman accused of a crime by a Norman had the choice of trial by combat or by ordeal, the Norman must meet the former if his English accuser thought fit to encounter him; but if he dared not, as the insolence of the victor seems to presume, it was sufficient for the foreigner to purge himself by the oaths of his friends, according to the custom of Normandy. (Thorpe, p. 210.)

We have next, in the Leges Henrici Primi, a treatise compiled, as I have mentioned, under Stephen, and not intended to pass for legislative,[1] numerous statements as to the usual course of procedure, especially on criminal charges. These are very carelessly put together, very concise, very obscure, and in several places very corrupt. It may be suspected, and cannot be disproved, that in some instances the compiler has copied old statutes of the Anglo-Saxon period, or recorded old customs which had already become obsolete. But be this as it may, the Leges Henrici Primi still are an important document for that obscure century which followed the Norman invasion. In this treatise we find no allusion to juries; the trial was either before the court of the hundred or that of the territorial judge, assisted by his free vassals. But we do find the great original principle, trial by peers, and, as it is called, *per pais;* that is, in the presence of the country, opposed to a distant and unknown jurisdiction — a principle truly derived from Saxon, though consonant also to Norman law, dear to both nations, and guaranteed to both, as it was claimed by both, in the 29th section of Magna Charta. "Unusquisque per pares suos judicandus est, et ejusdem provinciæ; peregriña autem judicia modis omnibus submovemus." (Leges H. I. c. 31.) It may be mentioned by the way that these last words are taken from a capitulary of Ludovicus Pius, and that the compiler has been so careless as to leave the verb in the first person. Such an inaccuracy might mislead a reader into the supposition that he had before him a real law of Henry I.

It is obvious that, as the court had no function but to see that the formalities of the combat, the ordeal, or the compurgation were duly regarded, and to observe whether the party succeeded or succumbed, no oath from them, nor any reduction of their numbers, could be required. But the law of Normandy had already established the inquest by sworn recogni-

[1] It may be here observed, that, in all probability, the title, Leges Henrici Primi, has been continued to the whole book from the first two chapters, which do really contain laws of Henry I., namely, his general charter, and that to the city of London. A similar inadvertence has caused the well-known book, commonly ascribed to Thomas à Kempis, to be called 'De Imitatione Christi,' which is merely the title of the first chapter.

tors, twelve or twenty-four in number, who were supposed to be well acquainted with the facts; and this in civil as well as criminal proceedings. We have seen an instance of it, not long before the Conquest, among ourselves, in the history of the monk of Ramsey. It was in the development of this amelioration in civil justice that we find instances during this period (Sir F. Palgrave has mentioned several) where a small number have been chosen from the county court and sworn to declare the truth, when the judge might suspect the partiality or ignorance of the entire body. Thus in suits for the recovery of property the public mind was gradually accustomed to see the jurisdiction of the freeholders in their court transferred to a more select number of sworn and well-informed men. But this was not yet a matter of right, nor even probably of very common usage. It was in this state of things that Henry II. brought in the assize of novel disseizin.

This gave an alternative to the tenant on a suit for the recovery of land, if he chose not to risk the combat, of putting himself on the assize; that is, of being tried by four knights summoned by the sheriff and twelve more selected by them, forming the sixteen sworn recognitors, as they were called, by whose verdict the cause was determined. "Est autem magna assisa," says Glanvil (lib. ii. c. 7), "regale quoddam beneficium, clementia principis de consilio procerum populis indultum, quo vitæ hominum et statûs integritati tam salubriter consulitur, ut in jure quod quis in libero soli tenemento possidet retinendo duelli casum declinare possint homines ambiguum. Ac per hoc contingit insperatæ et prematuræ mortis ultimum evadere supplicium, vel saltem perennis infamiæ opprobrium, illius infesti et inverecundi verbi quod in ore victi turpiter sonat consecutivum.[1] Ex æquitate autem maximâ prodita est legalis ista institutio. Jus enim quod post multas et longas dilationes vix evincitur per duellum, per beneficium istius constitutionis commodius et acceleratius expeditur." The whole proceedings on an assize of novel disseizin, which was always held in the king's court or that of the justices itinerant, and not before the county or hundred, whose jurisdiction began in consequence rapidly to decline, are explained at some length by this ancient author, the chief justiciary of Henry II.

[1] This was the word *craven*, or begging for life, which was thought the utmost disgrace

Changes not less important were effected in criminal processes during the second part of the Norman period, which we consider as terminating with the accession of Edward I. Henry II. abolished the ancient privilege of compurgation by the oaths of friends, the manifest fountain of unblushing perjury; though it long afterwards was preserved in London and in boroughs by some exemption which does not appear. This, however, left the favorite, or at least the ancient and English, mode of defence by chewing consecrated bread handling hot iron, and other tricks called ordeals. But near the beginning of Henry III.'s reign the church, grown wiser and more fond of her system of laws, abolished all kinds of ordeal in the fourth Lateran council. The combat remained; but it was not applicable unless an injured prosecutor or appellant came forward to demand it. In cases where a party was only charged on vehement suspicion of a crime, it was necessary to find a substitute for the forbidden superstition. He might be compelled, by a statute of Henry II., to abjure the realm. A writ of 3 Henry III. directs that those against whom the suspicions were very strong should be kept in safe custody. But this was absolutely incompatible with English liberty and with Magna Charta. "No further enactment," says Sir F. Palgrave, "was made; and the usages which already prevailed led to a general adoption of the proceeding which had hitherto existed as a privilege or as a favor — that is to say, of proving or disproving the testimony of the first set of inquest-men by the testimony of a second array — and the individual accused by the appeal, or presented by the general opinion of the hundred, was allowed to defend himself by the particular testimony of the hundred to which he belonged. For this purpose another inquest was impanelled, sometimes composed of twelve persons named from the 'visne' and three from each of the adjoining townships; and sometimes the very same jurymen who had presented the offence might, if the culprit thought fit, be examined a second time, as the witnesses or inquest of the points in issue. But it seems worthy of remark that 'trial by inquest' in criminal cases never seems to have been introduced except into those courts which acted by the king's writ or commission. The presentment or declaration of those officers which fell within the cognizance of the hundred jury or the leet jury, the representatives of the ancient échevins, was final and conclusive;

no traverse, or trial by a second jury, in the nature of a petty jury, being allowed." (p. 269.)

Thus trial by a petty jury upon criminal charges came in; it is of the reign of Henry III., and not earlier. And it is to be remarked, as a confirmation of this view, that no one was compellable to plead; that is, the inquest was to be of his own choice. But if he declined to endure it he was remanded to prison, and treated with a severity which the statute of Westminster 1, in the third year of Edward I., calls *peine forte et dure;* extended afterwards, by a crue interpretation, to that atrocious punishment on those who re fused to stand a trial, commonly in order to preserve their lands from forfeiture, which was not taken away by law till the last century.

Thus was trial by jury established, both in real actions or suits affecting property in land and in criminal procedure, the former preceding by a little the latter. But a new question arises as to the province of these early juries; and the view lately taken is very different from that which has been commonly received.

The writer whom we have so often had occasion to quote has presented trial by jury in what may be called an altogether new light; for though Reeves, in his "History of the English Law," almost translating Glanvil and Bracton, could not help leading an attentive reader to something like the same result, I am not aware that anything approaching to the generality and fulness of Sir Francis Palgrave's statements can be found in any earlier work than his own.

"Trial by jury, according to the old English law, was a proceeding essentially different from the modern tribunal, still bearing the same name, by which it has been replaced; and whatever merits belonged to the original mode of judicial investigation—and they were great and unquestionable, though accompanied by many imperfections — such benefits are not to be exactly identified with the advantages now resulting from the great bulwark of English liberty. Jurymen in the present day are triers of the issue: they are individu als who found their opinion upon the evidence, whether ora or written, adduced before them; and the verdict delivered by them is their declaration of the judgment which they have formed. But the ancient jurymen were not impanelled to examine into the credibility of the evidence: the question was not discussed and argued before them: they, the jurymen, were the witnesses themselves, and the verdict was substantially the examination of these witnesses, who of their own knowledge, and without the aid of other testimony, afforded their evidence respecting the facts in question to the best of their belief. In its primitive form a trial by jury was therefore only a trial by witnesses; and jurymen were distinguished from any other witnesses only by customs which imposed upon them the obligation of an oath and regulated their number, and which prescribed their rank and defined the territorial qualifications from whence they obtained their degree and influence in society.

"I find it necessary to introduce this description of the ancient 'Trial by Jury,' because, unless the real functions of the original jurymen be distinctly presented to the reader, his familiar knowledge of the existing course of jurisprudence will lead to the most erroneous conclusions. Many of those who have descanted upon the excellence of our venerated national franchise seem to have supposed that it has descended to us unchanged from the days of Alfred; and the patriot who claims the jury as the 'judgment by his peers' secured by Magna Charta can never have suspected how distinctly the trial is resolved into a mere examination of witnesses." (Palgrave, i. 243.)

This theory is sustained by a great display of erudition, which fully establishes that the jurors had such a knowledge, however acquired, of the facts as enabled them to render a verdict without hearing any other testimony in open court than that of the parties themselves, fortified, if it might be, by written documents adduced. Hence the knights of the grand assize are called recognitors, a name often given to others sworn on an inquest. In the Grand Coustumier of Normandy, from which our writ of right was derived, it is said that those are to be sworn "who were born in the neighborhood, and who have long dwelt there; and such ought they to be, that it may be believed they know the truth of the case, and that they will speak the truth when they shall be asked." This was the rule in our own grand assize. The knights who appeared in it ought to be acquainted with the truth, and if any were not so they were to be rejected and others chosen, until twelve were unanimous witnesses. Glanvil (lib. ii.) furnishes sufficient proof, if we may depend on the language of the writs which he there inserts. It is to be remembered that the transactions upon which an assize of modern disseizin or writ of right would turn might frequently have been notorious. In the eloquent language of Sir F. Palgrave, "the forms, the festivities, and the ceremonies accompanying the hours of joy and the days of sorrow which form the distinguishing epochs in the brief chronicle of domestic life, impressed them upon the memory of the people at large. The parchment might be recommended by custom, but it was not required by law; and they had no registers to consult, no books to open. By the declaration of the husband at the church door, the wife was endowed in the presence of the assembled relations, and before all the merry attendants of the bridal train. The birth of the heir was recollected by the retainers who had participated in the cheer of the baronial hall; and the death of the ancestor was proved by the friends who had heard the wailings of the widow, or who had followed the corpse to the grave. Hence trial by jury was an appeal to the knowledge of the country; and the sheriff, in naming his panel, performed his duty by summoning those individuals from amongst the inhabitants of the country who were best acquainted with the points at issue. If from peculiar circumstances the witnesses of a fact were previously marked out and known, then they were particularly required to testify. Thus, when a charter was pleaded, the witnesses named in the attesting clause of the instrument and who had been present in the folkmoot, the shire, or the manor court when the seal was affixed by the donor, were included in the panel; and when a grant had been made by parol the witnesses were sought out by the sheriff and returned upon the jury." (Palgrave, p. 248.)

Several instances of *recognition* — that is, of jurors finding facts on their own knowledge — occur in the very curious chronicle of Jocelyn de Brakelonde, published by the Camden Society, long after the "Rise and Progress of the Commonwealth." One is on a question whether certain land was liberum feudum ecclesiæ an non. "Cumque inde summonita fuit recognitio 12 militum in curia regis facienda, facta est in curia abbatis apud Herlavum per licentiam Ranulfi de Glanvilla, et juraverunt recognitores se nunquam scivisse illam terram fuisse separatam ab ecclesiâ." (p. 45.) Another is still more illustrative of the personal knowledge of the jury overruling written evidence. A recognition was taken as to the right of the abbey over three manors. "Carta nostra lecta in publico nullam vim habuit, quia tota curia erat contra nos. Juramento facto, dixerunt milites se nescire de cartis nostris, nec de privatis conventionibus; sed se credere dixerunt, quod Adam et pater ejus et avus a centum annis retro tenuerunt maneria in feudum firmum, unusquisque post alium, diebus quibus fuerunt vivi et mortui, et sic disseisiati sumus per judicum terræ." (p. 91.)

This "judgment of the land" is, upon Jocelyn's testimony, rather suspicious; since they seem to have set common fame against a written deed. But we see by it that, although parol testimony might not be generally admissible, the parties had a right to produce documentary evidence in support of their title.

It appears at first to be an obvious difficulty in the way of this general resolution of jurors into witnesses, or of witnesses into jurors, that many issues, both civil and criminal, required the production of rather more recondite evidence than common notoriety. The known events of family history, which a whole neighborhood could attest, seem not very likely to have created litigation. But even in those ages of simplicity facts might be alleged, the very groundwork of a claim to succession, as to which no assize of knights could speak from personal knowledge. This, it is said, was obviated by swearing the witnesses upon the panel, so that those who had a real knowledge of the facts in question might instruct their fellow-jurors. Such, doubtless, was the usual course; but difficulties would often stand in the way. Glanvil meets the question, What is to be done if no knights are acquainted with the matter in dispute? by determining that persons of lower degree may be sworn. But what if women or villeins were the witnesses? What, again, if the course of inquiry should render fresh testimony needful? It must appear, according to all our notions of judicial evidence, that these difficulties must not only have led to the distinction of jurors from witnesses, but that no great length of time could have elapsed before the necessity of making it was perceived. Yet our notions of judicial evidence are not very applicable to the thirteenth century. The records preserved give us reason to believe that common fame had great influence upon these early inquests. In criminal inquiries especially the previous fame of the accused seems to have generally determined the verdict. He was not allowed to sustain his innocence by witnesses — a barbarous absurdity, as it seems, which was gradually removed by indulgence alone; but his witnesses were not sworn till the reign of Mary. If, however, the prosecutor or appellant, as he was formerly styled, was under an equal disability, the inequality will vanish, though the absurdity will remain. The prisoner had originally no defence, unless he could succeed in showing the weakness of the appellant's testimony, but by submitting to the ordeal or combat, or by the compurgation of his neighbors. The jurors, when they acquitted him, stood exactly in the light of these; it was a more refined and impartial compurgation, resting on their confidence in his former behavior. Thus let us take a record quoted by Palgrave, vol. ii. p. 184: — "*Robertus* filius *Roberti de Ferrariis* appellat *Ranulfum de Fatteswarthe* quod ipse venit in gardinum suum, in pace domini Regis, et nequiter assultavit *Rogerum* hominem suum, et eum verberavit et vulneravit, ita quod de vitâ ejus desperabatur; et ei robavit unum pallium et gladium et arcum et sagittas; et idem *Rogerus* offert hoc probare per corpus suum, prout curia consideraverit; et *Ranulphus* venit et defendit totum de verbo in verbum, et offert domino Regi unam marcam argenti pro habenda inquisitione per legales milites, utrum culpabilis sit inde, necne; et præterea dicit quod iste *Rogerus* nunquam ante appellavit eum, et petit ut hoc ei allocetur, — oblatio recipitur. — Juratores dicunt quod revera contencio fuit inter gardinarium prædicti *Roberti*, *Osmund* nomine, et quosdam garciones, sed *Ranulfus* non fuit ibi, nec malecredunt eum, de aliqua roberia, vel de aliquo malo, facto eidem."

We have here a trial by jury in its very beginning, for the payment of one mark by the accused in order to have an inquest instead of the combat shows that it was not become a matter of right. We may observe that, though Robert was the prosecutor, his servant Roger, being the aggrieved party, and capable of becoming a witness, was put forward as the appellant, ready to prove the case by combat. The verdict seems to imply that the jury had no bad opinion of Ranulf the appellee.

The fourteenth book of Glanvil contains a brief account of the forms of criminal process in his age; and here it appears that a woman could only be a witness, or rather an appellant, where her husband had been murdered or her person assaulted. The words are worth considering: "Duo sunt genera homicidiorum; unum est, quod dicitur murdrum, quod nullo vidente, nullo sciente, clam perpetratur, præter solum interfectorem et ejus complices; ita quod mox non assequatur clamor popularis juxta assisam super hoc proditam. In hujusmodi autem accusatione non admittitur aliquis, nisi fuerit de consanguinitate ipsius defuncti. Est et aliud homicidium quod constat in generali vocabulo, et dicitur simplex homicidium. In hoc etiam placito non admittitur aliquis accusator ad probationem, nisi fuerit mortuo consanguinitate conjunctus, vel homagio vel dominio, *ita ut de morte loquatur, ut sub visus sui testimonio.* Præterea sciendum quod in hoc placito mulier auditur accusans aliquem de morte viri sui, *si de visu loquatur* (l. xiv. c. 3). Tenetur autem mulier quæ proponit se à viro oppressam in pace domini regis, mox dum recens fuerit maleficium vicinam villam adire, et ibi injuriam sibi illatam probis hominibus ostendere, et sanguinem, si quis fuerit effusus, et vestium scissiones; dehinc autem apud præpositum hundredi idem facit. Postea quoque in pleno comitatu id publice proponat. Auditur itaque mulier in tali casu aliquem accusans, sicut et de aliâ quâlibet injuriâ corpori suo illatam solet audiri." (c. 6.)

Thus it appears that on charges of secret murder the kindred of the deceased, but no others, might be heard in court as witnesses to common suspicion, since they could be no more. I add the epithet *secret;* but it was at that time implied in the word *murdrum.* But in every case of open homicide the appellant, be it the wife or one of his kindred, his lord or vassal, must have been actually present. Other witnesses probably, if such there were, would be placed on the panel. The woman was only a prosecutrix; and, in the other sex, there is no doubt that the prosecutor's testimony was heard.

In claims of debt it was in the power of the defendant to wage his law; that is, to deny on oath the justice of the demand. This he was to sustain by the oaths of twelve compurgators, who declared their belief that he swore the truth; and if he declined to do this, it seems that he had no defence. But in the writ of right, or other process affecting real estate, the wager of law was never allowed; and even in actions of debt the defendant was not put to this issue until witnesses for the plaintiff had been produced, "sine testibus fidelibus ad hoc inductis." This, however, was not in presence of a jury, but of the bailiff or judge (Magna Charta, c. 28), and therefore does not immediately bear on the present subject.

In litigation before the king's justices, in the curia regis, it must have been always necessary to produce witnesses; though, if their testimony were disputed, it was necessary to recur to a jury in the county, unless the cause were of a nature to be determined by duel. A passage in Glanvil will illustrate this. A claim of villenage, when liberty was pleaded, could not be heard in the county court, but before the king's justices in his court. "Utroque autem præsente in curiâ hoc modo dirationabitur libertas in curiâ, siquidem producit is qui libertatem petit, plures de proximis et consanguineis de eodem stipite unde ipse exierit exeuntes, per quorum libertates, si fuerint in curiâ recognitæ et probatæ, liberabitur à jugo servitutis is qui ad libertatem proclamatur. Si vero contra dicatur status libertatis eorundem productorum vel de eodem dubitatur, ad vicinetum erit recurrendum; ita quod per ejus veredictum sciatur utrum illi liberi homines an non, et secundum dictum vicineti judicabitur." (l. ii. c. 4.) The plea of villenage was never tried by combat.

It is the opinion of Lord Coke that a single accuser was not sufficient at common law to convict any one of high treason; in default of a second witness "it shall be tried before the constable or marshal by combat, as by many records appeareth." (3 Inst. 26.) But however this might be, it is evident that as soon as the trial of peers of the realm for treason or felony in the court of the high steward became established, the practice of swearing witnesses on the panel must have been relinquished in such cases. "That two witnesses be required appeareth by our books, and I remember no authority in our books to the contrary. And this seemeth to be the more clear in the trial by the peers or nobles of the realm because they come not *de aliquo vicineto*, whereby they might take notice of the fact in respect of vicinity, as other jurors may do." (Ibid.) But the court of the high steward seems to be no older than the reign of Henry IV., at which time the examination of witnesses before common juries was nearly, or completely, established in its modern form; and the only earlier case we have, if I remember right, of the conviction of a peer in parliament — that of Mortimer in the 4th of Edward III. — was expressly grounded on the notoriousness of the facts (Rot. Parl. ii. 53). It does not appear, therefore, indisputable by precedent that any witnesses were heard, save the appellant, on trial of peers of the realm in the twelfth or thirteenth century, though it is by no means improbable that such would have been the practice.

Notwithstanding such exceptions, however, sufficient proofs remain that the jury themselves, especially in civil cases, long retained their character of witnesses to the fact. If the recognitors, whose name bespeaks their office, were not all so well acquainted with the matters in controversy as to believe themselves competent to render a verdict, it was the practice to *afforce* the jury, as it was called, by rejecting these and filling their places with more sufficient witnesses, until twelve were found who agreed in the same verdict.[1] (Glanvil, l. ii. c. 17.) Not that unanimity was demanded, for this did not become the rule till about the reign of Edward III.; but twelve, as now on a grand jury, must concur.[2] And though this profusion of witnesses seems strange to us, yet what they attested (in the age at least of Glanvil and for some time afterwards) was not, as at present, the report of their senses to the fact in issue, but all which they had heard and believed to be true; above all, their judgment as to the respective credibility of the demandant and tenant, heard in that age personally, or the appellant and appellee in a prosecution.

Bracton speaks of afforcing a panel by the addition of better-informed jurors to the rest, as fit for the court to order, "de consilio curiæ affortietur assisa ita quod apponantur alii juxta numerum majoris partis quæ dissenserit, vel saltem quatuor vel sex, et adjungantur aliis." The method of rejection used in Glanvil's time seems to have been altered. But in the time of Britton, soon afterwards, this afforcement it appears could only be made with the consent of the parties; though if, as his language seems to imply, the verdict was to go against the party refusing to have the jury afforced, no one would be likely to do so. Perhaps he means

[1] By the jury, the reader will remember that, in Glanvil's time, is meant the recognitors, on an assize of novel disseizin, or mort d'ancestor. For these *real* actions, now abolished, he may consult a good chapter on them in Blackstone, unless he prefer Bracton and the Year-Books, digested into Reeves's History of the Law.

[2] In 20 E. III. Chief Justice Thorpe is said to have been reproved for taking a verdict from eleven jurors. Law Review, No. iv. p. 388.

that this refusal would create a prejudice in the minds of the jury almost certain to produce such a verdict.

"It may be doubtful," says Mr. Starkie, "whether the doctrine of afforcement was applied to criminal cases. The account given by Bracton as to the trial by the country on a criminal charge is very obscure. It was to be by twelve jurors, consisting of milites or liberi et legales homines of the hundred and four villatæ."[1] But it is conjectured that the text is somewhat corrupt, and that four inhabitants of the vill were to be added to the twelve jurors. In some criminal cases it appears from Bracton that trial by combat could not be dispensed with, because the nature of the charge did not admit of positive witnesses. "Oportet quod defendat se per corpus suum quia patria nihil scire potest de facto, nisi per præsumtionem et per auditum, vel per mandatum [?] quod quidem non sufficit ad probationem pro appellando nec pro appellato ad liberationem." This indicates, on the one hand, an advance in the appreciation of evidence since the twelfth century; common fame and mere hearsay were not held sufficient to support a charge. But on the other hand, instead of presuming the innocence of a party against whom no positive testimony could be alleged, he was preposterously called upon to prove it by combat, if the appellant was convinced enough of his guilt to demand that precarious decision. It appears clear from some passages in Bracton that in criminal cases other witnesses might occasionally be heard than the parties themselves. Thus, if a man were charged with stealing a horse, he says that either the prosecutor or the accused might show that it was his own, bred in his stable, known by certain marks, which could hardly be but by calling witnesses. It is not improbable that witnesses were heard distinct from the jury in criminal cases before the separation had been adopted in real actions.

At a later time witnesses are directed to be joined to the inquest, but no longer as parts of it. "We find in the 23rd of Edward III." (I quote at present the words of Mr. Spence, Equitable Jurisdiction, p. 129) "the witnesses, instead of being summoned as constituent members, were adjoined to the recognitors or jury in assizes to afford to the

[1] The history of trial by jury has been very ably elucidated by Mr. Starkie, in the fourth number of the Law Review, which, though anonymous, I venture to quote by his name. I have been assisted in the text by this paper.

jury the benefit of their testimony, but without having any voice in the verdict. This is the first indication we have of the jury deciding on evidence formally produced, and it is the connecting link between the ancient and modern jury."[1] But it will be remembered — what Mr. Spence certainly did not mean to doubt — that the evidence of the demandant in an assize or writ of right, and of the prosecutor or appellant in a criminal case, had always been given in open court; and the tenant or appellee had the same right, but the latter probably was not sworn. Nor is it clear that the court would refuse other testimony if it were offered during the course of a trial. The sentence just quoted, however, appears to be substantially true, except that the words "formally produced" imply something more like the modern practice than the facts mentioned warrant. The evidence in the case reported in 23 Ass. 11 was produced to none but the jury.

Mr. Starkie has justly observed that "the transition was now almost imperceptible to the complete separation of the witnesses from the inquest. And this step was taken at some time before the 11th of Henry IV.;[2] namely, that all the witnesses were to give their testimony at the bar of the court, so that the judges might exclude those incompetent by law, and direct the jury as to the weight due to the rest." "This effected a change in the modes of trying civil cases; the importance of which can hardly be too highly estimated. Jurors, from being, as it were, mere recipients and depositaries of knowledge, exercised the more intellectual faculty of forming conclusions from testimony — a duty not only of high importance with a view to truth and justice, but also collaterally in encouraging habits of reflection and reasoning (aided by the instructions of the judges), which must have had a great and most beneficial effect in promoting civiliza-

1 The reference is to the Year-Book, 23 Ass. 11. It was adjudged that the witnesses could not be challenged like jurors; "car ils doivent rien temoigner fors ceo qu'ils verront et oiront. Et l'assise fut pris, et les temoins ajoints a eux." This has no appearance of the introduction of a new custom. Above fifty years had elapsed since Bracton wrote, so that the change might have easily crept in.

2 The Year-Book of 11 H. IV., to which a reference seems here to be made, has not been consulted by me. But in the next year (12 H. IV. 7) witnesses are directed to be joined to the inquest (as in 23 Ass. 11); and one of the judges is reported to have said this had often been done; yet we might infer that the practice was not so general as to pass without comment. This looks as if the separation of the witnesses, by their examination in open court, were not quite of so early a date as Mr. Starkie and Mr. Spence suppose. But, perhaps, both modes of procedure might be concurrent for a certain time.

tion. The exercise of the control last adverted to on the part of the judges was the foundation of that system of rules in regard to evidence which has since constituted so large and important a branch of the law of England." (Spence, p. 129.)

The obscurity that hangs over the origin of our modern course of procedure before juries is far from being wholly removed. We are reduced to conjectural inferences from brief passages in early law-books, written for contemporaries, but which leave a considerable uncertainty, as the readers of this note will be too apt to discover. If we say that our actual trial by jury was established not far from the beginning of the fifteenth century, we shall perhaps approach as nearly as the diligence of late inquirers has enabled us to proceed. But in the time of Fortescue, whose treatise De Laudibus Legum Angliæ was written soon after 1450, we have the clearest proof that the mode of procedure before juries by *vivâ voce* evidence was the same as at present. It may be presumed that the function of the advocate and of the judge to examine witnesses, and to comment on their testimony, had begun at this time. The passage in Fortescue is so full and perspicuous that it deserves to be extracted.

"Twelve good and true men being sworn as in the manner above related, legally qualified — that is, having, over and besides their movable possessions, in land sufficient (as was said) wherewith to maintain their rank and station — neither suspected by nor at variance with either of the parties; all of the neighborhood; there shall be read to them in English by the court the record and nature of the plea at length which is depending between the parties; and the issue thereupon shall be plainly laid before them, concerning the truth of which those who are so sworn are to certify the court: which done, each of the parties, by themselves or their counsel, in presence of the court, shall declare and lay open to the jury all and singular the matters and evidences whereby they think they may be able to inform the court concerning the truth of the point in question; after which each of the parties has a liberty to produce before the court all such witnesses as they please, or can get to appear on their behalf, who, being charged upon their oaths, shall give in evidence all that they know touching the truth of the fact concerning which the parties are at issue. And if necessity so require, the witnesses may be heard and examined apart, till they shall have deposed all that they have to give in evidence, so that what the one has declared shall not inform or induce another witness of the same side to give his evidence in the same words, or to the very same effect. The whole of the evidence being gone through, the jurors shall confer together at their pleasure, as they shall think most convenient, upon the truth of the issue before them, with as much deliberation and leisure as they can well desire; being all the while in the keeping of an officer of the court, in a place assigned them for that purpose, lest any one should attempt by indirect methods to influence them as to their opinion, which they are to give in to the court. Lastly, they are to return into court and certify the justices upon the truth of the issue so joined in the presence of the parties (if they please to be present), particularly the person who is plaintiff in the cause: what the jurors shall so certify, in the laws of England, is called the verdict." (c. 26.)

Mr. Amos indeed has observed, in his edition of Fortescue (p. 93), "The essential alteration which has since taken place in the character of the jury does not appear to have been thoroughly effected till the time of Edward VI. and Mary. Jurors are often called testes." But though this appellation might be retained from the usage of older times, I do not see what was left to effect in the essential character of a jury, when it had reached the stage of hearing the witnesses and counsel of the parties in open court.

The result of this investigation, suggested perhaps by Reeves, but followed up by Sir Francis Palgrave for the earlier, and by Mr. Starkie for the later period, is to sweep away from the ancient constitution of England what has always been accounted both the pledge of its freedom and the distinctive type of its organization, trial by jury, in the modern sense of the word, and according to modern functions. For though the passage just quoted from Fortescue is conclusive as to his times, these were but the times of the Lancastrian kings; and we have been wont to talk of Alfred, or at least of the Anglo-Saxon age, when the verdict of twelve sworn men was the theme of our praise. We have seen that, during this age, neither in civil nor in criminal proceedings, it is possible to trace this safeguard for judicial purity. Even when juries may be said to have existed in name, the institution denoted but a small share of political wisdom, or at least provided but indifferently for impartial justice. The mode of trial by witnesses returned on the panel, hearing no evidence beyond their own in open court, unassisted by the sifting acuteness of lawyers, laid open a broad inlet for credulity and prejudice, for injustice and corruption. Perjury was the dominant crime of the middle ages; encouraged by the preposterous rules of compurgation, and by the multiplicity of oaths in the ecclesiastical law. It was the frequency of this offence, and the impunity which the established procedure gave to that of jurors, that produced the remedy by writ of attaint; but one which was liable to the same danger; since jury on an attaint must, in the early period of that process, have judged on common fame or on their own testimony, like those whose verdict they were called to revise; and where hearsay and tradition passed for evidence, it must, according to our stricter notions of penal law, have been very difficult to obtain an equitable conviction of the first panel on the ground of perjury.

The Chronicle, already quoted, by Jocelyn de Brakelonde, affords an instance, among multitudes, probably, that are unrecorded, where a jury flagrantly violated their duty. Five recognitors in a writ of assize came to Samson abbot of St. Edmund's Bury, the Chronicler's hero, the right of presentation to a church being the question, in order to learn from him what they should swear, meaning to receive money. He promised them nothing, but bade them swear according to their consciences. They went away in wrath, and found a verdict against the abbey.[1] (p. 44.)

[1] I may set down here one or two other passages from the same Chronicle, illustrating the modes of trial in that age. Samson offered that a right of advowson should be determined by the claimant's oath, a method recognized in some cases by the civil and canon law, but only, I conceive, in favor of the defendant. Cumque miles ille renuisset jurare, dilatum est juramentum per consensum utriusque partis sexdecim legalibus be hundredo, qui juraverunt hoc esse jus abbatis. p. 44. The proceeding by jurors was sometimes applied even when the sentence belonged to the ecclesiastical jurisdiction. A riot, with bloodshed, having occurred, the abbot, acceptis juramentis a sexdecim legalibus hominibus, et auditis eorum attestationibus, pronounced sentence of excommunication against the offenders.

The combat was not an authorized mode of trial within boroughs; they preserved the old Saxon compurgation. And this may be an additional proof of the antiquity of their privileges. A free tenant of the *celerarius* of the abbey, cui potûs et escæ cura (Du Cange), being charged with robbery, and vanquished in the combat, was hanged. The burgesses of Bury said that, if he had been resident within the borough, it would not have come to battle, but he would have purged himself by the oaths of his neighbors, sicut libertas est eorum qui manent infra burgum. p. 74. It is hard to pronounce by which procedure the greater number of guilty persons escaped.

Yet in its rudest and most imperfect form, the trial by a sworn inquest was far superior to the impious superstition of ordeals, the hardly less preposterous and unequal duel, the unjust deference to power in compurgation, when the oath of one thane counterbalanced those of six ceorls, and even to the free-spirited but tumultuary and unenlightened decisions of the hundred or the county. It may, indeed, be thought by the speculative philosopher, or the practical lawyer, that in those early stages which we have just been surveying, from the introduction of trial by jury under Henry II. to the attainment of its actual perfection in the first part of the fifteenth century, there was little to warrant our admiration. Still let us ever remember that we judge of past ages by an erroneous standard when we wonder at their prejudices, much more when we forget our own. We have but to place ourselves, for a few minutes, in imagination among the English of the twelfth and thirteenth centuries, and we may better understand why they cherished and panted for the *judicium parium*, the trial by their peers, or, as it is emphatically styled, by the country. It stood in opposition to foreign lawyers and foreign law; to the chicane and subtlety, the dilatory and expensive though accurate technicalities, of Normandy, to tribunals where their good name could not stand them in stead, nor the tradition of their neighbors support their claim. For the sake of these, for the maintenance of the laws of Edward the Confessor, as in pious reverence they termed every Anglo-Saxon usage, they were willing to encounter the noisy rudeness of the county-court, and the sway of a potent adversary.

Henry II., a prince not perhaps himself wise, but served by wise counsellors, blended the two schemes of jurisprudence, as far as the times would permit, by the assize of novel disseizin, and the circuits of his justices in eyre. From this age justly date our form of civil procedure; the trial by a jury (using always that word in a less strict sense than it bears with us) replaced that by the body of hundredors; the stream of justice purified itself in successive generations through the acuteness, learning, and integrity of that remarkable series of men whose memory lives chiefly among lawyers, I mean the judges under the house of Plantagenet; and thus, while the common law borrowed from Normandy too much, perhaps, of its subtlety in distinction, and became as scientific as that of

Rome, it maintained, without encroachment, the grand principle of the Saxon polity, the trial of facts by the country. From this principle (except as to that preposterous relic of barbarism, the requirement of unanimity) may we never swerve — may we never be compelled, in wish, to swerve — by a contempt of their oaths in jurors, and a disregard of the just limits of their trust!

NOTE IX. PAGE 278.

The nature of both tenures has been perspicuously illustrated by Mr. Allen, in his Inquiry into the Rise and Growth of the Royal Prerogative, from which I shall make a long extract.

"The distribution of landed property in England by the Anglo-Saxons appears to have been regulated on the same principles that directed their brethren on the continent. Part of the lands they acquired was converted into estates of inheritance for individuals; part remained the property of the public, and was left to the disposal of the state. The former was called *bocland;* the latter I apprehend to have been that description of landed property which was known by the name of *folcland.*

"Folcland, as the word imports, was the land of the folk or people. It was the property of the community. It might be occupied in common, or possessed in severalty; and, in the latter case, it was probably parcelled out to individuals in the *folcgemot,* or court of the district, and the grant attested by the freemen who were then present. But, while it continued to be folcland, it could not be alienated in perpetuity; and, therefore, on the expiration of the term for which it had been granted, it reverted to the community, and was again distributed by the same authority.[1]

"Bocland was held by book or charter. It was land that had been severed by an act of government from the folcland, and converted into an estate of perpetual inheritance. It might belong to the church, to the king, or to a subject. It might be alienable and devisable at the will of the proprie-

[1] Spelman describes folcland as terra popularis, quæ jure communi possidetur — sine scripto. Gloss. Folcland. In another place he distinguishes it accurately from bocland: — Prædia Saxones duplici titulo possidebant: vel scripti auctoritate, quod bocland vocabant — vel populi testimonio, quod folcland dixere. Ib. Bocland

tor. It might be limited in its descent without any power of alienation in the possessor. It was often granted for a single life, or for more lives than one, with remainder in perpetuity to the church. It was forfeited for various delinquencies to the state.

"Estates in perpetuity were usually created by charter after the introduction of writing, and, on that account, bocland and land of inheritance are often used as synonymous expressions. But at an earlier period they were conferred by the delivery of a staff, a spear, an arrow, a drinking-horn, the branch of a tree, or a piece of turf; and when the donation was in favor of the church, these symbolical representations of the grant were deposited with solemnity on the altar; nor was this practice entirely laid aside after the introduction of title-deeds. There are instances of it as late as the time of the Conqueror. It is not, therefore, quite correct to say that all the lands of the Anglo-Saxons were either folcland or bocland. When land was granted in perpetuity it ceased to be folcland; but it could not with propriety be termed bocland, unless it was conveyed by a written instrument.

"Folcland was subject to many burdens and exactions from which bocland was exempt. The possessors of folcland were bound to assist in the reparation of royal vills and in other public works. They were liable to have travellers and others quartered on them for subsistence. They were required to give hospitality to kings and great men in their progresses through the country, to furnish them with carriages and relays of horses, and to extend the same assistance to their messengers, followers, and servants, and even to the persons who had charge of their hawks, horses, and hounds. Such at least are the burdens from which lands are liberated when converted by charter into bocland.

"Bocland was liable to none of these exactions. It was released from all services to the public, with the exception of contributing to military expeditions, and to the reparation of castles and bridges. These duties or services were comprised in the phrase of *trinoda necessitas*, which were said to be incumbent on all persons, so that none could be excused from them. The church indeed contrived, in some cases, to obtain an exemption from them; but in general its lands, like those of others, were subject to them. Some of the charters granting to the possessions of the church an exemption from all services whatsoever were genuine; but the greater part are forgeries." — (p. 142.)

Bocland, we perceive by this extract, was not necessarily alodial, in the sense of absolute propriety. It might be granted for lives, as was often the case; and then it seems to have been called *læn-land* (præstita), lent or leased. (Palgrave, ii. 361.) Such land, however, was not feudal, as I conceive, if we use that word in its legitimate European sense; though *lehn* is the only German word for a fief. Mr. Allen has found no traces of this use of the word among th Anglo-Saxons. (Appendix, p. 57.) Sir F. Palgrave agrees in general with Mr. Allen.[1]

We find another great living authority on Anglo-Saxon and Teutonic law concurring in the same luminous solutior of this long-disputed problem. "The natural origin of folcland is the superabundance of good land above what was at once appropriated by the tribes, families, or gentes (mægburg, gelondan), who first settled in a waste or conquered land; but its existence enters into and modifies the system of law, and on it depends the definition of the march and the gau with their boundaries. Over the folcland at first the king alone had no control; it must have been apportioned by the nation in its solemn meeting; earlier, by the shire or other collection of freemen. In Beôwulf, the king determines to build a palace, and distribute in it to his comites such gold, silver, arms, and other valuables as God had given him, save the folcsceare and the lives of men — 'bûtan folcsceare and feorum gumena' — which he had no authority to dispose of. This relative position of folcland to bocland is not confined to the Anglo-Saxon institutions. The Frisians, a race from whom we took more than has generally been recognized, had the same distinction. At the same time I differ from Grimm, who seems to consider folcland as the pure alod, bôcland as the fief. 'Folcland im Gegensatz zu beneficium. Leges Edv. II.; das ist, reine alod, im Gegensatz zu beneficium, Lehen. Vgl. das Friesische câplond und bôcland. As. p. 15.' (D R. A. p. 463.) I think the reverse is the case; and indee we have one instance where a king exchanged a certain por

[1] The law of real property, or bocland, in the Anglo-Saxon period, is given in a few pages, equally succinct and luminous, by Mr. Spence. Equit. Jurisd. p. 20-25. The Codex Diplomaticus furnishes the best ancient precedents, and is of course studied, to the disregard, where necessary, of more defective authorities, by those who regard this portion of legal history

tion of folcland for an equal portion of bôcland with one of his comites. He then gave the exchanged folcland all the privileges of bôcland, and proceeded to make the bôcland he had received in exchange *folcland*." (Kemble's Codex Diplomaticus, i. p. 104.)

It is of importance to mention that Mr. K., when he wrote this passage, had not seen Mr. Allen's work; so that the independent concurrence of two such antiquaries in the same theory lends it very great support. In the second volume of the Codex Diplomaticus the editor adduces fresh evidence as to the nature of folcland, "the *terra fiscalis*, or public land grantable by the king or his council, as the representatives of the nation." (p. 9.) Mr. Thorpe, in the glossary to his edition of "Ancient Laws" (v. Folcland), quotes part of the same extract from Allen which I have given, and, making no remark, must be understood to concur in it. Thus we may consider this interpretation in possession of the field.[1]

The word folcland fell by degrees into disuse, and gave place to the term *terra regis*, or crown-land. (Allen, p. 160.) This indicates the growth of a monarchical theory which reached its climax, in this application of it, after the Conquest, when the entire land of England was supposed to have been the demesne land of the king, held under him by a feudal tenure.

NOTE X. Page 305.

"Amongst the prerogatives of the crown, the Conqueror and many of his successors appear to have assumed the power of making laws to a certain extent, without the authority of their greater council, especially when operating only in restraint of the king's prerogative, for the benefit of his subjects, or explaining, amending, or adding to the existing law of the land, as administered between subject and subject; and this prerogative was commonly exercised with the advice of the king's ordinary or select council, though frequently the edict was expressed in the king's name alone. But as far as can be judged from existing documents or from history, it was generally conceived that beyond these limits the consent

[1] It seems to be a necessary inference from the evidence of Domesday Book that all England had been converted into bocland before the Conquest, with the exception of the terra regis, if that were truly the representative of ancient folcland, as Allen supposes.

of a larger assembly, of that which was deemed the 'Commune concilium regni,' was in strictness necessary; though sometimes the monarch on the throne ventured to stretch his prerogative further, even to the imposition of taxes to answer his necessities, without the common consent; and the great struggles between the kings of England and their people have generally been produced by such stretches of the royal prerogative, till at length it has been established that no legislative act can be done without the concurrence of that assembly, now emphatically called the king's parliament." (Report of Lords' Committee on the Dignity of a Peer, p. 22, edit. 1819.)

"It appears," says the committee afterwards, "from all the charters taken together, that during the reigns of William Rufus, his brother Henry, and Stephen, many things had been done contrary to law; but that there did exist some legal constitution of government, of which a legislative council (for some purposes at least) formed a part; and particularly that all impositions and exactions by the mere authority of the crown, not warranted by the existing law, were reprobated as infringements of the just rights of the subjects of the realm, though the existing law left a large portion of the king's subjects liable to tallage imposed at the will of the crown; and the tenants of the mesne lords were in many cases exposed to similar exaction." (p. 42.)

These passages appeared to Mr. Allen so inadequate a representation of the Anglo-Norman constitution, that he commented upon the ignorance of the committee with no slight severity in the Edinburgh Review. The principal charges against the Report in this respect are, that the committee have confounded the ordinary or select council of the king with the *commune concilium*, and supposed that the former alone was intended by historians, as the advisers of the crown in its prerogative of altering the law of the land, when, in fact, the great council of the national aristocracy is clearly pointed out; and that they have disregarded a great deal of historical testimony to the political importance of the latter. It appears to be clearly shown, from the Saxon Chronicle and other writers, that assemblies of bishops and nobles, sometimes very large, were held by custom, "de more," three times in the year, by William the Conqueror and by both his sons; that they were, however, gradually intermitted by

Henry I., and ceased early in the reign of Stephen. In these councils, which were legislative so far as new statutes were ever required, a matter of somewhat rare occurrence, but more frequently rendering their advice on measures to be adopted, or their judgment in criminal charges against men of high rank, and even in civil litigation, we have, at least in theory, the acknowledged limitations of royal authority. I refer the reader to this article in the Edinburgh Review (vol. xxxv.), to which we must generally assent; observing, however, that the committee, though in all probability mistaken in ascribing proceedings of the Norman sovereigns to the advice of a select council, which really emanated from one much larger, did not call in question, but positively assert, the constitutional necessity of the latter for general taxation, and perhaps for legislative enactments of an important kind. And, when we consider the improbability that "all the great men over all England, archbishops and bishops, abbots and earls, thanes and knights," as the Saxon chronicler pretends, could have been regularly present thrice a year, at Winchester, Westminster, and Gloucester, when William, as he informs us, "wore his crown," we may well suspect that, in the ordinary exercise of his prerogative, and even in such provisions as might appear to him necessary, he did not wait for a very full assembly of his tenants in chief. The main question is, whether this council of advice and assent was altogether of his own nomination, and this we may confidently deny.

The custom of the Anglo-Saxon kings had been to hold meetings of their witan very frequently, at least in the regular course of their government. And this was also the rule in the grand fiefs of France. The pomp of their court, the maintenance of loyal respect, the power of keeping a vigilant eye over the behavior of the chief men, were sufficient motives for the Norman kings to preserve this custom; and the nobility of course saw in it the security of their privileges as well as the exhibition of their importance. Hence we find that William and his sons held their courts *de more*, as a regular usage, three times a year, and generally at the great festivals, and in different parts of the kingdom. Instances are collected by the Edinburgh Reviewer (vol. xxxv. p. 5). And here the public business was transacted; though, if these meetings were so frequent, it is probable that for the most part they passed off in a banquet or a tournament.

The Lords' Committee, in notes on the Second Report, when reprinted in 1829, do not acquiesce in the positions of their hardy critic, to whom, without direct mention, they manifestly allude. "From the relations of annalists and historians," they observe, "it has been inferred that during the reign of the Conqueror, and during a long course of time from the Conquest, the archbishops, bishops, abbots and priors, earls and barons of the realm were regularly convened three times in every year, at three different and distinct places in the kingdom, to a general council of the realm. Considering the state of the country, and the habits and dispositions of the people, this seems highly improbable; especially if the word barones, or the words proceres or magnates, often used by writers in describing such assemblies, were intended to include all the persons holding immediately of the crown, who, according to the charter of John, were required to be summoned to constitute the great council of the realm, for the purpose of granting aids to the crown." (p. 449.) But it is not necessary to suppose this; those might have attended who lived near, or who were specially summoned. The committee argue on the supposition that all tenants in chief must have attended thrice a year, which no one probably ever asserted. But that William and his sons did hold public meetings, *de more*, at three several places in every year, or at least very frequently, cannot be controverted without denying what respected historical testimonies affirm; and the language of these early writers intimates that they were numerously attended. Aids were not regularly granted, and laws much more rarely enacted in them; but they might still be a national council. But the constituent parts of such councils will be discussed in a subsequent note.

It is to be here remarked that, with the exception of the charters granted by William, Henry, and Stephen, which are in general rather like confirmations of existing privileges than novel enactments, though some clauses appear to be of the latter kind, little authentic evidence can be found of any legislative proceedings from the Conquest to the reign of Henry II. The laws of the Conqueror, which we find in Ingulfus, do not come within this category; they are a confirmation of English usages, granted by William to his subjects. "Cez sunt les leis et les custumes que li reis William grantad el pople de Engleterre après le conquest de la terre. Iceles mesmes que li reis Edward sun cusin tint devant lui." These, published by Gale (Script. Rer. Anglic. vol. i.), and more accurately than before from the Holkham manuscript by Sir Francis Palgrave, have sometimes passed for genuine. The real original, however, is the Latin text, first published by him with the French. (Eng. Commonw. vol. ii. p. 89.) The French translation he refers to the early part of the reign of Henry III. At the time when Ingulfus is supposed to have lived, soon after the Conquest, no laws, as Sir F. Palgrave justly observes, were written in French, and he might have added that we cannot produce any other specimen of the language which is certainly of that age. (See Quarterly Review, xxxiv. 260.) It is said in the charter of Henry I. that the laws of Edward were renewed by William with the same emendation.

But the changes introduced by William in the tenure of land were so momentous that the most cautious inquirers have been induced to presume some degree of common consent by those whom they so much affected. "There seems to be evidence to show that the great change in the tenure of land, and particularly the very extensive introduction of tenure by knight-service, was made by the consent of those principally interested in the land charged with the burdens of that tenure; and that the general changes made in the Saxon laws by the Conqueror, forming of the two one people, was also effected by common consent; namely, in the language of the charter of William with respect to the tenures, 'per commune concilium tocius regni,' and with respect to both, as expressed in the charter of his son Henry, 'concilio baronum;' though it is far from clear who were the persons intended to be so described." (Report of Lords' Committee, p. 50.)

The separation of the civil and ecclesiastical jurisdictions was another great innovation in the reign of the Conqueror. This the Lords' Committee incline to refer to his sole authority. But Allen has shown by a writ of William addressed to the bishop of Lincoln that it was done "communi concilio, et concilio archiepiscoporum meorum, et cæterorum episcoporum et abbatum, et omnium principum regni mei." (Edinb. Rev. p. 15.) And the Domesday survey was determined upon, after a consultation of William with his great council at Gloucester, in 1084. This would of course be reckoned a legislative measure in the present day; but it might not pass for more than a temporary ordinance. The only laws under Henry I., except his charter, of which any account remains in history (there are none on record), fall under the same description.

The Constitutions of Clarendon, in 1164, are certainly a regular statute; whoever might be the consenting parties, a subject to be presently discussed, these famous provisions were enacted in the great council of the nation. This is equally true of the Assizes of Northampton, in 1178. But the earliest Anglo-Norman law which is extant in a regular form is the assize made at Clarendon for the preservation of the peace, probably between 1165 and 1176. This remarkable statute, "quam dominus rex Henricus, consilio archiepiscoporum et episcoporum et abbatum, cæterorumque baronum suorum constituit," was first published by Sir F. Palgrave from a manuscript in the British Museum. (Engl. Commonw. i. 257; ii. 168.) In other instances the royal prerogative may perhaps have been held sufficient for innovations which, after the constitution became settled, would have required the sanction of the whole legislature. No act of parliament is known to have been made under Richard I.; but an ordinance, setting the assize of bread, in the fifth of John, is recited to be established "communi concilio baronum nostrorum." Whether these words afford sufficient ground for believing that the assize was set in a full council of the realm, may possibly be doubtful. The committee incline to the affirmative, and remark that a general proclamation to the same effect is mentioned in history, but merely as proceeding from the king, so that "the omission of the words 'communi concilio baronum' in the proclamation mentioned by the historian, though appearing in the ordinance, tends also to show that, though similar words may not be found in other similar documents, the absence of those words ought not to lead to a certain conclusion that the act done had not the authority of the same common council." (p. 84.)

NOTE XI. Page 305.

This charter has been introduced into the new edition of Rymer's Fœdera, and heads that collection. The Committee of the Lords' on the Dignity of a Peer, in their Second Report, have the following observations: — "The printed copy is taken from the Red Book of the Exchequer, a document which has long been admitted in the Court of Exchequer as evidence of authority for certain purposes; but no trace has been hitherto found of the original charter of William, though the insertion of a copy in a book in the custody of the king's Exchequer, resorted to by the judges of that court for other purposes, seems to afford reasonable ground for supposing that such a charter was issued, and that the copy so preserved is probably correct, or nearly correct. The copy in the Red Book is without date, and no circumstance tending to show its true date has occurred to the committee; but it may be collected from its contents that it was probably issued in the latter part of that king's reign; about which time it appears from history that he confirmed to his subjects in England the ancient Saxon laws, with alterations." (p. 28.)

I once thought, and have said, that this charter seems to comprehend merely the feudal tenants of the crown. This may be true of one clause; but it is impossible to construe "omnes liberi homines totius monarchiæ" in so contracted a sense. The committee indeed observe that many of the king's tenants were long after subject to tallage. But I do not suppose these to have been included in "liberi homines." The charter involves a promise of the crown to abstain from exactions frequent in the Conqueror's reign, and falling on mesne tenants and others not liable to arbitrary taxation.

This charter contains a clause — "Hoc quoque præcipimus ut omnes habeant et teneant legem Edwardi Regis in omnibus rebus adjunctis his quæ constituimus ad ultilitatem Anglorum." And as there is apparent reference to these words in the charter of Henry I. — "Legem Edwardi Regis vobis reddo cum illis emendationibus quibus pater meus eam emendavit consilio baronum suorum" — the committee are sufficiently moderate in calling this "a clause, *tending to give in some degree* authenticity to the copy of the charter of William the Conqueror inserted in the Red Book of the Exchequer." (p. 39.) This charter seems to be fully established: it deserves to be accounted the first remedial concession by the crown; for it indicates, especially taken in connection with public history, an arbitrary exercise of royal power which neither the new nor the old subjects of the English monarchy reckoned lawful. It is also the earliest recognition of the Anglo-Saxon laws, such as they subsisted under the Confessor, and a proof both that the English were now endeavoring to raise their heads from servitude, and that the Normans had discovered some immunities from taxation, or some securities from absolute power, among the conquered people, in which they desired to participate. It is deserving of remark that the distinction of personal law, which, indeed, had almost expired on the continent, was never observed in England; at least, we have no evidence of it, and the contrary is almost demonstrable. The conquerors fell at once into the laws of the conquered, and this continued for more than a century.

The charter of William, like many others, was more ample than effectual. "The committee have found no document to show, nor does it appear probable from any relation in history that William ever obtained any general aid from his subjects by grant of a legislative assembly; though according to history, even after the charter before mentioned, he extorted great sums from individuals by various means and under various pretences. Towards the close of his reign, when he had exacted, as stated by the editor of the first part of the Annals called the Annals of Waverley, the oath of fealty from the principal landholders of every description, the same historian adds that William passed into Normandy, 'adquisitis magnis thesauris ab hominibus suis, super quos aliquam causam invenire poterat, sive justè sive iniquè' (words which import exaction and not grant), and he died the year following in Normandy." (p. 35.)

The deeply learned reviewer of this Report has shown that the Annals of Waverley are of very little authority, and merely in this part a translation from the Saxon Chronicle. But the translation of the passage quoted by the committee is correct; and it was perhaps rather hypercritical to cavil at their phrase that William obtained this money "by exaction and not by grant." They never meant that he imposed a general tax. That it was not by grant is all that their purpose required; the passage which they quote shows that it was under some pretext, and often an unjust one, which is not very unlike exaction.

It is highly probable that, in promising this immunity from unjust exactions, William did not intend to abolish the ancient tax of Danegelt, or to demand the consent of his great council when it was thought necessary to impose it. We read in the Saxon Chronicle that the king in 1083 exacted a heavy tribute all over England, that is, seventy-two pence for each hyde. This looks like a Danegelt. The rumor of invasion from Denmark is set down by the chronicler under the year 1085; but probably William had reason to be prepared. He may have had the consent of his great council in this instance. But as the tax had formerly been perpetual, so that it was a relaxation in favor of the subject to reserve it for an emergency, we may think it more likely that this imposition was within his prerogative; that he, in other words, was sole judge of the danger that required it. It was, however, in truth, a heavy tribute, being six shillings for every hyde, in many cases, as we see by Domesday, no small proportion of the annual value, and would have been a grievous burden as an annual payment.

NOTE XII. Page 307.

This passage in a contemporary writer, being so unequivocal as it is, ought to have much weight in the question which an eminent foreigner has lately raised as to the duration of the distinction between the Norman and English races. It is the favorite theory of M. Thierry, pushed to an extreme length both as to his own country and ours, that the conquering nation, Franks in one case, Normans in the other, remained down to a late period — a period indeed to which he assigns no conclusion — unmingled, or at least undistinguishable, constituting a double people of sovereigns and subjects, becoming a noble order in the state, haughty, oppressive, powerful, or, what is in one word most odious to a French ear in the nineteenth century, aristocratic.

It may be worthy of consideration, since the authority of this writer is not to be disregarded, whether the Norman blood were really blended with the native quite so soon as the reign of Henry II.; that is, whether intermarriages in the superior classes of society had become so frequent as to efface the distinction. M. Thierry produces a few passages which seem to intimate its continuance. But these are too loosely worded to warrant much regard; and he admits that after the reign of Henry I. we have no proof of any hostile spirit on the part of the English towards the new dynasty; and that some efforts were made to conciliate them by representing Henry

II. as the descendant of the Saxon line. (Vol. ii. p. 374.) This, in fact, was true; and it was still more important that the name of English was studiously assumed by our kings (ignorant though they might be, in M. Thierry's phrase, what was the vernacular word for that dignity), and that the Anglo-Normans are seldom, if ever, mentioned by that separate designation. England was their dwelling-place, English their name, the English law their inheritance; if this was not wholly the case before the separation of the mother country under John, and yet we do not perceive much limitation nec essary, it can admit of no question afterwards.

It is, nevertheless, manifest that the descendants of William's tenants in capite, and of others who seized on so large a portion of our fair country from the Channel to the Tweed, formed the chief part of that aristocracy which secured the liberties of the Anglo-Saxon race, as well as their own, at Runnymede; and which, sometimes as peers of the realm, sometimes as well-born commoners, placed successive barriers against the exorbitances of power, and prepared the way for that expanded scheme of government which we call the English constitution. The names in Dugdale's Baronage and in his Summonitiones ad Parliamentum speak for themselves; in all the earlier periods, and perhaps almost through the Plantagenet dynasty, we find a great preponderance of such as indicate a French source. New families sprung up by degrees, and are now sometimes among our chief nobility; but in general, if we find any at this day who have tolerable pretensions to deduce their lineage from the Conquest, they are of Norman descent; the very few Saxon families that may remain with an authentic pedigree in the male line are seldom found in the wealthier class of gentry. This is of course to be taken with deference to the genealogists. And on this account I must confess that M. Thierry's opinion of a long-continued distinction of races has more semblance of truth as to this kingdom than can be pretended as to France, without a blind sacrifice of undeniable facts at the altar of plebeian malignity. In the celebrated Lettres sur l'Histoire de France, published about 1820, there seems to be no other aim than to excite a factious animosity against the ancient nobility of France, on the preposterous hypothesis that they are descended from the followers of Clovis, that Frank and Gaul have never been truly intermingled;

and that a conquering race was, even in this age, attempting to rivet its yoke on a people who disdained it. This strange theory, or something like it, had been announced in a very different spirit by Boulainvilliers in the last century. But of what family in France, unless possibly in the eastern part, can it be determined with confidence whether the founder were Frank or Gallo-Roman? Is it not a moral certainty that many of the most ancient, especially in the south, must have been of the latter origin? It would be highly wrong to revive such obsolete distinctions in order to keep up social hatreds were they founded in truth; but what shall we say if they are purely chimerical?

NOTE XIII. Page 318.

It appears to have been the opinion of Madox, and probably has been taken for granted by most other antiquaries, that this court, denominated *Aula* or *Curia Regis*, administered justice when called upon, as well as advised the crown in public affairs, during the first four Norman reigns as much as afterwards. Allen, however, maintained (Edinb. Rev. xxvi. p. 364) that "the administration of justice in the last resort belonged originally to the great council. It was the king's baronial court, and his tenants in chief were the suitors and judges." Their unwillingness and inability to deal with intricate questions of law, which, after the simpler rules of Anglo-Saxon jurisprudence were superseded by the subtleties of Normandy, became continually more troublesome, led to the separation of an inferior council from that of the legislature, to both which the name *Curia Regis* is for some time indifferently applied by historians. This was done by Henry II., as Allen conjectures, at the great council of Clarendon in 1164.

The Lords' Committee took another view, and one, it must be confessed, more consonant to the prevailing opinion. "The ordinary council of the king, properly denominated by the word 'concilium' simply, seems always to have consisted of persons selected by him for that purpose; and these persons in later times, if not always, took an oath of office, and were assisted by the king's justiciaries or judges, who seem to have been considered as members of this council; and the chief justiciar, the treasurer and chancellor, and some other great officers of the crown, who might be styled the king's confidential ministers, seem also to have been always members of this select council; the chief justiciar, from the high rank attributed to his office, generally acting as president. This select council was not only the king's ordinary council of state, but formed the supreme court of justice, denominated *Curia Regis*, which commonly assembled three times in every year, wherever the king held his court, at the three great feasts of Easter, Whitsuntide, and Christmas, and sometimes also at Michaelmas. Its constant and important duty at those times was the administration of justice." (p. 20.)

It has been seen in a former note that the meetings *de more*, three times in the year, are supposed by Mr. Allen to have been of the great council, composed of the baronial aristocracy. The positions, therefore, of the Lords' committee were of course disputed in his celebrated review of their Report. "So far is it," he says, "from being true that the term Curia Regis, in the time of the Conqueror and his immediate successors, meant the king's high court of justice, as distinguished from the legislature, that it is doubtful whether such a court then existed." (Ed. Rev. xxxv. 6.) This is expressed with more hesitation than in the earlier article, and in a subsequent passage we read that "the high court of justice, to which the committee would restrict the appellation of Curia Regis, and of which such frequent mention is made under that name in our early records and courts of law, was confirmed and fully established by Henry II., if not originally instituted by that prince." (p. 8.)

The argument of Mr. Allen rests very much on the judicial functions of the witenagemot, which he would consider as maintained in its substantial character by the great councils or parliaments of the Norman dynasty. In this we may justly concur; but we have already seen how far he is from having a right to assume that the Anglo-Saxon kings, though they might administer justice in the full meetings called witenagemots, were restrained from its exercise before a smaller body more permanently attached to their residence. It is certain that there was an appeal to the king's court for denial of justice in that of the lord having territorial jurisdiction, and, as the words and the reason imply, from that of the sheriff. (Leg. Hen. I. c. 58.) This was also the law before the Conquest. But the plaintiff incurred a fine if he brought his cause in the first instance before the king. (Thorpe's Ancient Laws, p. 85; and see Edinb. Rev. xxxv. 10.) It hardly appears evident that these cases, rare probably and not generally interesting, might not be determined ostensibly, as they would on any hypothesis be in reality, by the chancellor, the high justiciar, and other great officers of the crown, during the intervals of the national council; and this is confirmed by the analogy of the royal courts in France, which were certainly not constituted on a very broad basis. The feudal court of a single barony might contain all the vassals; but the inconvenience would have become too great if the principle had been extended to all the tenants in chief of the realm. This relates to the first four reigns, for which we are reduced to these grounds of probable and analogical reasoning, since no proof of the distinct existence of a judicial court seems to be producible.

In the reign of Henry II. a court of justice is manifestly distinguishable both from the select and from the greater council. "In the Curia Regis were discussed and tried all pleas immediately concerning the king and the realm; and suitors were allowed, on payment of fines, to remove their plaints from inferior jurisdictions of Anglo-Saxon creation into this court, by which a variety of business was wrested from the ignorance and partiality of lower tribunals, to be more confidently submitted to the decision of judges of high reputation. Some plaints were also removed into the Curia Regis by the express order of the king, others by the justices, then itinerant, who not unfrequently felt themselves incompetent to decide upon difficult points of law. Matters of a fiscal nature, together with the business performed by the Chancery, were also transacted in the Curia Regis. Such a quantity of miscellaneous business was at length found to be so perplexing and impracticable, not only to the officers of the Curia Regis, but also to the suitors themselves, that it became absolutely necessary to devise a remedy for the increasing evil. A division of that court into distinct departments was the consequence; and thenceforth pleas touching the crown, together with common pleas of a civil and criminal nature, were continued to the Curia Regis; plaints of a fiscal kind were transferred to the Exchequer; and for the Court of Chancery were reserved all matters unappropriated to the other courts." (Hardy's Introduction to Close Rolls p. 23.)

Mr. Hardy quotes a passage from Benedict Abbas, a contemporary historian, which illustrates very remarkably the development of our judicial polity. Henry II., in 1176, reduced the justices in the Curia Regis from eighteen to five; and ordered that they should hear and determine all writs of the kingdom — not leaving the king's court, but remaining there for that purpose; so that, if any question should arise which they could not settle, it should be referred to the king himself, and be decided as it might please him and the wisest men of the realm. And this reduction of the justices from eighteen to five is said to have been made *per consilium sapientium regni sui;* which may, perhaps, be understood of parliament. But we have here a distinct mention of the Curia Regis, as a standing council of the king, neither to be confounded with the great council or parliament, nor with the select body of judges, which was now created as an inferior, though most important tribunal. From this time, and probably from none earlier, we may date the commencement of the Court of King's Bench, which very soon acquired, at first indifferently with the council, and then exclusively, the appellation of Curia Regis.

The rolls of the Curia Regis, or Court of King's Bench, begin in the sixth year of Richard I. They are regularly extant from that time; but the usage of preserving a regular written record of judicial proceedings was certainly practised in England during the preceding reign. The roll of Michaelmas Term, in 9 John, contains a short transcript of certain pleadings in 7 Hen. II., "proving that the mode of enrolment was then entirely settled." (Palgrave's Introduction to Rot. Cur. Regis, p. 2.) This authentic precedent (in 1161), though not itself extant, must lead us to carry back the judicial character of the Curia Regis, and that in a perfectly regular form, at least to an early part of the reign of Henry II.; and this is more probable than the date conjectured by Allen, the assembly at Clarendon in 1164.[1] But in fact the interruption of the regular assemblies of the great council, thrice a year, which he admits to date from the reign of

[1] This discovery has led Sir F. Palgrave to correct his former opinion, that the rolls of Curia Regis under Richard I. are probably the first that ever existed, Glanvil giving us no reason to presume any written records in his time. English Commonw. vol. ii. p. 1.

Stephen, would necessitate, even on his hypothesis, the institution of a separate court or council, lest justice should be denied or delayed. I do not mean that in the seventh year of Henry II. there was a Court of King's Bench, distinct from the select council, which we have not any grounds for affirming, and the date of which I, on the authority of Benedict Abbas, have inclined to place several years lower, but that suits were brought before the king's judges by regular process, and recorded by regular enrolment.

These rolls of the *Curia Regis*, or the King's Court, held before his justices or justiciars, are the earliest consecutive judicial records in existence. The Olim Registers of the Parliament of Paris, next to our own in antiquity, begin in 1254.[1] (Palgrave's Introduction, p. 1.) Every reader, he observes, will be struck by the great quantity of business transacted before the justiciars. "And when we recollect the heavy expenses which, even at this period, were attendant upon legal proceedings, and the difficulties of communication between the remote parts of the kingdom and the central tribunal, it must appear evident that so many cases would not have been prosecuted in the king's court had not some very decided advantage been derived from this source." (p. 6.) The issues of fact, however, were remitted to be tried by a jury of the vicinage; so that, possibly, the expense might not be quite so considerable as is here suggested. And the jurisdiction of the county and hundred courts was so limited in real actions, or those affecting land, by the assizes of novel disseizin and mort d'ancestor, that there was no alternative but to sue before the courts at Westminster.

It would be travelling beyond the limits of my design to dwell longer on these legal antiquities. The reader will keep in mind the threefold meaning of Curia Regis: the common council of the realm, already mentioned in a former note, and to be discussed again; the select council for judicial as well as administrative purposes; and the Court of King's Bench, separated from the last in the reign of Henry II., and soon afterwards acquiring, exclusively, the denomination Curia Regis.

In treating the judges of the Court of Exchequer as officers of the crown, rather than nobles, I have followed the

[1] They are published in the Documens Inédits, 1839, by M. Beugnot.

usual opinion. But Allen contends that they were "barons selected from the common council of the realm on account of their rank or reputed qualifications for the office." They met in the palace; and their court was called Curia Regis, with the addition "ad scaccarium." Hence Fleta observes that, after the Court of Exchequer was filled with mere lawyers, they were styled barons, because formerly real barons had been the judges; "justiciarios ibidem commorantes barones esse dicimus, eo quod suis locis barones sedere solebant." (Edinb. Rev. xxxv. 11.) This is certainly an important remark. But in practice it is to be presumed that the king selected such barons (a numerous body, we should remember) as were likely to look well after the rights of the crown. The Court of Exchequer is distinctly traced to the reign of Henry I.

NOTE XIV. Page 326.

The theory of succession to the crown in the Norman period intimated in the text has now been extensively received. "It does not appear," says Mr. Hardy, "that any of the early English monarchs exercised any act of sovereign power, or disposed of public affairs, till after their election and coronation. . . . These few examples appear to be undeniable proofs that the fundamental laws and institutions of this kingdom, based on the Anglo-Saxon custom, were at that time against an hereditary succession unless by common consent of the realm." (Introduction to Close Rolls, p. 35.) It will be seen that this abstinence from all exercise of power cannot be asserted without limitation.

The early kings always date their reign from their coronation, and not from the decease of their predecessor, as is shown by Sir Harris Nicolas in his Chronology of History (p. 272). It had been with less elaborate research pointed out by Mr. Allen in his Inquiry into the Royal Prerogative. The former has even shown that an exception which Mr. Allen had made in respect of Richard I., of whom he supposes public acts to exist, dated in the first year of his reign, but before his coronation, ought not to have been made; having no authority but a blunder made by the editors of Rymer's Fœdera in antedating by one month the decease of Henry II., and following up that mistake by the usual assumption that the successor's reign commenced immediately, in placing some instruments bearing date in the first year of Richard just twelve months too early. This discovery has been confirmed by Mr. W. Hardy in the 27th volume of the Archæologia (p. 109), by means of a charter in the archives of the duchy of Lancaster, where Richard, before his coronation, confirms the right of Gerald de Camville and his wife Nichola to the inheritance of the said Nichola in England and Normandy, with an additional grant of lands. In this he only calls himself "Ricardus Dei gratiâ *dominus* Angliæ." It has been observed, as another slighter circumstance, that he uses the form *ego* and *meus* instead of *nos* and *noster*.

Whatever, therefore, may have been the case in earlier reigns, all the kings, indeed, except Henry II., having come in by a doubtful title, we perceive that, as has been before said in the text on the authority of an historian, Richard I. acted in some respects as king before the title was constitutionally his by his coronation. It is now known that John's reign began with his coronation, and that this is the date from which his charters, like those of his predecessors, are reckoned. But he seems to have acted as king before. (Palgrave's Introduction to Rot. Cur. Regis, vol. i. p. 91; and further proof is adduced in the Introduction to the second volume.) Palgrave thinks the reign virtually began with the proclamation of the king's peace, which was at some short interval after the demise of the predecessor. He is positive indeed that the Anglo-Saxon kings had no right before their acceptance by the people at their coronation. But, "after the Conquest," he proceeds, "it is probable, for we can only speak doubtingly and hypothetically, that the heir obtained the royal authority, at least for the purposes of administering the law, from the day that his peace was proclaimed. He was obeyed as chief magistrate so soon as he was admitted to the high office of protector of the public tranquillity. But he was not honored as the king until the sacred oil had been poured upon him, and the crown set upon his head, and the sceptre grasped in his hand." (Introduct. to Rot. Cur. Reg. p. 92.)

This hypothesis, extremely probable in all cases where no opposition was contemplated, is not entirely that of Allen, Hardy, and Nicolas; and it seems to imply an admitted right, which indeed cannot be disputed in the case of Henry II., who succeeded by virtue of a treaty assented to by the baronage, nor is it likely to have been in the least doubtful when Richard I. and Henry III. came to the throne. It is important, however, for the unlearned reader to be informed that he has been deceived by the almanacs and even the historians, who lay it down that a king's reign has always begun from the death of his predecessor: and yet, that, although he bore not the royal name before his coronation, the interval of a vacant throne was virtually but of a few days; the successor taking on himself the administration without the royal title, by causing public peace to be proclaimed.

The original principle of the necessity of consent to a king's succession was in some measure preserved, even at the death of Henry III. in 1272, when fifty-six years of a single reign might have extinguished almost all personal recollections of precedent. "On the day of the king's burial the barons swore fealty to Edward I., then absent from the realm, and from this his reign is dated." Four days having elapsed between the death of Henry and the recognition of Edward as king, the accession of the latter was dated, not from his father's death, but from his own recognition. Henry died on the 16th of November, and his son was not acknowledged king till the 20th. (Allen's Inquiry, p. 44, quoting Palgrave's Parliamentary Writs.) Thus this recognition by the oath of fealty came in and was in the place of the coronation, though with the important difference that there was no reciprocity.

NOTE XV. Page 329.

Mr. Allen has differed from me on the lawfulness of private war, quoting another passage from Glanvil and one from Bracton (Edinb. Rev. xxx. 168); and I modified the passage after the first edition in consequence of his remarks. But I adhere to the substance of what I have said. It appears, indeed, that the king's peace was originally a personal security, granted by charter under his hand and seal, which could not be violated without incurring a penalty. Proofs of this are found in Domesday, and it was a Saxon usage derived from the old Teutonic *mundeburde*. William I., if we are to believe what is written, maintained the peace throughout the realm. But the general proclamation of the king's peace at his accession, which became the regular law, may have been introduced by Henry II. Palgrave, to whom I am indebted, states this clearly enough. "Peace is stated in Domesday to have been given by the king's seal, that is, by a writ under seal. This practice, which is not noticed in the Anglo-Saxon laws, continued in the protections granted at a much later period, though after the general law of the king's peace was established such a charter had ceased to afford any special privilege All the immunities arising from residence within the verge or ambit of the king's presence — from the truces, as they are termed in the continental laws, which recurred at the stated times and seasons — and also from the 'handselled' protection of the king, were then absorbed in the general declaration of the peace upon the accession of the new monarch. This custom was probably introduced by Henry II. It is inconsistent with the laws of Henry I.; which, whether an authorized collection or not, exhibit the jurisprudence of that period, but it is wholly accordant with the subsequent tenor of the proceedings of the Curia Regis." (English Commonwealth, vol. ii. p. 105.)

A few words in Glanvil (those in Bracton are more ambiguous), which may have been written before the king's peace was become a matter of permanent law, or may rather refer to Normandy than England, ought not, in my opinion, to be set against so clear a declaration. The right of private war in the time of Henry II. was giving way in France; and we should always remember that the Anglo-Norman government was one of high prerogative. The paucity of historical evidence or that for records for private war, as an usual practice, is certainly not to be overlooked.

END OF THE SECOND VOLUME.

www.ingramcontent.com/pod-product-compliance
Lightning Source LLC
LaVergne TN
LVHW020115110826
845151LV00001B/164

* 9 7 8 1 4 2 5 5 4 3 1 8 1 *